Completing a Professional Practice Dissertation

A Guide for Doctoral Students and Faculty

Completing a Professional Practice Dissertation

A Guide for Doctoral Students and Faculty

by

Jerry Willis
Marist College

Deborah Inman
Manhattanville College
and

Ron Valenti
College of New Rochelle

Information Age Publishing, Inc.
Charlotte, North Carolina • www.infoagepub.com

Library of Congress Cataloging-in-Publication Data

Willis, Jerry, Deborah Inman, and Ron Valenti
  Completing a professional practice dissertation : a guide for doctoral
students and faculty / edited by Jerry Willis, Ron Valenti, and Deborah Inman
      p. cm.
  Includes bibliographical references.
  ISBN 978-1-60752-439-7 (pbk.) -- ISBN 978-1-60752-440-3 (hardcover) --
ISBN 978-1-60752-441-0 (e-book)
  1. Dissertations, Academic--Authorship. 2. Academic writing. 3. Doctoral
students--Psychology. I. Valenti, Ron. II. Title.
  LB2369.W534 2010
  808'.042--dc22

                                                              2010000949

Printed in the United States of America

CONTENTS

CHAPTER 1

A BIT OF HISTORY AND LORE ABOUT DOCTORAL PROGRAMS AND DISSERTATIONS

You are probably reading this book because you are a doctoral student, a professor who works with doctoral students, or a practicing professional who is involved in one or more doctoral programs. More specifically, you are involved in doctoral programs that prepare professionals who will graduate and enter or resume careers in one of the professions—in fields like education, business, psychology, social work, or the health professions. This book was written for you. It is about completing one of the major activities of most professional practice doctoral programs—the dissertation. It is a practical book, and that term applies to this chapter as well as the others. This chapter is an overview of the history of doctoral programs in general and of the dissertation in particular. We have included this chapter in the book because it is essential that you understand why some developments in Western doctoral programs are what they are. Do you, for example, know why there is an "oral defense of your thesis?" Do you know the original purpose of doctorates? Do you know how long the modern version of a dissertation has been a part of doctoral programs? These and many other questions are asked, and answered, in this chapter. The answers are important to you because they help you

Completing a Professional Practice Dissertation: A Guide for Doctoral Students and Faculty, pp. 1–22
Copyright © 2010 by Information Age Publishing

both understand current practices, and how procedures might, and perhaps should, be different when the doctoral program is preparing professional practitioners rather than academics or researchers.

FROM PLATO'S ACADEMY TO THE UNIVERSITY OF BOLOGNA

Before universities emerged as organized institutions during the Middle Ages, teachers often hung out their shingle, and students paid fees directly to the professors who taught them (or were taught free of charge). Hanging out a shingle was common in the early Middle Ages but it goes back to the Academy of Plato in Athens, which was founded around 385 BCE. The Academy was located in a grove of trees about a mile from the center of Athens. That is where Plato began meeting with his students. The location was named after a Greek mythical hero, Academus, and Plato's school thus acquired its name—The Academy.

In the 1,000 years between the founding of The Academy and the emergence of the first Western European university, many other schools emerged that were organized around a particular teacher/scholar. Then, as the Catholic Church became a dominant factor in the educational life of Western Europe during the Middle Ages, the schools that were created tended to be located in monasteries, churches, and nunneries, and all of these were more or less under the control of the church. (Often the children of nobles were taught by the priest who also oversaw the church on the noble's estate.) However, by the ninth century there was a growing need for alternative ways of preparing people for increasingly sophisticated professions such as law, medicine, and the clergy. To meet that need, a more organized institution of education, the university, emerged in Western Europe. These institutions offered degrees at several levels and they were organized around a central administration rather than individual scholars. The University of Bologna was created in 1088, the University of Paris followed in 1150, and Oxford University was created in 1264 (though this date could be set earlier or later, depending on how you define "was created"). By the end of the Middle Ages there were universities in major cities across Western Europe.

These early universities had a structure similar to that of modern universities, but their curriculum was quite different. Students typically entered a university when they were around 14 or 15 years of age, and they took 6 years to complete a bachelor's degree. In those years students studied the *seven liberal arts*: arithmetic, geometry, astronomy, music theory, grammar, logic, and rhetoric. Modern readers find the seven liberal arts familiar, but those familiar names hide a major difference between modern universities and the universities of the Middle Ages. What is not obvious in the list of subjects studied is the difference in what early universities considered valid sources of knowledge. Modern universities are based on the revolution that occurred during the Enlightenment period in the eighteenth century. The Enlightenment overthrew the dominance of two sources of knowledge—Catholic Church doctrine and Greek philosophy—and replaced them with a growing confidence in the ability of humans to discover truths for themselves through systematic searches for knowledge. The Enlightenment brought science to the forefront as a source of knowledge, and some of the most famous conflicts of that era— such as Galileo versus the Catholic Church on whether the Earth or the Sun was at the center of the universe—are reflections of that shift in preferred and worthy sources of knowledge.

In the Medieval universities the educational purpose was not to discover and teach new knowledge, it was to study and learn the existing knowledge found in the Bible and other church documents, and in the writings of the ancients. Thus students might take a course in one of Aristotle's books, which had been written over a thousand years before. The goal of that course would be to learn the truths in the book and how to interpret and apply them. There was little, if any, room to criticize or question Aristotle's views on, for example, astronomy or geometry. This approach to learning and knowledge was based on Scholasticism (see Figure 1.1).

Scholasticism and Medieval Universities

Scholasticism dominated Western intellectual thought from the twelfth to the fourteenth centuries. It was an effort to integrate two sources of knowledge, church teachings and Greek thought, particularly that of Aris-

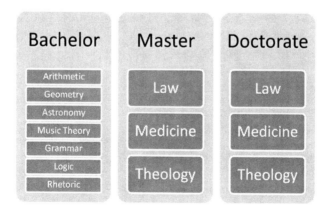

Figure 1.1.   The degree structure of early universities.

totle. Scholastics came to consider both church teachings and the newly rediscovered writings of Greek philosophers like Aristotle as sources of ultimate, God-given Truth. Reconciling these two sources was not easy, given that Aristotle and the other Greek thinkers were pagans, and their thought had to be coordinated with both the Bible and established church doctrine. The methods used by the Scholastics involved careful study of an established source of knowledge, careful reading of previous commentaries on that source, and the use of deductive logic to derive meaning from the source. Scholastics also needed strong skills in grammar and rhetoric because they had to convince others that their interpretations were correct. Thus, the seven liberal arts shown in Figure 1.1 were not treated equally in the first level (bachelor) of university degrees. *Logic* was emphasized because it was the method by which you developed knowledge from accepted sources. *Rhetoric and grammar* were also important because you needed them to be able to effectively communicate your thinking to others. And, because convincing others was often through oral rather than written means, rhetoric was especially important. Many classes in a medieval university involved students listening to their teachers use logic to derive meaning from a well-known source such as a church doctrinal statement, the Bible, or a book written by Aristotle. In those and other classes students would also be expected to make their own speeches on a set of issues or questions provided by the teacher. Their skills in the use of both logic and rhetoric were critical to progress toward their degree. "In medieval universities, exercises and exams were held in the form of disputations between students or between a student and a master" (Pironet, 2001, p. 109).

The "oral defense" that is still a part of the dissertation process in modern universities has its origins in the Medieval expectation that a student be able to present and defend his (women were not admitted to early universities) interpretations and positions. Because the emphasis was on the student's ability to defend his position against those who would argue alternative viewpoints, these oral defenses were called "disputations." One definition of medieval disputations is:

> In the scholastic system of education in the Middle Ages, disputations … offered a formalized method of debate designed to uncover and establish truths in theology and in other sciences. Fixed rules governed the process: they demanded dependence on traditional written authorities and the thorough understanding of each argument on each side. (from http://www.absoluteastronomy.com/topics/Disputation)

It is difficult for moderns to understand how important disputation was in the universities of the Middle Ages. A primary way of supporting your position on virtually any point was through disputation.

Medieval university life was strongly dependent on dialectical practices. Academic argumentation and consequently practically all intellectual reasoning was understood to take place in the contexts where someone is trying to convince another person by presenting a sequence of sentences. Such a conception of logic was of course deeply embedded in the ancient tradition. Aristotle's Topics, for example, put logic in the context of an encounter between an opponent and a respondent. (Yrjönsuuri, 2001, pp. vii-viii)

The oral defenses, or disputations, of different positions were not, however, ivory tower exercises that had little to do with what students would do after they graduated. Across the Middle Ages disputation, which is a form of debate with well-defined rules and procedures, was a highly prized way of seeking knowledge and truth. Often a disputation was about a religious issue. Learning the skills of logic and rhetoric needed to hold your own in a disputation was something you might well need in your professional life after leaving the university. Thus, much of the work at the bachelor's level prepared you for disputation. That continued at the masters and doctoral level where students focused on a particular profession.

The Doctorate in Early Universities

It may surprise you to know that while universities have existed for more than 1,000 years, the dissertation is not nearly so old. In its most common contemporary form, the PhD research dissertation has existed for only about 200 years. And, for almost half of that period, the research doctorate and required dissertation were common only in German and American universities.

Another surprise is that the early doctorates were not the high prestige doctorates that prepare graduates for careers as researchers and academics. The first doctorate was not a research or a scholarly degree. Instead, it was a teaching degree. The English word Doctor comes from the Latin word, *docere* which means "to teach." During the Middle Ages, universities in Bologona and Paris began to offer *doctores legum,* which were licenses to teach civil law. That began in the twelfth century, and was followed by a *doctores decretorum,* which was a license to teach canon law (Taylor & Beasley, 2005). Later, universities expanded their teaching degrees to include doctorates in medicine—which are still with us today as the MD but are now professional practice degrees rather than degrees that allow you to teach medicine to aspiring physicians.

Completing the Doctorate in Early Universities

We are so accustomed to the idea that work on a doctorate of any sort will end with the oral defense of a written dissertation that it is hard to think of a doctoral program that does not include those activities. However, as you will see in the next section, what we consider *normal and expected* is a relatively recent addition to the doctoral program. Early doctorates were professional practice degrees; they were licenses to either teach a particular discipline or a license to practice a particular profession. With that purpose in mind, plus the dominance of the scholastic method in early universities, the early traditions of doctoral work included an oral presentation by the candidate of their own ideas about a topic as well as an oral defense of those ideas. The oral defense thus developed before the written dissertation. This is not surprising, given that universities emerged in the ninth and tenth centuries while the printing press was not even invented by Johannes Gutenberg until 1440. Even when there was a written thesis, it was the oral defense that took precedence. The importance of "disputation" in the intellectual life of the Middle Ages is illustrated by the quote below:

> The Middle Ages laid great emphasis on disputations. "Such intellectual tournaments in which the students were taught to defend a thesis against attack, did more to enable them to grasp a subject than the mute and solitary reviewing and cramming of our modern examinations can possibly do. That method brought into play all the excitement of a contest, the triumph of success, and the disgrace of defeat, in order to emphasize the value of what had been learned, together with the importance of an alert wit and constant readiness to use it." (F. Paulsen). After the Middle Ages the weekly disputations declined in use and were largely succeeded by the Seminar system. The candidate for the doctorate published a thesis or theses and defended them against all comers, a custom which still prevails in some European universities. It was in keeping with this custom that Martin Luther posted his 95 theses. (Ayers, 1918, p. 168)

Note that this quote makes it clear that the term "defending your thesis" had a different meaning in the Middle Ages. Today when someone says they will defend their thesis next Friday at 1 P.M., we assume that a dissertation committee of about five people will convene a meeting to examine the student on the dissertation he or she has written. All the committee members will have received a copy of the dissertation, which is typically between 100 and 350 pages, at least one or two weeks before, and each member will be prepared to ask the student some questions about the research work presented in the dissertation. That is what "defending your thesis" means today. It is not necessarily what "defending your thesis" meant in the Middle Ages. Instead, it meant the student had developed a statement about a topic or issue. That was his thesis and the defense of the thesis was a meeting in which the rules of disputation were used in a relatively formal debate about that thesis. When, in 1517, Martin Luther

nailed his list of 95 "theses" to the door of the Castle Church in Witten-
berg, he titled his short document "Disputation on the Power and Efficacy
of Indulgences." Here are four of Luther's theses:

> 73. The pope justly thunders against those who, by any art, contrive the
> injury of the traffic in pardons.

> 74. But much more does he intend to thunder against those who use the
> pretext of pardons to contrive the injury of holy love and truth.

> 75. To think the papal pardons so great that they could absolve a man even
> if he had committed an impossible sin and violated the Mother of God—
> this is madness.

> 76. We say, on the contrary, that the papal pardons are not able to remove
> the very least of venial sins, so far as its guilt is concerned.

What Luther did was to lay out an argument, in an accepted form—
disputation, against what he considered a corruption of church practice—
the selling of indulgences so that those with money could go ahead and
"sin," and know that they were already pardoned for it. The original
meaning of the word "thesis" was not a long document you write about a
research study you have conducted for your master's or doctoral degree.
It was a statement of your position on a particular issue. In some ways that
type of thesis is very close to the idea of a hypothesis that is typically
required in dissertations today. A thesis, or hypothesis, is the beginning
point for a disputation or oral exam and discussion.

The oral defense remained very important even after the printing
press made the dissemination of printed copies of the defense of the thesis economically possible. One interesting document in the National
Archives of Hungary is a list of the doctoral disputations that would be
conducted during a particular month in 1686. These printed announcements were often highly decorated and embellished. You can see a photo
of one, which is from the Archives of the Prince Esterházy family, at the
Hungarian National Archives website (http://www.mol.gov.hu/
index.php?akt_menu=743).

Even as late as 1917 there was a famous statement of theses, in the old
sense of that term. On April 16, 1917 Vladimir Lenin returned from exile
in Switzerland. His train arrived at the Finland Station in Petrograd (formerly St. Petersburg) and he gave a speech at the railroad station that is
generally referred to as the *April Theses*. The *April Theses*, or more formally
"The Tasks of the Proletariat in the Present Revolution" spelled out what
the Bolsevicks should do now that the Czar had been overthrown and a
provisional government established. The *April Theses* were also printed in

party newspapers like *Pravda* and read out at a number of meetings. The second of Lenin's 10 theses was:

> The specific feature of the present situation in Russia is that the country is passing from the first stage of the revolution—which, owing to the insufficient class-consciousness and organisation of the proletariat, placed power in the hands of the bourgeoisie—to its second stage, which must place power in the hands of the proletariat and the poorest sections of the peasants.

> This transition is characterised, on the one hand, by a maximum of legally recognised rights (Russia is now the freest of all the belligerent countries in the world); on the other, by the absence of violence towards the masses, and, finally, by their unreasoning trust in the government of capitalists, those worst enemies of peace and socialism.

> This peculiar situation demands of us an ability to adapt ourselves to the special conditions of Party work among unprecedentedly large masses of proletarians who have just awakened to political life (from http://www.marxists.org/archive/lenin/works/1917/apr/04.htm)

Note that Lenin's thesis does not take quite the same format as Martin Luther's. Lenin couches his thesis in a particular theory, that of Karl Marx, about the historical progression of societies. Revolution, which occurs as a society moves from one predicted level of historical development to another, has several stages. Russia at that point was in the first stage—where the feudal power of the Czar had been overthrown and replaced by "power in the hands of the bourgeoisie." However, Marxist theory proposed that a second stage of revolution would take power from the bourgeoise and "place power in the hands of the proletariat and the poorest sections of the peasants." This thesis of Lenin is much closer to a form of hypothesis that is still required today in many dissertations. It involves taking a theory, applying the theory to a situation, and then developing an action that should be done that is an implication of the theory being studied. The reasons for this difference in the theses of Luther and Lenin is the Enlightenment and the elevation of the scientific method as a source of knowledge while religious and ancient sources became less important. Lenin considered himself a follower of "scientific communism" rather than a secular religion and he stated his theses in a way that showed he was basing his conclusion about what should be done on his understanding of Marxist theory. Lenin considered that theory to be a scientifically established fact.

However, while the disputation of the Middle Ages had given way to a different form of argumentation, rhetoric and logic were still important because oral rather than written presentations of theses and their defense were still a major avenue of influence. In responding to a critic who was also a member of his political party, Lenin had this to say:

> Mr. Plekhanov in his paper called my speech "raving". Very good, Mr. Plekhanov! But look how awkward, uncouth and slow-witted you are in your polemics. If I delivered a raving speech for two hours, how is it that an audience of hundreds tolerated this "raving"? Further, why does your paper devote a whole column to an account of the "raving"? Inconsistent, highly inconsistent! (from   http://www.marxists.org/archive/lenin/works/1917/apr/04.htm)

WILHELM VON HUMBOLDT AND
THE GERMAN UNIVERSITY REVOLUTION

One reason why Lenin's theses were different from those of Luther were developments in nineteenth century Berlin. Humboldt University in Berlin is sometimes called "the mother of all modern universities" because the scientist, scholar, and diplomat Wilhelm von Humboldt redesigned the German university system while he was in the German government. His model for the University of Berlin (later renamed Humboldt University after his death) had a profound influence on all modern universities. Put succinctly, his revolutionary redesign was a shift from Scholasticism to Humanism. Scholasticism has already been discussed. At its core was a reliance on established sources of knowledge. Humanism was different. Instead of putting its faith in God-given knowledge found in sacred books and the wisdom of the ancients, humanism put its emphasis on the ability of humans to learn things for themselves. Humanism also elevates the value and importance of humans as humans, rather than as servants of greater things such as a religion. Von Humboldt was a supporter of New Humanism, which was an intellectual movement that began in the mid-1700s and focused on the unity of the body and soul as well as nature and art. It emphasized the full and harmonious development of the individual. New Humanism was part of a move toward liberalism:

> Wilhelm von Humboldt holds a conspicuous place among the early progenitors of German liberalism, for in addition to being an able theoretician he was also an historical figure whose career left its imprint on German thought and culture: in the two decades from 1790 to 1810, Humboldt made a crucial contribution to the development and canonization of the German conception of self-formation or self-cultivation (Bildung). In his Limits of State Action (1791-92), Humboldt proposed the reduction of state power to the barest minimum in order to insure freedom for individual self-cultivation, and during a sixteen-month tenure as Head of the Section for Religion and Education in the Ministry of the Interior ... he revamped the

Prussian educational system in accord with the neo-humanist conception of Bildung. (Sorkin, 1983, p. 55)

One way to think about scholasticism and humanism is to treat them as two different ways to seek truth. Humanism, which emerged after the Enlightenment, is sometimes treated as a competitor to another Enlightenment movement, scientific empiricism. However, many scholars see these two movements as having more in common than their strong rejection of scholasticism. Von Humboldt's revision of the German education system broadened its foundations and created the model for the modern university. Our focus here, however, is specifically on how he changed doctoral work. Humboldt believed teaching and research should be intimately and carefully linked, for example. This led to some interesting developments in higher education as Don Barry, the President of the University of Limerick, noted in his 2007 inaugural address:

In 1810 Von Humboldt established a university in Berlin with the unity of research and teaching as one of its basic principles. The teaching efforts of all academics were geared to the kinds of specialised work that produces either future investigators or future professionals whose work depends upon a sophisticated knowledge base. This led to a downgrading of the importance of undergraduate teaching and indeed to the contracting out of the first two years of college work to local academies so that faculty could devote themselves to research and advanced level teaching. (from http://www2.ul.ie/web/WWW/Administration/PresidentsOffice/PresidentsInauguralAddress)

His focus on the importance of linking teaching to research is the foundation for what we now call the "research university" where professors are expected to pursue dual careers as teachers as well as researchers. He also advocated "academic freedom" (*lehrfreiheit*) which meant that faculty could pursue both teaching and research on topics that might be controversial without restrictions on the part of religious or government authorities.

However, in spite of Von Humboldt's neo-humanist views his emphasis on the professor as a researcher meant both he and his university emphasized the importance of research over teaching. Both were important but research was more important. And despite what viewbooks distributed to potential undergraduate students might say, most scholars of higher education today would agree that the primacy of research accomplishments over teaching success remains a characteristic of most modern research universities.

Von Humboldt's university was also the first research university in another way. Initially, it offered only one degree. Students were working on their doctorate and the purpose of the university was to teach and mentor students so they would become excellent scholars in their chosen field of research.

Humboldt believed PhDs should be scientists in search of universal truths and he created the curriculum that is used today in most American research universities. Students study the subject matter of their discipline for some years and are mentored in research skills by their professors who involve them in ongoing research projects. Then, near the end of their program, students take a "comprehensive" or "qualifying" exam that determines whether they know enough about their discipline, and the research methods of that discipline, to proceed to independent research work. If they "pass their comps" the next step is the dissertation—which is typically their first piece of independent research. The expert professors who have taught and mentored them, also work intensively with doctoral students during their dissertation phase to ensure they have the guidance and support needed. Once students have gathered and analyzed the data for the dissertation, written the dissertation, and defended it in an oral examination, they receive the PhD degree and are judged ready to join the discipline's community of researchers and lead their own research projects.

Humboldt's model of a research university was initially rejected by most European and U.K. universities. However, his ideas were enthusiastically adopted by leading universities in America, including Yale University which awarded the first American PhDs in 1861. The six page, handwritten dissertation of James Morris Whitton titled *Ars Longa, Brevis Vita* was written entirely in Latin.

The German models of both a research university and a research dissertation still dominate American doctoral education, but the American version of Von Humboldt's model is somewhat different from the model that was eventually adopted by universities in some European countries. Bowen and Rudenstein (1992) organized the American PhD program into three stages:

> The first [stage] comprises a period of formal course work that usually lasts two or three years. The second is a less defined interim period in which other stipulated requirements … are completed. This stage may involve passing a general examination or qualifying exam … as well as choosing a dissertation topic, and, in some cases, submitting an approved prospectus [proposal]. The last stage is one of intensive dissertation research and writing, including final defense of the dissertation. (p. 251)

America was the first nation to adopt the German or Humboldt model for PhD programs, but the model that emerged here is quite different from the one that was adopted in other countries. For example, in the United Kingdom, Cambridge University eventually began offering the "German"

PhD but most of the PhD programs at Cambridge, and Oxford, are not like American PhD programs. American programs are often referred to as "taught" PhDs because they generally require two or more years of coursework in addition to a dissertation. Some years ago, one of the authors of this book was visiting with a Cambridge professor and his new American PhD student who had not yet figured out that the Cambridge model was quite different from the typical American approach. The student mentioned something about the advantage of having the prestigious name of Cambridge University at the top of his transcript when he applied for an academic position. His professor politely pointed out that Cambridge does not issue "transcripts," or lists of courses, for the PhD programs because there are no required courses. Instead, when students apply for admission to a PhD program they include in their application the type of research they want to do. In essence, they start with a short proposal for their dissertation. If the student is accepted, one of the Cambridge professors in his or her area of interest will serve as major professor, and most of the student's time will be spent doing research, not attending classes. Students do receive reading assignments from their advisor and those readings are often discussed at regular meetings where they may sip glasses of sherry or port while discussing the readings. And, students may attend lectures offered by professors because the lectures are relevant to their research, or deal with a related method of research. However, the PhD at Cambridge is a "research degree" and PhD students spend much of their time being mentored on, and doing, research. The main result of a Cambridge PhD program is a dissertation. There is even a famous case where a young student from Vienna was the preferred candidate for a professorship in philosophy. His name was Ludwig Wittgenstein and the philosophers at Cambridge, including Bertrand Russell and G. E. Moore, had already concluded he was the genius who should be given the open faculty position in philosophy. Wittgenstein had written a book, *Tractatus Logico-Philosophicus,* which was published in 1921. It had set the world of philosophy on its ear, but he did not have a doctorate. Here is how Russell and Moore took care of that.

> Within a year of Wittgenstein's return [to Cambridge], Ramsey died, at the age of 26.... As Wittgenstein had already satisfied the statutory residence requirements, he was entitled to submit the Tractatus as his dissertation; in June 1929, Moore and Russell administered his oral examination and duly awarded him the PhD.... He began giving lectures in January 1930, and was regularly on the university's lecture lists in the years that followed. (Stern, 1996, p. 92)

Ironically, when Wittgenstein submitted his book as a dissertation in 1929 he had already begun to move away from the positions he advocated in the book. Yet, it remains a foundation for one approach to thinking about everything from meaning to the way research should be conducted in the social sciences. Wittgenstein's later book, *Philosophical Investigations,* was not edited and published until after he died in 1951. That book also continues to be a foundation, but for a different approach to philosophy and a quite different approach to research in the social sciences.

Quickly awarding Wittgenstein a PhD on the basis of having spent time "in residence" at the university, and a book he had written almost ten years previously, would have been much more difficult at an American university. In contrast to Cambrdige, most American PhD programs did and do require at least two years of coursework, followed by a research dissertation. As noted earlier, outside the United States, the American approach is sometimes called a "taught" degree because it involves extensive coursework.

On the surface, it might be tempting for an American to say that the American PhD is obviously better because it involves both advanced study of the discipline plus mentoring and practice in research. That quick conclusion may not be accurate however, for two reasons. The first is that in systems where the PhD degree work is mostly, or all, research, students typically start that degree with much more background in the discipline than is typical of American students at the beginning of their doctoral work. American students are often trained more broadly at both the bachelors and master's level, but they may not have studied their discipline in as much detail as students in other higher education systems. For example, a student beginning a PhD after finishing an U.K.-style "MPhil" or "Master of Philosophy" degree in the same discipline would typically have as much or more depth of knowledge in the discipline as a student finishing 2 years of coursework in an American PhD. Thus, it is hard to compare the American "taught" PhD with a "research" PhD from a U.K. university like Cambridge because the context of the degree is so different.

The second difficulty is with the purpose of the degree. In Humboldt's original plan for the PhD, the sole purpose was to produce researchers who could continue to make scientific and scholarly advances in their discipline. Many PhD students do just that—they graduate, find a position as a professor at a research university, and establish their own program of research. From 1810 when Humboldt founded the University of Berlin to the end of World War II, most PhD graduates probably did just that—they were prepared by researchers and scholars in research universities to become researchers and scholars in research universities.

However, over the last 60 years, the goals and purposes of PhD work in many disciplines has changed drastically. In more and more disciplines, the majority of doctoral students will not become professors. Instead they will become professional practitioners. Preparing practitioners was decidedly not the purpose of Humboldt's PhD program but in many PhD programs today, students who plan careers as academics are in the same PhD program as students who plan professional careers in the field. They take many of the same courses and complete the same type of dissertation. As you will learn in the next section, the "fit" of the traditional PhD program in America and elsewhere to the goal of preparing professional practitioners has been seriously questioned for at least the last 30 years. In the face of rising criticism, many PhD-granting colleges and universities have elected to make only limited adjustments in their programs to accommodate the changing career paths of their students. However, another popular option is the one we will focus on in the remainder of this chapter—the creation of professional practice doctoral programs designed specifically to meet the needs of students who plan careers as professionals rather than academics.

THE "PROBLEM" OF THE PhD AS
THE DOMINANT MODEL FOR DOCTORAL WORK

Beginning with Yale's first PhD in 1861, Morgan and Libner (2004) comment on the development of American doctoral programs:

> From that small start the process of dissertation research to what has been often described as the pinnacle of the U.S. educational system. Despite this success, beginning in the 1930s there have been undercurrents of criticism about the direction of graduate education in this country. In the past ten years, there has been renewed and concentrated critical discussion of the purpose and outcomes of the PhD program. The Carnegie Foundation's Initiative on the Doctorate, The Woodrow Wilson Fellowship Foundation's Responsive PHD Initiative, and the University of Washington's Re-envisioning the PhD are but three examples.

Although Morgan and Libner believe their criticisms of the traditional PhD program are appropriate, they caution that change in the procedures and processes of PhD programs, including the dissertation, will likely come slowly. "We might think of them as ritual objects in a complex rite of passage—the PhD degree—developed to anoint a kind of priesthood of scholars. They lie in a tight matrix of reciprocal relationships, academic standards, and perhaps even social norms. To change dissertation requirements or standards is to put pressure on that matrix. Therefore, change is likely to be a slow and difficult process." Damrosch (2007) agreed and suggested one reason for the difficulty in changing doctoral programs.

Our ability to confront the limitations of our programs is further dimin-
ished by the fact that the tenured faculty at doctorate-granting institutions
are all people for whom the present system has worked well. Possibly, we
could wish to move to some more prestigious institution or have some
added benefits where we are, but these are minor adjustments in a context
of overall success. (p. 36)

Despite the barriers to change, however, these authors are optimistic that
new forms of the dissertation are possible: "Meanwhile, 142 years after
the first dissertations were submitted in the United States, there is a rising
tide of commentary and discussion about the appropriateness of the dissertation as we have known it" (Morgan & Libner, 2004).

A thorough review of the literature on the problems of doctoral work
in modern universities, and the proposed solutions, is not the focus of
this chapter or this book. However, some attention to those criticisms
does provide useful background to a discussion of why professional
practice doctorates have become so popular today and how they, and
the dissertations produced by students in those programs, differ from
traditional PhD programs. The list below has been adopted from Taylor and Beasley (2005) and the Carnegie Foundation's book-length
treatment of problems and solutions in American doctoral education
(Golde & Walker, 2006).

Only Half of Those Admitted to Doctoral Programs Actually Graduate

This surprising finding is well established in the literature. Admissions
standards for doctoral programs are some of the most rigorous in higher
education. Yet, of the applicants who meet those stringent standards, only
one in two actually graduates. One of several major stumbling points is
the dissertation. Failure to complete the dissertation is so commonplace
that the abbreviation ABD has become popular. It is short for "all but dissertation" and some individuals list the result of their doctoral work on
their resume as "PhD (ABD)".

It Takes Too Long to Complete a Doctoral Program

The general consensus is that students, on average, take about eight
years to complete a doctorate. That means half the students who do finish
actually take *longer!* The general expectation is that a student should finish a program in 3 years but the reality is that students tend to take much
longer.

Doctoral Programs Do not Prepare Students for Future Jobs, Especially Professional Practice Jobs

Several of the national reports on the quality of traditional PhD programs have questioned their ability even to adequately prepare students for careers as academic researchers and scholars. These critics are thus concerned that traditional doctoral programs are failing to accomplish Humboldt's original purpose for PhD programs. Other critics have been more specific—they point out that doctoral students today have career goals outside academia and that programs have not responded adequately to this shift in the career paths of doctoral graduates. There is a "disjuncture between what PhD programmes were training students to be, namely academics, and what they were increasingly doing ... which was working in other forms of employment (Taylor & Beasley, 2005, p. 10). This point was also made in the Carnegie report on the future of doctoral education (Golde & Walker, 2007). "Many PhD recipients are ill-prepared to function effectively in the setting in which they work.... PhD recipients who work outside the academy struggle to make that transition" (p. 5). One estimate is that in the sciences, "no more than 10 percent will be faculty" (Prewitt, 2006, p. 5).

Present PhD Programs are Too Narrow

As Golde and Walker (2007) put it,

> every discipline is evolving, with its boundaries expanding and changing. The resulting redefinition of intellectual identity is often fraught with tension. The challenge for doctoral education is to help students be flexible and interdisciplinary, and to balance this with the enormous amount that students are expected to know. (p. 4)

While there is general agreement that doctoral programs in virtually all disciplines need to prepare students to be more flexible and to understand and work well with related disciplines, efforts to move in that direction contradict the tendency for doctoral programs to push students toward greater and greater specialization. Nevertheless, Elkana (2007) highlights the urgent need for programs to do just that:

> Doctoral programs should devote far less attention to work within the boundaries of a discipline's subfields and far more attention to the broader questions of the philosophical, sociological, and methodological contexts of work, thus combating overspecialization. This must be repeated regularly at all the important choice points in a doctoral program. (p. 66)

This issue—how to balance specialization with interdisciplinary work and a broader understanding of the context in which a discipline exists—has not been settled, and there are examples today of different doctoral program revision efforts that take programs in opposite directions—toward more specialization at some institutions and toward a more interdisciplinary perspective at others. In our view, broadening the boundaries of doctoral study trumps the need for more specialization.

PhD Programs No Longer Provide Close Mentoring and Support to Students

Humboldt's original plan was that the professors in a PhD program would work closely with students over a period of years. The full time job of the professor was to mentor the next generation of research professors while involving them intensely in the professor's research program.

> The old model presupposed a one-to-one relationship between student and sponsor, actually called the "Doktorvater" [doctor father] in German, as though the patriarchal sponsor was supposed to give birth, parthogenetically, to the newborn PhD. For many reasons, this old model no longer works well for many students—or even for many faculty. (Damrosch, 2007, p. 38)

Everything from the weakened financial state of higher education to growing diversity in student interests (and thus no suitable faculty person to serve as a sole mentor), to larger numbers of students without corresponding increases in the number of faculty, to the danger of Freudian oedipal problems impeding mentoring and support, and the increasing diversity of students, are all cited as reasons for the decline in quality and amount of support and mentoring for students in doctoral programs. Problems with limited mentoring, or the virtual absence of support and mentoring, tend to be concentrated around dissertation issues. Many students feel that while they received decent support for completing coursework, they had to do their dissertation virtually "by themselves." This is less a problem in fields such as chemistry or physics where professors at research universities tend to have both laboratory space for research and grants to support their research program and their doctoral students. As a result new students often join the research team and participate fully as junior and then more senior researchers in the laboratory's ongoing program of research. Thus, by the time students are ready to do a dissertation, they already have considerable research experience. Their dissertation, more often than not, is the next logical step in the major professors' research program. Students who work with a well-funded research professor conducting a significant program of research that involves many studies are thus likely to work closely with the professor and with other students who are working in the same laboratory.

Such a model is rare, however, in many disciplines. Research funding is much harder to come by, and less dependable, in the humanities, many of the social sciences, and in professional fields like education, business, and social work. In these fields, even doctoral faculty may find themselves doing research without funding and without a way of supporting doctoral students who will be doing their dissertation with them. The result can be a less than satisfactory situation in which students complete all their coursework without ever actually doing any prior research, either independently or under the guidance of a major professor. This approach, which is the norm in many doctoral programs, and in many disciplines, is the reality many students face. But it is not what Humboldt had in mind. Modern professors play many different roles, including teaching responsibilities that have little or nothing to do with their own programs of research. The number of committees, meetings, and other demands associated with being a professor in the large bureaucracy known as the *research university* will surprise many people. And, the trend toward higher teaching loads, even in research universities, will likely make things worse rather than better in the near future.

PhD Programs Discourage Collaboration and Interdisciplinary Work

As Prewitt (2006) put it, "At present ... the promise of doctoral preparation that is collaborative and interdisciplinary is hostage to a reward system tailored to individual achievement within a discipline" (p. 31). However, citing the work of the Carnegie Foundation, he concluded that "building doctoral training around practices that are interdisciplinary and collaborative is our future" (p. 31). The Carnegie Report on the future of doctoral education (Golde & Walker, 2006) is filled with comments about the need for interdisciplinary content that cuts across disciplines. There are examples of efforts to do just that but the growing amount of knowledge in each specialization works against this trend. Instead, it encourages subspecialization. Many doctoral programs give students little time or encouragement to study across disciplines or to work in collaboration with specialists from other disciplines. A recent article about the influence of neuroscience on the field of psychology (Glenn, 2008) raised the question of whether the traditional model of a primary mentor-professor and student-researcher will work today. Glenn quoted Alan Kraut, Executive Director of the Association for Psychological Science, who noted that "The individual investigator who has a great idea and can follow that idea with a couple of graduate students over a 10-year period—that era has probably gone." In discussing psychological research involving neuroscience, Kraut noted that "you can't know enough on your own," it is necessary to collaborate. That is true of many fields today in part because the field itself is complicated, and in part because the relevance of related disciplines has become much more obvious—as in the case of psychology and neuroscience.

The need for collaborative scholarship is even more important in professional fields like business, social work, nursing, education, and family therapy. In all these professional fields the issues of practice are rarely so narrowly focused that one discipline has complete ownership. For example, the problem of low student performance in urban schools has elements that relate to disciplines such as economics, sociology, psychology, curriculum theory, leadership, child development, family dynamics, anthropology, and political science. Many efforts to address a problem of professional practice will involve, at the least, attention to knowledge and procedures from several disciplines, and at the most, a collaborative team that includes knowledgeable specialists from many disciplines.

Current Problems Are Particularly Crucial to Students Who Plan Professional Rather Than Research Careers

A number of the issues noted above, such as the number of students who start but do not complete a doctoral program, and the number of years students take to finish a degree, are relatively universal. They cut across virtually all doctoral programs. Other problems, however, seem particularly unsatisfactory for doctoral students planning careers outside academe. Elkana (2006) pointed out that even in the sciences, a larger and larger percentage of doctoral students do not become academic researchers:

> More than half of those with a doctorate in science will not remain within academe.... Of those with doctorates in science and engineering who are currently faculty members (about 46%), half [23%] are in research universities and half are in other academic institutions.... The remaining working scientists and engineers are employed in government, industry, finance, business, transnational corporations, security-related research, and legal firms dealing with the growing issue of intellectual property rights. (p. 84)

Elkana proposes a number of changes, such as giving students a chance to learn how to use "local" knowledge, that would make PhD programs more suitable for doctoral students planning professional careers. Elkana's concerns are even more central to the structure of programs with the explicit goal of preparing students for professional rather than academic careers. At the doctoral level, these programs are generally called "professional practice" or "professional" programs. Elkana (2006) points out that becoming a strong professional in any discipline requires different types of knowledge (e.g., tacit knowledge" and "narrative" understanding) that are rarely addressed in traditional PhD programs but may be essential to practice. The same applies to certain habits of mind such as "reflective thinking" and methods of solving problems of professional practice (such as participatory action research). Few doctoral programs based on a traditional research PhD model in the Humboldt tradition give much attention to these "essentials" of professional practice. Further, professional practice is a social process and practitioners, whether they be a teacher, social worker, forensic chemist, clinical psychologist, or medical doctor, must learn to collaborate and work effectively with others, sometimes leading and sometimes working as a participant in collaborative efforts. Again, traditional PhD programs rarely invest much effort in developing these skills. This point was made directly about PhD programs in chemistry by Golde and Walker (2006):

> Ultimately, two-thirds of the PhD chemists work in industry and government labs, and about one-third work in academia. These strong connections with industry mandate that doctoral training prepare students for academic jobs and for industrial careers, which demand a somewhat different skill set. One criticism leveled regularly at doctoral programs in chemistry is that PhD students are not taught the kinds of skills necessary to succeed in the workplace. Other than technical and scientific competency, the attributes most prized by chemical employers include communication (both written and oral), information management, team work, product stewardship, understanding of principles of responsible care, independent thinking, creativity, flexibility, vision, and maturity. (p. 136)

This criticism applies to many doctoral programs, even those for professions. One of this book's authors' own doctoral program in child clinical psychology, for example, was based on the "scientist-practitioner model" that was adopted by American psychology in 1949. He received much more training in the area of statistical analysis of experimental data than in the "most prized" attributes listed in the quote above. And, while he and his fellow students were trained, on the professional side, primarily to individual psychotherapy and assessment, many of them ended up in administrative positions such as directors of mental health centers. A quite different skill set is needed to successfully manage and lead a mental health center with 30 or 40 employees versus spending the work week assessing patients and doing counseling and therapy with individuals and couples. There was a mismatch between the work done after graduation and the work they were prepared to do in the doctoral program.

Issues With the Dissertation

Finally, there has been a growing concern that the traditional 100 to 350-page dissertation, completed at the end of a students' doctoral program, does not serve the needs of doctoral students planning professional careers. As noted earlier, the written dissertation emerged late in the history of higher education. Before Humboldt created the University of Berlin in 1810, the emphasis was on a student's ability to use logic effectively and to be able to present and defend a "thesis" in a form of oral combat called disputation. The traditional five-chapter dissertation is relatively new. It typically includes:

- an introductory chapter followed by
- a review of the literature,
- a chapter on the methodology of the research,
- a chapter on the results of the data analysis, and
- a final chapter discussing the implications of the research

This format, which derives from Humboldt's model of PhD programs to prepare students to become novice professors and researchers, served its purpose, as a student's first independent piece of research. When dissertations became standard expectations for PhD work, there were publication outlets for dissertations. The traditional scholarly or research monograph format, which is typically about 100-150 printed pages, was a reasonable way of disseminating dissertation research. Often the review of the literature chapter would be shortened a bit for publication. Long literature reviews, however, made sense when students were expected to have read virtually all the relevant research on their particular topic. That was actually possible in 1810; it is rarely possible today.

A PhD graduate in 1810 could optimistically hope that his (women were not initially admitted to the University of Berlin) dissertation might soon appear as a monograph on the booklist of one of the many publishers of monographs. Indeed, for part of the twentieth century some European countries even required that a student's research monograph be published before a doctorate was awarded. Today that is rarely the case. Very few dissertations are published substantially intact, and the percentage of new PhDs who publish articles based on their dissertation is well below 10%. This has led to a number of efforts to reform both the process and the form of the dissertation. One option that developed first in the sciences and engineering is the TAD or *three article dissertation*. That chemistry doctoral student mentioned earlier who worked in his professor's lab for several years would naturally be involved with his or her professor and fellow students in publishing papers based on the laboratory's current research. Many PhD programs in the sciences now allow students to submit TADs. The heart of the dissertation is three articles authored or coauthored by the student and either published or submitted for publication. We will have more to say about different formats for dissertations later, but at this point it is important to note that the value of a traditional five-chapter dissertation for students planning professional careers has been questioned by many.

In the next chapter we will introduce one answer to the problems of both Humboldt-style PhD programs and dissertations for doctoral students who plan careers as professional practitioners. That solution is the professional practice doctoral program and dissertations that focus on the solution of a problem of professional practice.

SUMMARY

Doctoral programs have a long history, beginning in the Middle Ages when the first universities in Western Europe were created. Doctorates in the Middle Ages were based on the scholastic method, and doctorates were initially awarded as licenses to teach subjects such as law or medicine. Doctoral students "defended their thesis" in a process called disputation. However, the "thesis" was not a 200 page document, it was a statement or position succinctly stated and well articulated.

Modern dissertations, or theses, are different. They are part of doctoral programs designed to prepare academics and researchers. The structure of PhD programs, and the structure and purpose of modern dissertations, derive from the work of Wilhelm von Humboldt and his leadership in the creation of the University of Berlin in 1810. Modern research universities are based on the model created by Humboldt at the University of Berlin. Today this model of doctoral programs remains dominant in American higher education. However, the modern PhD program and the research dissertation are not well suited to preparing professional practitioners, even though increasing percentages of PhD students go into professional practice rather than becoming academics.

While traditional PhD programs have begun to make adjustments to meet some of the needs of students who will become professional practitioners, an even more radical approach to meeting those needs will be explored—doctoral programs designed specifically and purposely to serve the needs of professionals rather than academics.

CHAPTER 2

THE PROFESSIONAL
PRACTICE DOCTORATE

Doctorates for people who plan to practice a particular profession have been around for about a thousand years. In the Middle Ages the emerging universities of Western Europe created doctorates in law and medicine. And, while the nature of these two degrees has changed drastically over the intervening centuries, the *Juris Doctor* (JD) and the doctor of medicine (MD) have been around in their present form for at least a hundred years. These degrees differ considerably from the PhD degree discussed in some detail in Chapter 1. The PhD degree, and program of study, was created specifically for students who would become academics and researchers. From the beginning it was to be a "research degree."

The doctor of laws and the doctor of medicine are quite different today from the research PhD in terms of intent and curriculum. Both focus on preparing students to take their place as practicing members of a profession rather than find an academic post at a university and establish a program of research. From the Middle Ages until the 1970s, only a few new doctoral programs to prepare students for professional practice appeared. These include the EdD or doctor of education and the DPsy or doctor of psychology. That does not mean, however, that all the students who wanted to pursue doctoral work were planning careers as researchers and professors. But, for much of the twentieth century doctoral students who planned professional careers attended PhD programs originally

Completing a Professional Practice Dissertation: A Guide for Doctoral Students and Faculty, pp. 23–59

created to prepare researchers. However, as noted in Chapter 1, this situation became increasingly less acceptable. Taylor and Beasley (2005) found there was a "disjuncture between what PhD programmes were training students to be, namely academics, and what they were increasingly doing ... which was working in other forms of employment" (p. 10). As a result, a new form of doctorate began to emerge that has become known as the *professional doctorate* or the *professional practice doctorate*. As Green and Powell (2005) tell us,

> For many professionally related subjects, the traditional doctorate is of little significance. It is perhaps for this reason that the recent developments in Practiced-Based Doctorates and the Professional Doctorate have arisen.... The Professional Doctorate has filled a gap that the traditional PhD was unable to fill. (pp. 53-54)

If dissatisfaction with traditional, Humboldt-style PhD doctorates was one impetus for the creation of professional practice doctorates (PPD), another was the growing body of knowledge, skills, and expertise in many of the professions. In fields where a bachelor's degree might have been considered over-preparation 100 years ago, and a master's degree adequate preparation 50 years ago, the explosion of knowledge and expertise now justifies a doctorate in the practice of that profession.

FAMILY CHARACTERISTICS OF PROFESSIONAL PRACTICE DOCTORATES

The PsyD in psychology, EdD in education, DPharm in pharmacy, DNP (doctor of nursing practice) in nursing, and DPP or doctor of professional practice in business are all quite different. However, there is a set of "family characteristics" or "family resemblances" that are shared among professional practice doctorates (PPD). Few of these new PPD have all these characteristics but members of this family of doctorates are more likely to have these characteristics (Green & Powell, 2005) than doctoral programs from the PhD research family:

- Courses prepare students for professional practice in the field.
- The content and skills students learn are broader and more interdisciplinary than traditional PhD programs because professional practice requires a broader range of skills, expertise, and knowledge.

- The components of coursework, research, and field work are more integrated and connected in PPD programs.
- Faculty in PPD programs typically include more practicing professionals than is typical of traditional PhD programs.
- The curriculum includes more relevant field experiences that prepare students for professional practice.
- PPD programs may be the first professional degree as is illustrated by the DPsy in psychology or a midcareer degree as is the case with many EdD and DNP programs.
- PPD programs tend to rely on portfolios rather than qualifying or comprehensive exams for student assessment.
- PDD programs tend to emphasize "more integration with the professional workplace" and this can often "reduce the dominance of the university sector (the 'academy') and its tendency to privilege academic knowledge over professional knowledge" (Green & Powell, 2005, p. 88).
- "There is a strong practice element that, in turn, is mediated by intellectual understanding and reflection" (p. 90).
- Students in PPD programs are typically older, come from a wider range of backgrounds, pay their own program costs, and already have experience in their chosen profession.
- Students in PPD programs typically complete the doctorate part time while working full time and carrying family responsibilities.
- In recognition of the experience and expertise students can contribute to a doctoral program, PPD programs often accept students in cohorts that complete the program together and thus form a cooperating and collaborating group that provides support and encouragement to members of the cohort, and share expertise.
- Dissertations in PPD programs tend to be shorter and to focus on problems of practice.
- Dissertations in PPD programs are typically done "in the field" and are likely to use methods of research and scholarship suited to the context of practice.
- Traditional PhD research dissertations generally use a research model that involves conducting research to test the implications of a particular theory in tightly controlled settings; PPD dissertations generally address a real world problem and may develop or use theory but the goal may not be theory development. The goal may be to develop a solution to a real-world problem. The result of a traditional dissertation is theoretical knowledge; the result of a PPD dissertation is professional knowledge.

As you can see from this list, PPD programs focus heavily on the skills, knowledge and expertise needed to practice a profession. In the next section you will see how a PPD developed in the field of psychology.

The Case of the Psychology Doctorate

In our view, the Humbolt model of doctoral programs is not a good "fit" for programs that prepare students for professional practice. However, that view has not always been supported in professional doctoral programs. A debate about professional practice doctorates in psychology led to two "solutions" that now compete with each other in the academic marketplace. In the 1949 "Boulder Conference" the American Psychological Association (APA) decided that all doctoral level professional psychologists should be prepared in the *scientist-practitioner model*—which meant they were prepared as researchers or scientists and also as practitioners. Although generations of clinical psychologists have been trained under the "Boulder Model" it was controversial from the beginning because many felt the emphasis on producing scientists and researchers generally took precedence over preparing strong practitioners. Many critics argued that the result of the Boulder model was an overemphasis on becoming scientists, to the detriment of efforts to prepare students to become practicing professionals. As Gelso (2006) put it,

> The scientist–practitioner model of graduate education in the fields of professional psychology … has been a source of great controversy over the 40 years since its inception. Although the causes of the controversy are many, one of the bottom-line issues is whether it is viable to train students to be scientists generally and psychological researchers specifically when, at the core, these students enter training with the wish to be practitioners and not researchers. (p. 3)

Gelso argued that clinical psychology programs should continue to try and produce scientist practitioners, which is typically the goal of PhD programs in clinical psychology today. On the other hand, after reviewing the research on the career patterns of clinical psychologists trained as scientist practitioners, Dick (1996) summarized the research this way: "The majority of clinical psychologists didn't publish articles. For that matter, they didn't present conference papers, prepare manuscripts, write research papers for internal circulation, or write reviews." As you might expect, Dick does not hold positive views of the scientist practitioner model for preparing professional practitioners. He is not alone.

The continuing criticism finally resulted in the Vail Conference, held in 1973. At Vail, Colorado, the APA formally endorsed a professional practice doctorate, the PsyD or "doctor of psychology" which was to focus on the preparation of practitioners, not scientists. The newer model of doctoral preparation for professional psychologists is the *scholar practitioner model* that was created at the Vail Conference in 1973.

> The Vail conferees endorsed different principles, leading to an alternative training model.... Psychological knowledge, it was argued, had matured enough to warrant creation of explicitly professional programs along the lines of professional programs in medicine, dentistry, and law. These professional programs were to be added to, not replace, Boulder-model programs. Further, it was proposed that different degrees should be used to designate the scientist role (PhD) from the practitioner role (PsyD—Doctor of Psychology). Graduates of Vail-model professional programs are scholar—professionals: the focus is primarily on clinical practice and less on research. (Norcross & Castle, 2002, p. 22)

Today the PhD and the PsyD are both available. In New York the professional practice degree in psychology (PsyD) is offered by Adelphi University, Alfred University, Hofstra University, Long Island University, New York University, Pace University, SUNY-Albany, and Yeshiva University. Also, perhaps because some smaller institutions put a larger portion of their energy into developing strong links with practicing professionals in the community, there are a number of accredited PsyD programs at small colleges and universities around the country. They include Alliant University-Fresno, Antioch University-New England, Azusa Pacific University, Biola University, Carlos Albizu University-Miami, Chesnut Hill College, Fuller Theological Seminary, George Fox University, Immaculata University, Loyola College in Maryland, Marywood University, Our Lady of the Lake University, Regent University, Wheaton College, Widener University, and The Wright Institute.

Today, the scientist-practitioner model of professional preparation continues to be offered by many departments of psychology and typically leads to a PhD. While the goal is to prepare professional practitioners, most of the programs using this model, which are accredited by the American Psychological Association (APA), are clearly adaptations of the Humboldt model of doctoral preparation. However, many of the DPsy programs, also accredited by the APA, represent a rejection of the von Humboldt model. They put much more emphasis on professional work in the field, they expect students to do a dissertation that deals directly with an issue of professional practice, they involve practicing psychologists in teaching, mentoring, and supervising students to a greater degree, and they more tightly link coursework to professional practice. This "scholar-practitioner" model that leads to a DPsy is an example of what we are calling a professional practice doctoral program. Today scientist practitioner PhD programs in professional psychology exist alongside DPsy programs. However, you need only to study the curriculum of a few DPsy programs to see that they have a different emphasis. That is not the case with another doctoral degree, which is the most common doctorate in America today, the EdD.

Is the EdD a Professional Practice Doctorate?

One of the most popular specialized degrees that *seems* to be a professional doctorate is the EdD or doctor of education. However, the parentage and purpose of the EdD is somewhat questionable. It should, logically, be a degree offered by schools and colleges of education for students who plan professional careers in education. The equivalent in a college of business would be the DBA or doctor of business administration and the DPS, or doctor of professional studies, which are always PPD programs. That is not how it has worked out in education, however.

Today, schools and colleges of education that want to offer one or more doctoral degrees must decide between the PhD (first awarded in education at Teachers College, Columbia University in 1893) or the EdD (first offered in America at Harvard in 1920 and in the world at the University of Toronto in 1881 (Green & Powell, 2005, p. 87). Theoretically, the curriculum of a PhD program in education was supposed to prepare scholars and researchers who would work primarily in schools and colleges of education. The EdD curriculum was to prepare practitioners. From the beginning, however, there have been intense discussions, to put it mildly, about the relationships between the PhD and the EdD—what they *should be* and what they *actually are*. (That the Harvard education faculty only opted for an EdD after the rest of the faculty at Harvard rejected their petition to offer a PhD in education set the tone for discussions over the last 90+ years.) Today there is very little, if anything, that can reliably distinguish between virtually all PhD programs in education and virtually all EdD programs. For example, the University of Houston's Department of Curriculum and Instruction offers only the EdD to doctoral students, regardless of whether they are preparing to become researchers or practitioners. This is due to an initial decision by the state of Texas to restrict the department to EdD degrees. However, many of Houston's doctoral students go on to take academic positions at research universities. On the other hand, the equivalent department at Louisiana State University offers only the PhD, regardless of career goals, because the state of Louisiana initially required the department to select one, and only one, doctoral degree. They selected the PhD.

Shulman and his colleagues (2006) summarized the current state of affairs this way:

> Instead of having two separate entities that effectively accomplish distinct functions, we have confounding and compromise, a blurring of boundaries, resulting in the danger that we achieve rigorous preparation neither for practice nor for research. (p. 26)

We will have more to say about this later, but it is clear that in schools and colleges of education, whether the degree offered is a PhD or an EdD provides absolutely no reliable information, by itself, as to whether the program is designed to prepare professional practitioners or academic researchers. The situation is further complicated by the fact that many programs, some offering a PhD and some an EdD, advertise that they are preparing professionals but actually require students to complete a program that is much more suited to a career as an academic researcher. Fortunately, there is currently an effort on the part of the Carnegie Foundation to address this problem. The Carnegie Project on the Education Doctorate (http://www.carnegiefoundation.org/programs/index.asp?key=1867) is a coalition of doctoral granting institutions supported by the Carnegie Foundation, that has the goal of developing appropriate and distinctive models for professional practice doctorates in education.

The Acceptance of Professional Practice Doctorates

The Humboldt doctorate, with its emphasis on research, is well established in American higher education, and any attempt to expand the range and type of doctorates offered will likely face opposition. Often, the opposition is based on tradition and inertia. "We have always done it *this* way, and that has worked well for us." A variation on this is the idea that focusing more on practical and professional matters somehow diminishes the quality of the degree. For example, when the State of California decided to allow California State University campuses to offer doctoral degrees in areas of professional practice, a major criticism was that the expansion made no sense—the doctoral degree was for scientists and researchers, not for practitioners. The term "credential inflation" was tossed about in the debate over whether to allow the California State University system to offer professional doctorates in areas like education. Before the decision, doctoral programs in California public universities were essentially limited to the other major university system in the state, the University of California. The plan for expanding the right to offer doctorates to California State University campuses generated resistance in favor of the other system, which had been offering PhDs and EdDs for many decades. In an article titled, *Credential Inflation and the Professional Doctorate in California Higher Education* (La Belle, 2004) the Center for Studies in Higher Education at the University of California Berkeley (CSU) argued for the expansion and against the idea that the new doctoral programs merely contributed to the undesirable trend toward "credential inflation" that meant people who wanted to enter certain professions had to complete more years of education. California did authorize the new professional practice doctorates at CSU campuses and it did so primarily because the state recognized that in all professions there have been unprecedented increases in both the knowledge base and the skills base that students need in order to become outstanding professional practitioners. Just 200 years ago, for example, teachers could graduate from high school, take a summer of teacher education coursework, and begin the Fall semester as a licensed elementary teacher. In the 1800s, however, the standards were increased and many teachers spent a year, then 2 years, and finally 4 years in a "normal" school where teachers were prepared. In the late 1800s and early 1900s, most of those normal schools were converted to colleges and universities where teachers were required to earn bachelor's degrees before beginning their careers as teachers. Today, many school districts expect to fill the ranks of their teaching staff with educators who have a master's degree. That pattern of increased requirements has also occurred in other professions and most agree that this is not an example of "credential inflation." Rather it is an example of the increasing requirements needed to reflect the growth and development of the profession. Medical education has followed a similar path. Before the Flexner Report in 1910 which resulted in much higher standards, medical schools might require as little as 1 year of study past a high school diploma before awarding the MD degree, and the typical length of medical study was 2 years after high school graduation.

Another example of the "credential inflation" argument was made in 2005 by Arthur Levine, then President of Teachers College, Columbia University. Levine was concerned over the status of the EdD versus the PhD in educational leadership. Levine's suggested solution to what he considered an unsatisfactory state of affairs was to eliminate the EdD completely and offer, instead, an education degree like the MBA. Levine's line of argument would have made von Humboldt proud. He argued that no professional practice doctorates should be offered in educational leadership. The doctorate should be limited to the PhD and awarded to students planning careers in research. Coincidentally, he argued that the proper places to offer those PhDs in educational leadership were research institutions like his own Teachers College. He saw the elimination of professional practice doctorates in educational leadership as both sensible and economical. They would be replaced by masters of educational leadership based on the MBA model from business.

Both Levine's conclusions and his logic seem oddly out of step with current trends in higher education and the development of the professions. At the same time Levine (2005) was recommending the elimination of the professional practice doctorate in educational leadership, a great many other professions are adding new options to the doctoral possibilities for students with professional aspirations. "The main growth area in doctoral studies over the past two decades has been in professional doctorates" (Taylor & Beasley, 2005). For example, at Levine's own Columbia University, the School of Nursing was the first to offer a doctor of nursing practice or DNP, beginning in 2004. The School of Nursing website describes the development and purpose of this professional practice doctorate:

> Columbia University School of Nursing faculty developed the DNP degree to educate nurses for the highest level of clinical expertise, including sophisticated diagnostic and treatment competencies.
>
> The degree builds upon advanced practice at the master's degree level and prepares graduates for fully accountable professional roles in several nursing specialties. The program is comprised of 30 credits of science underpinning practice, a year of full-time residency, and the completion of a scholarly portfolio of complex case studies, scholarly papers and published articles. (from http://sklad.cumc.columbia.edu/nursing/news/newsItem.php?newsID=1)

The School of Nursing at the University of Utah also voiced the conclusion that professional practice doctorates are playing an increasingly important role in the preparation of professionals:

> Nursing is moving in the direction of other health professions in the transition to the DNP. Medicine (MD), Dentistry (DDS), Pharmacy (PharmD), Psychology (PsyD), Physical Therapy (DPT) and Audiology (AudD) all offer practice doctorates. (from http://www.nurs.utah.edu/programs/dnp/index.html)

The School also explains why a doctorate in nursing practice is preferred over a master's degree:

> Over recent years, the increasing complexity of health care, the growth in scientific knowledge, and the use of increasingly sophisticated technology have required master's degree programs preparing nurses for advanced practice roles to expand the number of didactic and clinical clock hours far beyond the requirements of master's education in virtually any other field. Many nurse-practitioner master's programs around the country now exceed

60 credits and cannot be completed in less than three years; they often carry a credit load equivalent to doctoral degrees in the other health professions. College faculty have been forced to add content and clinical time to the program, increasing the intensity of the academic experience for students. Additional specific content areas have been identified as needed by advanced practice nurses, particularly new scientific information, genetics, informatics, and practice management. Furthermore, advanced practice nurses themselves identify content areas where they feel additional training is needed, including practice management, health policy, use of information technology, risk management, evaluation of evidence, and advanced diagnosis and management.

And the School distinguishes between the role of the PhD and DNP:

Doctoral programs in nursing fall into two principal types: research-focused and practice focused. Most research-focused programs grant the Doctor of Philosophy degree (PhD), while a small percentage offers the Doctor of Nursing Science degree (DNS, DSN, or DNSc). Designed to prepare nurse scientists and scholars, these programs focus heavily on scientific content and research methodology; and all require an original research project and the completion and defense of a dissertation or linked research papers. Practice-focused doctoral programs are designed to prepare experts in specialized advanced nursing practice. They focus heavily on practice that is innovative and evidence-based, reflecting the application of credible research findings. The two types of doctoral programs differ in their goals and the competencies of their graduates. They represent complementary and alternative approaches to the highest level of educational preparation in nursing.

The list of professional practice doctoral degrees today goes well beyond health care doctorates such as the MD, DNP, DO, DDM, and DVM. They include the:

(DM) Doctor of Music—Louisiana State University

(DCP) Doctorate in Clinical Practice—University of Southampton (United Kingdom)

(PharmD) Doctor of Pharmacy—St. Johns University, Purdue University

(DPT) Doctor of Physical Therapy—Melbourne University (Australia), Northern Arizona University

(DProf) Doctor of Professional Studies in executive leadership—Pace University

(DCS) Doctor of Consumer Science—Liverpool John Moores University (United Kingdom)

(DAEPsy) Doctor of Applied Educational Psychology—Newcastle University (United Kingdom)

(DSW Clinical) Clinical Doctor of Social Work—University of Pennsylvania

(EngD) Doctor of Engineering—Bristol University (United Kingdom)

This list is illustrative but by no means exhaustive; there are many, many other professional practice doctorates available today. The universities listed as offering a particular degree are also only illustrative. Hundreds of colleges and universities all over the world offer professional practice doctorates today, with new programs being added each year. There have also been a number of national initiatives to create groups of professional practice doctorates in a field. For example, in the United Kingdom, the "Engineering Doctorate (EngD) Scheme" was created in 1992 to encourage engineering departments to create exemplary professional practice doctorates in various fields of engineering. To date, over 20 doctoral programs have been developed.

Over the next 20 years, the type of doctoral degree that is generally termed a *professional practice doctorate* (Green & Powell, 2005) or *professional doctorate* (Scott, Brown, Lunt, & Thorne, 2004) will become an even larger percentage of the doctoral programs offered in the United Sates as well as the United Kingdom and Australia. Professional practice doctorates are now, and will likely continue to be, offered at two points in a person's career:

- As the initial degree preparing a student to independently practice a profession. Examples are the DPsy in psychology and the MD in medicine.
- As an advanced or midcareer degree designed to enhance the capabilities, skills, and abilities of students who are already prepared for and practicing in their chosen field. Examples include some DNP and EdD programs.

In their analysis of the current state of professional practice doctorates in education, Shulman et al. (2006) rejected Levine's position that they should be eliminated and instead endorsed the idea of a "new doctorate for the professional practice of education.... A new degree can help restore respect for the excellent work of education practitioners and leaders" (p. 28). The authors refer to this new degree as a professional practice doctorate or PPD, but they are not very concerned about the name; they are more concerned about the experiences of students who complete a new degree program.

We believe that, properly understood and designed, the highest professional degree in education deserves to be a doctorate—but not one so readily confounded with the doctorate needed to prepare education scholars.... In our judgment, the extent to which the professional practice doctorate requires a new vision demands a "zero-base" approach to design, without any of the assumptions that characterize the status quo. Tinkering toward the ideal is much less likely to succeed than starting with a clean slate. (p. 28)

In our view, higher education is in a state of flux regarding doctoral education. The traditional PhD, based on Humboldt's model and purpose, currently retains the prestige high ground primarily because it is the most established doctoral degree and it has the weight of history on its side. With the exception of the doctorates in law and medicine, which have existed even longer than the PhD, professional practice doctorates do not yet have the general prestige of a PhD. However, in our opinion, this will change rapidly as the public, and employers, become aware of the difference between PhDs and professional practice doctorates. As professional practice degrees become more established, and more familiar, the comparison between the PhD and the PPD will shift from one based on general prestige to a question of the "fit" between the degree program and career path. Students who plan careers as researchers and scholars in a particular discipline will continue to complete PhD degrees while students interested in professional practice will opt for PPD degrees.

PROFESSIONAL PRACTICE CAPSTONE EXPERIENCES: DISSERTATION? CAPSTONE PROJECT? PORTFOLIO? OR?

Professional practice doctorates typically have some form of capstone experience. That is, there is an activity or project, often near the end of the program, that requires students to use all of what they have learned to deal with one or more issues of professional practice. In some PPD programs this capstone is a dissertation; in others it is a portfolio. PPD programs, in fact, offer a variety of capstone experiences that are quite different from the traditional, Humboldt-style PhD dissertation. Even PPD dissertations are often quite different from the traditional PhD dissertation. In this section we will explore the characteristics of the most popular form of capstone experience in PPD programs today, the professional practice dissertation, and also look briefly at other types of capstone experiences that replace the dissertation.

What Distinguishes the PhD Research Dissertation From the PPD Dissertation

Figures 2.2 and 2.3 summarize the difference between the traditional dissertation model and a PPD dissertation model. Figure 2.3 is based on the assumption that a dissertation or some other form of capstone experience is required in the professional practice doctoral program. That is usually, but not always, the case. For example, St. John Fisher College in Rochester, New York offers a doctor of nursing practice that does not have a dissertation requirement. Instead, the College requires 1,000 hours of supervised clinical practice in a variety of settings. By way of comparison, the nearby University of Rochester also requires 1,000 hours of supervised clinical practice plus a "capstone project" in its DNP program.

> At the completion of the program, students defend an evidence-based capstone project, which they design as they progress through their practicum experiences and implement through their residency. The capstone project is the practice equivalent to a PhD research dissertation. (from http://www.son.rochester.edu/son/prospective-students/programs/dnp-phd-ms-phd/doctor-of-nursing-practice-dnp-program

A capstone experience like the one used at the University of Rochester is common in PPD programs. Generally students will produce a written description of a project or program they either initiated or evaluated, and defend the document at an oral exam. Duquense University in Pittsburgh described its capstone experience requirement for the doctor of nursing practice this way:

> This is a practice focused doctorate, not research focused. As a result the culminating work is not a dissertation but a capstone project which will demonstrate the ability of the graduate to contribute to the transformations needed in health care in creative and innovative ways by developing systems, programs of evaluation, or nursing interventions that improve health outcomes for populations of patients. (from http://www.nursing.duq.edu/gradDNP.html)

The standards for professional practice doctorates in nursing developed by the American Association of Colleges of Nursing (AACN, 2004, 2005, 2006) allow programs with no dissertation requirements or requirements that involve a less intensive "capstone project." However in all cases, AACN requires that the dissertation or similar experience be focused on clinical practice and address either a problem in practice or directly inform practice.

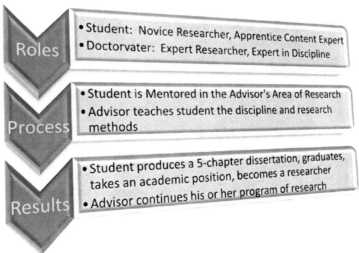

Figure 2.1. The traditional dissertation model.

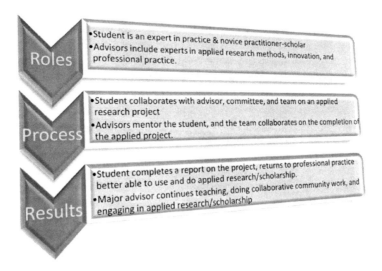

Figure 2.2. An alternative approach for the professional practice dissertation.

As illustrated in Figures 2.1 and 2.2, the traditional PhD model is simpler and more straightforward. A student usually works primarily with one major professor who helps the student select a topic, pick a research method, conduct the research, analyze the data, and write the dissertation. In this model the role of the major professor is similar to the *Doctorvater* in the original Humboldt model at the University of Berlin. The student learns both disciplinary content and research methodology from the major professor. The dissertation itself is typically 100 to 350 pages long and has five chapters: "Introduction," "Review of the Literature," "Methodology," "Results," and "Discussion."

The intellectual structure of the traditional dissertation is also well-defined (see Figure 2.3). This structure derives from the scientific method, particularly the method based on a philosophy of science called postpositivism that was first developed by Sir Karl Popper. From the perspective of postpositivism, the goal of the dissertation research, or any research, is to find laws or rules that can be generalized to other settings. However, you do not, in a single study, find ultimate truths or laws. There are always alternative explanations of why the results were what they were. The generalizations and laws are thus stated as theories and the implications of theories. That is because it is not possible to be 100% sure the theory is true. The great majority of PhD dissertations use this framework.

To illustrate this type of dissertation we will use Thai Nguyen's (2005) dissertation in the area of engineering. He was concerned that the current methods used to keep rotary grinding tools cool while in use were harmful to the environment. His dissertation was a study of an alternative to current grinding coolants. One alternative involved the use of very cold air and a vegetable oil mist mixture. Another focused on using liquid nitrogen as a coolant medium. His dissertation included several studies but one of them was a comparison of the grinding efficiency of his new mist method with conventional methods. The end result of the dissertation was a model for using alternative cooling methods that "offers a practical guideline for the optimal use of grinding coolants in achieving a balance between the demands of productivity and care for the environment." Dr. Nguyen's dissertation is available online at http://ses.library.usyd.edu.au/handle/2123/1689.

A very similar approach was used by Eileen Britt (2008) in her dissertation. In this case the innovation was a short-term educational therapy method called motivational enhancement therapy that was designed to increase the likelihood that adults with diabetes would manage their disease effectively. One aspect of her dissertation compared the effectiveness of the new therapy with that of the standard patient education method used at the hospital where the research was conducted.

A professional practice dissertation may use the traditional model shown in Figure 2.3, but many adopt a very different model (see Figure 2.4). As Figure 2.4 indicates, professional practice dissertations typically begin with a problem or issue of professional practice rather than a theory. Also, you must decide why you want to do the dissertation. That decision is made for you if you do a traditional dissertation. In the traditional model you are to conduct research to test the validity of a theory or the practical implications of a theory. However, that need not be the purpose of a professional practice dissertation. In Chapter 3 you will learn that there are many reasons for doing a professional practice dissertation.

Your reason or purpose for doing your dissertation research will have a significant impact on the research method you adopt, but regardless of the method used, many professional practice dissertations are conducted in real-world work environments and therefore call for involvement and participation on the part of professionals working in that context as well as program faculty at your institution. In fact, your supporting team may include professionals in your field who are both working practitioners and doctoral program faculty.

In addition to the focus on finding solutions to practical problems rather than theory development, there are other differences between traditional and professional practice dissertations:

- PPD dissertations tend to be done in the field, often in the setting where the doctoral student works.

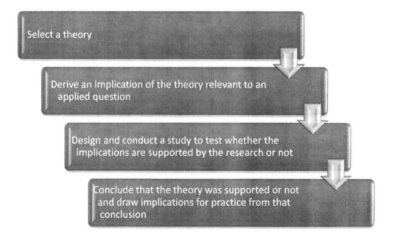

Figure 2.3.   The intellectual structure of a traditional dissertation about an applied issue.

- PPD dissertations tend to be done collaboratively rather than by a lone researcher because most of the significant issues of professional practice call for collaboration.

- PPD dissertations are more likely to use traditional qualitative, alternative quantitative, and nontraditional research methods because traditional experimental methods are not as well suited to research "in the field" nor are they as strong at addressing some of the types of questions that concern professionals. Often PPD dissertations are more concerned with "local" success than with finding universal laws while the goal of PhD research dissertations is often to test whether a theory is universally applicable or not.

- The format of the dissertation varies more in PPD programs than in PhD programs. The capstone experience may not even be called a dissertation. An e-portfolio, a capstone experience, or some other type of culminating experience may take the place of a traditional dissertation. However, the "article dissertation" is becoming more popular in both traditional and PPD programs. It will be discussed in more detail later in this chapter.

- The approach to mentoring dissertation students and for assessing the dissertation varies more in PPD than in traditional research PhD programs. The dissertation committee on some PPD dissertations may be much more involved as colleagues and co-researchers, and there is often more participation by professional practitioners than is typical of PhD dissertation committees.

These are some of the differences between research dissertations in PhD programs and professional practice dissertations. Several of the differences noted in this list deserve more attention because they have such a strong impact on the dissertation work of PPD students.

Use of a Wider Range of Methodologies

There are significant differences in the range of research methods that are accepted and encouraged in PPD dissertations. Pacific University's DPsy program, for example, has these dissertation guidelines for students:

The doctoral dissertation provides evidence of scholarly competence representing an original contribution to psychology. In keeping with the practitioner-scholar model of the School, dissertations are not confined to traditional experimental studies, but may use a variety of formats: single case experimental designs, case studies of individuals, groups or systems;

program development or evaluation; experimental or correlational research; or a synthesis and extension of scholarly literature. The complete dissertation is defended in an oral examination. (from http://www.pacificu.edu/spp/clinical/dissertation.cfm)

Antioch College's guidelines for their DPsy dissertation are even broader:

The PsyD dissertation is viewed primarily as an educational vehicle that contributes to the development of a practitioner with the knowledge and skills of a scholar, capable of bringing scientific inquiry into the various realms of professional psychology. Purposive, disciplined inquiry and formal research for the PsyD are seen as integral to, rather than distinct from, his or her professional practice in real, locally meaningful situations. The dissertation is viewed as both an educational process, contributing to the practitioner's professional development, and a distinct contribution to identifiable domains of professional psychological practice and/or scholarship.

The dissertation process asks students to integrate specific areas of psychological theory and research, which are consonant with their professional mission, with a repertoire of scholarly and scientific methodologies in order to develop answers to a set of problems. Our students are encouraged to tap into a broad range of research questions and methods in their consideration of the dissertation design. Examples of projects a student might pursue include empirical studies, theoretical papers, program evaluations, integrative case studies, design and implementation of innovative programs, and public policy issues. The dissertation should seek to inform an identifiable audience. Students are expressly required to identify exemplars within the current psychology and social science professional literature (e.g., published journal articles and book chapters) upon which to model their dissertations. These dissertations range in length from approximately sixty to one hundred pages. (from http://www.antiochne.edu/cp/dissertation.cfm)

Antioch expects students to address a relevant issue of professional practice, but the acceptable methods to do that are diverse, ranging from empirical research to evaluations of existing programs, case studies, documentation of design and implementation projects, and dissertations on public policy issues. In fact, the only restriction on how you go about doing a DPsy dissertation at Antioch appears to be that you must be able to "identify exemplars within the current psychology and social science professional literature." If you can find journal articles or book chapters that use the approach you want to use, that is a potential format for a DPsy dissertation at Antioch.

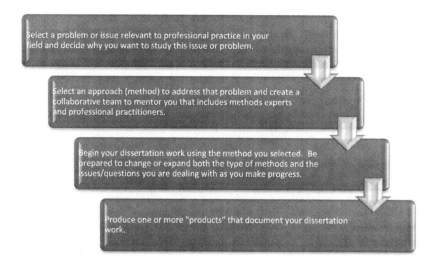

Figure 2.4. A model for a professional practice dissertation.

Options for Mentoring and Assessing PPD Dissertations

In terms of providing support to students while they complete their dissertation, there are several models in widespread use.

The Doctorvater Model

The most common model in PhD research programs involves collaboration almost exclusively with a major professor (Chair) until the student is ready to defend the dissertation in a final oral exam. In this model, other members of the dissertation committee may not see the dissertation until the major professor believes the current draft is very close to the final version. While there are advantages to this approach, especially to busy dissertation committee members who must budget their time carefully, we think a more inclusive model is desirable, particularly in PPD programs where students do applied or project dissertations. We base our opinion on the fact that PPD dissertations are typically done in real world settings such as offices, factories, schools, and hospitals. Successful dissertations done in work settings generally calls for collaboration and teamwork. The dissertation committee should reflect that need by operating as a collaborative team. Using a collaborative model makes the dissertation committee function more like the typical professional workplaces in which most PPD graduates will be expected to work.

The Inclusive Committee Model

In a more inclusive model of dissertation mentoring and assessment, students work primarily with their major advisor (Chair) as they develop their dissertation concept, do the research, and write the dissertation, but the other members of the dissertation committee will also be kept abreast of developments and have the opportunity to offer their own advice and suggestions about how to proceed. Where necessary, the dissertation committee may meet as a group to resolve issues and help the student make decisions about methods, procedures, problems, and theoretical issues.

In the *Doctorvater* and Inclusive model, the culminating evaluation of the dissertation is an oral examination in which the student defends the dissertation. This is a holdover from the disputation model in the Middle Ages but it is such an established component of doctoral programs that the oral defense will likely survive for many more decades. The examining committee will typically consist of the three or four members of the dissertation committee and a an additional member who is appointed by the graduate school or some other administrative unit. That additional member often does not participate heavily in the examination but does have the responsibility for seeing to it that the student is appropriately treated and that the guidelines and rules for dissertation defenses are followed. Generally, the additional member of the committee does not have a vote unless there is a tie. In that case, he or she can cast the deciding vote according to the rules at some institutions. Votes to approve a dissertation will usually be conditional on specified changes that need to be made by the student. The committee may elect to supervise that process as a group, with each member rereading the dissertation and approving the changes, or the committee may delegate that task to the major professor (Chair).

A Collaborative Model

Although it is not yet widely used, the collaborative model of dissertation supervision is more common in newer PPD programs. In the collaborative model, members of the dissertation committee are also collaborators on the research project. A student studying a new method for providing professional development education to the nursing staff of a large hospital might have a committee made up of a major professor from the PPD program, the director of nursing education at the hospital who is also a teaching professor and internship supervisor for the program, another professor at the university who has experience in the research method being used in the study (participatory action research, for example), and one of the nursing educators at the hospital who has extensive experience delivering professional development education at that hospital. In this model, members of the dissertation committee are also colleagues and coresearchers with the student. They are much more heavily involved and invested in the dissertation research than is typical of committees in either the *Doctorvater* or Inclusive model. Some consider this a violation of the purpose of the dissertation—to be a student's first independent research project. That criticism is based on the implicit assumption that the lone researcher model of research is good for the dissertation because that is the typical model of scholarship after graduation. However, like the Lone Ranger' s approach to law enforcement, the lone researcher's approach to applied research is becoming more a topic of historical discussion than a contemporary reality. As noted earlier, a more effective and increasingly more common approach to the solution of professional practice problems involves collaborative rather than individualistic work.

Alternative Purposes for a PPD Dissertation

Most universities define the purpose of the dissertation in research PhD programs as the production of *independent, original, and significant scholarship*. However, many studies of dissertations have shown that this is far more often stated than achieved as a working requirement for PhD dissertations. In her study of the PhD dissertation Barbara Lovitts (2006) found that faculty and administrators often say dissertation research must be original and significant, but in practice they do not expect it of graduate students and they rarely get it in a dissertation.

> Although significance is frequently stated as a requirement for the PhD, faculty do not expect graduate students to make significant contributions. Indeed, they noted [the faculty who participated in her study] that graduate students rarely make them. Instead, faculty look for evidence that the student has the ability to make a significant contribution in the future. (Lovitts, 2006, p. 173)

While the stated purpose of research PhD dissertations is usually defined as making an original and significant contribution to the scientific knowledge of a field, universities that offer doctorates in professional practice often define the professional practice dissertation as an effort to solve a problem rather than discover universal knowledge. For example, the University of Illinois defines the purpose of its EdD dissertation this way:

> The EdD dissertation should demonstrate the EdD candidate's ability to relate academic knowledge to the problems of professional practice. The dissertation should be characterized by the kind of synthesis of experiences that is the hallmark of a highly qualified professional. The demonstration of these

qualities may take a variety of forms such as: (a) a field study; (b) a scholarly, original paper dealing with the interpretation and evaluation of the work of a particular writer whose findings have a significant bearing on any aspect of the educational enterprise where the significance has not been clearly indicated by earlier studies; or, (c) an analytic report demonstrating the student's ability to carry a project through from conceptualization to evaluation. (quoted from http://www.ed.uiuc.edu/saao/grad/handbook/edd.html)

These expectations are typical of PPD dissertations in many fields. Essentially, a PPD dissertation must involve thoughtful and considered approaches to issues that are relevant to professional practice.

Acceptable Formats for a PPD Dissertation

There is one established and several emerging formats for a dissertation today. Several of the options will be briefly discussed here. Two of the options, the five-chapter dissertation (five-CD) and the three-article dissertation (TAD) are dealt with in detail in later chapters.

The Five-Chapter Dissertation

For many decades the traditional five-chapter dissertation format has been the only acceptable option in the majority of American doctoral programs. The five chapters typically focus on these topics:

- Overview
- Literature Review
- Methodology
- Results
- Discussion

The great majority of the many *how-to* books on doing a dissertation assume the five-chapter format will be used. Most also assume that the dissertation will be based on the dominant empirical, positivist/postpositivist approach to research that emphasizes the goal of testing a theory.

While the five-chapter dissertation (five-CD) has been around for a long time, there are reasons to seriously consider other options. As noted, the five-chapter dissertation is deeply embedded in postpositivism, which is one of the three major philosophies of science that undergird research and scholarship in the social sciences, the helping professions, education, and business. The other two contemporary philosophies of science, *interpretivism* and *critical theory* (Willis, 2007), are increasingly popular alternatives to postpositivism. Graduate students whose dissertations are based on one of these two alternative paradigms—interpretivism and critical theory—and particularly students in PPD programs, often do dissertations that are poorly suited to the traditional five chapter, positivist, format. Slattery (1997) follows Stanford University's Elliot Eisner in pointing out that the traditional research models, and the traditional research article format, do not work well when the scholar is using a postmodern framework (which may be critical or interpretive). Common components of a postmodern analysis such as multiple understandings and multiple forms of representation, for example, are often better presented in formats more at home in the humanities than in the hard sciences.

In an article published in *Educational Researcher,* Duke and Beck (1999) made a case for "alternative formats for the dissertation." They define the traditional dissertation format this way:

A lengthy document (typically 200-400 pages in length) on a single topic presented through separate chapters for the introduction, literature review, methodology, results, and conclusions. (p. 31)

Duck and Beck conclude that:

The dissertation in this format is ill-suited to the task of training doctoral students in the communicative aspects of educational research, and is largely ineffectual as a means of contributing knowledge to the field. (p. 31)

The Article Dissertation

Much of the Duke and Beck paper is devoted to an analysis of the problems with the traditional format. Other authors have made similar critiques. Gerber (2000), for example, pointed out that the traditional 200+ page dissertation in education is "written for a very limited audience, the candidate's committee" and that "library shelves are filled with dissertations that have never been opened." He also criticizes the effort put into training students to write in a format "they will probably never use again"—a criticism also made by Krathwohl (1994) more than a decade ago. Writing a traditional dissertation requires "students to spend months writing at length and in great detail about every aspect of the research." However, once they graduate most of the scholarly and professional writing they will do requires very different styles. Gerber mentions three types of writing students do after graduation:

1. Writing journal articles,
2. "Communicating with practitioners," and
3. "Writing for external funding."

For professional practitioners we would add additional types of writing such as:

4. Communicating with the public,
5. Writing to influence policy,
6. Creating training and educational materials, and
7. Writing to develop collaboration with groups such as patients, customers, clients, or parents.

However, Gerber's conclusion applies to these additional types as well: "The writing style required of the traditional dissertation does not prepare students for the type of writing necessary for the post-dissertation stage of their careers." He proposes that the time and effort invested by students and mentors on dissertations should be invested in developing writing skills that will be useful to the student after graduation.

Gerber's (2000) preferred alternative is to use the "article format" for dissertations. Ironically, he points out that while the great majority of faculty in many disciplines still believe the traditional five chapter format is the *only* acceptable format, the "notable exception" to this comes from faculty in the *hard* sciences. In this bastion of traditional postpositivist research, dissertations based on articles written for publication in refereed journals have long been accepted as an alternative dissertation format. Adopting this format in a PPD program gives students more training in a style of writing closer to the type that will be needed after graduation. It also means more dissertation studies are published. "Much dissertation research [reported in the traditional five-chapter format] never gets published since many students have lost the motivation to examine the same work another time" (Gerber, 2000). Article dissertations would expand the audience for the student's study considerably as "few researchers, teachers or administrators to which the research may be of use read the lengthy dissertations archived on university library shelves" (Gerber, 2000).

Typically, the "article" dissertation, often referred to as a TAD (three-article dissertation), has five elements:

- Introduction—introduces and explains the articles that follow.
- Article 1
- Article 2
- Article 3
- Conclusion—ties the three papers together and proposes both general implications and future scholarship that naturally follows from the work already done.

For examples of detailed guidelines on how to produce "article dissertations" see:

- the Clark University website for information on their "three article dissertation or TAD (http://www.clarku.edu/departments/geography/phddis.cfm),
- the Harvard Graduate School of Arts and Sciences (http://www.gsas.harvard.edu/publications/hb-govt.php)
- the Louisiana State University website for thesis and dissertation guidelines (http://appl003.lsu.edu/grad/gradschool.nsf/$Content/ETD+Guidelines+pdf/$file/ETDguidelines.pdf),
- the University of Alabama guidelines for "article-style dissertations" (http://graduate.ua.edu/thesis/)
- the University of Utah, health sciences website (http://www.health.utah.edu/HealthEd/PhD2006.pdf)

Many other universities in North America, the United Kingdom, and Australia encourage the use of TADs in both traditional and PPD programs, but the links above illustrate the general approach to this type of dissertation.

A variation on the "standard" TAD format for a dissertation involves documents associated with a project. For example, if a student in a PPD program for educational leadership did a dissertation on a project involving additional services for new immigrant children and parents, the documents in the dissertation might include:

1. The proposal that obtained funding for the project.
2. The collaboratively developed curriculum plan for the program.
3. Recruiting and support materials developed for parents including both print as well as video (e.g., a video of a presentation the student made at a parent's group, or a video clip of a television spot announcement encouraging participation in the program).
4. An article on the evaluation of the project.

A dissertation consisting of these four documents with short introductory and concluding sections would meet the goals of Gerber and others because they would demonstrate the student's ability to communicate effectively with several different audiences and for different purposes. Variations on this model seem particularly appropriate for PPD students.

An Emerging Option: Electronic Dissertations

Taking the dissertation off the page and putting it online, on a DVD, or on some other electronic media makes many options possible. For example, the linear sequence of a dissertation—Chapter 1, then Chapter 2, then Chapter 3, and so on—is no longer required. Dissertations can be created that have many different structures other than the traditional linear framework. The second advantage is that students are no longer restricted to black ink-on-paper. Electronic dissertations can include video, audio, animation, 3D graphics, links to other online materials, and much more.

Dissertations of this type are generally referred to as *electronic theses and dissertations (ETD)*. For over a decade the *International Symposium on Electronic Theses and Dissertations* (http://epc.ub.uu.se/ETD2007/) has served as a meeting place for innovators interested in developing methods, guidelines, and procedures for expanding the format of dissertations beyond the traditional black ink on white paper. A number of universities are already experimenting with "electronic theses and dissertations" or ETD. They include Harvard University, Humboldt University (Berlin), Massachusetts Institute of Technology, Michigan State University, University of New Brunswick (Canada), University of Arizona, University of Georgia, University of Iowa, University of Waterloo (Canada), Virginia Commonwealth University, Virginia Tech University, and West Virginia University. Some universities are simply placing traditional ink-on-paper dissertations on the Internet so they are freely available to anyone with Internet access. Others are going much further and allowing the inclusion of many types of data such as audio, video, and high resolution still and animated graphics. This has made some alternative formats for dissertations, such as documentary films possible. While this option is not widely available to doctoral students, significant progress is being made on all the remaining issues related to ETD. For example, to ensure the long-term availability of ETD, Virginia Tech University's Digital Library and Archives (http://scholar.lib.vt.edu/theses/) now has archive copies of over 10,000 ETDs from many different universities. The site also has links to other ETD archives at institutions such as the Economic University of Vienna, MIT, North Carolina State University, Louisiana State University, Uppsala University (Sweden), California Institute of Technology, Humboldt University of Berlin, and the Technical University of Dresden.

PORTFOLIOS, CAPSTONES, AND PROJECTS: ALTERNATIVES TO DISSERTATIONS AND EXAMS

A common component of traditional PhD doctoral programs is a comprehensive examination that assesses a student's mastery of the content taught in the courses and an understanding of the research methods students were expected to know and use. These examinations often involve a series of questions that students must answer on a specific day, or days. Students typically take these exams when they are finished, or almost finished, with their doctoral coursework. These are "high stakes" exams that make or break a students' doctoral career. Students generally have two chances to "pass the comps" before they are dropped from the doctoral program. In professional practice doctoral programs such exams have been used for years, in part because they have been used for even longer in traditional doctoral programs. However, despite the fact comprehensive exams are still widely used in PPD programs, many of the recently revised programs are now shifting to some form of portfolio assessment in place of a comprehensive exam. For example, the required portfolio in the community college leadership doctoral program at Oregon State University requires a portfolio that serves three purposes:

1. It is an alternative to preliminary written examination
2. It provides written documentation of student's understanding of major field (mastery of outcomes for community college leadership program)
3. It documents the student's capability for research (adapted from http://oregonstate.edu/education/programs/docs/ portfolio_guidelines.doc)

At Iowa State University the educational leadership doctoral program combines a portfolio requirement with a capstone experience to meet several requirements. Iowa State describes the capstone experience this way:

> When coursework is substantially completed, students participate in a Capstone Experience in which they use their knowledge, skills, and abilities in a specific problem-based situation in a public or private sector organization. The purpose of the capstone is twofold: 1) to engage students in doing educational leadership and 2) to collaboratively support educational organizations with assistance in addressing a need.
>
> The experience can be completed individually or in a team of students working in the same organizational setting. The length of time is variable, depending on the nature of the experience. The student works within the framework of the organization, assists in carrying out its mission, and engages in reflective and scholarly endeavors suitable to advanced graduate studies. (quoted from http://www.elps.hs.iastate.edu/Academics/document/ PhD_ELPS.pdf)

Iowa State's portfolio includes several types of information:

There are two key components of portfolio assessment for ELPS [Educational Leadership and Policy Studies] doctoral students. The first is the portfolio assessment process, and the second is the presentation portfolio.

The portfolio assessment process has been designed to support learning and development in the six major program domains throughout the doctoral program. Through this process, students monitor and reflect on their learning in each domain. Portfolio assessment is an opportunity for students to understand and celebrate their own learning, to set goals for improvement, and to receive feedback from important stakeholders such as the major professor, committee members, and other individuals who may be involved in the student's program.

As part of the portfolio assessment process, ... each student reviews his/her learning in the six domains three times during the program. At each review, the student assesses the current level of proficiency in each domain, selects an example of work he/she has produced in the domain, writes a reflective self-assessment about learning in the domain, and seeks feedback from the major professor.

After the third self-assessment, the materials from all the reviews are compiled in a presentation portfolio, using the guidelines below. The presentation portfolio is submitted to the Program of Study (POS) committee so that it can be discussed at the prelim orals. The discussion at the meeting should focus not only on the student's current level of achievement but also on the student's learning history, i.e., the process through which current achievement was developed. (In addition to discussing the presentation portfolio at the prelim orals, the POS committee will also discuss the capstone project.)

The presentation portfolio is a learning portfolio rather than a professional portfolio.... In contrast, a professional portfolio is a summative collection of best work that might be presented to potential employers. Although the ELPS portfolio assessment process focuses on portraying the learning process over time, it should assist students in identifying materials that could be useful in developing a professional portfolio. (quoted from http://www.elps.hs.iastate.edu/Academics/document/portfolio_assess.pdf)

Note that at Iowa State the portfolio does not substitute for the preliminary exam, but in a growing number of programs, it does. However, at Iowa State the "prelim" is not the traditional exam where students sit for the exam for many hours, or days, and answer essay questions developed by the faculty. Instead, the exam is a meeting with faculty that focuses on the capstone experience and the portfolio:

The meeting to satisfy the requirement of the preliminary oral examination will be scheduled when the project is completed. In addition to the POS committee, a representative from the capstone placement site is encouraged to attend either in person or via speakerphone. A student will bring his/her learning portfolio to the meeting. The student will present his/her capstone project and describe how the experience related to the six program component areas. The portfolio will be circulated to the committee and used as a basis for additional discussion. (quoted from http://www.elps.hs.iastate.edu/Academics/document/capstone_experience.pdf)

In some professional fields, the portfolio even substitutes for the dissertation. This is not yet common in PPD programs, but it is becoming more and more popular. For example, at New York University, students in the professional doctoral program in occupational therapy receive a DPS, or doctor of professional studies. They do not complete a separate dissertation. Instead, they prepare a professional portfolio:

At the completion of the DPS degree, students will defend an evidence-based professional electronic portfolio ("e-portfolio"). The e-portfolio will document how the student has integrated knowledge and skills learned in the curriculum to his/her specialty practice area. (quoted from http://steinhardt.nyu.edu/depts/ot/programs/23)

There are three steps to the NYU portfolio development process:

First, students complete an analysis of their current practices to determine career goals consistent with their area of specialization.

Second, students use their academic coursework and clinical experience to collect "artifacts" that demonstrate advancement of knowledge, skills, and abilities gained through the integrated academic and clinical work within the program.

Third, students organize and catalog their artifacts. In the final course, Professional Portfolio: Advanced Practice E40.3310, students present their e-portfolio to a panel of three faculty members. Faculty review the e-portfolio based on the original, professional development plan and its consistency with the evidence-based knowledge in the field of inquiry. (quoted from http://steinhardt.nyu.edu/depts/ot/programs/23)

Today, only a few professional practice doctoral programs require students to submit a professional portfolio in lieu of a dissertation. There are, however, a number of professional practice doctoral programs where portfolios, or some other form of documentation, take the place of a dissertation. For example, the Texas A&M Health Sciences Center in Houston allows students to do a traditional dissertation and defend it in an oral exam or to do a series of papers based on their coursework and field experiences and to defend at least one of them in an oral defense similar to a dissertation defense (see http://tamhsc.edu/education/catalog/srph/ phdgrad.html for more information).

Changes in the dissertation requirement are more commonplace in new professional practice doctoral programs. Many have modified their dissertation requirement so that it is more closely integrated into the other experiences within the program. A good example is the University of Connecticut. Its recently revised EdD program does require a dissertation, but it is based on a series of case studies students develop in experiences across the doctoral program:

> The dissertation would take the form of a cross-case analysis that provides a comprehensive integration and synthesis of the four case situations students prepared in the program. In the cross-case analysis students would adhere to a methodology that would ensure trustworthiness and credibility of their analyses. In doing so the students' analyses would integrate and synthesize theoretical frameworks, findings from research studies, and data from their own case studies into a comprehensive and thorough articulation of key perspectives on systemic school reform. The skills required to conduct such a cross-case analysis are similar to the situational assessment analogical reasoning and structural thinking capabilities that characterize the reasoning process of experts. (quoted from http://www.education.uconn.edu/ departments/edlr/edadmin_EDD_course.cfm)

The University of Connecticut justifies this approach on the basis that the work done will help develop skills and understandings that will be very useful in the professional settings where students will spend their careers after graduation.

The University of Connecticut's School of Education is ranked number 1 in New England and 31st nationally in the 2008 *U.S. News and World Report* rankings. Another highly ranked university has also taken a different approach to the educational leadership dissertation. Ranked 21st nationally, the University of Maryland's EdD program in leadership allows students to complete a traditional dissertation or a "doctoral research study." A *doctoral research study*:

> addresses a problem of practice, where the focus is upon the integration of knowledge or its application. A variety of research methods may be used, resulting in a number of alternative forms of scholarly study, such as a program design study, a curriculum evaluation study, a policy analysis study, or a knowledge synthesis study. A dissertation generates or confirms knowledge and may be more linked to theory than practice, but may also use a variety of research methods, including empirical, interpretive, or critical. All doctoral research studies and dissertations will result in a substantial written document. (quoted from http://www.education.umd.edu/EDPL/areas/ prog5-a.htm)

Finally, third ranked George Peabody College of Education at Vanderbilt University offers another interesting variation in the mix of portfolio, qualifying exam, and dissertation. The EdD program in educational leadership requires a day-long qualifying exam that occurs near the end of the student's coursework. However, no portfolios and no dissertation are required. Instead, there is a "capstone experience" that takes up the last year of the 3 year doctoral program. The year long, collaborative, capstone experience "is an independent research and analytic activity embedded in a group project. The group project is designed to integrate theories and tools learned throughout the program, and should demonstrate mastery of concepts and methods" (quoted from http://peabody.vanderbilt.edu/x3810.xml).

It begins with a set of problems:

> Students will be presented with a panel of problems of practice originating from external practitioners and policymakers, generated through the suggestion and review of LPO faculty [Leadership, Policy, & Organizations] members. LPO faculty will select final capstone problems.

> Each individual problem will correspond to areas of LPO faculty expertise and disciplines ingrained in the program curriculum (e.g., sociology of education/higher education; governance and politics of education/higher education; economics of education/higher education). Three or four problems will be developed each year for each program specialty, with the assumption that no more than three to four students will select any one problem of practice.

> During the capstone course, students will develop a document that outlines the scope of responsibilities for each member of the team. This contract between students and faculty will inform individual evaluations at the end of the capstone experience. (quoted from http://peabody.vanderbilt.edu/x3810.xml)

The capstone experience ends with a paper, collaboratively written by a small team of students, that is examined by the faculty:

> A final capstone product, which will be presented to the faculty in the last half of the final semester of course work, will measure approximately 50-75 pages in length (plus appendices) and will be comprised of multiple sections including: contextual analysis, data analysis, program recommendations, implementation strategy, conclusions, appendix, and references.

> Faculty will evaluate individual components as well as the whole of the final product. Final passage will be based upon a combination of these two evaluations and will be granted to the group, not to individual group members. In those cases where the final product requires substantial revision, all

group members will participate in a revision process. (quoted from http://peabody.vanderbilt.edu/x3810.xml)

The Peabody approach is collaborative, it provides a focus for the capstone work that replaces the dissertation in the final year of the program, and it assures there are faculty experts interested in the topics selected because the faculty choose the topics. We see that last characteristic as a weakness as well as a strength. We believe a capstone experience should allow students to explore areas of professional practice that interest them rather than having to select only from a set of topics picked by faculty. Nevertheless, the Peabody approach remains an interesting way of supporting a capstone experience in a professional practice doctoral program that replaces the traditional dissertation requirement.

Article dissertations and portfolios seem to be the most popular alternatives to traditional dissertations today but there are others such as the group research study used at Vanderbilt in the educational leadership program. Some others seem to be relatively minor variations on the traditional five-chapter model. For example, the Department of Curriculum and Instruction at the University of Nevada Las Vegas allows some students to use an alternative four chapter dissertation format that eliminates traditional *Chapter 2: Review of the Literature*. However, the department's website (http://ci.unlv.edu/doctoral/general/proposal_alternate) notes that students using that format must add "a more extensive appendix that includes supporting material such as the literature review." More revolutionary alternatives to the traditional dissertation include those that go well beyond "ink-on-paper" and include many different types of media. The trend toward electronic theses and dissertations (ETD) was discussed earlier in this chapter, and we believe variations on this innovation will become much more widely accepted in 10 years than they are now. A current example of an ETD is the dissertation of Ray Bird. This is actually a British MA dissertation, but it shows how serious scholarly work can be presented in a multimedia format. If you would like to "read" this dissertation, which has many video components (stored on YouTube.com), it is online at http://raysdocudrama.wordpress.com/about/. As you can see from the web address, the dissertation itself, completed in 2008, is stored on one of the popular, and free, blog sites, WordPress.

YOUR FIRST DISSERTATION DECISION: TIMING AND SEQUENCE

The first major decision a doctoral student makes about his or her dissertation is when they will begin working on it. There are two common answers to this question. One comes in the form of advice given to students and the other comes from studies of what students actually do. The advice most commonly given to students is to start early. Begin working on your dissertation while you a completing coursework. For example, when you have a paper or project assignment in a course, select writing topics and projects that can become part of your dissertation. If you are doing a traditional five-chapter dissertation, for example, you could do a literature review by writing papers for several courses. Each paper would cover a certain type of literature and the papers could then be combined to make a suitable literature review in a traditional five-chapter dissertation. Courses on statistics and research methods also typically require students to write papers about a research idea or simulated project. One or more papers from those courses could be the methodology chapter of a traditional dissertation.

As easy as this may sound, it is rarely done. One reason is students' interests change as they progress through a doctoral program. An idea for a dissertation that seems excellent in the first year of doctoral work is often rejected as uninteresting, or unworkable, or too time consuming by the third year. Another reason is that many doctoral students, particularly in the social sciences, education, and business, must find "dissertations of opportunity" when they are ready to do their research. That is, they must find an organization where they can do research, and find a topic that is sufficiently interesting to the host organization that they are allowed conduct the research. These opportunities emerge and disappear quickly which means students will sometimes do an available dissertation to meet graduation requirements rather than do a dissertation that really interests them. This brings to mind the somewhat cynical lyrics of a Crosby, Stills, and Nash (1970) song: "If you're not with the one you love, love the one you're with."

The Serial Dissertation Dilemma

The problems noted above that keep many students from starting their dissertation work early in their doctoral program are particularly severe when the doctoral program is based on a serial model. A doctoral program based on a serial model follows a linear sequence. A typical example is completing general and required courses first, followed by specialty courses and field experiences, followed by work on the dissertation. Some traditional programs even have serial requirements built into their operational rules. In some, for example, you cannot write and defend a dissertation proposal until you have completed 85% of your coursework and passed a comprehensive exam. If your program has such rules, you may be forced to follow the required, linear sequence of the program.

Under those circumstances, combining work on the dissertation with other activities such as coursework and field placements will be a hit and miss affair, and most doctoral students end up doing the bulk of the work on their dissertation or capstone experience at the end of their doctoral program.

When A Concurrent Approach is Possible

As noted above, serious work on the dissertation is often not begun until a student has completed most or all of the coursework. This approach can be counterproductive because it may lead to students working virtually alone on their dissertation research because there are few organized support systems other than the major advisor and the dissertation committee. A further disadvantage to putting the bulk of dissertation work at the end of the program is that the unique demands and requirements of a dissertation often become apparent to students only after they have begun their research. That, unfortunately, is generally after they have completed most coursework and other experiences. Thus there is little opportunity for the student to master skills and procedures that were only recently recognized as important to finishing the dissertation.

An alternative to the end-of-program dissertation is to imbed preparatory work, and actual dissertation work, into experiences spread across the entire program. Some professional practice doctoral programs actually build in opportunities for doing dissertation work concurrently with other components of the program. For example, they build in course assignments that help students start work on aspects of the dissertation. Other programs create research teams that work under the mentorship and leadership of a faculty member who helps students develop and conduct professional projects and studies that can become part of a student's dissertation.

Nova Southeastern University's School of Education (2005) expects students to do their dissertation concurrently with their coursework. "You must complete an applied dissertation as part of your doctoral degree requirements. The applied dissertation is developed and implemented concurrently with your course work." This is particularly appealing in programs that support article dissertations. An opportunity that comes up in a student's first year of doctoral work may lead to an article (that may also be submitted as part of a course or internship requirement). Projects completed in the second or third year may produce two more articles that, with the paper from the first year of study, become the core of the student's dissertation.

A growing number of PPD programs (but still only a few) allow students to develop collaborative research and project teams to complete work that may become the dissertations or capstone projects for a number of team members. Still other programs integrate coursework, fieldwork and research work in ways that encourage students to do much of the work on a dissertation or capstone project well before the end of the program. Where programs allow it, and especially where programs actively encourage and support it, we strongly advise you to do your dissertation/capstone work concurrently with other components of the doctoral program. The result is often a better learning experience for you as a student.

An Even Better Option: An Integrative, Collaborative Dissertation/Capstone Project

One of the criticisms of traditional PhD research doctoral programs is that they tend to separate different aspects of the program so much that students have difficulty applying what they learn in, for example, courses on professional practice, to their work in the field (e.g., field placements, internships, etc.). One unfortunate result of that is what the philosopher Alfred North Whitehead (1929) called "inert knowledge."

In Whitehead's (1929) view inert knowledge is knowledge that is taught and learned in isolation, without links to other, related knowledge and certainly without an exploration of how it can be used in an applied context.

> Theoretical ideas should always find important applications within the pupil's curriculum. This is not an easy doctrine to apply, but a very hard one. It contains within itself the problem of keeping knowledge alive, of preventing it from becoming inert, which is the central problem of all education. (p. 17)

More recently, MIT's Seymour Papert (1994) has written about "school math" and "kitchen math" to illustrate the point that when schools teach mathematics in the abstract, students often acquire inert knowledge they cannot apply to real world problems. He contrasts "school math" to "kitchen math" which is learned in the context of practice. A problem in kitchen math may be, at its conceptual base, the same as a school math problem. However, when students learn the procedures for solving a problem in their mathematics classroom, they often do not make the connection between those procedures and the solutions to problems in other parts of their lives. Thus, they cannot use their school math knowledge to solve a real world problem, such as making correct measurements when they adjust recipes in the kitchen. One established way to deal with this problem is to link the learning of concepts to solving problems in the real world. Cognitive science, constructivism, and several other theories of how humans learn (Bransford, Brown, & Cocking, 2002) emphasize the importance of learning "in context" so that students can use what they learn in the classroom to solve meaningful problems in context. This is as much a problem in a graduate program for professional practitioners as it is for fourth grade children learning basic mathematics. Approaches to teaching and learning such as authentic instruction, problem-based learning, collaborative learning, anchored instruction, virtual reality learning, and case studies are all examples of teaching methods that help us avoid the inert knowledge problem and help students build what Rand Spiro (Spiro, Coulson, Feltovich, & Anderson, 1988; Spiro, Feltovich, Jacobson, & Coulson, R., 1995) calls *cognitive flexibility*, which could be considered the opposite of inert knowledge.

Although the authors did not use the term, the inert knowledge problem was discussed in many chapters of the Carnegie Foundation's report on *Envisioning the Future of Doctoral Education* (Golde & Walker, 2006). The lack of connection and integration between different components of a doctoral program appears to be commonplace both in research PhD programs and in professional practice doctoral programs. To address this issue, more and more programs are taking a "blended" approach. Across the curriculum the theoretical, scholarly, and professional practice issues are approached together, in blended activities, rather than separately (e.g., having a course on relevant theory, another on relevant research data, and another on professional practice expertise, and still another that is an internship experience). Further, PPD programs often link experiences such as internships to coursework as well as to both the consumption and conduct of applied research. An integrative or blended approach to developing a PPD curriculum is a practical application of the work of Iran-Nejad, McKeachie, and Berliner (1990), who argued that the traditional approach to learning anything is based on the idea of "simplification by isolation" (p. 509). This approach is criticized by the authors who trace it to the research design work of the pioneering British statistician, M. S. Bartlett, in the 1930s. Bartlett proposed that the research environment be simplified by isolating one variable for study while holding everything else constant. For example, in a study of different methods of fertilizing fields of wheat, the researcher might create a series of plots planted with wheat. These plots would be as close to identical as possible—similar soil fertility, soil moisture, exposure to the sun, depth of frost line, wind patterns, and so on. The planting and cultivation procedures would also be identical across all the plots. The *only* difference would be the methods of fertilization. In such a study, the yields from each plot would be statistically analyzed to discover whether one or more of the fertilization methods was better than others. This is a classic example of research based on "simplification by isolation." When applied to curricula it leads doctoral program designers to create programs where students study theory, research and professional practice in separate "plots" with very little interaction between the plots.

Iran-Nejad et al. (1990) believe that *simplification by integration* is a more promising approach to building both research and learning environments. Such environments are based on the assumption that "the more meaningful, the more deeply or elaborately processed, the more situated in context, and the more rooted in cultural background, metacognitive, and personal knowledge an event is, the more readily it is understood, learned and remembered" (p. 511). PPD programs that do this often make it possible for students finish their coursework, their field work, and their dissertation/capstone project at the same time because these three types of activities are integrated rather than separate, discrete activities. In programs where the "article dissertation" or TAD is an option, an integrated curriculum often allows students to finish their coursework having already written three papers on professional practice issues that become the core of their dissertation. Adding a short introduction and a short concluding section may be the only additional intellectual work they must do on their dissertation.

SUMMARY

Professional practice doctoral programs serve the needs of students who plan careers as professionals rather than academic researchers. One of the differences between PhD research doctoral programs and PPD programs is the purpose and nature of the capstone experience. In PPD programs the capstone experience may take many forms—from an e-portfolio to a traditional five-chapter dissertation. Other options include article dissertations, group projects or papers, and dissertations or projects that address a significant problem of practice.

CHAPTER 3

SELECTING YOUR
TOPIC AND PURPOSE

In Chapter 2 we discussed one of the first decisions you must make about your dissertation. That decision involves the timing and sequencing of your dissertation work. In a typical program, doctoral students complete most of their coursework, take and pass their comprehensive exam, and then are officially "admitted to candidacy" which means they have permission to officially begin working on their dissertation. This is the "serial" approach to completing a doctoral program—basic or foundational coursework, followed by specialty coursework, followed by an internship or similar experience if the program prepares professionals, and finally concluding with dissertation work. Two other options we discussed in Chapter 2, concurrent and integrative, let you mix coursework, fieldwork, and research with work on your dissertation.

Where possible we advise you to adopt a concurrent or integrative approach to doing a dissertation, but no matter what the timing and sequencing of your dissertation work, there are two other important questions you must address at the beginning. One is the topic of your dissertation and the other is the purpose of the dissertation. Students often mix these two decisions but they are actually quite different, and a decision on one does not necessarily restrict your decisions on the other. Figure 3.1 shows how decisions about your topic and purpose can be broken down into four related considerations: two for topic and two for purpose.

Completing a Professional Practice Dissertation: A Guide for Doctoral Students and Faculty, pp. 61–93
Copyright © 2010 by Information Age Publishing

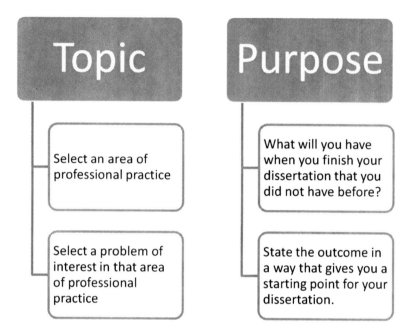

Figure 3.1.   Aspects of selecting a topic and purpose for your professional practice dissertation.

The first step in selecting a topic is to narrow down your interests to an area of professional practice in your field. Any field of practice can be divided into different areas and types of responsibility. For example, a doctoral student in an educational leadership program might begin to focus on a dissertation topic by selecting an area of responsibility such as:

- Community relations
- Leading learning organizations
- Transitional leadership
- Student achievement
- Special education services
- Curriculum reform
- Staff development
- Teacher leadership
- High stakes testing
- The policymaking process
- Or any of a hundred other areas of responsibility for an education leader

The areas of responsibility in your profession may be quite different from those in the, admittedly incomplete, list above for education leaders. However, most professions require expertise and decision-making across many different areas of responsibility. Those areas are a good place to start your search for a dissertation topic. Are there areas that interest or concern you?

The second step in selecting a topic is to identify an interesting problem or issue within an area of professional practice. For example, an educational leadership doctoral student might select community relations as his or her area of interest and then select the problem/issue of engaging new immigrant parents in the education of their children as the issue of interest.

Once you have the general area of practice and a problem or issue, the next step is to decide what you want to accomplish (your purpose) through your dissertation. A convenient way of establishing your purpose is first to decide what you will have when you finish your dissertation. Will it be a new theory? A more skilled group of practicing professionals? More knowledge about whether a program or process works or not? A new professional development unit? An evaluation of an existing program? Implementation of a new program? What you will have when you finish your dissertation could be knowledge, a product, or a procedure, to name but a few purposes for doing a dissertation. Before you have completed the process of deciding what the purpose of your dissertation is, you should be able to say in a general way what the outcome of your dissertation will be.

At this point, the difference between a Topic and a Purpose may still be a bit fuzzy. To help you begin to think this way, several examples from different professions are discussed below. The first is in the area of nursing.

Figure 3.2 is one example of the decisions a student in a DNP (doctor of nursing practice) program might make about his or her dissertation. The general area of interest is nursing practice on a hospital floor for surgery patients. That, however, is still too broad. The problem is more specific. There are many, many different types of bandages or wound dressings and the decisions about what bandage to use on a wound can make the difference between a smooth surgery and recovery period versus one that takes much longer and is fraught with complications and problems. A burn patient undergoing skin grafts, for example, requires different dressings than someone with a deep puncture wound, or a large, ragged wound from an accident. This doctoral student is interested in enhancing the quality of patient care by focusing on the way decisions about bandages are made. In terms of purpose, the student hopes to enhance the process of making bandage decisions and thus enhance wound care on a surgical floor. The outcome of the dissertation will be an

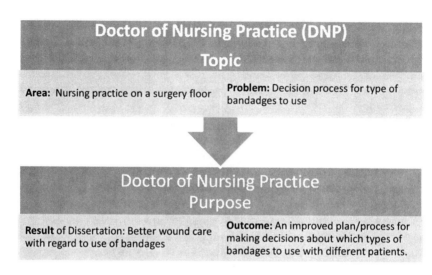

Figure 3.2.   An example of the decisions about the dissertation topic and purpose a student in a DNP program might make.

improved plan and process for deciding what type of bandages should be used for patients on the floor.

The second example (Figure 3.3) comes from a DPsy program for counseling psychologists. The general topic is how to help victims of natural disasters such as tornados, hurricanes, or earthquakes. The problem is that the staff members of the mental health center where the doctoral student will do the dissertation are not trained to do this type of counseling and support.

The DPsy dissertation will attempt to address that shortcoming and enhance the skills of the staff as well as volunteers who will be prepared to help in emergency situations. This will be accomplished by developing a 2-day staff development program on disaster counseling and creating a disaster response plan. Both these outcomes—the staff development program and the response plan, are complex products that will not only need to be developed but tested by being implemented and evaluated. The staff development program could be offered once with an intensive evaluation that leads to major revisions and improvements. A second trial run might also be done to evaluate the revised version. The response plan might also be tested in a simulated disaster to locate weak points and problems.

Depending on the amount of work devoted to creating and evaluating the staff development program, or the response plan, either of these would actually be a strong professional practice dissertation by itself!

Doctor of Psychology (DPsy)
Topic

Area: Short-term counseling for victims of natural disasters

Problem: Lack of expertise among counselors at a mental health center when it comes to this type of counseling

Doctor of Psychology
Purpose

Result of Dissertation: Enhanced disaster counseling skills for the staff and volunteers of a local mental health center.

Outcome: A two-day staff development program on disaster counseling plus a disaster response plan for the mental health center.

Figure 3.3.   An example of a topic and purpose for a professional practice dissertation in counseling psychology.

The third example is a further exploration of the educational leadership dissertation discussed earlier.

This third example is not like the first two that focused on the direct solution of a problem. In this third example, the result of the dissertation will be a document that synthesizes the scholarly and professional literature on parent involvement. This particular literature is fairly large and it is spread across many different journals and books. Also, some of the more successful parent involvement programs are not written up in either the scholarly or professional literature. Educators know about them through word of mouth. A doctoral student doing this dissertation would likely need to make visits or phone calls to get detailed information on those "lost" programs that are successful but not well known outside their local area. The result would be a dissertation document that would inform educators about the issues and problems associated with increasing parent involvement, myths and mistakes schools often make in parental involvement projects, characteristics of successful projects, and examples of successful projects that have worked well with new immigrant parents. A well-written document on this topic would be useful to many education leaders.

FACTORS TO CONSIDER WHEN SELECTING YOUR TOPIC

Now that we have explored the basics of making decisions about your topic and your purpose, it is time to explore both of these decisions in more detail.

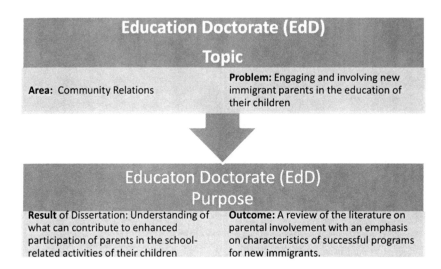

Figure 3.4.   Example of a professional practice dissertation in educational leadership.

What constitutes a good topic? When that question is answered for traditional PhD research dissertations, the answer often centers on two things: the specific area of research you have been prepared to do research in, and the current "hot" topic in that area. The research methods in academic fields like psychology, biology, or engineering have become so specialized that doctoral students must often limit their dissertation topic to one that requires research methods and technical skills the student already knows. Mastering the research methods in some fields can take years.

When it comes to the question of a "hot topic" in a field, that is not necessarily answered at a global or national level. It may be answered at the local level. What is the hot topic of your major professor (Chair)? The answer to that question often answers the question, What constitutes a good topic? This is not necessarily a bad or a cynical approach to selecting a research topic. Having someone to mentor you who is heavily invested in a type of research usually means you get more support and help, and you are more likely to do research on the cutting edge of your discipline. That is important if you hope to become a professor at a research university.

Selecting a topic when you are planning a professional practice career is different. While there are many and varied research methods for studying questions of professional practice, they tend to be more common across different professions and different problems. In addition, while there are "hot topics" it is not so crucial that your dissertation be about one of the hot topics in your professional field. If you are completing a professional practice doctorate, here are six suggestions about selecting a topic:

1. **Select a topic that interests you.** Perhaps the most important aspect of selecting a dissertation topic is to pick something you will enjoy becoming intimately involved with. A dissertation calls for a significant investment of time and effort. If you don't have much interest in your topic, you may well find the work irritating, boring, and frustrating by the time you defend the dissertation, or you may not even finish! The term ABD—all but dissertation—was coined because thousands of doctoral students every year finish all their doctoral work except the dissertation and never graduate.

2. **Select a topic that interests others.** Most professional practice dissertations are done in work settings and that means, at a minimum, you will need permission to do the study. That is the minimum; the administration and staff in the setting will have to decide your work is worthy enough to disrupt their work routine. You will more likely need more than permission, however. Consider the nursing dissertation about bandage selection that was mentioned earlier. This study would likely require the cooperation of floor nurses, the charge nurse, the director of nursing education, the physicians who have patients on the floor, and many others. Gaining both permission and enthusiastic participation on the part of stakeholders sets a higher standard for a topic, but if doing the dissertation involves others, you will want to use that higher standard to assess the topics you are considering.

3. **Does the Topic Pass The Resume Test?** One of the authors often tells his doctoral students to ask this question about their dissertation topic. "When I apply to that "ideal" job after I graduate, will my dissertation help move my application from the big pile of all applicants to the smaller pile of semi-finalists?" I do not suggest that this be the only criteria for your dissertation topic but it can be one of them. For example, if you want to become the superintendent of an urban school district, would a dissertation about the problems of small rural schools meet the resume test? Probably not. On the other hand, a dissertation on the characteristics of successful public schools in high-poverty urban areas would probably pass the resume test for this student. Of course, every doctoral student will have a different "ideal job" in mind, but matching your dissertation to your ideal job makes sense.

4. **Does the Topic Pass the Time and Effort Test?** Doctoral students tend to be idealists, especially with regard to their dissertation topic. They want the dissertation to make a difference, a Big difference. That often means they propose, and are sometimes approved, to do research that may consume years of their lives. If you are independently wealthy, and not in a hurry to complete your doctoral program, the time and effort involved in completing a "really good" dissertation that takes years may not be a concern. For most of us, however, time and effort is an issue. As you make choices between topics, take into consideration how long it will take to complete a dissertation on a particular topic. Will it require a year? Two years? More? How does that fit into your life and career plans? Often the decision you make with regard to time and effort will not necessarily be to reject a topic out of hand. Instead, if you really want to do your dissertation on a particular topic, you can cut back on the ambitious agenda you set for the dissertation and do only part of the grand plan. There will be time to do other work later, after you have your doctorate.

5. **Consider the Format and Topic Match.** We strongly favor article dissertations when that is possible. Combining work on your dissertation with coursework and fieldwork makes sense. Will your topic work as an article dissertation that is done as part of your coursework and fieldwork? That is, could three or so papers written in courses or as part of fieldwork become the core of your dissertation? Can you see how a dissertation on the topic could be done across two or three years of part-time study in your doctoral program? On the other hand, if you will be doing a traditional dissertation at the end of your coursework, or a traditional dissertation completed while you are completing your coursework, can you see ways to make course assignments do "double duty" as assignments and components of your dissertation? Regardless of whether you will do an article or five-chapter dissertation, ask yourself if the format matches the topic well.

6. **Is the Topic Worthy?** A few years ago when one of the authors was looking at a lot of dissertations in the area of educational technology, he noticed that many students did a survey dissertation. Typically, they asked a group of teachers or teacher educators what they thought teachers should know about technology, and they often asked respondents if they thought colleges of education were doing a good job preparing students to use technology in their classrooms after they graduated. The first 10 or so questionnaire dissertations like that were probably OK. After that, unless there was something unique about the survey, there was little rea-

son to do another survey. We already knew that teachers and teacher educators thought students should know more about the integration of technology into the classroom, and we already knew that graduates of colleges of education as well as employers of new graduates, did not think teachers were, on average, being prepared very well. Doing the 56th survey study confirming that conclusion was probably done because the doctoral student hoped it would be an "easy" study rather that because he or she thought it would make a significant contribution to the field.

To some extent, what is "worthy" is in the eye of the beholder, but there are trends and fads in dissertation research that seem to come and go without having much impact on either basic or applied scholarship. One often suggested way of deciding whether a topic is worthy or not is whether it is "original." One of many websites about how to successfully finish your dissertation offers a list of guidelines like the list you are reading. Item 8 in their list is:

8. **Make Your Research Topic Original—Has It Been Done Before?**
    The prerequisite for finding a new research topic is to be informed because most things have been studied before. Staying on top of the current debates in your academic field puts you in a position to identify the gaps in knowledge. After identifying the gaps, all you need to figure out is what kinds of information will fill these gaps. (from http://tadafinallyfinished.com/dissertation-topics.html)

This is not a very realistic suggestion for either a "research dissertation" or a "professional practice dissertation." For students doing research dissertations it is possible but highly unlikely that they will do a piece of original research that has "never been done before." It is more likely they will do a variation on existing studies with an eye toward expanding or more thoroughly testing the conclusions of earlier research. Research that confirms previous findings, and replications of important and controversial research, are both important aspects of the modern scientific method. Finally, as noted in an earlier chapter, the research on dissertations generally confirms that while the demand for "original" research is a commonly stated expectation of dissertations, it is rarely actually required, expected, or obtained.

The reason for not making "original" a strong requirement for professional practice dissertations is different from the logic of traditional research dissertations. The main reason for being less concerned about original or unique contributions is that most applied dissertations are trying to solve a "local" problem. The 2005 applied dissertation guide in the

School of Education and Human Services at Nova Southeastern University (http://www.schoolofed.nova.edu/arc/pdf/guidead.pdf), explains that an applied dissertation will "permit you to address research questions in your work setting." At Nova Southeastern University the applied or professional practice dissertation is thus a demonstration that the doctoral student can approach a problem of practice in an organized and meaningful way. The problem, and the solution or perspective developed, may be relevant and applicable in other settings, but that is not generally the primary goal of a professional practice dissertation—to find and verify "universal" laws, solutions, or perspectives. Instead, the primary goal is to address a problem of professional practice in a particular context. Some paradigms of research in education, health care, and the social sciences contend that all research does that (e.g., deal with local rather than universal meaning), and when a researcher claims to do more than that he or she is simply wrong or engaging in wishful thinking (see Willis, 2007; as well as Denzin & Lincoln, 2005 for more detailed treatments of this question). We will not debate the merits of this form of skepticism here, but the important point is that the oft stated but rarely achieved goal of "originality" in a dissertation is more often a distraction than a useful guideline or requirement. For most professional practice dissertations a more useful guideline is that the dissertation contribute to the solution and/or understanding of a significant problem of professional practice in a particular context or setting.

7. **Decide Whether Your Professional Practice Dissertation Should Be "Theory-Based" or "Theory-Informed."** The dissertation guide at Nova Southeastern University that was mentioned above includes this definition of an applied dissertation:

> The term applied research refers to research that examines the relationship and applicability of scientific theories to the resolution of practical problems. Gall, Gall, and Borg (2006) explicated the difference between basic and applied research. Basic research is intended to "understand basic processes and structures that underlie observed behavior" while applied research seeks to "develop and test predictions and interventions that can be used directly to improve practice." (p. 6)

This is a definition of what we are calling a "theory-based" dissertation. It begins with a theory, derives implications or predictions for practice from the theory, and then develops a research project about the validity of those implications or predictions for practice. In such a dissertation, the focus is on a theory and its implications. Both theory and implications are stated before the dissertation begins and provide the framework for doing the dissertation. This is the core concept of a theory-based dissertation and it is also the core of the most commonly used form of the scientific method. Many people simply refer to it as the "scientific" approach to problem solving in professional practice. Critics (Schön, 1995) call it the technical-rational approach because it reduces professional practice decisions to following the implications of a theory and the empirical research based on that theory.

You will learn about many other reasons or purposes for doing an applied or professional practice dissertation in the last section of this chapter, but for now we will simply note that some applied research scholars consider the "theory-based" approach to be misleading and inappropriate for professional practice research. A basic argument against this approach is that solutions to professional practice issues are not always neatly confined within the boundaries of one theory. Scholars who support this view typically advocate the wider use of qualitative research methods and an emphasis on "emergent" methods. The idea of emergent research means you may start your research with a problem that interests you but the theoretical explanation of the problem, or the development of a "solution" to the problem, may emerge across the research rather than be stated explicitly before dissertation research begins. Advocates also often see work in an applied setting as a way to develop new theory, or as a way to develop solutions that may cut across theories rather than stay within the boundaries of an existing theory. *The SAGE Handbook of Qualitative Research* (Denzin & Lincoln, 2005) is one of many books that contain chapters on this issue.

An option to a "theory-based" dissertation is a theory-informed dissertation. When you do a theory-informed dissertation you are aware of the major theories relevant to your professional practice issue or problem, and you make use of the literature on those theories and their implications for practice. However, you do not necessarily work within the implications of one theory, and you do not necessarily begin your research with a theory-based "solution" to your professional practice problem. Thus the goal of your dissertation is not to "support theory." Instead, it is to deal with a significant problem of professional practice. That may involve a solution that emerges from a particular theory, but it could also emerge from collaboration with practitioners in the setting where you are doing your research. We will have more to say about this in later chapters but the point here is that "theory-based" is not the only approach to doing a dissertation. There are others and many of them focus on the purpose of your dissertation. We will deal with that issue after discussing a practical but crucial issue—how to handle the issue of compatible and conflicting paradigms among dissertation committee members.

PARADIGMS, PROBLEMS, AND DISSERTATION COMMITTEES

In the popular literature on "scientific research" it is common to present research as a monolithic entity with one set of rules and procedures. However, it is not true of traditional theoretical research and it is not true of professional practice research. In each field that offers a professional practice doctorate there are several, if not many, paradigms for doing applied research and scholarship as well as many frameworks for doing professional practice. Some of these paradigms are compatible with other paradigms. However, there are theories that advocate quite different, even contradictory, guidelines for how to do "good" research or practice. For example, doing a dissertation according to the guidelines of the postpositivist paradigm can result in research decisions that are virtually the opposite of decisions made for a dissertation on the same topic based on an interpretivist or critical theory paradigm. How are these competing and conflicting paradigms handled in PPD (professional practice doctorates) programs? Your program probably fits one of four common patterns and the way you create your dissertation committee will vary, depending on how your program handles different paradigms for research and practice:

- **One Dominant Paradigm.** Many doctoral programs are dominated by one paradigm and virtually all the faculty prefer that paradigm. The paradigm influences the content of courses, the framework of research, the preferred methods of professional practice, and the types of questions that are considered appropriate to try to answer through research. If your doctoral program is this type, you should think seriously before trying to do a dissertation that does not fit within the dominant paradigm.

- **Ecumenical With One Preferred Paradigm.** This approach is more and more common today. Faculty in the program tend to prefer a particular paradigm, but they are open to exploring other paradigms and to accepting research based on alternative, even contradictory, paradigms. If you do a dissertation organized around a different paradigm, you should make sure that:

  o At least one member of your dissertation committee, preferably your major advisor (Chair), is familiar with, and comfortable with, the paradigm you will use.

  o When you write a dissertation proposal, or the dissertation itself, make sure you supply "extra" explanation and support for elements of your dissertation that do not fit the program's preferred paradigm. For example, suppose your program is based on a positivist, postpositivist, or empiricist paradigm that prefers quantitative and experimental research methods. However, you want to use a case study method in your dissertation and collect primarily quantitative data. Be sure to provide more explanation and background on case study methods and do not forget to include descriptions of several case studies from reputable sources that focus on issues similar to the ones you want to study. A case study dissertation from a prestigious university, for example, or one published in a refereed journal that is respected by the program faculty, may help reassure your committee that you are not trying to do some wild and crazy thing that will embarrass them and the program.

- **Multiple Paradigms in Conflict.** Unfortunately, there are programs where different faculty, or faculty groups, support opposing paradigms and there is very little respect or acceptance between the groups. Occasionally, faculty in programs like this are in open warfare, and the atmosphere is often uncomfortable for both students and faculty. More often, faculty maintain at least a surface level of civility and it is harder for new students to see that under the surface there is quite a bit of conflict and turmoil. Doing a dissertation in such a program calls for considerable tact and diplomacy. A critical factor in navigating the tricky cross currents, sand bars, and shoals of such a program is to select your dissertation committee very, very carefully. The committee should be compatible and be able to work together without making your dissertation the scene of another battle between competing paradigms. Once you have selected a major professor, be sure to listen to her or his advice on who the other committee members should be. Some advocates of competing paradigms may be good members of your committee, but others may make every step in the process an ordeal without actually enhancing the quality of your dissertation. Again, make sure you have a compatible dissertation committee, and, if possible, the person who is most supportive of your approach should be your major advisor and/or the most respected or highest ranking member of the committee. If that is difficult or impossible, try to create a committee with no deep and ongoing conflicts that are likely to become issues in the planning and execution of your dissertaton.

  Perhaps the ideal in programs like this is that your dissertation committee consist entirely of members who support and encourage the paradigm you are using in your dissertation. Some of our dissertation students have worried about creating a committee made up solely of members of one faction in a department. They often worry that the faculty who are strongly opposed to the paradigm they are using will somehow rise up and disapprove of their dissertation. We generally point out that the vote on whether a dissertation is approved or not is a vote of the committee. There is no "faculty vote" and no Faculty Inquisition committee that can enforce orthodoxy on dissertation committees. We also challenge doctoral students to select any dissertation they wish and we claim that we can find four faculty members on the campus who would vote against approval as well as four other faculty members who would consider it a very acceptable dissertation. The point is that there are no universal, paradigmatic standards for dissertations, but any dissertation committee may have its own set of standards. It is not important that your dissertation be universally approved of at your institution, or even in your program. That is rarely possible unless faculty are relatively ecumenical. It is, however, important that your dissertation committee is comfortable with the paradigm you use and approve your dissertation.

- **Ecumenical Acceptance of Multiple Paradigms.** Programs with faculty who have their different paradigm preferences, but who recognize the value and merits of alternative paradigms, or at least accept that other reasonable people may value alternative paradigms, are much easier on students when it comes to doing a dissertation. With less chance that your dissertation will become another battleground in ongoing paradigm wars, you can afford to create a committee with representatives from other paradigms. While these committee members may not determine the basic structure and format of your dissertation, they can offer advice and suggestions, raise concerns and issues, and critique your writing, in ways that advocates of the paradigm you have selected cannot. Getting input from "outside the paradigm" often results in a better dissertation. One of the authors was on the committee of a dissertation a few years ago written by a student who was a critical theorist (also sometimes called neo-Marxist or Frankfurt School theorists). He was writing about the impact of educational technologies in an urban school district and I was on the committee because that was a specialty of mine. His major professor was a critical theorist in the feminist tradition, but I was an interpretivist. The two paradigms, critical theory and interpretivism, have some different and some compatible foundational assumptions, but I did not see my role on the committee as one of insisting that the dissertation research reflect the foundations of my preferred paradigm. Instead, I saw my role as one of giving advice to the student and his major advisor. They, being quite capable scholars and knowledgeable critical theorists, should, in my opinion, be the ones to decide whether to consider my advice or not. However, my decision on whether to approve the dissertation was not based on whether they took my advice or rejected it. My vote was based on whether the dissertation was a "good" one within the paradigm the student was using. If committee members from alternative paradigms have this philosophy of committee membership, they can often make useful contributions to your dissertation research without becoming total pains to deal with. Your Chair and fellow doctoral students should be able to give you advice on the committee membership philosophy of potential members.

WHAT IS THE PURPOSE OF YOUR DISSERTATION RESEARCH?

In the previous section we discussed the impact of paradigms on the structure of your dissertation committee. In this section we will explore another critical aspect of your dissertation that is heavily influenced by paradigms. That is the basic purpose of your dissertation. There are seven basic answers to the question, "What is the purpose of your dissertation research?" While different paradigms or perspectives on research may support more than one purpose, the support for each purpose ranges from outright rejection to enthusiastic support, depending on the paradigm of research you adopt. Depending on what your dissertation committee expects in your proposal and your dissertation, you may need to justify your general purpose by linking it to a paradigm or by showing that it is a common purpose of research on your topic.

We have organized the purposes for doing a dissertation along a continuum that begins with the established and traditional purposes (e.g., theory testing) and ends with emerging and innovative purposes (e.g., narrative inquiry/storytelling).

Test A Theory and Develop Implications for Practice

The purpose of basic research guided by the postpostivist paradigm of research is to discover general laws or law-like relationships. There is, however, no way to discover and "prove" a general law in a single research study. No matter how careful you are, or how well designed the study is, there is always a possibility, even a likelihood, that factors unknown to you have had at least some influence on the results. Thus, your data, and your interpretation of it, may not reflect what is "actually happening in the real world." For that reason the result of a traditional, postpostivist research study is a theoretical explanation of how the world works. It is theory because we cannot be absolutely sure the conclusions are True. Thus, within the traditional model of research, you do a study to test a theory about how the world behaves. The local context in which the research study is conducted is important only to the extent that it does not interfere with our efforts to generalize the results of the research to a larger and more broadly dispersed population.

An example of this type is the dissertation of Brad Hastings who completed his doctorate in psychology at Kansas State University in 1995. He was looking for characteristics that predict wife abuse. Hastings cites three theories of what leads to wife abuse—sociological, feminist, and psychological. He collected data that would permit him to compare the power of these three theories to predict wife abuse. (See the text box on the next page for details on this dissertation.) Although Hastings' dissertation is a reasonable example of the Support-A-Theory approach based on a postpositivist paradigm, as professional practitioners we find this approach to research done to guide professional practice troubling. First, the research, like many other research studies in this tradition, is based on a limited sample that was selected more for its convenience that for its relevance. Students in two settings, a military base in Kansas where college classes were offered and a community college in Kansas, were asked to volunteer and were given extra credit for participating. Second, the measure of wife abuse was a self-report questionnaire, the Conflict Tactics scale. Thus, this research drew conclusions by comparing the responses of adult college students on a set of questionnaires. This is quite different from, for example, gathering data on a group of men who have been charged with or convicted of wife abuse. Third, some of the results relate to the question of whether growing up in the southern part of the United States is associated with higher rates of wife abuse. However, of the 149 males in the study, only 9 were from the South. Basing conclusions about Southerness and wife abuse on 9 people then living in Kansas seems to be quite a stretch.

Brad Hastings (1999)
Cognitive, Contextual, and Personality Factors in *Wife Abuse (Psychology Dissertation, Kansas State University*

The purpose of this dissertation was to explore the relationship between selected personality characteristics (right wing authoritarianism, sex-role attitudes), cognitive variables (self-consciousness, hostile attribution bias) and contextual factors (military experience and regional background) to wife abuse. Most of these variables are self-explanatory but one, hostile attributions bias, may need further explanation. Hastings defined it as "the tendency to perceive hostile intent in others apart from the actual presence or absence of it" (p. 39). However, he did not have a direct measure of this personality characteristic so he used the Adversarial Sexual Beliefs Scale instead because it seemed to measure a similar characteristic in adult relationships.

Dr. Hastings gathered data on 149 males who completed a range of questionnaires (e.g., the Conflict Tactics Scale, the Adversarial Sexual Beliefs Scale, the Attitudes Toward Women Scale and several others). He also collected several types of demographic data.

The purpose of this dissertation was to compare the accuracy of several general theories about the relationship between several types of variables and wife abuse. Dr. Hastings was not trying to evaluate a treatment procedure nor was he attempting to deal with a problem in a particular context such as a suburban area where wife abuse appears to be increasing. Instead, he was looking for "universal" or widely applicable knowledge about what seems to be associated with wife abuse. The result was a set of conclusions that Dr. Hastings presented as starting points for making decisions about how to address the problem of wife abuse. He summarized his findings this way:

Results suggest three principal conclusions. First, they show that the hostile attributional bias is the most powerful predictor of verbal and physical abuse. Analyses consistently indicated that subjects possessing hostile attributions toward women are the most likely to verbally and physically abuse their present partner.

Second, the contextual norms and demographics emphasized in past models of abuse were found to interact with personality and cognitive variables. The effect of military experience, Southerness, and alcohol use were mediated by personality and cognitive variables.

Finally, the present results are consistent with past studies showing that abusers consume more alcohol, are younger, and earn less than non-abusers.

Insofar as the results show significant relationships between relevant cognitive, personality, and contextual factors, they provide a new, more accurate description of the problem, and may allow more effective forms of prediction, intervention and treatment.

This is a typical postpositivist approach to linking basic research to professional practice. Hastings states his conclusions in terms of universal relationships between the various variables studied. The statistical analyses, which involved a number of sophisticated statistical procedures including analysis of variance (ANOVA), leads to conclusions that are the foundation for recommendations for practice. Hastings concluded that his results support an existing theory of wife abuse, the "cycle of abuse" model, and that this model is based primarily on a particular psychological theory—social learning theory. Also at the theoretical level Hastings concluded that "the findings show that feminist, sociological, and psychological approaches to the study of wife abuse should be integrated into a more comprehensive model of abuse" (p. 116). At the professional practice level, Hastings concluded that his research "can provide a new, more accurate description of the problem" and "this should allow better prediction and lead to more effective forms of intervention and treatment (pp. 116-117).

In social science doctoral programs designed to prepare researchers, many doctoral students complete dissertations designed to support a theory. However, when research deals with the behavior of humans, it is very, very difficult to do empirical research that meets even most of the stringent criteria for such work. Dr. Hastings' dissertation is not an extreme example of work in this tradition; it is a reflection of the difficulties a doctoral student faces—in finding an appropriate sample to study, in selecting ways of measuring the variables under study, and in making choices about how to interpret the results. Dissertation committees often allow students considerable flexibility when it comes to meeting the criteria for this type of research, but a study that does not meet many of the basic criteria will be more difficult to publish and the implications you draw from the study may not be readily accepted.

Doing a dissertation to support a theory, and to draw implications for practice from such a study, is an option in many professional practice doctorates, but other purposes are more and more common in PPD programs. Within the postpositivist paradigm, another acceptable purpose for a dissertation is to evaluate a professional practice.

Evaluate the Universal Effectiveness of a Professional Practice

Professional practice research based on a postpositivist paradigm has a similar purpose to basic, postpositivist research. However, instead of testing a theory, or the implications of a theory, the purpose of a postpositivist professional practice dissertation is to validate the effectiveness of a particular professional practice. That does not mean, however, that you can leave theory behind. Most forms of professional practice are derived from theoretical foundations. For example, a therapist working from a psychoanalytic perspective must, of necessity, have some faith in the psychoanalytic theories of human thinking and behavior. An educator who ardently supports problem-based learning and student-centered pedagogies is likely to adopt a progressive or constructivist theoretical perspective on how humans learn. The same is true of virtually every field of professional practice—from leadership and training to health care, engineering, and business.

The difference between these first two types of purposes for doing a dissertation are not based on whether theory plays an important role. It does in both. The difference is in the level of focus. Dr. Hasting's dissertation, which was used as an example of how to test theory and draw implications for practice, gathered data on the relationships between variables that are important components of the theories under study. The three theories he studied—feminist, sociological, and psychological—predict different relationships between the variables he studied, such as sex-role attitudes, right wing authoritarianism, self-consciousness, hostile attribution bias, alcohol consumption, age, and military experience. Hastings compared his empirical findings to the predictions of the three theories and then concluded that a psychological theory of wife abuse, particularly social learning theory, is best supported by his data.

A dissertation that focuses on the validation of a particular professional practice shifts the focus away from the foundational theories of practice and concentrates on the professional practice itself. Dr. Hasting's dissertation, for example, concluded that a psychological theory was superior to other theories in explaining wife abuse—which is perhaps not surprising as he was completing a doctorate in psychology. He also selected a particular psychological theory, social learning. He further selected what might be called a "mini-theory," the cycle of abuse, as the explanation of wife abuse best supported by his research. He then used this line of reasoning to talk about how therapists should treat wife abuse.

Another approach would be to select a particular form of treatment, use it to provide treatment to individuals who are wife abusers, and to assess the effectiveness of that particular treatment. One such dissertation was done by Stephen Brannen at the University of Texas—Austin in 1994. A journal article based on the dissertation was published by Brannen in 1996. Dr. Brannen studied the effectiveness of two common forms of spousal abuse treatment. One involved treatment of couples in a group therapy setting. The other was also group therapy but this time males attended one group and females attended another. Brannen used a combination of quantitative and qualitative measures of outcomes to compare these two forms of treatment. He concluded that overall there were no differences in outcome between the two methods except for abusers who had a history of alcohol abuse. For those participants the couples group therapy had a better outcome.

Doing a research study of how well a particular treatment or procedure or method works is one way to do a professional practice dissertation of this type (evaluate the effectiveness of a professional practice). Another is to conduct a literature review of the existing research on treatment effectiveness. That is what Julia Babcock and her colleagues (Babcock, Green, & Robie, 2002) did. They used a method called meta-analysis to evaluate a set of 22 research studies of the effectiveness of treatments for "domestically violent males." Meta-analysis is a quantitative approach which means that only research studies that met many, or most, of the criteria for experimental quantitative research, were included in the analysis. The authors looked at the effectiveness of a treatment method called the Duluth model, another approach called cognitive-behavioral therapy, and a few other approaches that were the subject of empirical research. On the official website for the Duluth model, it is described this way:

> The Duluth Model holds that public intervention in domestic violence cases should include several key elements. It must protect victims of ongoing abuse (battering), hold perpetrators and intervening practitioners accountable for victim safety, offer offenders an opportunity to change (including punishment if it enhances victim safety) and ensure due process for offenders through the intervention process. The focus of intervention is on stopping the violence, not on fixing or ending interpersonal relationships. (http://www.theduluthmodel.org/duluthmodelonpublic.php)

Babcock and her coauthors described cognitive behavioral therapy this way:

> Cognitive behavioral batterers interventions, developed primarily by psychologists, tend to make violence the primary focus of treatment. Since violence is a learned behavior, nonviolence can similarly be learned according to the cognitive behavioral model.... Violence continues because it is functional for the user, reducing bodily tension, achieving victim compliance, putting a temporary end to an uncomfortable situation, and giving the abuser a sense of power and control.... Recognizing the functional aspects of violence, the cognitive-behavioral therapist points out the pros and cons of violence. In addition, they use skills training (e.g., communication, assertiveness, and social skills training) and anger management techniques ... to promote awareness of alternatives to violence. (p. 1027)

In this study, the authors concluded that the meta-analysis of existing quantitative research on treatment showed that "effects due to treatment were in the small range, meaning that the current interventions have a minimal impact on reducing recidivism beyond the effect of being arrested." If you would like to read another research study based on a review of the existing literature, Feder, Wilson, and Austin's (2008) review of "court-mandated interventions for individuals convicted of domestic violence" also used a meta-analytic approach but in a somewhat different way than Babcock and her colleagues. It is available online at http://db.c2admin.org/doc-pdf/Feder_DomesticViolence_review.pdf.

Both types of the universal effectiveness research, (1) a study of the effectiveness of a professional practice such as a treatment method and (2) a review of the literature such as a meta-analysis (a comprehensive analysis of the available empirical research) are common methods of doing research to establish the efficacy of a professional practice. Both research methods are usually based on a positivist or postpositivist approach to research and the goal is to add to the literature on whether the practice is, in general, effective or not. Again, the purpose is to make assertions about "universal" or general effectiveness. Later in this section we will present purposes for dissertations that focus on "local effectiveness."

Objective Description

A third form of positivist/postpositivist research that many students use for their dissertation is objective description. This type of research also has a "universal" purpose—the accurate and objective description of an event, characteristic, phenomenon, or type. For example, in the area of spousal abuse, Derrick Tollefson did his dissertation on the characteristics of men who continued to batter their spouse after treatment versus those who did not. He completed his dissertation, *Factors Associated with Batterer Treatment Success and Failure* at the University of Utah in 2001 and he published a paper based on his dissertation in 2006. Basically he collected data on 197 male batterers who were required by the court to complete a domestic violence program. Tollefson's purpose was to identify what of many factors he analyzed were associated with recidivism. He used a statistical process called bivariate analysis as well as logistic regression to analyze his data. He found four factors that predicted who would continue to batter their domestic partner. They were psychopathology (personality disorders), a psychiatric history, substance abuse, and child abuse in the batterer's own family history. These four variables, and particularly a diagnosis of psychopathology and a history of substance abuse, were such strong predictors of continued battering that they appeared to overwhelm any effect due to the treatment provided.

Tollefson's dissertation did not look at the effectiveness of treatment and it was not primarily a study designed to test the validity of a theory. Instead, it had the practical goal of objectively describing the characteristics of batterers who reoffend versus those who do not. Tollefson's dissertation is postpositivist because he was looking for universals and he proposes the predictive factors he found as universal characteristics of batterers. And because he makes this assumption about his findings, he is also able to provide the implications of the research and make general recommendations about how develop policies and practices for dealing with batterers.

Dissertations with this general purpose, objective description, can be found in virtually every field of professional practice. There are many things we need to know more about and such research is an example of efforts to systematically study phenomena and develop, at least tentatively, objective descriptions of the phenomena. Often, this type of study also involves creating typologies or categorical schemes that help us think about the phenomena being studied.

Objective description is the last of the positivist/postpositivist purposes for doing a dissertation. The next purpose for dissertation research is less ambitious and is typically based on a different paradigm.

Evaluate the Local Effectiveness of a Professional Practice

The difference between evaluating local effectiveness of a professional practice, and evaluating the universal effectiveness of a practice, begins with the attitude you take toward your research. Beginning a search for universal answers to any question requires you to have considerable confidence in the ability of your research method to separate out the influence of local factors from factors that are universal and present in all the contexts you wish to generalize to. For example, if battering is heavily influenced by cultural traditions and social norms that vary considerably from one culture to another, and if the reasons and patterns of battering vary considerably from one social class to another, and if they vary from one economic situation to another, and from one historic epoch to another, there is a poor chance of coming up with a definitive and universal "objective description" of the characteristics of batterers, a definitive and universal statement about what treatment "works best," or what theoretical explanation of battering or spousal abuse is "most accurate." It will be difficult because of the complex interplay of so many causal factors from so many levels (e.g., from cultural, social and historical variables to the psychological characteristics of individuals).

Whether you believe that a goal such as providing an objective description, or identifying the best treatment, is possible or not depends on your paradigmatic and theoretical foundations. The postpositivist paradigm is based on the assumption that universals can be discovered by good research, but the interpretivist paradigm tends to be much more skeptical and to doubt that many, if any, universals will be discovered about human behavior. That means a dissertation based on the interpretivist paradigm is likely to be concerned with "local effectiveness" rather than "universal effectiveness" when the research involves an evaluation of a professional practice. The actual study may be quite similar in form and procedure to one done by a postpositivist doctoral student, but the results will be interpreted differently. Actually, the interpretive dissertation will be "similar" but will also be different in a number of respects. For example, interpretivists looking at local effectiveness are likely to provide much more detail about the characteristics of the local context because they believe that context is important to understanding how a practice works. For that reason, qualitative research methods, such as case studies, are more likely to be used than are straightforward quantitative methods that focus on one

or two quantitative outcome variables such as the likelihood that a batterer will continue to batter after treatment.

Another difference is that the interpretivist doctoral dissertation is
likely to present more than one view of the professional practice. For
example, in a study of the effectiveness of a treatment for battering, quantitative outcome data would likely be gathered, but the views and opinions
of the battered spouse, the batterer, the therapists involved in providing
the therapy, and others such as the court officers involved in adjudicating
cases, may all be sought and incorporated into the results. This approach,
called "multiple perspectives," will often provide readers of the dissertation research with a number of viewpoints on the professional practice
under study. Such an approach requires readers to do their own analysis
before they can either accept the findings reported in the dissertation or
decide what might be useful in their own practice.

This last issue, who and how findings and conclusions are generalized,
is another example of how different the search for an understanding of
local effectiveness is different from the search for universal effectiveness.
If you believe your research tells you something that is universal, it is relatively easy to use the findings as a starting point for proposing obviously
needed changes in policy and practice. On the other hand, if you believe
your research, at best, helps you and readers understand the local effectiveness of a practice, then the decisions about what can be generalized
must be left in the hands of the readers, who know their own contexts of
practice much better than you do as the author of the dissertation. Your
job is not to tell them how to practice, it is to provide enough detail and
information about your research so that they can make informed decisions about what may apply to their own context.

If you do a dissertation with the purpose of evaluating the local
effectiveness of a professional practice there are several different
methodologies that can be used. Many dissertations with this purpose use
a case study method which is discussed in Chapter 6. Other dissertations
adopt ethnographic methods that involve field observations, interviews,
and the collection of artifacts such as work products that would be expected
to change if the new professional practice is effective. These are also
discussed in Chapter 6.

Another common methodology for this type of dissertation is program
evaluation, and one of the most useful guides to doing program evaluation
is free. The W. K. Kellogg Foundation funds many projects each year in
education and related fields, and it has developed a handbook that is available online. The *W. K. Kellogg Foundation Evaluation Handbook* (1998) is
available at http://www.wkkf.org/pubs/Tools/Evaluation/Pub770.pdf. This is
a relatively eclectic handbook that recommends the collection and analysis
of several types of both quantitative and qualitative data. There are, of

course, many other guides to program evaluation including one developed for the National Science Foundation that also recommends the use of both qualitative and quantitative data. The *User-Friendly Handbook for Mixed Method Evaluation* (NSF, 1997), is available online at http://www.nsf.gov/pubs/1997/nsf97153/start.htm.

Develop a Solution to a Local Problem or Issue

Developing a solution to a local problem/issue is another popular approach to doing a professional practice dissertation. And, like dissertations that evaluate the local effectiveness of a professional practice, there are a number of different methodologies to choose from when your goal is to develop a solution. These include several forms of action research as well as a group of designs that are called instructional design or ID. Both action research methods and ID methods will be discussed in more detail in Chapter 7, but there are a number of general issues that should be considered when doing this type of dissertation. Perhaps the most important is to keep in mind that the purpose is to create an outstanding solution to a local problem or issue, not to create a universally applicable solution that can be used "everywhere." An example of this type of dissertation is *A Program Assessment in Domestic Violence* by Alice Smith. She completed her dissertation at Tennessee State University in 2001. The dissertation is accessible online at http://e-research.tnstate.edu/dissertations/AAI3024633/.

Dr. Smith described the general purpose of her dissertation research this way: "to seek relevant data that will permit planning and implementing more effective treatment programs for African-American male perpetrators of domestic violence." Thus far the purpose seems to not to be the solution to a local problem. It sounds more like an effort to find universal rather than local solutions. However, she narrows her focus by further clarifying the purpose of the dissertation: "To that end, an investigation was undertaken of what was, and what was not, effective treatment in the Kelly Miller Smith Center Against Abusive Behavior." Dr. Smith explicitly acknowledged the complex nature of the factors that influence battering in the African American culture:

> While poverty and minority status alone may not accurately predict family violence, cultural differences appear to require attention in the treatment of the offender. If indeed, the effects of such conditions as poverty and racism are causally linked to violent behavior in the family setting, we need to understand precisely what that link is and under what conditions it may arise. For, like domestic violence itself, remediation of the problem cannot be studied independently of the legal, cultural, political, and situational facets of social life.

Dr. Smith used ethnographic methods (which are discussed in Chapter 6 of this book) to do a case study based on six men who completed the existing treatment program at the Miller Center. Three were recidivists who continued to batter their partner after treatment and three were nonrecidivists. She conducted an extensive series of individual interviews with each male, audiotaped and transcribed them, and then analyzed the interviews for clues that suggested what contributed to the success or failure of treatment. This dissertation took into consideration the unique characteristics of the clients of the Miller Center and of their African American heritage. Dr. Smith's conclusions are couched in terms of the specific context in which the Miller Center operates and they are most applicable to that Center. In her discussion she does make broader generalizations but we would suggest that this dissertation is best considered an example of an effort to enhance the quality of a local professional practice —in this case the treatment program from male batterers at the Miller Center in Tennessee. There is much in this dissertation that might generalize to other settings but we would argue that those generalizations are best made by the readers of the dissertation. The primary and direct contribution of this dissertation is information and perspectives that can enhance professional practice at the Miller Center. That is a worthwhile and valuable contribution to professional practice!

Alice Smith's dissertation gathered information that would be helpful in revising and improving a professional practice. Other dissertations focus directly on the creation of a new professional practice. Brandi Colon's dissertation did just that using an instructional design model. It is discussed in Chapter 9 of this book.

Hermeneutic (*Verstehen*) Understanding

Hermeneutics will be discussed in Chapter 9, but for our purposes here, consider it a qualitative method borrowed from the humanities that has the goal of developing a better understanding of a "text." The German word for understanding, *verstehen*, is often used in relation to hermeneutic methods because of the influence of several German philosophical traditions on hermeneutic methods. The term text may mean an actual text or it may mean a cultural tradition, a business practice, or virtually anything else that has been developed by humans.

A dissertation with the purpose of better understanding a particular context or situation is usually based on either interpretive or critical theories of research and meaning. Understanding is the interpretive/critical equivalent of a positivist dissertation that proposes to provide an "objective description" of something. The difference between these two types of dissertation purposes lies primarily in two areas—one is the tendency to emphasize quantitative data when the purpose is objective description, versus the use of more qualitative measures (see Chapters 6-9) if the goal is understanding of a local context. The other major difference is that hermeneutics is not positivist when it comes to the search for meaning and understanding (*verstehen*). First, because hermeneutics looks closely at context and history to develop a better understanding, the result may be more than one possible meaning. Second, because people with different backgrounds, experiences, and values may interpret the data differently, there is always the likelihood of multiple perspectives on the meaning or significance of a text. Third, hermeneutics is part of a movement in the social sciences that is quite skeptical about whether traditional research methods can lead us inexorably toward a clearer and clearer vision of Truth in any absolute sense. Thus, the alternative goal of understanding or *verstehen* in a particular local context is often the purpose of a hermeneutic dissertation rather than the discovery of universal Truths.

An example of a dissertation based on hermeneutic theory and hermeneutic methods of developing understanding is Amy Voida's (2008) study, *Exploring a Technological Hermeneutic: Understanding the Interpretation of Computer-Mediated Message Systems*, which was done in the School of Interactive Computing of the College of Computing at Georgia Tech University. The full text of Dr. Voida's dissertation is available online at http://smartech.gatech.edu/handle/1853/24744 and it is worth exploring for two reasons. The first is that she applies the hermeneutic methods of research to an applied topic—understanding the users' perceptions of computer-mediated messaging systems such as camera phones, instant messaging systems, and mobile messaging systems such as Blackberries. She proposes that prior research suggests that "individuals can hold different interpretations of a technology" (p. XIV) and that what she has done in her dissertation is to "explore the question of where these different interpretations come from. What influences an individual's interpretation of a technology? And what is the nature of these interpretations" (p. XIV)? She uses the methods of a branch of hermeneutics called philosophical hermeneutics (see Chapter 9 in this book) to study the "nature of interpretation," and she presents what she calls a "technological hermeneutic" which is "a descriptive theory of how individuals interpret technology—how they come to understand the meaning of technology in their own lives" (p. XIV). Dr. Voida does not offer a set of absolute answers to questions such as how users of Blackberries understand their technology. Instead she proposes her "technological hermeneutics" as a way of gaining

> insight into the nature of the interpretive process. Interpretations are dynamic and evolving; individuals continually draw from new experiences,

reengaging and reinterpreting technology. Interpretations are also hybrid and synthesized; individuals draw from multiple resources in an active process of interpretive bricolage. (p. XIV)

In another section of her dissertation she commented that

> I had to allow that the answers I would hear would be fundamentally subjective. Why someone uses technology in the way that they do is an intensely personal and subjective question. Anyone who is interested in the design and use of technology ought to care deeply about what people believe ... even if they do not share the same beliefs and even if they think some of those beliefs are bizarre or baseless. (p. 2)

Here Dr. Voida is making it clear that she is not a postpositivist researcher looking for universal and general answers to her primary questions. She works from what some call a phenomenological perspective. Phenomenologists are concerned with the perceptions and beliefs of individuals and groups rather than with finding what postpositivists would call the truth of the matter. Phenomenological research thus emphasizes developing an understanding of how people and groups experience their lives and how they build their understanding of that experience. Hermeneutics is one way of accomplishing such a purpose. This researcher is not a total skeptic, however, who believes no other person can "really" understand how someone else can view the world. She believes that meaning and understanding have a significant and critical social component and that allows us to use subjective understanding for professional purposes such as designing better information technologies:

> But the subjective individual experience is not a constructive ending point for research that aims to influence subsequent generations of computational technology. One cannot pragmatically design and release technology for one individual's subjective beliefs.... Although I firmly believe in the primary importance of individual perspectives, I also believe that many individuals will share similar or similar enough beliefs about technology, as a result of having shared cultural experiences, for example, to suggest more generalizable lessons for design. (p. 3)

How Dr. Voida (2008) used hermeneutic theory and methods, based primarily on the work of philosopher Paul Ricoeur, is one reason to read this dissertation if you are interested in hermeneutic research methods.

The second reason to read it is that this is an example of an modified "article dissertation." The bulk of the dissertation is a series of chapters that are revisions of papers the author wrote over her 7 years as a student at Georgia Tech University. The dissertation also includes other chapters because as Dr. Voida (2008) notes,

I had not originally set out to contribute a technological hermeneutic. I had set out more simply to understand the use of computer-mediated messaging systems. Much of the research I discuss in this text has been published elsewhere in an original form that, in fact, makes no mention of hermeneutics or even of interpretations. The clues were all there. It took me seven years to see them and to find the right language with which to discuss them. (p. 6)

In this 10 chapter dissertation, 6 of the chapters were previously published, all with coauthors. Several early chapters provide theoretical background information on hermeneutics and Chapters 9 and 10 focus on synthesis.

Amy Voida's (2008) dissertation was a direct effort to develop understanding (*verstehen*) through hermeneutic methods, and it turned into a project to create a hermeneutic framework for helping others involved in the design of information technology resources to pursue their own understanding of the ways people fit technologies into their lives. Lee Brodie's (2001) dissertation in the Department of Curriculum Studies at the University of Saskatchewan had a different purpose which is explained in the title, *The Hermeneutic Approach to Museum Education Program Development*. Museums are places where people develop understanding through interaction with the exhibits, and with the educational programs of a museum. That process is in many ways a hermeneutic process and Dr. Brodie used hermeneutic research methods to develop education programs at two museums. The dissertation is an introduction to hermeneutic theory as a framework for creating museum education programs and a description of how Dr. Brodie worked with museum educators at two museums to help them create programs. His dissertation emerged from a dissatisfaction with traditional methods of creating museum education programs that were based on a positivist epistemology and a behaviorist theory of learning. He had been taught this approach to curriculum development and lesson planning but as he worked as a practicing museum educator he found the behavioral objectives, regular testing, and group goal setting unsatisfactory. A hermeneutic approach offered another option and his dissertation is the story of his journey from a behaviorally-trained museum educator to a museum educator who can advocate and mentor other museum educators in the development of programs that are based on constructivist, interpretivist, and hermeneutic approaches to both the process of instructional design and the content and methods incorporated into the programs. Dr. Brodie's dissertation is available online at http://library2.usask.ca/theses/available/etd-10212004-002539/.

Before moving to the last purpose for doing a professional practice dissertation we want to mention another hermeneutic dissertation that used methods very close to those used in traditional hermeneutic studies of literature and sacred texts. That is Gunnel Svedberg's (2002) dissertation at the Karolinska Institutet in Sweden. Translated into English the title is *Nursing Traditions in Swedish Psychiatric Care During the First Half of the 20th Century*. She conducted interviews with 22 nurses who worked in psychiatric care facilities before 1953 and she also used "literary works, contemporary scientific literature and medical archives" as sources of data. She described her research method as "phenomenological hermeneutics based of Paul Ricoeur's philosophy." Her dissertation is available online at http://diss.kib.ki.se/2002/91-7349-106-3/thesis.pdf. An extended abstract is in English but most of the dissertation is in Swedish. It is, however, another dissertation based on a series of articles the author had previously published.

Storytelling and Narrative Inquiry

As a purpose for doing research, hermeneutic understanding is closely related to this purpose—telling a story. The more scholarly term for storytelling is narrative inquiry and while the two terms are not equivalent, there is considerable overlap. A dissertation that "tells a story" is more like a novel or short story and it incorporates the characteristics of novels or short stories in the format. Narrative inquiry may also be called "storytelling" but most narrative inquiry dissertations will be organized around issues and points that are relevant to the topic, with "stories" told to support what the author is saying. Chapters 7 and 8 in this book both cover the methodology of storytelling and narrative inquiry scholarship. The argument for considering this approach revolves around how humans learn. The humanities have always considered stories a primary means of learning. Homer's *Illiad* and *Odyssey* are epic poems that taught Greeks what it meant to be Greek and what was honorable and dishonorable in their lives. In the past 40 years in American social sciences, European influences, especially from France and Germany, have helped us become more aware of the importance of narrative and metaphor in the way humans make meaning. Some scholars suggest that much of what we know comes from stories. Note, for example, how often political candidates try to communicate their message through stories. Many social scientists also argue that the process of telling a story is also part of the meaning making for the story teller as well. They do not have all the meaning worked out when they begin a story. Instead, they build meaning as they tell their stories. These are some of the reasons why storytelling or narrative inquiry has become both a method of collecting data and a method of communicating results.

Paige Averett's (2004) dissertation, *Parental Communications and Young Women's Struggle for Sexual Agency*, which was completed at Virginia Tech University, relies on the story as an organizing structure. Her data was the written narratives of 14 young women that focused on their emerging sexuality and the influence of "messages communicated from their parents and the quality of the parent-child relationship." Dr. Averett used a theoretical framework she described as postmodern and feminist, and her dissertation is more organized around the stories of the young women she interviewed. For example, Chapter 2 in Dr. Averett's dissertation is titled, "My Narrative: Beginning with Me," and she tells her own story of developing sexual awareness and parental communication and relationships. She realizes, however, that this is not necessarily the norm in dissertations:

> Many researchers do not position themselves in their research for several good reasons. One reason being the attempt of scientific objectivity, a noble goal but in my opinion, impossible. Another reason is professionalism. Many researchers, in an attempt to separate qualitative research from other traditions such as journalism or non-fiction writing create boundaries that include exclusion of the personal voice. For some researchers it is fear of exposure, and I respect that.
>
> However, for other researchers the inclusion of the self is a priority in research. I am such a researcher. My reasons include my commitment to transparency. For me transparency replaces objectivity and gives qualitative research more creditability. In my humble opinion, transparency on the part of the researcher is a more realistic, honest and more authentic goal. Also, it is a longstanding moral standard of mine. As a therapist, social worker, case manager, teacher, and now researcher I have never asked a client to give of themselves, that which I would not be willing to give. In this instance I was asking my participants to share a written narrative of their sexual development and the impact of their family upon it. Thus I feel compelled as a researcher attempting transparency to do the same. (p. 7)

In Chapter 2 she does just that. In her methods chapter, she describes her purpose this way:

> In the study, I sought not Truth but insight into the complexity that is adolescent female sexuality. I believe that this work is an attempt to move to a deeper understanding, by immersing myself in the complexity of what women know from their own experiences, while not abandoning what I know about myself. (p. 18)

She uses the stories told to her by 14 female students in a course on Human Sexuality at a Southeastern university. In the class she asked each student to write a narrative and before the students wrote their narrative she read parts of her own narrative (Chapter 2 of the dissertation) to them. She used the14 narratives and the data from 14 follow up interviews as her data. Dr. Averett made no pretense of remaining objective and keeping her distance from her participants.

> Having social constructivist leanings I believe in the idea of being co-constructors of knowledge with my participants. I would like to believe we could interact and learn as equals. However, the power of ultimate authoring and responsibility for a dissertation placed me in a position of higher power, not to mention my education, age and experiential background.... As such I saw my role as one of negotiator and facilitator. In my search to give voice to oppressed populations such as adolescents, minorities, women, I strove to make my research a negotiated process. (p. 23)

Averett's results section is organized around a set of general themes such as "Parents Have Influence in the Sexual Lives of their Daughters" but there is a story structure to the dissertation. Much of her understanding is expressed through the stories being told by her participants.

A third dissertation in the tradition of narrative inquiry and storytelling takes us even further along the continuum toward storytelling versus narrative inquiry format. Angelik Grigoratos (2006) is a South African of Greek origin who completed her master's dissertation at the University of Pretoria. The title is *A Narrative Exploration Into the World of Ill Fathers Who Have Lost a Limb Due to Diabetes.* The author advocates the use of discourse as both a means of understanding and as a means of communicating understanding. Her dual topic was the "subjective experiences of fathers who have encountered the world of illness from a South African context" and "knowledge relating to fatherhood and disability." Her participants in the study were three men who were fathers and who had lost limbs because of the complications of diabetes. She interviewed each participant five times with different goals ranging from establishing rapport to exploring fatherhood and disability to reflection and feedback. In her dissertation Ms. Grigoratos introduces the topic through her experience with her own father, who lost a leg because of diabetes. He was one of her participants. In fact, he was the primary participant. Her purpose was not "objective description." Instead it was to provide fathers with the opportunity to deliver "an alternative narrative against the oppressive weight of the dominant cultural grand narratives that these fathers have been living" (p. 16). She did this through interviews in which fathers could tell their stories. From this "narrative framework," she

> investigated the personal narratives about being a father who has lost a limb due to diabetes and what meanings were constructed thereof.... Through

the exploration of the narrative illness of fathers I gained understanding of how they conceptualized being a father with a disability, against the various discourses that silence, stereotype and marginalize them. The telling of these narratives constructed new perceptions and new maps of their relationships in the world. (pp. 16-17)

Ms. Grigoratos takes the position that

As human beings we are organizing, narrative-telling, meaning-making creatures that are constantly trying to make sense from our experiences.... Narrative is a crucial human way of giving meaning to experience. Through the action of telling and consequently interpreting experiences, narration serves as a mediator between the inner world of thoughts and feelings and the outer world of observational actions. (p. 57)

With this as a foundation for her research, she not only gathered narrative data, she reported her results in narrative form. In fact, she organized the story of her father's experience around the sequence of phases in Homer's *Odyssey* and she integrated the stories of the other two fathers— one African and one Afrikans—into the middle phase. More specifically, much of her results and discussion sections consists of a series of "letters" to the fathers "wherein I reflect certain aspects of their narratives" (p. 74). A portion of first of those letters is reprinted below:

Dear Dad

In Search of Ithaca

You set out on a passage through the wild seas of life, past the magnanimous barriers of constraint, the tight grip of the chronology of devious illnesses and discouraging discourses about fathers. From time to time you were exposed to blind alleys of recovery. You have salt in your blood, like a captain you fought your way through stormy seas and wild winds. When considering your passage through the sea of life, this comment gathers a certain authority. I thought of many a ways to depict your experience and eventually chose Odysseus' journey to reach Ithaca. I reflected back on the story written by the epic poet Homer ... so as to re-tell your journey accordingly. Your journey began from a young age and dwells in our memory till today. (p. 75)

In some of the letters, Ms. Grigoratos (2006) quotes or summarizes the narrative of a father but the way both the letter and the quotes and summaries are presented always serves the purpose of answering the question, "How do fathers make sense of limb loss due to diabetes, through narrative" (p. 122)? Thus her letters in the results chapter are less efforts to move the conversation to a higher level of generalization than to effectively communicate the subjective and personal viewpoint of each father. After the results chapter there is a short "Interpretation and Recommendations" chapter but the core of this dissertation are the stories told in the results chapter.

All three of the dissertations used as examples of storytelling and narrative inquiry are available online in their complete version. If you are interested in exploring this type of study for your dissertation, reading each of these recent dissertations would give you an excellent overview of three different ways such a dissertation can be done.

SUMMARY

Selecting what you will do your dissertation "on" is not a simple process and for some doctoral students it is one of the most difficult decisions that must be made. We have tried to reduce the complexity of the process by suggesting that the decision actually involves two choices—one about topic and one about purpose. However, as we explored both these choices, particularly purpose, it also became clear that one complication in the process is that there is no single standard for what is a "good" topic or a "good" purpose. The American social sciences, and many fields of professional practice, are influenced today by three broad, general paradigms that guide both research and practice. They are postpositivism, interpretivism, and critical theory. These three broad paradigms and many others that are associated with them, compete for attention in many fields today. Choices about topic and purpose are often also choices about preferred paradigms and that complicates the process of putting together a dissertation committee that will guide and mentor you. Terms like "paradigm clash" and "paradigm wars" were coined to describe what can happen when scholars take hard line opposing views because they operate from different paradigms. It is not easy to negotiate the process of choosing a topic and purpose and at the same time avoid the pitfalls and frustration of having a dissertation that becomes another battle in a departmental paradigm war. In this chapter we have made a number of suggestions about how to accomplish that and we have noted that the seven purposes—from supporting a theory to telling a story are supported by some paradigms more than others.

CHAPTER 4

CONSTRUCTING YOUR
DISSERTATION TEAM

Throughout the history of graduate study, students engaging in research, and more specifically, writing a dissertation, have placed great emphasis on relations developed with those who mentor their work. During dissertation research, students work closely with faculty who have expertise, experience, and an interest in the doctoral student's topic. Therefore, one of the most important decisions a student makes is the selection of who will serve on their dissertation committee. The relationships developed with, and the mentoring provided by, members of a dissertation committee can have a life-long impact.

The structure of dissertation committees varies among universities. In some universities these committees consist of four members (typically three inside members who are faculty in the college or discipline, and an outside member who is from a different college or discipline). Other institutions may have five committee members with one serving as a "objective observer" who is added to the committee just before the final oral exam. This person reports back to a dean or academic vice president that the oral examination was conducted appropriately.

Even across departments within the same institution, the structure of dissertation committees may vary. Traditionally there is a Chair of the committee and 2-4 other members, with the Chair working most closely with the student. There are many variations on this general pattern, but

Completing a Professional Practice Dissertation: A Guide for Doctoral Students and Faculty, pp. 95–122
Copyright © 2010 by Information Age Publishing

in professional practice doctoral programs, two common variations are a requirement that

1. someone with experience developing and/or designing, as well as evaluating, new innovations for practice be included on the committee, and
2. that at least one member of the committee be a practitioner who currently works in the field.

These two variations are a response to the fact that many professional practice dissertations are applied research studies done in the workplace.

Another factor you should consider when developing your dissertation committee has to do with the possibility that some, or all, of your committee may move to another institution while you are completing your dissertation. Today professors are relatively mobile; they do not tend to stay at one university for 30 years and then retire. However, if your chair leaves the university, you will have to find another chair and this can be frustrating because it means having to start over developing this relationship and finding someone who is compatible with your interests. One way of anticipating the possibility that your committee will change because of moves, retirements, and other factors such as the health of members, is to have both a chair and a methods specialist. Committee structures that include a chair and a research design specialist offer the student the opportunity to work closely with two members of the committee. Then, if one member should leave the institution, you can continue to work with the other, and progress on your dissertation may not be interrupted.

Finally, an option that is required, or at least encouraged, in some professional practice doctoral programs is the inclusion of a practicing professional on the dissertation committee. Some institutions require that this person hold a doctorate, but regardless of the requirements the inclusion of a practicing professional is generally highly desirable. We will have more to say about this option later in this chapter.

In the mid-1990s, a professional practice doctoral student, Laurie Hernandez (1996), described her approach to building her dissertation committee. She was a student in a family therapy professional practice doctoral program and she wanted to do a qualitative dissertation. She was concerned about creating a committee that could support her during the dissertation process. She also wanted a committee that would be a facilitator of progress rather than a barrier. At her university a dissertation committee was made up of at least three faculty members, one of which is the Chair.

Dr. Hernandez commented that while she had progressed through the program without major problems she did not find the process of selecting her committee easy.

> I did not feel prepared to make a decision. This surprised me; I had expected the choosing to be an easy process. It wasn't. I realized I had no idea how to get started on the process. I was not sure what it meant to work with a committee and a chairperson on a dissertation, and I was confused and overwhelmed with all of it.

She had worked successfully with many of the faculty in her doctoral program but when it was time to select a committee there was no professor who seemed to be a natural as her Chair, and no group of three that stood out as the best choices for a committee.

She decided to approach the process of selecting a chair and committee members as if it were a qualitative research study. She began with a question, "What do you think are the most important qualities to have in a dissertation committee?" However, that question was refined as she collected her data and ended up being more specific and personal: "What are the most important qualities for *me* to have in *my* dissertation committee?" Here are a few of the comments she made about her search for a great chair and search committee:

> The dissertation is only a part of the picture albeit a major feature. Your chair can also be your mentor, someone who can help you take the next few steps in your career.... The dissertation process can be a very intense one so you want to be able to feel comfortable with your chair. Of course there will be times when both sides feel stressed out with the process.... If you know a faculty person now and feel like you can talk to that person, then you have a good sense that the relationship part of chairing is there.

> You want the chair to bring experiences and expertise which will add to yours and at the same time, you want to have some simpatico with the person too.

As she talked with potential committee members she asked herself the following questions:

- What are my needs?
- What sorts of things do I need in a relationship?
- What is my timeline for completing the dissertation?
- What do I want to do after my dissertation?

These were excellent questions because they forced me to be clear about what I needed in the dissertation experience, and what my expectations were during a dissertation as well as after graduation. I had learned enough about "committee life" to begin acknowledging my part in the committee process and think more openly about my tacit knowledge. I needed a committee [that] would help me complete the process but ... would not take my motivation for granted and would push me to work harder and reach farther. I needed a chair who could challenge and surprise me into doing things I never thought possible. I needed a committee who was always accessible, yet also comfortable with not hearing from me when I couldn't be bothered because things were rolling along just fine without them. I needed committee members who were experts on qualitative research but could talk to me about it in an understandable way. I needed a committee ... willing to risk exploring my ideas, and ... speak authentically and legitimately about those ideas, despite their sometimes unusual nature.... I needed a committee [with] ... experience guiding other students through long projects. I needed to be, as my consultant said, "simpatico" with my chairperson: For instance, during a dissertation meeting, I needed to be comfortable enough to either revel in the excitement of my project or be openly miserable when I felt stuck.

Openly thinking these thoughts allowed me to experience a kind of self-aware conversation:

Expertise in systemic thinking, qualitative research, and academic writing absolutely necessary. Interest in student's content area (general now but to be refined later) extremely helpful. Sense of humor, creativity, and ability to generate visionary ideas necessary for this position. Members must be authoritative yet collaborative, patient yet assertive, and inspirational yet practical. Must be accessible in case of emergency (such as writer's block, flight of ideas, or delusions of grandeur), yet able to "back off" and provide "space" when necessary. Benefits are not guaranteed; however, benefit potential (in admiration, gratitude, and productivity) is great.

IS THERE A DIFFERENCE BETWEEN A "RESEARCH" PhD DISSERTATION AND A PROFESSIONAL PRACTICE DISSERTATION?

Laurie Hernandez (1996) did her doctorate in an applied field, family therapy, but she was interested in a career that included working as a professor. While her process and her conclusions about the characteristics of good committee members are reasonable, they may not always fit the needs of a person who plans a career as a professional practitioner—such as a family therapist in a regional mental health center.

While the answers you come up with, and even the questions you decide to ask, may be different from those of Dr. Hernandez, the process of posing questions about yourself (and potential dissertation committee members), and answering them, can be very helpful. Do you like/need a great deal of feedback from faculty on early ideas or drafts? Do you need this feedback in written or oral form? Or, do you prefer to work by yourself, or in discussion with your friends, professional colleagues, and other graduate students, and only discuss your work, or have it read by committee members, once it is quite polished? Do you find advice about making your way in the profession helpful or anxiety provoking (or perhaps distracting)? Most faculty will adapt to some degree to what works best for you, but faculty also have their own styles, and the faculty may find it more difficult to adapt to you if you either do not know or cannot articulate what works best for you.

As noted in earlier chapters, the research PhD dissertation is a product of a revolutionary change in German higher education in the early nineteenth century. That change was designed to produce better professors and researchers. In contrast, the professional practice doctorate, and the many forms of dissertations associated with it, are a product primarily of developments in the last half of the twentieth century. Scott, Brown, Lunt, and Thorne (2004) argue that a defining feature of a professional practice doctorate, including the dissertation, is a focus on the development of individuals in relation to their professional work. Consequently, practice-rooted research projects, work-based learning, employment related skills and cohort-driven pedagogies distinguish professional practice doctorates from research/academic doctorates.

Because research doctorates are well established in higher education, and have been for over a hundred years, they tend to be considered the "standard." Newer approaches often have to contend with the discomfort and resistance that any innovation is likely to face when it calls for fundamental shifts in the way both organizations and individuals do their work. Scott and his colleagues make that point and note the one major shift that almost all professional practice doctorates require is from an "academy-based research environment" to an approach that thinks of knowledge production as occurring within the workplace environment. This shift suggests the traditional model, which was a centerpiece of the nineteenth century German revolution in higher education, that involved a close mentorship between one doctoral student and one senior researcher with a track record of research success, is no longer the "ideal" approach. Instead, the development of knowledge within the workplace environment calls for the involvement of a diverse team that works with the student completing a dissertation. That team will include faculty, professional practitioners from the field, and other stakeholders who bring complimentary expertise and experience to the dissertation work (Scott, Brown, Lunt, & Thorne, 2004).

The term "Ivory Tower" has become a part of higher education slang and it is an expression of the traditional idea that universities purposely isolate themselves from the real world so the professors and graduate students can devote themselves to research that, when completed, will be shared with the public at large. The origins of the term Ivory Tower are hazy and disputed but one credible explanation is that in the early twentieth century a new research building was constructed on the campus of Princeton University. Funds for the building came from a family whose business interests included the Ivory soap brand. Thus, the building soon became known as the "Ivory Tower" in local parlance, and the term gradually acquired its current, much broader meaning. We think that broader meaning stuck because universities have presented themselves that way—as separate and apart from the ordinary worlds of commerce, business, industry, and social life. However, the development of more and more professional practice doctorates represents a shift in the other direction—toward more engagement, more involvement, and more collaboration with the "real world."

This shift is not simply a shift in the locus of dissertation research—from the university research laboratory to schools, hospitals, businesses, and factories—it is also a shift in the purpose of the dissertation. Professional practice dissertations more often address contemporary problems of practice in a specific context than traditional dissertations, and they are less often undertaken to discover universal laws of nature. They also tend to use methods that are more suited to the less controlled and more open environments of professional practice as opposed to traditional research methods that may be best suited to laboratory studies where virtually every aspect of the experiment can be tightly controlled.

These three differences between professional practice and traditional dissertations call for a different approach to creating a dissertation committee. For example, if your dissertation will be done in a work-based environment, there is an advantage to having your chair be a "practitioner scholar" who is both a successful practitioner and an experienced researcher. For example, suppose you are completing a professional practice doctorate in psychology and you want to do your dissertation on bipolar disorders. Further, suppose that one of your potential dissertation chairs is an experimental psychopathologist who does basic research on bipolar disorders. The other potential chair is a clinical psychologist who has been a therapist in inpatient and outpatient facilities that treat bipolar disorders and has published papers on the treatment of bipolar disorders as well as directed a mental health center. This second option is a practitioner scholar and may be a better choice as chair because he or she has experience doing applied research in professional settings.

A second potential difference in your committee structure is the possible need for what some have called an executive mentor. An executive mentor is someone drawn from the work environment where you will do your dissertation. If you are completing a dissertation in your own workplace, this person will likely be one of your supervisors. As a doctoral candidate, you may need direct mentoring and support from a practitioner who knows the setting where you will complete your dissertation. He or she should understand your role and responsibilities, and, if you are fortunate, also take a professional interest in your doctoral research. One of the authors of this book currently directs and teaches the St. John Fischer College (SJFC) professional practice executive leadership doctoral program. The program operates at two locations and he directs the program offered at the College of New Rochelle in Westchester County, New York. In the SJFC model, each doctoral student selects a highly qualified professional practitioner from their workplace or organizational environment who serves as an executive mentor for from one to four semesters while the student completes the doctoral program. Some executive mentors work with students for four semesters but it is the student's option to keep or change mentors at the end of each semester. The role of executive mentors is primarily to function as a field supervisor and "critical friend" whose executive experience and expertise assists a student with practical responsibilities while complementing the academic and scholarly contributions for the doctoral program faculty. Although executive mentors do not chair the dissertation committee nor necessarily participate as one of the official committee members, their role, and their expertise and experience in professional settings, can be very valuable to a student's dissertation work. As you can see the "practitioner scholar" concept mentioned earlier and the executive mentor model have much in common. This person will be familiar with your career goals, your work experience, and will also understand the process of developing working relationships in professional settings.

As noted earlier, another type of dissertation committee member to seriously consider when you are doing a professional practice study is a methodology expert. A student completing a traditional research dissertation on the way to becoming a researcher and academic should have had a number of research experiences before beginning a dissertation. Such a student will probably already be familiar with the research method appropriate to his or her dissertation. In addition, the Chair of the dissertation committee may well be an expert on the research method as well as the topic of the dissertation. All of that, however, is less likely with professional practice doctoral students. You may have selected a dissertation topic that interests you because it is relevant to your career goals as a practitioner. That means you are less likely to be proficient in the appropriate research methods for that topic. Further, many of the research methods most suited to research in the field are relatively new and easy to do poorly but difficult to do well. All this points toward two conclusions: (1) having someone on your committee who knows the research method you will use and who is capable of tutoring and mentoring you on how to use that method, and (2) doing "trial runs" of your study under the supervision of that committee member until you have developed the skills required to appropriately use the research method, or methods.

We offer this advice regardless of whether you will be using qualitative or quantitative methods. Advanced quantitative methods, such as path analysis, multiple regression, and so on, are complex and require many decisions that help determine whether your data analysis is meaningless or insightful. Many qualitative methods rely heavily on the researcher as the "method" because he or she makes so many decisions about what data to collect, how to analyze it, and how to interpret it. There are fewer hard and fast rules, and much more reliance on the experience and expertise of the researcher. Thus, in the case of both qualitative and quantitative dissertations, it is important that your committee contribute to your strengths when it comes to the research methodology you have decided to use.

We will return to the topic of dissertation membership several more times in this chapter but at this point another important issue deserves consideration—the style of interaction between you and the committee.

WHY HAVE A COMMITTEE?

Some students end up like Laurie Hernandez. They arrive at the point in their program when it is necessary to select a committee and not only are they unsure about who to select, they are not sure what questions they should ask to make the decision. We think the place to start is with the reasons – the reasons for having a committee. There are four major reasons for having a dissertation committee (other than the obvious one that your doctoral program requires you to have a committee).

Reason 1. To Help You Finish a "Good" Dissertation.

The key word in the heading is "good" because you are the one who has to define what is good when it comes to your dissertation. Here are three definitions of good that fit at least one dissertation student mentored by one of the authors of this book:

1. **A good dissertation is one that breaks new ground on the edge of professional practice about a significant problem**. It is publishable

in a major journal and is likely to be cited by the next generation of researchers studying this problem. Many doctoral programs with a traditional focus would probably agree with this characterization of what a good dissertation is. If this is your definition then your committee should be made up of scholars and practitioners who work on the cutting edge of your field, who are intimately aware of the current body of scholarship related to your topic, who are experienced, and well-published, researchers well connected in your field, and who have a track record of helping doctoral students position their dissertation research so that it addresses issues at the raw edge of current knowledge and practice.

2. **A good dissertation is one that successfully addresses a significant problem of professional practice in the local context.** It can be publishable in a major journal but the emphasis is on solving a local problem rather than searching for universal knowledge. This is quite a different goal. It reflects a trend, particularly in the social sciences, based on the idea that the 150 year search for universal laws about human behavior has not been very productive and that both basic and applied research in the social and behavioral sciences, as well as the professional fields based on those sciences, might be more profitably directed toward addressing real-world problems in a particular context. If this is your definition of a good dissertation, then your committee should be made up of applied scholars and experienced practitioners who are deeply concerned about collaborating with others to find solutions to real problems in the context of practice. At least some members should be practicing professionals, preferably in the practice environment where you will do your dissertation research, and committee members who do not work in that environment should have strong track records of working collaboratively with practicing professionals. Further, all the members of the committee should understand and "buy into" your idea of what a "good" dissertation is. They should also be comfortable with, and able to help you refine, research methods that are most suited to this type of dissertation study. The methods often include close collaboration and participation of a sizable group of stakeholders and collaborators using methods like participatory action research or emancipatory research methods.

3. **A good dissertation is one that is relevant to my career goals, can be completed in a reasonable amount of time, and contributes to my overall preparation for the career path I have selected.** The first definition of a "good" dissertation is most often found in the minds of research professors. This third definition is most often found in the minds of doctoral students who want to do a decent

dissertation but who see the dissertation as one of several important components of their doctoral work. Relevance, reasonable effort and time commitments, and career-support, are the three core components of this idea of a good dissertation. By "career-support" we mean that when a search committee looks at your resume and sees that you did your dissertation on topic XXX using methods YYY, they are much more likely to slide your resume over into the "further consideration" pile than put it in the larger "not interested" pile. If this is your idea of a good dissertation, you need a chair who has an excellent and up-to-date understanding of your career goals and who can help you narrow you initial "save the entire world" idea for a dissertation down into a manageable, relevant, and focused topic and purpose.

4. **A good dissertation is one that gives me an opportunity to serve an apprenticeship with a scholar-practitioner who is an expert in a critical area of professional practice research.** Doctoral faculty vary considerably from program to program but most faculties include some very strong generalists who have particular interests but have the breadth of expertise and experience to work with students in several areas of professional practice. Most programs also have a few "specialists" who have developed a strong area special interest to the point where they have achieved regional and national recognition. Suppose, for example, that you are completing a doctorate in social work practice and a member of the doctoral faculty is a specialist in reducing truancy and absences in inner city schools. If your goal is a career in school social work, a dissertation on how to reduce truancy in inner city schools may be very appropriate. Your dissertation might be part of a larger involvement, an apprenticeship or mentorship, with the doctoral faculty member who is a specialist in that area of practice. In such cases, your dissertation committee should be chaired by the specialist and the other members should add additional strengths, such as research methodology or subject matter expertise, to the strengths of your major professor.

However, this type of dissertation can be problematic because you are working with a chair who has extensive and cutting edge knowledge about your topic. Make sure your own theoretical and professional perspectives are compatible with those of your chair— otherwise the dissertation experience can be a difficult one fraught with conflicts and impasses. However, it is almost as important that the other committee members you select also be compatible with the chair. It is not unheard of for a dissertation to become a point of conflict between strong willed committee members who use the dissertation as a battleground where theoretical disagreements, opposing value judgments, and departmental political conflicts become the feedstock for arguments that have little to do with the dissertation itself. Because the chair on such a dissertation generally takes a very strong role, it is sometimes helpful to have one or more committee members who are content to take a "back seat" role and give the chair more freedom to work with you. Sometimes faculty do this for each other, especially in programs where several faculty have highly developed research interests and students often select a chair based on a desire to learn more about that specialty.

Reason 2: To Keep You Out of Trouble and Save You Time

In their book on doctoral supervision Taylor and Beasley (2005) rightly point out that one of the major responsibilities of your chair and the committee is to communicate a clear understanding of the institutional requirements for both you and the committee, and to make sure that you are both aware of and follow all the detailed, hard-to-find, and difficult to understand rules that must be followed by students who complete a dissertation at your institution. These guidelines include tedious but common rules about the size of the margins for your dissertation (often 1" on all sides or 1.5" on all sides, but there are many variations) to the deadlines for defending your dissertation and submitting a final copy if you plan to graduate in a semester. At some institutions there are hundreds of rules and because you are doing this for the first, and generally final, time, you are likely to miss some of those rules and run afoul of the people who check to make sure that you have crossed every *t* and dotted every *i* correctly. At least some members of your dissertation committee should have served on a number of other committees at your institution, and thus can help you work through the bureaucratic process of doing a dissertation.

Reason 3: To Protect and Support You When Trouble Arrives

A third reason to have a committee, and a chair, is to help you deal with problems and troubles when they arrive. Even when a research project has been approved as meeting all the ethical and practical guidelines for appropriate practice, there can still be problems. For example, you are doing research in five classrooms in a local school district and the parents of a child complain that he is being "experimented upon" without permission. You have gotten signed releases from all the parents and the text of the release was approved by both the school board and the Institutional Review Board (IRB) on your campus that approves all research studies. Then, you learn that this child moved into the district after the releases went out to parents and that the parents are correct—they did not sign a release. Such problems, which can end up being big or small, depending on how they are handled, are just the sort of thing you need a committee for. Their experience, and their ability to vouch for you as a reasonable and careful scholar, can be critical in helping you deal with trouble. Of course, it is even better if they note early on that your parent release process does not include a way of identifying new students who come into the experimental classroom after the releases were sent to parents and require you to modify your system in anticipation of that eventuality. Committees and chairs will do that but no one can anticipate every possible eventuality. Thus, somewhere in the process of doing your study you are likely to run into "trouble" and need the wise counsel and support of your committee. One of the authors of this book remembers a graduate student doing a study at a summer camp for emotionally disturbed children. Her study involved asking students to play a game that involved moving the lever of a sort of game controller to one of several positions. The experimental apparatus automatically collected the data as children responded and it ran on standard electrical power from a wall socket. The camp was on top of a mountain in the foothills of the Smokey Mountains and the study was done in the summer. In the middle of one phase of this student's study, a powerful electrical storm produced lots of lightning strikes on the mountain and one of them hit the power line, made its way into the experimental apparatus and delivered a painful but not lethal shock to all the children who had their hands on the metal levers. This is an example of unanticipated "trouble" that you are not likely to anticipate and plan for. It calls for some serious talk with your committee and/or chair about what to do with the study.

Reason 4: To Speak on Your Behalf To Others

Professional practice dissertations generally happen in a work environment such as a hospital, business, school, or office. Gaining entry to that setting and developing good working relationships with the professionals and staff can be one of the most demanding, and difficult tasks, you must accomplish. That task will be less daunting if members of your committee are comfortable with your ability to do your dissertation in an applied setting. They will gain confidence that you can do that by working with you as you plan your work. And, if they believe in you they will also be willing to vouch for you to the people who must decide whether you can do your dissertation in their work environment. The willingness of committee members to smooth the way, to talk to potential collaborators about your research, and to sing your praises to them, can significantly reduce the amount of time and effort you must spend getting set up to do your dissertation in an applied setting.

And, that type of help does not end with the dissertation. Once you finish your doctoral work you may continue in your current position for the rest of your working career. Most people do not do that, however. They eventually move to another position and they thus need references from people who know them well and can thus speak knowledgeably about their professional expertise and patterns of work and interaction. For many doctoral students, the members of their dissertation committee, especially the chair, will be a source of references for the next ten or twenty years. Committee members have much more interaction under a wider range of circumstances than faculty who teach you one or two courses. They have a better foundation from which to evaluate your work. They also tend to form closer friendships with you and thus be more reliable when it comes to writing references or accepting requests from your potential employers for telephone interviews about you. They, as friends and colleagues, also tend to become your advocate rather than a detached and "objective" reference. All this is in your favor. And, even if you do not change jobs and need employment references, you may be surprised at the number of times over your career that you need a reference—as part of a grant application to launch an interesting project, for membership in a prestigious professional organization, and for much more. It is, therefore, a good idea to keep this potential role for your committee members in mind as you complete your dissertation.

WORK THE COMMITTEE AND CHAIR SHOULD DO

Now, having identified some of the reasons for having a committee and a chair, we will look at some more of the roles of a chair and a committee. Some of these roles will be important, very important, in your dissertation. Others will not be as important. If you are having some difficulty selecting members of your committee, you might want to look over our list and create your own list of the four or five most important roles of your particular committee and chair. Then evaluate the potential members relative to those roles. Make sure at least one person on the committee can handle each important role and that as many members as possible have strengths in those areas.

Accessible and Available for Consultation

Will your chair and other members be accessible? Are appointments difficult to get? Or, will you be able to stroll in during office hours most of the time and be able to talk to your chair or another committee member? Faculty accessibility varies amazingly from one professor to another and while finishing your dissertation you need easy access. If you are unsure about accessibility, ask other students who work, or have worked with the faculty member. Ask the professor as well. And check to be sure that members are not likely to take a year-long sabbatical to Timbuctu in the middle of your dissertation work. One of the authors remembers working with a doctoral student a few years ago who was on her third dissertation committee because virtually all the members of the previous two had moved to other universities, had died, were on medical leaves, or were on sabbaticals.

Another issue related to accessibility is how to set up appointments. Is a quick e-mail enough? Should you phone? Is there a gatekeeper such as a secretary you must deal with in order to make sure you get a quick appointment? Can you call the professor at home to chat about something, or to make an appointment?

Setting up appointments can be especially tricky when one or more of the committee members lives and works some distance away. One of the authors recently served on a dissertation committee where the chair resided in Boston and a third committee member lived and taught in the Midwest. Both the candidate and your author lived and worked in New York. There are certainly advantages to having the best people possible serve on your dissertation committee, even if they do not live and work in close proximity. And, the growing number of information technologies that can connect people and groups who are geographically distant from each other makes can support a widely dispersed committee. However, in this case there were times when some substantial and technical decisions had to be made by the dissertation student and committee member living in the New York area. If your committee is dispersed you and the members should probably discuss how communication between you and the committee, and between committee members, will be handled and supported before the dissertation research even begins. If you plan on using methods such as blogs, forums, and video conferencing, make sure you try them out and verify that they both work well and are acceptable to all the members of your committee.

Involvement in Planning and Adapting

In the sciences and engineering fields, faculty often have "research programs" that are well funded through grants. As a result students often join a research team in the faculty member's laboratory and work their way up from novice assistant researcher to the senior researcher on one or more projects. Faculty who have consistent grant funding typically plan their research projects several years in advance. Thus, when you join a team as a first year doctoral student, your major professor may already know the likely research study you will do in three or four years for your dissertation.

The research programs described in the previous paragraph are one extreme. The opposite extreme is a doctoral program in the social sciences, education, business or another professional practice area where there is little, if any, grant funding for research, and few faculty have research programs. Instead, they do individual research studies as opportunities present themselves. In such a setting a doctoral student may be expected to take virtually full responsibility for selecting his or her research topic, designing the research study, and conducting the research. The chair and the committee play minimal roles and offer very little mentoring or support. Some students find this approach acceptable because it gives them a great deal of freedom. We generally advise against such an extreme approach. A doctoral student is usually a novice scholar-practitioner and will benefit from the thoughtful guidance and mentoring of a chair and committee that is knowledgeable and invested in the student's success.

We recommend regular meetings with your chair and committee, even if they are often short and focus on quick updates about the progress of your dissertation work. Whether these are scheduled well in advance or not depends on you and your needs. Some students find that regular, scheduled meetings keep them on track and focused on the work they need to do to finish their dissertation in a reasonable amount of time. Other students prefer to schedule meetings as needed with their committee and chair. There is even a tradition in some programs to work exclusively with the chair of your committee between approval of your dissertation proposal and the final defense of the finished product. That, we think, is dangerous because most of the committee is kept in the dark about your progress, and any changes you had to make. It also prevents you from benefitting from the expertise and experience of the committee members. This approach can occasionally be a recipe for disaster, or at least unnecessary difficulties, during the final oral defense of your dissertation when a committee member learns about a change in the way the dissertation was done that he or she cannot accept. Our advice is to keep all members of your committee updated and involved in the dissertation process so that there are no surprises for them when they read your dissertation and come to the oral defense.

A related issue is whether members of your dissertation committee, especially the chair, receives authorship credit should you publish articles based on your dissertation. Each field has criteria for determining who should be the first author and whether someone should receive authorship credit or not. Generally speaking, if your chair or someone else contributed significantly to the creative and innovative components of your research, they may deserve second or third authorship credit should you publish a paper. For example, suppose your major professor suggests the general framework of a research study and you follow that framework to do your dissertation. You should probably offer to add your major professor to the list of authors for the paper. Many will politely decline because they want you to publish your dissertation independently, but there will be times when having the name of your major professor on a paper with yours will be an advantage to you.

Writing and Editing Your Dissertation

There are probably as many ways of writing and editing a dissertation as there are students completing a dissertation. Some write a complete rough draft and only then present it to his or her chair. Others write a section, get feedback from the chair, and perhaps other members of the committee, make changes based on that feedback, and then get feedback on the new version. The way you handle the writing process should probably depend on your personal style and that of your chair and committee members. At a minimum, however, we recommend that you:

1. Get advice and suggestions at least from your chair about the format and structure of each section of your dissertation.
2. Write a rough draft and get detailed editorial feedback from your chair and one other member of the committee (at a minimum). Make revisions based on the feedback and get feedback on the new version. Continue in this cycle until your chair feels no further major revisions are needed.
3. Once you have a decent draft of the dissertation, submit it to all members of your committee, schedule a meeting with each one individually, and during that meeting ask for feedback and suggestions. Hopefully, the committee member will have written recommendations and changes on the dissertation. If not, take very good notes and use them to make revisions after talking over the recommended changes with your chair.

4. Make sure that when you get feedback on your writing, you cover three levels: (A) the technical aspects of whatever formatting style guide you use. Most professional practice doctoral programs use the American Psychological Association (APA) guidelines; (B) general writing quality that addresses everything from grammar errors to structural and organizational problems that make it difficult for readers to understand what you are trying to communicate, and (C) quality of writing based on the conceptual, theoretical and professional content of the dissertation. You will find that different committee members are good at different types of editing and review. One of the authors of this book remembers, for example, a professor who was often asked to be on dissertation committees because he was an expert at APA guidelines and often spotted hundreds of mistakes that needed to be corrected before the dissertation would be accepted by the graduate school. Don't expect a single reader to be good at all three levels of review and editing. Few are. But, make sure you have readers who are good at each level. Perhaps the most difficult to get is level B readers who can help you with general issues of writing. Faculty often feel a student should have developed minimally acceptable skills before entering a doctoral program and that doing much work at this level is above and beyond the call of duty. Faculty may have a point about this but in our work as editors of many different types of documents, including journals, over the past 20 years we know that the general writing skills of the professoriate is not always high, or even minimally acceptable. If your chair and committee feel your writing does not meet minimal quality standards do not try to "fix" it by yourself and do not ask your mother, husband, wife, or cousin to give you a little help because they are a "good" writer. Instead, hire an expert who knows how a dissertation should be written in your field and who has experience teaching others how to do it. We recommend against "ghost writers" who take your faulty prose away, fix it themselves, and return it to you so that you can submit it to your committee. There are quite a few companies and many individuals who offer such services. Some are good at it, some are not. However, our problem with this approach is not with quality, it is with the lack of learning. A fixer does just that; he or she fixes your dissertation and brings it up to acceptable levels of quality. However, the next time you write something you will be writing at the same level of quality you were before. Having your dissertation doctored by a specialist fixes the dissertation but not your writing. If your dissertation needs rewriting, make the experience a learning opportunity. Hire someone who helps you write a better disser-

tation. The result should be a good dissertation and better writing skills on your part.

5.   Finally, when your committee feels you, and your dissertation, are ready for the final oral defense, schedule the defense, print your dissertation, and distribute it to all the committee members well in advance of the data of the defense. Expect a few more changes to emerge from the defense, but if you have followed this five step process, there should not be many surprises that emerge during the final oral defense.

Supporting The Oral Defense

As noted in Chapter 1 the oral defense of a dissertation is left over from the Middle Ages when the ability to defend a position about statements from a holy book or ancient authority was considered a critically important skill for a new doctor. Today the oral defense varies from a rigorous and stressful rite of passage at some institutions to a celebratory meeting of committee, friends, and relatives where the doctoral candidate is the center of attention. A typical defense has five parts:

1.   The committee asks everyone to leave the room except the committee members and agrees on the guidelines and format for the defense.

2.   Everyone is welcomed back into the room, including the candidate and any guests. Then the candidate delivers a 10 to 15 minute summary of the dissertation, often supported by a PowerPoint presentation. Students often take much longer—as much as 45 minutes in our experience—but shorter is often better because the committee has read several versions of the dissertation already and is familiar with it.

3.   Once the candidate completes the presentation, members of the committee ask questions and the candidate attempts to answer them. The question phase usually begins as a round robin where a committee member asks one or more questions, then passes the baton to the next committee member. As things progress, however, the round robin format falls away and committee members feel comfortable following up on questions asked by others. Debates among committee members are not uncommon, but the focus is generally on the candidate. The role the major professor or chair takes varies. If a chair feels another committee member is not handling the questioning appropriately he or she may intervene by

raising issues, clarifying positions or issues, or guiding the candidate through judicious questioning.

4. When the committee members have had all their questions answered, or they have run out of time or energy to ask additional questions, the questioning phase ends and the candidate as well as guests are again asked to leave the room. Once they are alone members of the committee discuss the outcome of the oral defense. There are typically three options: failure (rare), accept the dissertation with revisions (common), accept the dissertation without revisions (not so common). Outright failure is rare for understandable reasons. Unless there is considerable conflict among committee members, or most of the committee is seeing the dissertation for the first time, issues should have been worked out and attended to well before the oral defense. There is little reason to allow a student to attempt an oral defense if it is clear a majority of the committee will vote against the current version of the dissertation. A decision to accept the dissertation without revisions happens occasionally but it is not very common either. There is almost always something one or more of the committee members wants changed before the final version is submitted for formal acceptance by the university. There are, however, two versions of the "accept with revisions" decision.

   One requires all the changes to be read and accepted by all or most of the committee. This can complicate your revision efforts because it requires more than one person to agree on changes. One person, for example, can approve one change while revising another, but it may be your luck that another committee member does just the reverse. You then have to go through another round of revisions and try to get agreement between all the committee members who are looking at your revisions. This can be tedious. A more desirable version of the *accept with revisions* decision is for the committee to entrust the supervision of the revisions to your chair. Each member agrees that the chair will make the decision for the committee and that he or she will sign the document that allows the dissertation to be submitted to the university once the revisions are satisfactory. Under this option, many students can complete the revisions for their dissertation in a few days, and we have served on committees where students only needed a few hours to make the required revisions and have them approved by the chair.

5. Once a decision has been agreed upon, there will usually be a set of documents or cards to be signed that indicate the decision and whether each committee member approved it. Then the candidate and guests are called back and the committee congratulates the

candidate on a successful defense (whether revisions are required or not). At some institutions it is traditional that the chair of the committee is the first one to address the candidate as "Doctor." This is often the end of the formal oral defense and local traditions vary concerning what happens next. There may be a party organized by friends, fellow students, or family for the candidate. Or, the candidate may go home and collapse for 24 hours in an effort to begin catching up on all the sleep and rest missed in the final phases of the dissertation process.

6. Two optional but not uncommon components of an oral defense are refreshments and a small post-defense party in the same room, and an opportunity for guests to ask questions. Neither of these are common, but in some departments the candidate or friends will bring drinks and snacks to the room before the examination, set them up and make them available to everyone, including the committee. Then, after the defense the guests, and committee, remain for a short party to celebrate the candidate's success. At one institution where one of the authors taught for a number of years we eventually had to restrict these parties somewhat because each doctoral candidate felt he or she had to outdo the previous one in terms of the luxuriousness of the drinks and edibles provided. The faculty felt this put an undue financial burden on doctoral students. The other optional component is an opportunity for guests in the room to ask their own questions of the candidate after the committee has completed their questioning. In some places the dissertation oral defense is virtually a private event and no one except the candidate and the committee are encouraged to attend. We think that is a mistake. For more than 800 years these have generally been open events and we think they should remain public events open to anyone, but especially open to fellow students and colleagues of the candidate. When they are open and questions are invited, the result is usually a few questions that are friendly in tone and nonadversarial in nature.

HOW DO YOU DECIDE WHO
YOU SHOULD ASK TO BE ON YOUR COMMITTEE?

When you think about the composition of your committee, it is important to have faculty with different strengths so you have all of the possible resources you may need. All members of your committee will participate in shaping the dissertation proposal, although the chair is usually the most involved. All will read and comment on the final dissertation and attend the defense. However, on a typical committee, different members play different roles in the process based on their strengths and your needs. We will discuss both the different roles members of the committee play, and the style of the interaction, in this section of the chapter. However, from the beginning it is important to note that the special characteristics of professional practice dissertations call for committee members with some skills, experiences, and inclinations that may not be as important in traditional research dissertations.

The first difference is that, traditional research dissertations, are often attempts to support a particular theoretical perspective. Many professors have never served on a dissertation committee where the purpose was not to test a theory. While professional practice dissertations may also focus on theory testing, a great many do not. Instead, they focus on developing a workable solution to a practical problem. That solution may actually draw on several theories and several traditions of practice. If you are not testing theories, make sure your committee is comfortable with a more practical or applied purpose.

A second difference that has been mentioned earlier relate to conducting dissertation research in the real world instead of in a controlled environment. Work in the field may involve the use of different research methods, and almost always requires additional effort to comfortably fit the research into the ongoing routines of an organization. Further, professional practice dissertations frequently have professional practitioners on the team and they are treated as valuable and worthy sources of guidance and advice. All this calls for committee members who are open, flexible, and capable of working respectfully with a diverse team. And, of course, faculty members who have considerable professional experience, especially recent or ongoing, can be very valuable members of a committee.

The third difference is that traditional research models tend to insist that once a study's plan has been agreed upon there should be few, if any, deviations from that plan. If the planned study is not successful, the appropriate path is to go back to the beginning and plan a different study. Many qualitative research methods, and many methods that are widely use in applied, field-based research, take the opposite approach. The initial plan of the research is only tentative, and everyone expects that it will change, sometimes drastically, as work proceeds. Some people make the point that the beginning of a research study is probably the point where you are the most ignorant about how the study should proceed. As you become involved in the research you learn more and more about both your topic, the research methodology, and the data. It makes sense to use that new knowledge to make adjustments that may enhance the usefulness of your study. This more flexible and open approach is practiced by many applied scholars today but not everyone is comfortable with it. Make sure your committee is comfortable with your approach to planning your dissertation research. Far more dissertations than necessary are problematic and frustrating experiences for the student because the student's expectations—with regard to topic, methodology, process, and many other things—were not in line with the expectations of their committee members. Students often approach the dissertation on the assumption that there is one Right Topic, and one Right Method to address that topic. They see any potential problems as involving a failure to make the Right choices. Our approach is to tell them that if they put one of us on the campus of virtually any large university with a diverse faculty, we can find three faculty on campus who will say that a particular dissertation was either not worth doing (topic) or done improperly (research method). And, on the same campus, we say that we can find three other faculty who will say that not only was the topic a good one, the methods used were fine as well. We say we can do that for *any* dissertation. The point is that there is no universal set of standards for research that everyone agrees on. That applies as well within particular disciplines or fields. What one historian considers a breakthrough in historical research methods, another considers a serious mistake that distracts the field from what it ought to be doing. Thus, when you do a dissertation you are not going to do a study that everyone will agree with and support. That is an impossible goal. What is reasonable, however, is that you select a committee with enough care and attention that the members of that committee find both the topic you have selected and the methods you will use acceptable. So select carefully, and make sure the committee actively participates in helping you select your topic and your methods.

THE STYLE OF INTERACTION BETWEEN YOU, YOUR CHAIR, AND THE COMMITTEE

Until recently questions about style of interaction were not something a doctoral student might comfortably ask in many programs. Aspland (2002) concluded that much of the literature on doctoral supervision deals with how students need to "adjust" to the supervisory style of their chair and committee while there was precious little on how a chair or committee member can adjust to the particular needs of a student. Hill (2002) went so far as to lament the dominance of the apprenticeship model throughout doctoral supervision, which epitomizes the medieval notion of the apprentice adapting to the master's lead, whims, and dictates.

While a traditional, authoritarian model based on the apprenticeship concept still dominates many programs, there are alternatives today. For example, in a study of the quality of graduate supervision Chapman

(2002) suggested that the essential role of the committee chair should be that of "critical friend." This model, which has much in common with the idea of a colleague, is preferred by many doctoral students over the more traditional model of dissertation chair that some have characterized as a "parent-child relationship" (Hill, 2002).

There is still quite a bit of disagreement about the proper relationship between the doctoral supervisor/chair and candidate. Aspland (2002) continues to argue that candidates must adapt to the supervisor's preferred style. On the other hand, Pearson and Breen (2002) contend that supervisors must adapt their style to the candidate's needs and expertise.

While there is no question the supervisor must understand his or her preferred style, the dynamic relationship of supervisor and candidate probably requires, not one, but a repertoire of supervisory styles. With that in mind, Brown and Atkins (1988) and Moses (1992) developed a self-administered questionnaire to measure supervisor's preferred styles, which while helpful to supervisors, took no account of candidates. That work was later extended to include the style and preferences of doctoral candidates as well (Taylor & Beasley, 2005). Taylor and Beasley further contend that a harmonious and good working relationship between supervisor and candidate can only be achieved when both expend the necessary time and energy to adjust their personal styles to each other.

A major component of the relationship between a doctoral student and a chair, or a dissertation committee, is the "balance of power" when it comes to making major decisions about the dissertation. Table 4.1 is a questionnaire from Flinders University in Australia that is based on the original work of Moses (1992), later developed by M. Kiley and K. Cadman of the Advisory Center for Education, University of Adelaide, and finally adapted by Mike Lawson of Flinders University. We do not necessarily recommend that you ask all your potential chairs and committee members to complete this questionnaire but it is often helpful to consider your views, and the views of your chair and committee members about each of the 19 different but major decisions related to your dissertation work. If you find that a potential chair prefers to have the last word on most of these questions while you prefer to work with a chair who mentors and guides you, but gives you much more flexibility, that is an important component (but not the only one) in a decision about who should be your chair.

Expectations in Research Supervision

This questionnaire is designed to facilitate discussion of expectations held by postgraduate research students and supervisors. The questions cover many of the issues that arise during supervision of a research degree.

It is recommended that the form be completed independently by supervisor and student and that the responses be the topic of discussion at a supervision meeting. The major objective of this process is seen to be in assisting the student and supervisor to establish an effective working relationship for the duration of the research degree.

Table 4.1.   A Questionnaire About the Relative Roles of Supervisor and Doctoral Student Developed at Flinders University in Australia

WHOSE RESPONSIBILITY IS IT?

Indicate your view of issues in the first table by circling a point on the line in the middle column. Make any comments or clarification in the right hand column.

Who should have responsibility for: **Comments**

1. Selection of the students' research topic.

        1   2   3   4   5

    Supervisor   Student

2. Establishing the theoretical framework for the thesis research .

        1   2   3   4   5

    Supervisor   Student

3. Identifying a program of background reading or study for the student.

        1   2   3   4   5

    Supervisor   Student

4. Developing a schedule for completion of tasks that the student will undertake during the degree.

        1   2   3   4   5

    Supervisor   Student

5. Organizing regular meetings between student and supervisor.

        1   2   3   4   5

    Supervisor   Student

6. Making the student aware of facilities and resources in the department and university.

        1   2   3   4   5

    Supervisor   Student

7. Preparing the student for public presentations of research ideas or results.

        1   2   3   4   5

    Supervisor   Student

8. Providing resources that will support the student's research.

        1   2   3   4   5

    Supervisor   Student

9. Developing a network of fellow students or staff for the student.

1	2	3	4	5
Supervisor			Student	

10. Ensuring that the student's programs is on track and on schedule.

1	2	3	4	5
Supervisor			Student	

11. Providing emotional support and encouragement to the student.

1	2	3	4	5
Supervisor			Student	

12. Maintaining an effective working relationship between supervisor and student.

1	2	3	4	5
Supervisor			Student	

13. Ensuring that the thesis will be of an acceptable standard when examined.

1	2	3	4	5
Supervisor			Student	

14. Ensuring that the current research literature has been identified and read by the student.

1	2	3	4	5
Supervisor			Student	

Other issues	1	2	3	4	5
5	Supervisor			Student	

DO YOU AGREE?

Circle the point on the line that represents your view on the following issues. Please note that "1" indicates you strongly agree with the statement and "5" indicates you strongly disagree:

Comments

15. A strong personal relationship between supervisor and student is advisable during candidature.

1	2	3	4	5
Agree			Disagree	

16. The supervisor should assist the student in writing of the thesis if necessary.

1	2	3	4	5
Agree			Disagree	

17. The supervisor should see all drafts of the student's written work.

1	2	3	4	5
Agree			Disagree	

Table continues on next page.

18. The supervisor should provide detailed commentary on all written work submitted by the student.

1	2	3	4	5
	Agree		Disagree	

19. The supervisor's written comments should normally be returned within 2 weeks from the time of submission.

1	2	3	4	5
	Agree		Disagree	

Other issues

1	2	3	4	5
	Agree		Disagree	

Adapted by Mike Lawson, Flinders University, from a questionnaire developed by M. Kiley and K. Cadman, Advisory Centre for University Education, The University of Adelaide, from work by I. Moses, Centre for Learning and Teaching, University of Technology, Sydney.

Table 4.1 focuses on the balance of power but that is a relatively crude component of the relationship. In our view, Table 4.1 is helpful but it does not get at many components expressed in the rich diversity of supervisory styles that may come into play across the process of completing a dissertation. The work of two other Australian researchers may help us get a handle on other, more subtle, components of the chair-student and committee-student relationship.

Toward an Adaptable Supervisory Style

Some of the most interesting work on style of supervision in doctoral programs has been done by two Australian scholars, Gatfield and Alpert (2002). They call for a new model of doctoral supervision. To help us understand doctoral supervision better, Gatfield and Alpert (2002) developed a four-quadrant management grid to examine supervisory style changes over time. Their model is conceptually built on the principle of Blake and Moulton's "Managerial Grid" (1964), a classic and pioneering work which studied management styles using two axes, one for "Concern for People" on the y-axis and the other "Concern for Production" on the x-axis.

In constructing their doctoral supervisory model Gatfield and Alpert (2002) replace Blake and Moulton's "Concern for People" with "Support" and they replaced "Concern for Production" with "Structure." These two key dimensions of style, "Structure" and "Support," play crucial roles in defining the supervisor's perception of role. Broadly speaking, "Structure" refers to the supervisor's approach to the management of the dissertation research project. "Support" refers to the supervisor's style of providing encouragement, help, guidance, and resources to the candidate to assist in completion of the dissertation research project.

If you simplify things and say that a supervisor may be High or Low on Structure and High or Low on Support, the result is a managerial grid with four supervisory styles, as depicted in Figure 4.1.

Consider these four types of doctoral supervision—from Directorial to Laissez-Faire. Which approach would you prefer? Why? Are your preferences in line with your needs, and will a supervisor who meets those needs help you complete a strong dissertation? These are complex decisions in part because our preferences and likes are not always perfectly aligned with what is best for us. This is, however, a very important aspect of your decision about your chair and your committee members.

There is also another related issue that complicates your choice of committee members. Suppose, for example, that your chair is in the lower right quadrant—Directorial. Do you want two other members of the committee who are also high in that quadrant? Probably not because the three may have difficulty compromising or working well together. Thus, you need to consider both how a chair or committee member's style will fit you and how it is likely to interact with the styles of other members of the committee.

We do not present Gatfield and Alpert's (2002) work on supervisory styles as the final word, but it is helpful in advancing an initial understand-

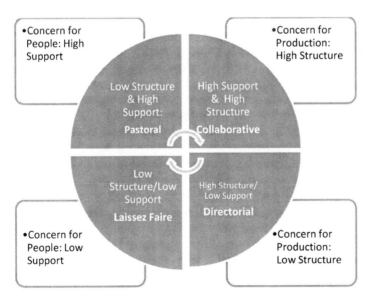

Figure 4.1.   Gatfield and Alpert's (2002) managerial grid for doctoral supervision.

ing of preferred supervisory styles and how flexible they need to be based on a doctoral candidate's changing needs. We use their framework here to focus your attention on two important elements of supervisory style—Structure and Support. We have also hinted at another aspect of chair-doctoral student and committee-doctoral student relationships that is not addressed by Gatfield and Alpert. That is the "Readiness Level" (Hersey & Blanchard, 1988) of the student to benefit from various supervisory styles. An aspect of Gatfield and Alpert's model implies that supervisory styles are relatively static and that one of the four styles is typically the "best" (e.g., Contractual). That is probably an oversimplification of the relationship. Different styles may be called for in different phases and for different aspects of the dissertation process. And, as Hersey and Blanchard have noted, doctoral students are at different levels of readiness to benefit from different supervisory styles. Thus, the choice of a chair and committee members is not quite the same as buying a new car by writing down all the characteristics you need in a vehicle and then finding the one that best matches your list. The chair-doctoral student relationship is a dynamic and changing process that is influenced by the participants and their interactions as well as by the tasks that must be accomplished.

SUMMARY

Some of the more important decisions you must make about your dissertation is the selection of a dissertation chair and the creation of a dissertation committee. While there are technical standards at your institution concerning the number of committee members, the process of creating your dissertation team is probably more artistic than scientific. It calls for active participation on your part and for simultaneous consideration of many factors—from your work habits and preferred methods of supervision and mentoring to the major roles you want your committee to play, to the personalities of both program faculty and the doctoral program itself.

As you explore alternatives and make choices, keep in mind that there are many factors to consider. Naturally, the expertise and competence of a potential committee member is important. However, the member's personality, their interest in your topic, and their beliefs about the relationship between student and committee are also important. These and other factors are especially important when it comes to selecting a committee chair who, through the dissertation research and writing process, may become your critical friend, mentor, and, eventually, primary advocate for your dissertation research. Additional committee members and optional readers will bring added dimensions, ranging from expert knowledge in your area of professional practice or research, to specialized skills in particular research methods or statistical procedures.

CHAPTER 5

SOURCES OF KNOWLEDGE AND PERSPECTIVE

Completing a dissertation involves both knowing and doing. As part of the process you should finish knowing a lot more than you did when you began your dissertation. What you *do* across the entire dissertation process determines both the type of knowledge and understanding you personally develop and what you can share with others.

We roughly divide what you do to complete a dissertation into two interacting and intertwined parts—(1) developing a deeper and more sophisticated understanding of the topic you have decided to study, and (2) conducting a research study on that topic. In this chapter we will focus on the first activity—increasing your understanding of the topic. This is traditionally accomplished by doing what has come to be called a *literature review*. However, we want to argue that in professional practice dissertations the concept of a traditional literature review may be too narrow. A broader concept may be needed because the sources of knowledge and perspective are broader that just the formal literature on a topic.

What Warrants Our Attention?

For almost any topic that interests you there will be many, many sources of information. Too many, in fact, for you to consult and use all of them.

Completing a Professional Practice Dissertation: A Guide for Doctoral Students and Faculty, pp. 123–175

So you must decide what sources warrant your attention and what sources do not. For example, if your physician tells you that tests confirm you have a serious disease such as Type 2 diabetes or stomach cancer, the people you pass on the street or sit next to at a restaurant will likely have opinions, and perhaps some information, about the disease. However, you are not likely to strike up a conversation with them in the hope of obtaining useful information. You are more likely to read books about the disease, consult other health care professionals, and check out websites about the disease that are sponsored and run by organizations you trust, such as the American Diabetes Association. You cannot use all the *potential* sources of information, so you decide which ones warrant your attention and you concentrate on them.

When it comes to doing a professional practice dissertation, there are two major types or families of sources that may be tapped to enhance your understanding of the topic: *scholarly* sources and *professional* sources. Traditional approaches such as a literature review have tended to emphasize scholarly sources over professional sources but we will argue that both types are very important and should be included in your professional practice dissertation work. A typical scholarly source is an article published in a scholarly or "academic" journal. Typical professional sources include articles published in professional practice journals and an interview with a practicing professional who has expertise related to the topic of your dissertation. Traditional literature reviews often privilege scholarly sources and ignore or deprecate the many sources of professional knowledge.

We suggest that both scholarly and professional sources of knowledge and perspective be respected and used. Figure 5.1 is a diagram of the sources that warrant your attention.

Scholarly Sources

The four major scholarly sources are generally disseminated via scholarly journals, academic books, and conference presentations:

- **Basic Research.** Typically basic research is done to test a theory that has been proposed to explain some aspect of the world. Very broad theories, such as psychoanalysis or neo-Marxist (e.g., critical) theory, apply to virtually all types of human and social interaction. Narrower theories such as behavioral learning theory, cognitive constructivism, or Beck's theory of depression, try to explain a much more restricted range of human behavior, such as how we learn, or the causes of depression. In a professional practice disser-

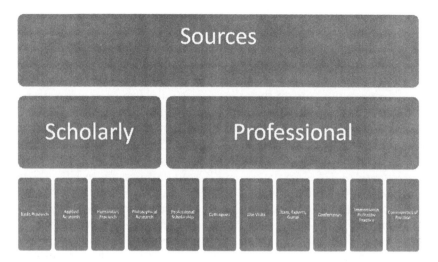

Figure 5.1. Sources of knowledge and perspective for a professional practice dissertation.

tation the theories that are the focus of basic research often provide a background for the research but they are typically not the focus. You might, for example, be studying what influences whether AIDS patients stick to the strict regimen for taking the cocktail of medicines that may save their lives. Several broad theories and some narrow theories, such as intrinsic versus extrinsic locus of control, or the social learning theory of personality, or attribution theory, or learned helplessness, have been used to explain health related behaviors and you might use one or more of these theories as a broad organizing structure for your dissertation research. For example, Kenneth Wallston's Multidimensional Locus of Control Health Scale (Wallston, Wallston, & DeVellis, 1978) might be an appealing source of data if you believe locus of control theory may explain why some HIV positive patients successfully take their medicines according to the detailed and time-sensitive regimen. The literature of basic research includes actual research studies, papers and books on the theories that are being studied, literature reviews, and attempts to synthesize or analyze the theoretical and empirical literature. However, this literature generally provides the background rather than the foreground for a professional practice dissertation.

- **Applied Research.** The difference between basic and applied research typically depends on the purpose. The purpose of basic research is to study a broad question or issue and to come up with answers that apply to many different contexts and settings. For example, suppose you are interested in autism and your research addresses the question of whether there is a genetic basis to autism. Research (e.g., studies of identical twins and whether one child being autistic means the other twin is more likely to be autistic even if the twins were reared apart from birth) to answer such as question is basic research because that question is a broad, fundamental question about the origins of autism. The answer has many different implications at several levels. On the other hand, suppose your interest focuses on the issue of how to improve the social and communicative skills of autistic children and there are three different theories that explain why autistic children tend to have poor social and communicative skills. Naturally, these three theories contradict each other on the reasons or causes, and they lead to different approaches to treatment and education. You might do a dissertation that looks at the impact of one or more of the most popular treatment alternatives on the social and communicative skills of autistic children. Or, you might compare the impact of different treatment and education programs. In either case, these are examples of applied research "in the basic research tradition" because you are still focused on theories—in this case theories that explain and have implications for treatment of the social/communicative aspects of autism. Applied research in the basic research tradition is an attempt to apply the broad or "universal" conclusions of basic research. These universal conclusions are expressed in theories. If this type of applied research shows that a particular type of treatment or innovation is effective then the theory that treatment or innovation is based on will also be supported. Thus, this type of applied research is also "theory-centric" just as basic research is.

Another approach to applied research is not so theory-centric. It focuses, instead on the solution of a problem or issue in professional practice and does not attempt to frame potential solutions within a single theory. Theories are certainly considered but solutions may combine approaches from several theories or may not fit comfortably into any theoretical framework. This type of applied research is thus "theory aware" or "theory informed," but it is not "theory centric." Some action research methods, which are discussed in later chapters, are theory aware research methods rather than theory-centric. Such methods also tend to accord more respect to professional practice sources of knowledge.

There are other ways to approach applied research that will be discussed in later chapters, but the point here is that you are concerned about questions of professional practice. While theory may "inform" or "guide" or "have implications for" the questions you are asking, the validation of existing theories, or the creation of new theories, is not the primary focus of applied research. Instead, the focus is on understanding or solving a problem or issue of professional practice. Some types of applied research begin with a theory and develop potential solutions to real world problems based on that theory. Others use theories as one of many potential sources of guidance in the process of trying to solve a problem of professional practice.

- **Humanities Research:** Over the past 20 years several areas of professional practice research have begun to use methods from the humanities. Each year, for example, there are a number of professional practice dissertations that are based on an approach called "narrative inquiry." This research method will be discussed in detail later in this book, but the basic approach involves exploring issues, problems, or patterns of professional practice using methods that allow you to "tell the story" of what has happened in a particular context of practice. The goal of this approach is to help readers of your research understand that context better. Narrative inquiry is one method for developing better understanding of particular professional practice contexts. Hermeneutic research is another. Both are contemporary methods from the humanities and both are now popular in the social sciences and in professional practice research.

- **Philosophical Research:** This type of scholarship focuses on foundational issues such as what sources we should use when trying to understand human behavior, the methods that are appropriate to study human behavior, and the nature of what we call "truth" or "knowledge." Philosophical research tends to use rhetoric, logic, and examples or cases to try and convince you that the preferred position of the author is the one you should adopt. The literature tends to fall into two broad groups of publications—those supporting a particular position and those that mainly argue against an established position. Professional practice dissertations typically take some philosophical positions as givens—the foundations upon which theories and professional practice decisions are based. That often means your literature review will include some coverage of your philosophical foundations. There is also the occasional professional practice dissertation that is philosophical. Such dissertations tend to focus on an analysis of alternative philosophical positions and their implications for practice.

Professional Sources of Knowledge and Perspectives

Scholarly sources, typically published in journals and books, or presented at conferences, have been acceptable sources for dissertation literature reviews virtually since dissertations became a part of the research doctorate in Germany in the early part of the eighteenth century. On the other hand, professional sources do not have a long history of acceptance in fields like psychology, education, and health care. For example, Sigmund Freud's use of case studies based on patients he was treating was often criticized as invalid and worthless because they were not "scientific" and thus not worth our attention. They were not "objective" and thus not valid sources of scientific knowledge. Most of this criticism came from researchers and scholars who were also opposed to Freud's theories, but the basic issue is whether the thoughtful analysis of professional practice is a valid source of knowledge and perspective. Those who believe the only source of worthwhile knowledge is scientific research will say "No!" Those who believe many sources of knowledge should be used when making professional practice decisions will say "Yes!" These are actually philosophical answers to the question, "What counts as a valid source of knowledge and perspective about professional practice?" We take a broad view and thus believe that there are many important sources that go beyond the traditional scholarly sources such as research journal articles.

Professional Scholarship

In every field of professional practice there are journals that publish papers based on practice. The papers in these journals use a variety of formats, from case studies to clinical notes about a particular patient or client, to discussions based on the author's experience of how to implement a new professional practice. Until recently much of this type of literature would not have been acceptable sources in quite a few dissertations because the philosophical foundations of the doctoral programs were so narrow that only empirical research studies based on the scientific method were considered high quality sources. That has changed drastically over the past 30 years. First, qualitative research has become much more widely accepted in the social sciences and in professional fields of practice. At the same time, the professional practice knowledge developed through reflection on practice has also become much more accepted and valued. As a result, many more professional practice doctoral programs not only accept professional sources of knowledge, they expect students to use them when they do their dissertation. The result is more use in dissertation literature reviews of professional journals like *Applied Psychology and Criminal Justice, Clinical Psychology Review, Distance Learning,*

Educational Leadership, Education and Treatment of Children, Electronic Journal of Knowledge Management, English Teaching: Practice and Critique, Health Research Policy and Systems, Journal of Professional Nursing, Journal of Technology and Teacher Education, Middle School Journal, Professional Case Management, and the Professional School Counseling Journal.

Colleagues

Colleagues are one of the major sources of new ideas and innovations for practicing professionals but this source is often ignored, or at least not acknowledged, when doing a dissertation. When a colleague influences what you do in your dissertation research, cite them! Explain their view and their area of expertise. If the influence was via an informal conversation you can site it as "personal communication" (see your APA guide for how to structure the citation and reference). If the influence was through something more formal, such as an interview, e-mail message, or formal response to questions you posed there are also APA guidelines for citing them.

If you have not considered citing colleagues ask yourself if you are missing some opportunities to learn from colleagues. The expertise of colleagues is a valuable but underused resource for professional practice doctoral students.

Site Visits

Another underutilized source of knowledge and perspective is the site visit. If you have ever read a published paper on an interesting project or innovation and then visited the organization or agency where the project operated, you may have been surprised by the difference between what you learned from the journal article and what you learned from the site visit. While the journal article often presents a formalized explanation of the project or innovation along with some outcome data, what you learn on a site visit tends to be more informal, more contextualized, and more situated in stories and examples that are less abstract and more detailed. Sometimes you will even learn that the view of the project described in the journal article is just one of several views of the project. These multiple views may represent the different, and even conflicting, viewpoints of different stakeholder groups. Site visits can enrich your understanding of an innovation or approach to professional practice in ways that are difficult to obtain simply by reading the available literature. Knowledge and perspectives developed from site visits can be very valuable. Consider them as valid sources and use them in your dissertation if they were significant sources for you. Some dissertations, in fact, are about what the author learned through site visits!

Stars, Experts, and Gurus

Another important source of knowledge and perspective is the expert—someone who has extensive experience with the topic your are studying and who has carefully reflected on that experience. You can, naturally, read the articles and books of many stars, experts, and gurus. However, even if the experts have written books or papers you can read, there may be reasons to seek an interview as well. For example, you may have questions specific to your dissertation work that are not answered or addressed in formal publications. If you can meet the expert face to face, arrive with a set of questions you want to ask and get permission to audio or videotape the interview so you can concentrate on the interview without having to write notes and at the same time obtain specific information from the expert that can be used in your study. Recording the interviews with experts also means you can quote them accurately in your dissertation where needed.

If you cannot meet the expert face to face, there are several ways to get responses to your questions. For example, if your expert agrees, you can submit a set of questions to the expert and ask them to answer them via e-mail. The downside of this is that it takes quite a bit of time to answer questions by typing responses. A better approach is to ask the expert to answer questions via audio. A simple microphone connected to the microphone input on their computer, and a free program like Audacity (http://www.audacity.sourceforge.com) is all that is needed to produce an audio file that can then be e-mailed to you as an attachment. Experts who find responding via typing e-mail messages too much effort may be willing to respond to your questions if they can talk rather than write.

Later in this chapter we will also introduce some free and inexpensive online ways to do interviews with experts who are not in your area. Video conferencing software, for example, is one way to do that.

Conferences

The cost of attending conferences is high, particularly if they are not within driving distance. If you live in New York and the major conference on your topic is being held in Los Angeles or Vancouver that year, the cost of attending can easily slide well above $1,500 even when you economize. On the other hand, attending a major conference often lets you attend presentations, seminars, and workshops where you are exposed to information and ideas that will not be in the printed literature for a year or more. You also have an opportunity to hear some of the major players in your field and perhaps even ask them questions about their work.

Conferences also immerse you in your field providing you with a feel of the current *zeitgeist*. Trends, issues, theories, and movements that are emerging in the field will be more apparent at conferences than elsewhere, and that can be important to you as you design and conduct your dissertation research.

With all the advantages of attending highly relevant conferences, the cost is still a serious consideration that may prevent you from attending some, or all, of the meetings that interest you. One option is to purchase the conference proceedings. Reading proceedings is not the same as attending the conference but if that is not possible the articles and abstracts in conference proceedings do provide cutting edge information and give you a feel for what the issues and hot topics were at the conference. More and more conferences are placing their proceedings online with free access to anyone. Also, some organizations include free access to online proceedings to members. The cost of an annual membership may be low compared to the total cost of attending a distant conference.

Immersion in Reflective Professional Practice

Another often ignored source of understanding and perspective is your own professional experience. Reflection on your own professional practice has become respectable and in many professional practice programs is considered a valid source in your doctoral research. There are many guides for analyzing your own practice and experience, but most of them fall into two general categories: narrative and reflective. These are similar approaches to thinking seriously about professional practice and one book that integrates narrative and reflection is Christopher Johns' (2007) book, *Engaging Reflection in Practice: A Narrative Approach*. However, a search on a book site like http://www.amazon.com will turn up books about reflective practice for practitioners in most fields, including education, nursing, psychology, social work, and business. An example is another book by Johns (2004) titled *Becoming a Reflective Practitioner: A Reflective and Holistic Approach to Clinical Nursing, Practice Development, and Clinical Supervision*.

Communities of Practice

A final source of professional practice knowledge is what is sometimes called "communities of practice." These are collaborative groups of professionals who share their experiences, their ideas, and their concerns about successful practice. Underlying the idea of communities of practice are several basic assumptions. One is that learning and understanding is fundamentally a social process—that humans learn and understand better in a social context where ideas and thoughts can be shared with others who have similar goals and concerns. We do not create our professional identities and our patterns of professional behavior as individuals. We do that as active, participating members in communities. Thus the development of ourselves as professionals is a deeply social process.

There are several popular models for this type of professional development. One is Wenger's (1988) view of what a community of practice (CoP) should be. Peter Senge's (2006) concept of learning communities is another along with Heron's (1996) cooperative inquiry. Communities of practice often serve as sources of knowledge and perspective for professional practice dissertations because they are powerful ways for professionals to explore their work and to develop new ideas, new approaches, and new perspectives on that work. If your dissertation integrates the work of a community of practice into your research project, you may find yourself citing the conclusions and perspectives developed through that community of practice. Communities of practice are also the focus of dissertation studies. Your dissertation may actually be the story of how a community of practice developed and worked toward the solution of a problem or issue of professional practice. Although any CoP may be the focus of a dissertation, two types are most often studied in dissertation research. One is CoP that use an action research methodology (Stringer, 2007), particularly participatory action research (PAR) where the leadership of the community and the decision-making responsibilities are shared across the participating groups (McIntyre, 2008). The other is Narrative Inquiry (Clandinin & Connelly, 2000). The Clandinin and Connelly book has several summaries of dissertations about CoP that used narrative inquiry as a means of professional development and discovery.

If your dissertation is about the work of a CoP you will naturally be including a lot of data taken from the meetings, explorations, and deliberations of that CoP. If there is one, or more, CoP involved in solving the problem or addressing the issue that is the focus of your dissertation, don't hesitate to use the conclusions and perspectives of CoP as sources in your dissertation. CoP is one of the more powerful ways for professional practitioners to advance thinking about practice and it is thus a valid and worthy source of guidance and knowledge.

Ways of Locating Relevant Sources

If you look at older guides to locating relevant sources for your dissertation, the approach presented will likely be what we call the "traditional approach." We will present that approach first and then suggest an alternative that is broader, more inclusive, and one that uses electronic sources that were not considered appropriate just a few years ago.

The "Traditional" Knowledge Search Process

Traditional searches of the literature begin with reading relevant books and using the standard abstract databases to find summaries of articles that seem appropriate. Abstract databases let you search for articles, and books, using several different approaches including the name of the author, the title, and keywords that are relevant to your topic.

The result will be a list of abstracts that summarize the contents of the paper or book chapter. If you are interested in reading the entire article, the traditional approach is to go to your college or university library, locate the journal where the paper was published, make a copy, and add it to your growing pile of papers. If your library does not subscribe to the journal, which is increasingly the case as the cost of journal subscriptions continues to rise, two other traditional options are to request a copy through interlibrary loan systems or go to a library that has the journal and make a copy there. One of the authors of this book fondly remembers spending two days at the Library of Congress in Washington, DC making copies of papers for a research project from journals that did not seem to be anywhere else in the country. Fortunately, as you will see in the next section, making a trip to Washington is seldom necessary today even if the papers you need are not in your library.

There are hundreds of abstract databases and virtually every field has at least one; most have many. For example, in psychology the American Psychological Association (APA) has the Psychological Abstracts database along with several others. Until 2006 Psychological Abstracts was a huge print index to the psychological and educational literature that took up several bookcases in the reference section of most college and university libraries. APA discontinued the print version in 2006 and now only supports the PSYCInfo online database. Most college and university libraries subscribe to this database and you can generally access it using your university ID and password. Directions may be on your institution's website but if not the reference librarians can help you connect. In education the ERIC database plays a similar function. ERIC is short for Educational Resources Information Center and this government funded system was substantially revised during the last Bush administration. In fact, it was dismantled and put together in a very different way with commercial, profit-making partners taking more control of the system while the roles of non-profit groups such as universities and professional organizations were either eliminated or substantially decreased. The home page of ERIC is http://www.eric.ed.gov and you can do ERIC searches from that website. Your institution may have other ways to connect to and use ERIC, however, that are easier. The ERIC database has abstracts of hundreds of thousands of published papers as well as books, but it also has electronic, full-text documents that come primarily from practitioners who submit their work directly to ERIC for inclusion in the database. Thus, ERIC does what PSYCInfo does for the psychological (and some educational) literature—provide abstracts but not full text—and it hosts some full text documents submitted directly to ERIC.

We should note, however, that PSYCInfo is not the only database available from APA. PsycARTICLES is a database of articles published in the many APA journals. If your library subscribes to this database you have access to the full text of articles in APA journals. PsycBOOKS is, as you might expect from the title, a database of the full text of books published by APA, and PsycCRITIQUES is a database of reviews and commentary on books relevant to topics in psychology. APA even has a database named PsycEXTRA with information on the "grey literature" of psychology that is published outside the traditional publication outlets of peer reviewed journals and scholarly books.

Every professional field has abstract databases. For example, PubMed (http://www.pubmed.gov) is a huge health care database that includes abstracts as well as a growing number of full-text papers. In fact, if your work is funded by the National Institutes of Health, your research papers must be made available through PubMed even if they are published in journals as well. You will want to familiarize yourself with the major abstract databases in your field and become familiar with how they work as well as what they offer.

Basic Versus Advanced Searches

Most abstract databases, and most of the full-text databases that will be discussed later in the chapter, have several options for doing searches. One of them will be a *basic* search function that is simple and uncomplicated but offers few options. There will also be one or more *advanced* search options that let you be much more specific about what you are looking for. The advanced functions and how they work vary considerably from one database to another but both basic and advanced search options use Boolean operations like AND, OR, and NOT to define your search. These will be discussed later in this chapter. Advanced searches also give you many additional options, which are often needed because there may be hundreds of thousands of documents on your general topic. You need ways of narrowing the list of hits to those documents that deal with your specific interests. Advanced search options may, for example, include the following:

- Year of publication or a range of years.
- Section of the documents to be searched such as title, abstract, author name, institution where authors work, or full text.
- Wildcard options that let you look for terms where any characters are acceptable for part of the term. For example, the search term "psychological" would only find documents containing the term

psychological. However, a search for "psychol*" would find documents with terms that begin with "psychol" including psychology, psychologist, and psychological. The * is a common wildcard character but some systems use other characters and some may have several wildcard characters that operate in different ways.

- Publication type such as research article, book, research paper, report, literature review, and so on.

These are just a sample of the different options available in search systems. Learning the options available in the databases and search engines you use will help you find the most relevant documents without being overwhelmed by thousands of hits that are not relevant.

What Do You Do After Reading the Abstracts?

Once you read abstracts of potentially interesting articles, how do you read the complete text of a document? There are several ways. If the document is a journal article you can go to your library, find the journal, and read the paper (or make a copy to take with you). If your library does not subscribe to the journal the librarians can help you get a copy through a traditional interlibrary loan service. Interlibrary loan also works for other documents such as books. If you can't find the document locally and interlibrary loan takes too long, you can also get copies of articles through Internet-based article reprint services such as UnCover (http://uncweb.carl.org/). For a fee UnCover will download a copy of the document quickly and efficiently. A number of scholarly databases, usually associated with specific publishers, also have options for paying a fee to get a copy of a particular paper. Those fees generally range from $20 to $45 per article which is too high for regular use if you need copies of many papers. Interlibrary loan is a much less expensive way of getting copies, and your library may offer that service to you at no charge.

Writing A Traditional Literature Review

Once you have a good start on collecting relevant articles and books, the next traditional step would be to write a dissertation chapter that reviews the relevant literature. The format of that literature review will vary from dissertation to dissertation but one format might look like this:

1. **The Problem of XXX**. XXX can be an issue, a problem, a barrier, or a challenge that faces practitioners in a particular field. In this section you introduce XXX, show why it is something that warrants our attention, and why you have selected it as the focus on your dissertation. Your goal is to help readers understand XXX as well

as the broader context in which XXX operates and influences the outcomes of professional practice.

2. **Theoretical Frameworks.** Introduce the major theoretical frameworks currently used to organize and guide thinking about your topic. Provide some historical perspective about how and why each of the major theories developed and show, briefly, how they influence the policies and procedures of professional practice.

3. **Professional Practice Applications.** This section of your literature review looks at XXX from the perspective of practice. What does the literature tell you about XXX and how it is being addressed in practice? Are there approaches or policies tied to theories? What are they and how are they implemented? What does the research say about their effectiveness? Are there blended approaches that cut across theories? How do they work, what does the research say about their effectiveness? In this section of the review you should organize approaches to professional practice into families or groups that share common approaches, theories, and/or perspectives. Then, if there are variations and alternatives within each family, introduce and explain them as well. At the end of this section, readers should begin to see there are questions that have not been fully answered in the literature and that your dissertation research will address one or more of them.

4. **Approaches to Research on the Topic.** Although you will be citing and explaining research studies throughout the literature, this section should focus on the methods and procedures commonly used to study XXX. Discuss them in some detail and analyze both the strengths and weaknesses of each major research method used. If there are differences in methods based on the ideology of the researchers—those who prefer qualitative, quantitative, or emancipatory ideologies, for example—point that out. If certain types of questions are typically addressed using particular research methods, note that as well. Then draw some conclusions about whether it is better to use the standard methods for answering certain types of questions, or is there some appeal in using different methods because they let you approach the question from different perspectives?

5. **What is Needed.** The first four parts of your review should bring the reader to this section with some understanding and expectation of what you want to do in your dissertation. In this final section of the literature review, make your plans explicit. Explain what you want to do and why. Do this briefly, in one to four pages, and leave the details for other chapters. Your goals in the

literature review, however, are to (1) convince your committee that you know and understand the relevant literature, and (2) show that the research you want to pursue for your dissertation is worthy of doing and that you are capable of doing it.

If you would like to read more about how to conduct a traditional literature review there are many online resources. The staff at Central Queensland University in Australia has developed a very good tutorial which is at this Internet address: http://www.library.cqu.edu.au/litreviewpages/#. Another tutorial is available at http://www.lib.rmit.edu.au/tutorials/litreview/ ha455a.html which was developed by the Royal Melbourne Institute of Technology. Another website with material on how to conduct a review of the literature was created by the Collaborative Research Network (http://kancrn.kckps.k12.ks.us/guide/literature.html).

THE "NEW" SEARCH FOR KNOWLEDGE AND PERSPECTIVE

Since the turn of the century two major developments have changed the way researchers look for relevant material on their research topic. One of those developments is the expansion of "what counts" as valid and worthy sources of information. As the grip of positivism weakened in many fields, a growing respect for sources beyond the empirical research article, and the theoretical paper based on research, developed. The second major development is, in part, a result of that expanded range of acceptable sources as well as the development of new technologies, both hardware and software, that support both traditional and "new" ways of searching for information. In fact, the traditional approaches to doing searches have not been replaced by new ways. It is more accurate to say that new approaches have added to, rather than replaced, traditional methods. In this section we will explore a number of the newer tools and approaches. We will begin with full-text databases.

Full-Text Databases

Traditional databases for searching the scholarly and professional literature provide only the abstracts of articles, papers, books, and other documents. Once you found a relevant document, there was still the additional step of locating a printed copy of the full document that you could read. Full-text databases changed all that. For example, the SAGE

Journals Online database is an example of a commercial full-text database that contains both abstracts and the full-text of articles published in SAGE's 520 journals. These journals cover a range of disciplines including business, the humanities, science, social science, technology, and medicine. You can search specific journals or all the journals in this database, find relevant articles, and then either read the papers online or download them to your own computer and print them if you prefer to read paper copies instead of from your computer screen. Several of the large journal publishers offer access to virtually all the papers in the journals they publish through an online database that includes full-text access. However, since these are mostly for-profit publishers there is generally a substantial fee for access to these databases and they typically cover only the journals (and sometimes books) from that publisher. The Association of Computing Machinery's (ACM) Digital Library is an example of this type of database that is from an organization rather than a publisher. If you are a member of ACM you have access to the Digital Library of conference papers and journal articles published by the organization. Another example of a publisher's full-text database is Emerald Management Extra, a database of the 175 business management related journals published by Emerald plus summaries of articles in 300 other business management journals from other publishers.

Another type of full-text database covers journals and other types of publications from more than one publisher. Some of these databases are huge and provide full-text access to thousands of journals that can be searched electronically. An example of this type of full-text database is Academic Search Elite which is from an established company, EBSCO, serving the library market. Academic Search Elite contains the full-text of papers published in about 2,100 different journals from many different publishers plus the abstracts of papers in an additional 1,550 journals. Other databases like this include JSTOR which is strong in the humanities, Educational Administration Abstracts which despite its title contains some full-text resources for some journals, ProQuest Direct that covers thousands of journals and lets you specify whether you want to search only for papers available in full-text, and Project Muse that covers over 400 journals mainly in the humanities and social sciences from 150 different publishers.

There are many, many other full-text databases, some of them focused on a particular area of professional practice. These databases are particularly useful to professional practice doctoral students because they can be accessed from your computer at home at any time of the day or night. This saves the time and energy required to drive to your college or university library to do either hand or electronic searches. Since most professional practice doctoral students complete their degree part time and have a full time job, the ability to search at any time, and from home, is a decided advantage. We suggest you explore the full-text options available in your field and make heavy use of them. However, since almost all of these databases are for-profit, you may be limited to those your institution subscribes to. If you need to use a database that is not available through your campus library, check with a reference library about ways to get access. There may be an institution nearby with an exchange agreement with your university. Or, you may be able to go to the library of an institution and use the computers in that library to connect to the database you need to use.

Online, Open Access Journals

Full-text databases are one recent development that makes searching the literature easier. Another is online and open access journals. Until recently, journals were printed—ink on paper—and having an article published in a journal gave it more status than a paper that was distributed in any other way. Scholarly journals began in the seventeenth century, and they did not change much over the next 250 years. Today, however, a new form of journal is beginning to replace the traditional print journal. Today there are thousands of E-journals (also called online journals, electronic journals or just ejournals) on the web. They use the same review process to select articles for publication as traditional print journals, but many e-journals give authors the opportunity to use media other than text and black and white graphics. Many of the online journals require that either you or your institution has paid a subscription fee before you can access the full text of papers published in that journal. There are, however, a growing number of what are called "open access" journals that do not charge a subscription fee. The costs of publishing online journals is less than print versions and even those costs are paid for in different ways—volunteer editors and reviewers; sponsorship by an organization, institution, or library, or grant funding. The result is that users of open source journals have free and open access via the Internet. If you would like more information on open access scholarly and professional journals the Directory of Open Access Journals website (http://www.doaj.org/) lists almost 5,000. The list is organized by broad discipline (e.g., agriculture, arts, life sciences, business, literature, mathematics, science, social science, and so on).

While e-journals are relatively new, there are already thousands and many of them are relevant to the different fields professional practice. A few of the ones available on the World Wide Web are:

- *Current Issues in Education.* http://cie.ed.asu.edu/
- *The Electronic Journal of Communicative Psychoanalysis.* http://www.ejcpsa.com/
- *Contemporary Issues in Technology and Teacher Education.* http://www.citejournal.org
- *Interactive Multimedia Electronic Journal of Computer-Enhanced Learning.* http://imej.wfu.edu/
- *International Electronic Journal for Leadership in Learning.* http://www.ucalgary.ca/~iejll/
- *International Journal of Educational Technology.* http://www.outreach.uiuc.edu/ijet/
- *Journal of Asynchronous Learning Networks.* http://www.aln.org/alnweb/journal/jaln.htm
- *Journal of Statistics Education.* http://www.amstat.org/publications/jse/
- *Journal of Technology in Counseling.* http://jtc.colstate.edu/
- *Online School Library Media Research* http://www.ala.org/aasl/SLMR/ This is a publication of the American Association of School Librarians.
- *Psycoloquy.* http://www.princeton.edu/~harnad/psyc.html This journal, sponsored by the American Psychological Association, publishes papers on cognitive science, behavioral psychology, behavioral biology, and philosophy.
- The Online Journal of Issues in Nursing. http://www.nursingworld.org/MainMenuCategories/ANAMarketplace/ANAPeriodicals/OJIN.aspx
- *Techne: Journal of the Society for Philosophy and Technology* http://scholar.lib.vt.edu/ejournals/SPT/
- *The Turkish Online Journal of Distance Education.* http://tojde.anadolu.edu.tr/

These are only a few of the thousands of e-journals available. To look for other journals on the web you can use several sites that keep track of currently active ejournals. In addition to the Directory of Open Access Journals mentioned earlier there are:

- *NewJour.* http://gort.ucsd.edu/newjour/index.html NewJour is a list of electronic journals. It includes both newsletters and other forms of scholarly and professional communication as well as refereed journals.

- *Electronic Journal Miner.* http://ejournal.coalliance.org/
  Enter a term or phrase at this website and it will search for journals and other types of publications relevant to your keywords.
- *Ejournal Siteguide: a MetaSource.* http://www.library.ubc.ca/ejour/
  This is a gateway site to other websites that carry general and subject lists of ejournals.
- *Serials in Cyberspace.* http://www.uvm.edu:80/~bmaclenn/ This site at the University of Vermont has a list of ejournals as well as links to other lists.
- Canadian Electronic Scholarly Network. http://www.schoolnet.ca/vp-pv/cesn/e/ This site has links to Canadian ejournals as well as to other sites that have ejournal lists from all over the world.
- Australian Journals Online. http://www.nla.gov.au/ajol/ This site, at the Australian National Library, has information on over a 1,000 Australian ejournals.

Ejournals are both sources of information and potential publication outlets for your own research. We predict that over the next two decades ejournals will gradually replace traditional print journals. The number of ejournals available is growing rapidly as print journals add electronic versions and hundreds of new electronic-only journals come on line each year.

Free or fee, ejournals are an important part of the future in every area of research and professional practice.

Accessible General Publications

Some dissertations call for reviews of publications for the general public like newspapers and magazines. Many such publications have searchable databases that may contain the full-text of articles and papers, that go back more than a 100 years. *The New York Times, Wall Street Journal,* and *The Washington Post* have online, searchable databases that include what has been published in the papers over the past few decades. There are also newspaper databases such as Infotrac Custom Newspapers Online with articles published from 1980 to present in well over a 1,000 newspapers from around the world. And, if you want to restrict your search to a particular geographic area, there are databases of newspaper articles like Infotrac's New York State Newspapers database.

In addition, the New York Times Historical Newspapers database covers articles published from 1851 to 2001, the Wall Street Journal Historical Newspapers database has full-text access to articles published between

1889 and 1992, and the Washington Post Historical Newspapers database covers 1887 to 1988.

Google Scholar

The Internet is so huge and changes so quickly that it is impossible to simply "browse" the Internet and find relevant resources. The solution to that problem is to use one or more of the many Internet search engines. The Google search engine, which will be discussed later, is currently the dominant search engine. The success of the search engine took Google from a bright idea to a multibillion dollar company with thousands of employees in a matter of years. Google, however, has not been content to rest on its laurels as the search engine company that has remained at the top of the heap for longer than any other. It has used some of its resources to create other, related, tools that serve particular markets. One such service is Google Scholar, a search service that allows you to restrict your search to the scholarly and professional literature. The web address of Google Scholar is: http://scholar.google.com. Google Scholar searches work the same as regular Google searches, but the search is limited to "peer-reviewed papers, theses, books, abstracts and articles, from academic publishers, professional societies, preprint repositories, universities and other scholarly organizations" as noted on the Google Scholar website. When you search for relevant literature the resulting list of hits is organized according to a set of criteria that puts the most important and influential documents first. Many of the hits in Google Scholar will be the full-text of documents but some of them will be abstracts or summaries. Google Scholar is an excellent resource when you want to search the online scholarly literature without limiting yourself to the literature in a particular area. Google Scholar's database includes virtually all areas of scholarship. The Google Scholar website has tutorials on how to conduct effective searches that you should read before undertaking major searches.

Google Books

You may have read about Google's efforts to digitize all the books in some of the largest and oldest academic libraries. The Google Books project (http://books.google.com) is controversial because copyright law does not make it clear whether it is legal to make digital copies of books that are still under copyright protection and to put the digital copies in a database that anyone can search for relevant keywords. When a book contains keywords you searched for, Google Books does not give you access to the entire book if it is still under copyright. However, you will typically get access to the page where the keyword, or keywords, appear, as well as pages before and after. Sometimes that is enough, but it is almost always sufficient to tell you whether you need to find a copy of the book in your university's library or through interlibrary loan. Although relatively new and still in development, Google Books has already digitized over seven million books. The full text of books that are out of copyright is available but even if a book still has copyright protection Google Books does use the complete text of that book when you do a search.

One useful trick when using databases like Google Books is to find newer resources by looking for publications that reference the most relevant and topical of older resources. If a book published in 2010 references a critical and influential paper published in 1998, for example, that may be a book you want to check out more carefully. The same goes for articles and other types of documents that can be searched for in other databases. The Science Citation Index and the Social Science Citation Index are two databases that are particularly suited to finding newer publications that cite earlier papers and books.

INTERNET SEARCHES

Thus far we have mostly been discussing tools for locating information resources that are specialized. They were created for use by academics, scholars, and professionals. However, one of the revolutions of the digital age is the growth of the Internet and the development of tools such as search engines for finding information. Search engines have become indispensable tools for finding what you need on the Internet and that applies to researchers and professionals just as much as it does to someone looking for a great buy on a 1957 Edsel, or for information about how to make an authentic Ukrainian borsch. That is not, surprising, however, as the person who developed the concept of the Internet, Tim Berners Lee, was a scientist. His goal was to create an effective way for scientists to communicate electronically. He certainly accomplished his goal! And more!

Search Engines and Metasearch Engines

The World Wide Web is made up of "sites" where data is stored. Those sites can contain anything from an electronic storefront that sells books (like http://www.amazon.com) to electronic journals (such as http://

www.citejournal.edu where the journal *Current Issues in Technology and Teacher Education* is located). If you are sitting at a computer connected to the Internet, you could run a browser like Firefox, Opera, or Internet Explorer, type a web address like http://www.citejournal.edu into the address box at the top of the screen, press Return, and go to that website.

The World Wide Web dominates the Internet today. Most of the content on the Internet is housed on World Wide Web sites. The "www" in the two addresses mentioned already stands for "World Wide Web" and it has become so popular that it is generally referred to simply as "the Web." Today many scholars, journals, institutes, universities, and organizations have websites where resources of interest to someone completing a dissertation are housed.

In the early days of the Internet, documents that were available tended to be specialized papers and reports that appealed to small groups of scholars who shared an interest in one form of very specialized research or another. However, the problem with the Internet today is not that there isn't likely to be anything on a topic that interests you. The problem is that there are billions of documents on the web and sometimes it is hard to find exactly what you're looking for because the other two billion documents keep getting in the way. This embarrassment of riches led to the creation of a special form of software—*search engines*. Search engines let you type a word or two and then tell the engine to find sites on the Internet that have relevant information. A search engine is a system that has two parts:

1. A specially constructed database of the content of documents available on the Internet. (Some search engines only have World Wide Web sites in their databases; others include other types of Internet resources as well.)
2. A user interface that lets you specify terms you want to look for on the Internet.

Search engines vary in many different ways and there are several types of search engines. However, the basic way they are used is similar from one search engine to another.

- Go to the search engine's website,
- Type a word, phrase, or set of words, and
- Click the Search button.
- The engine will display a list of "hits" on your screen. Then you can click the name or title of a hit and go to that website.

To illustrate the process, we will walk through a real search one of the authors did recently in connection with writing an article. To make a particular point in the article he needed to know when the typewriter was invented, so he went to the website of the Go search engine (formerly called Infoseek) at http://www.go.com. He typed these two words: +*typewriter* +*invented*. He put a plus sign in front of each word to indicate that he wanted the search engine to locate sites that included that word before counting it as a hit. (Without the + signs Go would look for sites that contained either the word *typewriter* or the word *invented*.) When he told Go to find sites with these two words it located several hits. The second or third site he looked at told him the typewriter was invented in 1800. It took about 2 minutes to find this bit of information, but finding the same information from traditional print resources would have taken much longer even if the resources were available in the room where he was working. Usually, they are not, which means a trip to the library. Using a search engine reduced what would probably have taken hours to 2 minutes.

An Overview of Some Popular Search Engines

Even if you are reading this section a few months after this book was published, the information here is almost guaranteed to be obsolete by the time you read it. Search engines come and go with increasing regularity today. Even more quickly they are bought by other companies, renamed, and relaunched. Search engines, because they are used by millions if not billions of people every day, are very appealing to advertisers. A company that owns a popular search engine can earn billions of dollars in fees from advertisers whose ads appear on the screen while you search for information.

One reason search engines are potential moneymakers is the ability to customize the ads a user sees. For example, suppose you enter the search terms, *spring break* and *beach*. The search engine may put an ad for hotels around the Texas beach area of South Padre Island at the top of your screen. On the other hand, someone who types *car*, *new*, and *purchase* may get an ad from an Internet auto seller that offers low prices on new cars.

The smell of profit in the search engine industry means we have a lot of engines to choose from, and the competition is intense to make them easy to use as well as powerful because those two characteristics will attract more users. Below are brief descriptions of just a few of the current crop of search engines, beginning with one of the largest and by far the most popular search engine—Google. Keep in mind, however, that this is one of the most competitive and active markets, and a search engine that is on the leading edge of innovation and popularity today may be an also-ran a year later.

Google http://www.google.com/

Google was the new kid on the block in 1999, and it quickly became a popular search tool. It ranks websites on the basis of popularity, and it puts the most popular sites at the beginning of the list of hits. We use Google when we want to search a large index (Google has one of the largest) and when we are searching for information on a topic that many other Internet users would be interested in.

The way Google displays the results of a search illustrates a common procedure called "results clustering." A simple search engine may produce a list of results with 15 or 20 of the top hits from the same large website. You do not generally want that. It is better to have a diverse collection of relevant websites at the top of your list. Results clustering does that. It limits the number of hits displayed from the same website. Google will typically list no more than two hits from the same website, and it will indent the second one under the first to tell you these are from the same location. This is generally the preferred approach to creating a list of hits. However, there may be times when you want to see all the hits from a particularly useful website. To do that on Google, just click the "More Results" button that will be displayed below the second hit from that site. Other engines also use results clustering and they generally have options like "More from this site" that let you look at additional hits from the same location if that is what you want.

Another very good feature of Google is the *cache* command. It is not uncommon to click on the address of a hit and get a message saying that site is no longer available. Websites come and go, they move, and they are removed from the web. This can be disconcerting, but Google has a neat fix for that. Click the Cache command below a hit in your list of results and Google will retrieve that page from its own database. You will see the text of the page on your screen with your search terms highlighted. Remember, however, this is NOT the website for that hit. It is only the page from the site that Google stored on its own computer when it indexed the page and added it to the Google database.

Finally, when you do a Google search the search engine usually looks for your keywords anywhere on the Internet. However, if you look at the top of the Google home page, there is a list of options that limit either the locations searched (e.g., Gmail, groups, books, Google Scholar database, blogs, YouTube, and Google Reader which will be discussed later) or the type of content you want to find (e.g., images, video, maps, news, shopping, finance, calendar, photos, documents). There are so many options for where or what to search for that the menu has two extensions (*more* and *even more*). Because of Google's ease of use, a huge database, and the many options, this is currently (2010) the most popular Internet search engine.

Bing http://www.bing.com/

Bing is one of the newer search engines that claims to take a different approach to the search process. Bing, the search engine formerly known as Kumo, is also the latest effort on the part of Microsoft Corporation to capture a significant share of the search engine market. Bill Gates, and Microsoft, came late to the realization that the Internet was the future of personal computing and the company lagged behind others when it came to providing Internet software and services. Like Google, Bing lets you search for different types of content such as video or images as well as different types of locations. Bing also organizes hits when you do a search. For example, if you search for a term like "Educational Technology" a list on the left side of the screen will let you pick a subset of the hits such as those that define the term, or hits on the history of educational technology, or sites about a particular source such as the *Journal of Educational Technology.*

Bing is a useful alternative to Google but thus far Microsoft's advertising for Bing is more innovative than Bing itself. It is not the revolutionary search engine that will attract Google users in droves, though that is precisely what Microsoft would like. That said, the deep pockets of Microsoft mean they can create new versions that perhaps will accomplish their goal. Windows, which now dominates the operating system market, was a pitiful imitation of the Macintosh operating system until about version 3.1. Bing may evolve into a worthy competitor to Google.

Yahoo Search Engine http://search.yahoo.com

Until the summer of 2009 the third major search engine we planned to review briefly was Yahoo. The regular Yahoo website, http://www.yahoo.com, is a busy place with access to everything from news feeds to special interest groups on everything from classic cars to medical specialties and abstract art, to shopping services, horoscopes, and e-mail access. However, Yahoo's search engine has struggled to attract a sizable following, due in part to the success of Google. Over 70% of the searches are done on Google, which leaves 30% or less to all the other Internet search engines. After months of rumors, however, Yahoo and Microsoft announced in July of 2009 that they were combining their efforts in the area of Internet searching. Yahoo will handle the marketing side of things and sell the advertising that allows users to do searches at no cost other than the inconvenience of dealing with the ads on the search engine site. Yahoo will continue to support a Yahoo search engine on its site, and Microsoft will continue to support and develop Bing. But, if you look under the hood of Yahoo's search engine you will find Bing software rather than software Yahoo developed itself. This is an effort by the second and third ranked search engine companies to try and gain some ground on Google. To check out the Bing/Yahoo search engine go to either www.yahoo.com or www.search.yahoo.com to see the result.

Search Engines Not Enough? Try Metasearch Engines

Different search engines produce different results, sometimes drastically different results. That does not present a problem if you are simply looking for a few sources of information about a particular topic and you don't want a comprehensive list. Most searches fall into this category. But what if you want to find all the sites about the philosopher Ludwig Wittgenstein that are also relevant to social work practice? You could use each of the 15 or so most popular search engines. However, you would have to deal with many duplications because different search engines would probably find some of the same websites. An easier and quicker way to do this type of search is with a *metasearch engine,* aka *metasearch tool.* Metasearch engines use the databases of several different search engines and then compile a list of hits that *should* not contain duplicates. (Unfortunately, some metasearch engines don't eliminate the duplicates either.) A few of the better metasearch engines that were popular in 2010 are described below.

Mamma http://www.mamma.com
The slogan "mother of all search engines" tells you this metasearch tool has been around since the first Iraqi war. Mamma does a decent if not outstanding job but one annoying feature is that the first page or so of your list of hits is likely to be advertisements for sites that have paid to be the first hits you see.

Ixquick http://www.ixquick.com/
Ixquick has some significant strengths as well as some weaknesses. The main weakenss is that it does not always eliminate the duplications in hits from the 14 search engines it uses. On the other hand, it will accept and use sophisticated search options such as Boolean (explained in the next section) and "natural language" searches. It knows which search engines will accept different types of searches and adapts to them. A few search engines accept natural language searches which are searches that let you use English-language style search requests such as "I need information on home schooling educational materials." Another nice feature of Ixquick is the ability to select which search engines are used. There are ten options at the top of the screen, from Ask and Bing to Gigablast and Yahoo.

AskJeeves *http://www.askjeeves.com http://www.ask.com/*

Originally named after the efficient but slightly caustic valet in the short stories and novels of P. G. Wodehouse, this metasearch engine is now just called ASK. It is often recommended for beginners because it is easy to use and productive. It does eliminate duplicate hits from the resulting list. If you use the advanced search options, it also allows you to select where to look for your keywords—in the web address, in the title of the page, or anywhere on the website. You can also specify that you only want hits that have changed within a certain period of time, from within the last week to the last 2 years or unlimited.

Proteus *http://www.thrall.org/proteus.html*

This is another metasearch engine that has a number of options. This one uses over 30 different search engines and reference sources to create a list of hits. It also lets you select which search engines to use and it includes some options that are particularly useful for doing searches related to dissertation research. The ERIC database of documents about education and related topics is one of the sources you can specify. The Google database of U.S. government documents and Google Scholar are two others.

Infocom *http://www.info.com*

This metasearch engine returns results from the five major search engines including Bing, Google, and Yahoo.

Surfwax *http://www.surfwax.com*

Surfwax is a metasearch engine that has a number of useful options including choices about which hits to put at the top of your list and the maximum number of hits you want (from 25 to 500 to "maximum"). It also lets you select from quite a few options what parts of the Internet you want to search—from syndicated websites to blogs to news sites to the huge online encyclopedia, Wikipedia.

As with Internet search engines, many of the current "top" metasearch systems are likely to be also-rans in a year or so, and new types of both search engines and metasearch tools will soon be available that do a far better job of helping you find relevant hits on the Internet. They, like the current crop of engines and tools, will vary along many dimensions. Some search engines, for example, return hits only from paying participants, which makes them virtually useless for most scholarly searches. Be suspicious of the results from any search tool that only gives you hits from sites that paid for the privilege. Some metasearch tools eliminate duplications, and some don't. Some organize their list of hits by aggregating the relevancy ratings from all the search engines used, which is very desirable.

Still other differences between metasearch tools include the number of search engines used, whether you can select which engines are used in your search, and the ability to use advanced search strategies as well as simple ones.

Because search and metasearch engines are changing quickly we recommend you consult one of the sites on the Internet that try to keep up with current developments. We have already mentioned Search Engine Watch (http://www.searchenginewatch.com). A few more are listed below:

Findspot http://www.findspot.com/

This site contains a directory of search engines as well as links to a number of tools for searching the Internet.

Somewhere http://www.ekdahl.org/search.htm

This is another directory of search engines.

Advanced Search Straegies: The Legacy of George Boole

George Boole invented a new form of mathematics that includes operators other than the traditional plus, minus, multiply, and divide. To those familiar operations he added AND, OR, and NOT. These are sometimes called logical operators, Boolean logic, or Boolean algebra. To do sophisticated searches of abstract databases, full text databases, and the Internet, you must understand George Boole's operators and how they work with text. For example, AND lets you be more specific about the topic that interests you. It requires more than one search term to occur in a document before it is considered a "hit." For example, a search on the terms anorexia AND adolescent would only find documents where both anorexia and adolescent are in the document (or some section of the document such as the abstract if the database you are using lets you specify what part of the documents to search).

The OR operator works in just the opposite way. It broadens instead of narrows your search. For example, a search on terms "instructional technology" OR "educational technology" would find hits where one of the terms, instructional technology or educational technology, appeared. OR is most often used when there are several terms that have similar meanings and you want to search for documents that include any of the terms.

If you want to eliminate documents containing a specific term, you can use the NOT operator. For example, a search on the terms discipline NOT secondary would retrieve information about documents on discipline that made no mention of secondary. A more complex search such as discipline NOT (secondary OR "high school") combines the rules of regular algebra with Boolean algebra. This search tells the computer to find all the websites that contain the word discipline and then to eliminate from the list any sites that have the word secondary or the phrase high school. The quotation marks around "high school" tells the search engine to pay attention to the phrase high school rather than the separate words high and school. Therefore, the NOT would eliminate from your list a site that has the sentence "I attended Middleton High School in Middleton, Tennessee." However, it would not eliminate a site with the sentence "Attending school in Paris was a high spot of my educational experience" because the words high and school do appear but not as a phrase.

AND, OR and NOT are just a few of the special terms you can use to make your search more precise. Most sophisticated search engines support complex searches that make use of Boolean logic and/or special characters to help you formulate a very precise search. Boolean logic is used by search engines in two ways—with Boole's original terms like AND, OR, and NOT or with mathematical expressions. The Internet search engine Infoseek, for example, uses the + sign as a rough equivalent of AND. Below are some examples that work with Infoseek, but other search engines have similar features.

The search +*social_constructivism* + *secondary* has two components in it. Putting a + in front of each term means a hit must have that term in it. Because both terms have a +, this search will only report hits that contain both the term *social constructivism* and the word *secondary*. The underline character (_) between *social* and *constructivism* is a connector. It puts the two words together to indicate you want social constructivism [a term often used to describe educational theories based on the work of Lev Vygotsky] treated as one term instead of two different words. If you left the underline out and there was a space between social and constructivism, the search engine would look for hits with the word *social* and the word *constructivism* as well as the word *secondary*.

Some search systems uses quotation marks the way InfoSeek uses the underline character. Consider a search for "International Business Machines." Without quotes this search would locate websites that have the three words in the search term (e.g., an OR search). However, they would not necessarily be in the order listed in the search. Put quotes around the three terms and the search will select only documents (or websites if you are using an Internet search engine) that have the term *International Business Machines*. A site with *business* in one paragraph, *machines* in another, and *international* in yet another, would not be considered a hit.

These are only a few of the many different search options that let you precisely specify what you are searching for. In the following section we will present a summary of some of the other popular options and explain how they work. Keep in mind, however, that not all of these options work

with all search engines. And, even if they do, the way they are implemented may be different from the examples we use here. Use this section
as a general introduction to advanced searching and then read the
instructions for advanced searches on the web page of your preferred
search tool.

(the minus sign) and NOT. Use the minus sign when you are trying to
eliminate or exclude some sites from your list of hits. For example, I (JW)
developed an instructional design theory named R2D2 but when someone searches for websites about that theory using the term R2D2 they are
overwhelmed with sites about the Starwars movies. You can use the minus
sign to eliminate those hits (e.g., *+R2D2 – StarWars*). NOT works the
same way (*R2D2 NOT StarWars*). A common variation, by the way, of NOT
is AND NOT. When using the AltaVista search engine, for example, you
must use this format: *R2D2 AND NOT StarWars.*

Match Any Term (OR). If you input three search terms like *R2D2
movie StarWars*, some search engines (AltaVista, Infoseek) look for sites
that refer to any of the three terms. Others look for sites that have all
three (Google). It is important to know how a search engine handles multiple terms. Some assume the Boolean operator AND. *R2D2 AND movie
AND StarWars* tells the engine to find the sites that have all three of these
terms. Others assume the Boolean operator OR. *R2D2 OR movie OR Star-
Wars* means find the sites that contain one, or more, of these terms. A site
with the term movie in it will be listed as a hit even if it does not have the
terms StarWars or R2D2. This can be very handy when the same topic is
referred to by different terms (e.g., *high school OR secondary; elementary OR
primary; middle_grades OR junior_high*). Some engines require you to use
the + or – symbol, some accept the Boolean operators AND and OR, and
some have menus where you can select the option you want.

NEAR. Quotation marks, or the underline mark, are generally used to
specify a phrase. *"high school"* and *high_school* both tell the search engine
to find the phrase high school rather than find sites that have the word
high and the word *school* somewhere on the site. There is an intermediate
between these to extremes that some search engines support. If you
search for *problem_solving NEAR creativity* using the AltaVista search
engine it will find sites with the term problem solving and then it will look
for the word *creativity* in the 10 words before and after problem solving.
Only sites with the word *creativity* within 10 words of the term *problem solving* will appear in your list of hits. Some engines like AOL Search even let
you specify the number of words to search before and after the first search
term. The *search problem_solving NEAR/35 creativity* tells the search engine
to find sites with the term creativity within plus or minus 35 words of the
term *problem_solving.*

Limited Searching. There are times when you want to find resources that have your search terms in a particular location such as the title or name of a website. Some search engines allow you to do that. On AltaVista and a number of other search engines, for example, the search *Title: Math AND Simulations* will find sites that have these two words in their titles. There are other ways of limiting the search but they vary considerably from search engine to search engine. The advanced search options on the online bookseller site, www.amazon.com, are particularly helpful when you are searching for books about a particular topic, or for books written by a particular author. The Amazon database also includes quite a few journal articles as well but those are limited to papers that can be purchased for a fee and downloaded through the Amazon website.

Nesting (). Traditional algebra would be very limited if there were not ways of organizing the operations within a particular formula. Algebra, and Boolean searching, use parentheses () to clarify what is to be done to what, and when. Consider this search specification: *(High_School OR Secondary) AND (Science or Math) AND (problem-based_learning).* This search uses parentheses to organize the way the search is to be done. Things inside the parentheses are done first. The search engine finds sites that refer to *high school* or *secondary*, and it finds sites that have either the word *science* or *math* (or both). It also locates sites that contain the term *problem-based learning*. Finally, it creates a list that includes only sites that are hits on all three of the searches within the three parentheses. This is called nesting and it is a powerful way of organizing your search. The *search High_school OR Secondary AND Science OR math AND problem-base learning* will produce unpredictable results, but adding parentheses makes it clear what you want to do.

Capitalization. Most search engines ignore capitalization, but a few like Go pay attention to it. On Go the search term high_school and the term High_School are different. Also, some search engines only recognize Boolean operators such as AND, OR, and NOT if they are in all capitals. Otherwise they are treated as terms to be searched for.

Stemming. Suppose you are searching for information on tests and you know that some relevant sites will use the term *testing* while others will use *test* or *tests*. Some search engines match exact terms. If you specify *test* in your search, a site with the word *testing* (but not *test*) will not be included in your list of hits. Other sites will do the opposite. If you search for *test*, the engine will find all words for which test is the stem, including *testing* and *tests*. The Go search engine automatically uses stemming. Several others have an option that lets you switch stemming on.

Fuzzy searches: The WildCard character *. The * is sometimes called the "don't care" character or the wildcard. For example, searching for *test** will find *testing* and *tests* as well as the base term (test). Any word that begins with t e s t will be a hit regardless of the characters that come after that. Some search engines support both stemming and fuzzy searches using the * character. Others support one or the other, and some support neither. Unfortunately, searching for *test** will find not only *tests* and *testing* but *testicular* and *testosterone* as well. You may have to use AND or NOT to make your search more specific when you use stemming or a wildcard. Although * is commonly used as a wildcard in searches, some systems use ? and still others have several wildcard or "don't care" characters, each of which works a little differently.

The advanced search options discussed in this section are only a sample of the features available, but they are enough to get you started. Keep in mind what we said earlier. New and revised search engines regularly become available and may offer additional advanced features. Also, the options discussed thus far are not available on all search systems and, if available, may work differently than the examples. After you have used a search engine for simple searches, you may want to explore the help functions and tutorials for it. As noted earlier, many search engines actually divide their search options into basic and advanced. To do an advanced search you must click a button that says something like "Advanced Search." Search engines generally offer extensive help on how to use their advanced features.

SOCIAL NETWORKING, SCHOLARSHIP, AND PROFESSIONAL PRACTICE DISSERTATIONS

If the last decade of the twentieth century established the Internet as a powerful and necessary tool for "information workers," and almost everyone else as well, the first decade of the twenty-first century is when a particular type of Internet resource, *social networking*, emerged, matured, and became a part of contemporary life. Social networking websites like Facebook and MySpace were created to facilitate communication and interaction between individuals and groups with shared interests. These services are now used for professional communication and sharing as well. Professionals and scholars sometimes use general purpose social networking sites such as Facebook to create online environments where they can collaborate and interact with a community of like-minded scholars or professionals. There are also dedicated sites that were created specifically to support professional practitioners or researchers. An example is the Labmeeting (http://www.labmeeting.com/) site where scholars in the life sciences can create groups and use the site's tools to share documents and collaborate. Another site with a similar purpose and even more tools, is Nature Network (http://network.nature.com/) which has the motto, "connecting scientists." Academic.edu (www.academic.edu) is yet another that takes an interesting "family tree" approach to linking scholars. You can join groups organized around academic departments in universities (e.g., the human computer interaction group at Iowa State University or the Curry School of Education at the University of Virginia) as well as topics such as the medieval scholar Giambattista Vico or "continuing professional development." Other sites serving a similar purpose include SciLink (http://www.scilink.com/start.action) and epernicus (http://www.epernicus.com/).

Using social networking sites to support professional and scholarly work is a natural extension of the large network of collegial relationships, organizations, groups, journals, and conferences that form the support infrastructure for professions and scholarly disciplines. Social networking tools were added to this traditional mix of options for keeping up with your profession and your research interests. We will introduce some of the most popular types of social networking and scholarly support sites in the final sections of this chapter.

Mailing lists, NewsGroups, Forums, Discussion Groups, ...

Most of the tools in this section have been around for several years, long enough for scholars and professionals to begin using them to support their research and practice. However, while all of them support communication and collaboration, there are real differences in the way they work and thus each one is best suited to meeting specific needs.

Mailing Lists. A mailing list is a logical extension of simple e-mail, and there are thousands of mailing lists on topics relevant to professional practice dissertation work. For example, one popular mailing list for qualitative researchers is named ETHNO HOTLINE. If you send an e-mail message to this mailing list your message will be distributed to all the "members" of that list. If the message interests some of the other members of the list, they may reply to it, and those replies will also be sent to all members of the list. Lists are one-way people interested in a particular topic can "meet" electronically and discuss mutually interesting topics. Here are a few examples of mailing lists:

> *Biographical Methods Discussion List.* This discussion is for social scientists interested in the use of biographical research methods based on the interpretive paradigm of research. To join this discussion, send an e-mail message to *mailbase@mailbase.ac.uk*. In the body of the message (not in the header or "title" of the message) send this message,

substituting your first and last names for the general terms in the message: *join biog-methods yourfirstname yourlastname*

ETHNO HOTLINE. This discussion list emphasizes ethnographic research and frequently carries lively discussions of current issues. To subscribe, send an e-mail message to this address: *COMSERVE@CIOS.ORG.* Your message should say: JOIN ETHNO YOURFIRSTNAME YOURLASTNAME.

Qualitative Research for the Human Sciences. This is a general qualitative research list that supports ongoing conversations about current issues and needs. To subscribe, send a message to *listserv@uga.cc.uga.edu.* In the body of the message type the following: *subscribe qualrs-l yourfirstname yourlastname.*

Mailing lists are easy to use. There is no new software to learn because you send messages to a list using your e-mail program, and the messages you get from the mailing list arrive in your e-mail box. The information provided above about how to subscribe to a list may be enough to get you started. Using lists is not difficult, and it is becoming even easier as more and more mailing lists set up websites where, in a few simple steps, you can subscribe. Web-based mailing lists do not even require you to send an e-mail message to start the subscription process. However, finding appropriate lists to join is not always so easy.

Finding Relevant Mailing Lists

The mailing lists described earlier are a tiny sample of the thousands available. We will not attempt to list or describe even a small portion of them here, in part because they change so quickly. It is possible, for example, that by the time you read this, none of the lists mentioned earlier will be in operation. However, there are several ways to find out about active lists. One simple way is to use do a regular web search that includes the term "mailing list." For example, you could do a search with these terms:

Education "factor analysis research" "mailing list"

if you wanted to find mailing lists about the use of factor analysis in educational research.

Another way to find lists is to use some of the special websites that have information about lists. For example, information on mailing lists about topics in psychology is available at:

http://www.ucm.es/info/Psyap/iaap/psicored.htm

You can find information about education lists at http://edweb.gsn.org/lists.html, about nursing at http://nursing.buffalo.edu/mccartny/nursing_discussion_forums.html, about business at http://www.jiscmail.ac.uk/mailinglists/category/Business_Studies.htm, and there is a very long list of lists about statistics at http://www.stats.gla.ac.uk/cti/links_stats/lists.html.

Finally, there are a number of general mailing list websites that have information on thousands of lists. Three of the most useful of these are:

http://www.egroups.com

http://www.listbot.com

http://www.tapioca.com

All three provide plenty of information on how to use mailing lists as well as descriptions of currently active lists. *Tapioca* has information on many mailing lists for researchers, and it has a search option that lets you enter a few topics and get a list of lists that deal with the topics. Two other websites where you can search for lists are http://www.neosoft.com/internet/paml and http://www.tile.net/lists/.

Some Suggestions for Using Lists

The first thing you should do when you decide to join a list is find out how to *unjoin*. There are few e-mail problems more frustrating than joining a list, discovering that it is not of interest to you, but finding 50 or 60 messages from the list in your mailbox every day because you can't figure out how to unsubscribe. Generally, you will need to send a message like *unsubscribe listname yourfirstname yoursecondname* to the same address you used to subscribe, but the precise method of unsubscribing varies. The first or welcome message you get from the list may tell you how to unsubscribe. If it does, we suggest you create a folder named Unsubscribe on your hard disk and store the text of that message in the folder, using a title that tells you which list it refers to. (Yes, we know you won't do what we suggest here. But when you do decide to unsubscribe to a list and can't figure out how to do it just remember what good advice we gave.) Fortunately, some lists have websites where information on how the list operates as well as how to unsubscribe is available.

Once you have joined, you should begin to receive messages from the list. The first time you read messages you may be tempted to jump right into the conversation. There is an etiquette to participating in a list, and we suggest you *lurk* (read what other people are saying but do not reply yourself) until you feel sure you have a grasp of the rules of the list as well as appropriate topics for discussion. Many lists have a set of guidelines or FAQ (frequently asked questions) that tell you about the list and how to behave on it. Guidelines may be sent to you via e-mail or they, as well as answers to FAQ, may be on a website operated by the mailing list.

Polite, thoughtful, and respectful participation in a group is usually welcome. Undesirable and unappreciated on most lists is flaming. Flaming involves attacking people or otherwise being disruptive on the list. Flaming generally leads to other flames and many lists have died because flaming, once begun, became so entrenched that many people simply unsubscribed. Because you do not see the people you are responding to, it is easier to be much stronger and harsher than you would ever be in a face-to-face discussion. Resist that temptation and also resist the inclination to respond in kind when you are flamed. (It is generally a good idea to wait a day before responding to something that made you very angry, and even then it is often better to decide not to respond at all.)

Once you decide to stay subscribed to a list, a major question is what to do with the messages once you've read them. Most people simply delete the e-mail messages from a list after reading them. Some use the sorting and storing features of their e-mail software to create a folder where they place some, or all, of the messages from a list. If a message contains particularly useful information that has a long "shelf life" consider storing it so you can retrieve it later. Storing it in a folder other than the incoming mail folder where all your new mail resides will make it easier to find the message when you need it. Create a folder and give it a name that tells you what types of messages are stored in that folder.

Whether you store messages from a list will also depend on whether the list maintains a searchable *archive* of prior messages. Some lists keep an archive of all the messages posted to the list for the past few years. There may not be a need to save messages from those lists on your own computer because you can go to the list's website and search the archive if you need to reread a message.

Good and Poor Uses of Mailing Lists

Subscribe to mailing lists that cover topics that are very important to you, so important, in fact, that you want every message about them sent to your electronic mail box where you must do something with each one (read and/or delete them). For example, suppose you are doing your dissertation research on the impact of telecommuting rather than working every day in a company office. Your focus is on the patterns of social inter-action between telecommuters and other workers. A mailing list about research related to telecommuting would naturally be one you want to subscribe to, but a mailing list about research on the social relationships within business organizations might also be a good choice.

Subscribe also to lists that supply information you do not want to miss. Mailing lists send all the messages from the list to your mailbox. You don't have to do anything; they just come rolling in on their own. That is a good thing if the list disseminates information that is vital to you. This feature is also the main reason people unsubscribe. They get tired of their mailbox filling up with messages from the lists they have subscribed to. Thus, be judicious and subscribe only to lists that are especially important to you—and remember to keep track of how to unsubscribe!

Finally, lists are good for disseminating information and for answering queries that have brief, to-the-point answers. For example, one of the authors had a problem connecting a certain type of peripheral to a Mac-intosh computer, and posted a message on one of the mailing lists for educational technologists. He received several detailed and helpful answers. Lists are probably best at this type of Request-for-Help/Respond-With-Help format. They are also good for supporting groups interested in a very narrow topic.

Lists are not very satisfactory when you want to support several ongo-ing discussions that will last more than a few responses. Because all the messages on a mailing list are sent to your mailbox in the order they were received, messages about different topics are mixed together. There is no way to separate messages about *Topic A* from those about *Topics B* and *C*. That is a significant weakness of lists. Where extended discussion of more than one topic is important, newsgroups, which are discussed next, are better than mailing lists.

NEWSGROUPS

The term newsgroup is a bit misleading. It implies that these websites are all from news services like CNN and ABC News. There are such news-groups but a more informative name might be "Interest Groups" because newsgroups are just another way for people who share an interest to com-municate. Newsgroups, however, differ from mailing lists in two very important ways. First, messages are not delivered to your mailbox. Instead, all the messages for a newsgroup are stored on a server. When you want to read messages in a particular newsgroup you can use a pro-gram called a newsreader to display messages and, if you wish, reply to messages. This approach keeps messages out of your mailbox, but it means you must remember to regularly use your newsreader software to keep up with newsgroups. There are several ways to use newsreader software but we will only cover one of the easier methods here, in part because the next section will show you how to use a newer system, called RSS or really simple syndication, to access both newsgroups and several other types of websites.

The second difference between mailing lists and newsgroups is perhaps more important. Newsgroups allow you to have *threaded* discussions. Suppose, for example, that you read a message in a newsgroup about a particular statistical procedure, such as path analysis. Path analysis is a specialized and rather complicated extension of correlational statistics, and the message about it may be in a newsgroup where many forms of statistical analysis are discussed. If it were a mailing list instead of a newsgroup, messages on all the topics would be mixed together. The one on path analysis might be followed by one on analysis of covariance, for example. Fortunately, newsgroups thread their messages. If someone replied to that first message on path analysis you can go right to that reply without having to read all the messages in other threads. If forty people have responded to the path analysis message, you can read all 40 responses, one right after the other without messages on other topics interfering. Threading makes it possible for a newsgroup to support many different conversations at the same time. Each one is kept in its own thread.

Using Web-Based Newsreaders

A number of e-mail programs such as Outlook have newsreader software built in and there are also specialized newsreader programs like Free Agent (http://www.forteinc.com). Another option is to use what is called a web-based newsreader. Some people prefer to go to a site on the World Wide Web and use the software on that site to read newsgroup messages. Some Internet providers, in fact, don't have a news server and if you provider doesn't you have no other option than to use a web-based reader. Also, some providers may not carry the newsgroups you want to use. Here are the addresses of three websites where you can read newsgroup messages:

http://www.groups.google.com

http://www.easynews.com/

http://www.newsguy.com

These three web-based news readers work in slightly different ways but all will help you find, read, and post messages to newsgroups that are part of the relatively standard collection of newsgroups that is distributed world-wide through the usenet system. You will not, however, generally be able to access special newsgroups run by your university nor will most regional groups be available.

Finding Relevant Newsgroups

Once you have your newsreader set up and working, it will have a list of all the newsgroups available from your news server. A simple way to find relevant newsgroups is to use the commands in the newsreader program to list all the news groups and then browse through them to see which ones look interesting. It will be time consuming to look at every single one of the thousands available, however. The Usenet newsgroups are organized in categorical hierarchies. For example, you will see that the MISC (miscellaneous) category has thousands of newsgroups in it. Click MISC and your newsreader will display the next level of categories under MISC. One of those will be Education, which will have hundreds of news-groups. Click Education and you will see some newsgroups that you can explore as well as some additional categories that have more than one newsgroup in them. This process can be tedious but it is one way to get a complete idea of what groups are out there.

Another way is to use your newsreader program to search for news-groups that include discussions of the topics that interest you. For exam-ple, if you were interested in a research method called participatory action research, you could use the search function of your newsreader to find newsgroups that are discussing that method. Or, if you were interested in a particular theory, such as cognitive flexibility theory, or a particular theoretician, such as Ludwig Wittgenstein, most newsreader programs have search functions that help you locate relevant newsgroups.

Threading Your Way Through Newsgroups

Newsreader software lets you subscribe to as many news groups as you like. Once you are subscribed to a group you can read the messages in it any time you wish. Click on the name of the group in the newsreader soft-ware window and the message threads will be displayed. Then you click on a message in a thread to display it. Once you have read a message you have several options.

Read the next message in the thread

Read a message in another thread

Reply to the message by adding your own message to the current thread

Reply to the author of the message directly (which means the message will not go to the newsgroup)

Start a new thread

There are simple commands for all these options in most modern newsreader programs. As you decide what to do and how to behave in a newsgroup, keep in mind that the suggestions we made about participating in mailing lists also apply to newsgroups. Be sure you understand the purpose and acceptable topics before posting a message to a group. Lurk for a while and study the personality of the group before becoming an active participant. Some groups are *unmoderated* which means anything sent to the group is distributed to subscribers. Other groups are *moderated* which means someone looks at each message submitted and decides whether it will be posted or not. Finally, some groups are restricted. You may be able to read messages without being a member but not post. Some are even more restricted, you must apply for membership and be accepted before even reading messages from the group!

Blogs

Mailing lists and newsgroups are ways for groups with shared interests to communicate, and they have been around for a long time. A newer online form of communication is the blog. Blogs also support communication between members of a group but they were created to support a particular type of communication. Blogs are ideal when one person, or a small number of people, want to communicate with a large number of people. Among the 25 most popular blogs in 2010 were these:

TMZ.com—which has 6 million visitors a month and tends to carry gossip about famous people.

GIZMODO.com—which has about 6 million visitors a month, calls itself "the gadget blog" and has articles like "23 new gadgets that would make summer even more fun."

CROOKSANDLIARS.COM—which has about a quarter of a million visitors a month and concentrates on tabloid-style stories related to politics.

The very popular blogs don't provide much encouragement to someone doing a professional practice dissertation but we estimate there are well over 15 million active blogs on the Internet today and some of them may be of interest to you. The trick is finding them. RSS is one solution to both finding relevant blogs (and more) as well as keeping the messages from them organized.

RSS—Really Simple Syndication. Blogs, newsgroups, and several other types of online group communication systems such as forums and discussion groups each have their own web address. You could, therefore, use the bookmarks tool in your web browser to store the addresses of every site that may cover topics relevant to your dissertation research. You could even create a bookmarks folder named "Dissertation Web Sites" and create subfolders under that such as "Research Methods," "Research Studies," and so on to organize the bookmarks. Many dissertation students use just such an approach and it works for them. One drawback to this approach, however, is that you must go to those sites regularly and check to see if any new information has been added that is relevant to your dissertation. That takes time. Really Simple Syndication (RSS) turns the process around. This method notifies you when anything new is added to a site that you have on your list.

RSS is a system for accessing blogs and other types of Internet sites, including mailing lists and newsgroups. There are three parts to the system. One is a *reader*. The reader lets you subscribe to all sorts of websites— blogs, forums, newsgroups, and much more. Any site that has signed up for RSS service, which is free, can be added to the list of sites that your reader keeps track of. Although there are several very good readers or managing RSS feeds, we recommend using Google Reader which is free. When you sign on to your Google Reader you see your list of sites on the left of the screen and when you click a site, anything new that has been added to that site will appear in the larger window on the right. Google Reader has many options and commands for organizing, archiving, and tracking material from the sites you are monitoring. You can sign up by going to http://reader.google.com and completing the application form. Once you have signed up, you can begin to add blogs and other types of websites to your list. There is a button labeled *Add a Subscription* on the top left of the screen. Click that and you can either enter the web address of a site you want to monitor or enter a set of keywords and let Google Search find sites for you. For example, when I searched for "qualitative research" Google Search generated a sizable list of blogs and other websites relevant to qualitative research methods. Some were specialized such as Qualitative Research in Psychology and Qualitative Research and Occupational Medicine while others were more general. To subscribe to a site all you need to do is click the subscribe button below the description of the site. After that, Google Reader will monitor the site for you.

If you already know the web address of a site you want to monitor you can enter the address by clicking the *Add a subscription* button and either typing or pasting the web address in the text box that opens. Then click *ADD*. For example, any of the gateway sites discussed in the next section can be added to Google Reader this way.

Gateway or Portal Sites

In August of 2009 we used a popular *search engine*, Google, to look for World Wide Web sites that contained the term "qualitative research." There were 2,420,00 hits. Each hit represented a website containing the term *qualitative research*. When we did a search for "ANOVA" the abbreviation for Analysis of Variance, there were over 5,600,00 hits!

The World Wide Web (WWW or just web) has become a rich information resource for researchers and practitioners in many fields. The web is so rich, in fact, that the sheer volume can be overwhelming. What do you do with over 5 million hits on the term ANOVA? You can deal with that problem in several ways. One approach is to narrow your search. Longer and more specific searches produce smaller and more manageable lists of hits.

Narrowing your search criteria is a very good way to locate Web-based content on a specialized topic. But what if you have a general interest in exploring qualitative research but don't want to wander through the 2 million hits a search produced? There is, fortunately, a simple solution— *portal* or *gateway websites*. There are several portal websites about, for example, qualitative research. They contain many different types of information as well as annotated lists of other useful and interesting websites. The best of these is QUALPAGE, which was created by a nursing faculty member, Dr. Judy Norris, at the University of Alberta. Today the site is maintained by Dr. Judith Preissle at the University of Georgia. The content of QUALPAGE is divided into 13 different categories and the site has links to everything from introductory material on relevant theories and research methods to conference papers that report the latest research. It is probably the most useful and best known general web resource for qualitative researchers. The address for QUALPAGE is http://www.qualitativeresearch.uga.edu/QualPage/.

A second qualitative research gateway website, run by Ron Chenail, a professor in the School of Social and Systemic Studies at Nova Southeastern University, is another excellent portal to the online resources about qualitative research methods. The Web address of The Qualitative

Inquiry Project is http://www.nova.edu/ssss/qualinq.html. At that location you will find two different resources. *The Qualitative Report* (http://www.nova.edu/ssss/QR/index.html) is an electronic journal that is available to everyone via the Internet. It publishes papers on the use of qualitative methodologies and theory. Chenail also supports a website called Qualitative Research Resources on the Internet (http://www.nova.edu/ssss/qualinq.html) which has annotated links to hundreds of sites about qualitative research methods. Chenail's site has one of the largest lists of discussion groups and websites relevant to qualitative research.

For most of the resources listed on these gateway sites, the links are "hot." For example, if you click the listing for *The Participant Action Research Network* at Ron Chenail's website, you will be taken to the home page of the Participatory Action Research Network. Participatory action research is a form of action research based on interpretive and critical theories instead of empirical and positivist paradigms. This site contains introductory information on participatory action research as well as coverage of advanced topics, discussion groups, and links to other websites about action research and participatory inquiry.

Together, the two qualitative research gateway sites introduced here provide a beginning qualitative researcher with connections to hundreds of resources that have been reviewed and recommended by people with expertise in the field. You may still want to search the web for specialized resources, but we recommend that when you start exploring a general topic such as a research method or a professional practice, consider starting with gateway sites. You may find such sights through an online search but other sources include recommendations from colleagues, professors who specialize in the topic, questions posted to forums or mailing lists, and practicing professionals.

Virtually every major area of research and professional practice, and most research methodologies, have portal sites where you can begin looking for relevant information. For example a portal site for content analysis methods is Content Analysis Resources at Georgia State University (http://www.gsu.edu/~wwwcom/content.html). Content analysis is a very specialized research method. Bill Trochim's website, by contrast, covers a very broad range of research methods used in the social sciences. It is at http://trochim.human.cornell.edu. The Educational Research Resources Links website serves a similar purpose for education (http://jarl.cs.uop.edu/~cpiper/research.html). In disciplines with many specialties that use a wide range of research methods, some gateway sites even provide information on other gateway sites. That is true of the Psych Web Site at http://www.psywww.com/www.

These are only a few of the many gateway or portal websites about research methods. In your field of professional practice there will likely be a number of portal websites that introduce you to many valuable sites that focus on issues of practice, and/or research methods, relevant to your dissertation work. Using portal or gateway sites as a beginning point in your Internet search for material relevant to your dissertation can save you time compared to doing internet searches when the searches produce thousands of hits. The advantages of gateway sites are that a knowledgeable expert has usually judged each link to be worth using, and the gateway sites often include a brief description of each link that helps you decide whether to check the link out or not.

Collaborative Tools

Most of the Internet tools and sites discussed thus far in this chapter are either sources of information or sites with lists of that type of site. In this final section of the chapter we will introduce a group of Internet-based tools that were created for a related but different purpose. These tools are all designed to support collaboration with other individuals and groups. Some tools are widely used for "social networking" which is currently the "hot" use of the Internet with sites like Facebook and MySpace. You create your own site on a social networking site like Facebook or MySpace and then populate it with whatever you want—stories about what is happening in your life, pictures, information you want to share, whatever. Then you invite your friends to join your group and also to create their own sites. The result is a network of links between your social networking site and those of your group of friends.

Social networking sites are now being used by academics, professionals, and researchers in addition to teens and undergraduate college students. For example, the Facebook site named *Teaching & Learning With Facebook* is one of many that deal if teaching and learning. Facebook organizes its groups into 11 broad categories including business, common interest, organizations, and student groups. You can search among the relevant categories to find groups that fit your interests, including the topic and research methods of your dissertation. If you decide to join a group you send a request to the person who created the group and that person decides whether to add you to the group or not.

Forums, Conferences and Virtual Communities

Terms like *forum* and *conference* are often used to describe online sites that work much like newsgroups but are not necessarily a part of the *usenet* set of newsgroups. Another term, *virtual communities*, typically refers to websites that offer a significant range of services to people interested in a particular topic. A virtual community website may have all sorts of services—from conferencing tools and mailing lists to online newsletters and databases where members can search for relevant information. Some sites for researchers even publish electronic journals.

There are several virtual communities, also called "online communities" for students working on their dissertation. One is www.phinished.com and it has many different resources and tools as well as opportunities to communicate with other dissertation students. When we looked at the site, the discussion forums had over 160,000 messages spread over 19,000 threads.

There is also a new type of virtual community that combines the concepts of virtual reality with those of social networking. The best known of this type of site is Second Life, a huge and growing site where individuals, groups, and organizations can create virtual communities that appear on your screen as if they were real communities with virtual buildings and land. The description of Second Life on the home page (http://www.secondlife.com) is "Second Life is an online, 3D virtual world imagined and created by its residents." There are a number of education and research related communities operating on Second Life and several colleges and universities have created virtual campuses there. If you would like more information on the SecondLife virtual reality communities related to education and to research, there are several websites with relevant information:

- http://www.simteach.com/wiki/ index.php?title=Second_Life_Education_Wiki
- Second Life Researcher Mailing List (go to this website, http://list.academ-x.com/listinfo.cgi/slrl-academ-x.com, to join the mailing list.
- http://secondliferesearch.blogspot.com/ This is a blog about research being conducted on Second Life.
- http://www.victoriagloucester.net/ Second Life residents are asked to create a new name for their persona on Second Life and Victoria Gloucester is the name used by Catherine Parsons, the Assistant Superintendent of Curriculum at Pine Plains Central School District in New York. This site has several resources about the use of SecondLife in education and about related research.
- http://www.secondlife.intellagirl.com/ This is a site created by Sarah Robbins (AKA Intellagirl), a doctoral student in rhetoric and composition at Ball State University. Here you can read drafts of some of the chapters for her dissertation and some interesting reflections

on the process of completing the dissertation as well as her thoughts about teaching college composition courses.

Many of the forum and conference sites that would interest you are RSS aware and can thus be added to your list of feeds for Google Reader. Emerging developments in the area of virtual reality, on the other hand, will likely bring substantial changes to the way we communicate and interact with colleagues and do research. It would be very interesting to be able to peer over the technology horizon and see just what will be possible, and customary, in three or four years!

Video and Audio Conferencing

You are probably already familiar with Internet based telephone systems such as Skype that let you call all over the world without having to pay long distance fees. Skype and similar services were a boon when long distance charges, even within the United States, were too high for struggling doctoral students to spend hours on the phone interviewing experts scattered around the country. Today Internet telephone services have become mainstream and the cost of long distance calls is often built into your base monthly fee for telephone service. Long distance telephone service within the United States and Canada is often free of additional charges and the cost of calling other regions such as Western Europe may also be free or cost just a few pennies a minute. However, using Internet-base telephony like Skype is still useful if you want to interview someone in the few nations where corruption, backward technology, corporate greed, or unreasonable government taxes still keeps the price of ordinary international long distance service prohibitively high.

Our focus here is not so much on ways of conducting audio-only interviews with potential sources of knowledge and perspective. It is on video conferencing. Today there is a growing list of video conferencing services that let you contact and interact with one or more people over the Internet. Many of these services are highly sophisticated and were designed for corporate users with substantial budgets. It is not uncommon for a corporation to spend hundreds of thousands of dollars a year on video conferencing services. Fortunately, there are also video conferencing services designed for users with limited budgets. Many of them are, in fact, free.

To run a basic video conference that links you via audio and video to another person, you need three things: (1) a video camera that will connect to your computer, (2) video conferencing software installed on your computer or access to a video conferencing website that works through your Internet browser such as Firefox, Opera, or Internet Explorer, and (3) a person at another location who has a compatible setup on their computer. Web cameras, as they are called, cost as little as $15, and very good ones can be had for under $50. Some laptop computers even have video cameras built in, and video conferencing software is available for free.

A basic video conference lets you see the person you are having a video conference with on the screen of your computer and hear what they say through your computer speakers or via earphones plugged into the audio-out connector on your computer. Of course, the person you are conferencing with hears and sees you via their computer. This is the basic service that all video conferencing systems support. Even the free version of Skype (http://www.skype.com), which is marketed as a replacement for long distance telephone service, does this. The next step up in features is video conferencing with more than two participants, and the number supported by a system ranges from three or four to a virtually unlimited number. Beyond that, there are additional features such as:

- **Whiteboard space** where you and other participants can write or draw on your computer screen and everyone else can see your work and edit it if they wish
- **Desktop sharing** including sharing documents and computer software so that a document is on the screens of all participants and can be edited by anyone. Or a computer program can appear on all the screens with control of the program given to any participant.
- **Automatic recording** of the video conference so it can be replayed later. Otherwise, you must use a program like Camtasia to capture the computer screen as a video.
- **Web Browser Only Video Conferencing**. Some programs let you set up video conferences with people who do not have the same software. Many do this through options that allow participation using only a compatible web browser.

Although there are hundreds of video conferencing systems available today, we recommend the following because at least their basic systems are free, they have the features you are likely to need to do online interviews as part of your "review of the literature," and they do not require expensive equipment be added to your computer to work:

ooVoo. (http://www.oovoo.com/). ooVoo is a free videoconferencing software system.

DimDim. (http://www.dimdim.com). DimDim is a videoconferencing service with three levels. Two, with more features, cost $19 and up per month to use. The third level is free and allows up to 20 participants in a video conference and the use of one webcam.

Fuzemeeting (www.fuzemeeting.com). This is another multilevel service with one free, if limited, level.

Yugma (https://www.yugma.com/). The Yugma video conferencing service has nice tools for recording video conferences for later replay.

Wikis, Google Docs, and Other Collaborative Writing Tools

A wiki is a website here you can create a document collaboratively with a selected group of colleagues. Wiki sites can either be private, with access limited to those who have a password and ID, or public. The most famous public wiki is Wikipedia, a huge online encyclopedia with over 3 million different entries. Wikipedia is written and edited by volunteers who both update and add to entries already in this online encyclopedia as well as create new entries. Some academics are critical of Wikipedia because anyone can write and edit entries. Some professors even forbid students from citing material from Wikipedia because of that. They insist that material cited in anything from course papers to dissertations be from *reliable* sources such as refereed journals or published books. Despite the suspicion about the validity of Wikipedia content, several research studies have suggested (1) that the content is relatively accurate, and (2) that when someone deliberately adds biased or false content it is generally corrected quickly by another Wikipedia user. We don't think any source of knowledge and perspective should become so trusted that there is little or no consideration of the motives, context, intent, and possible bias that might influence the writer. Thus, we urge our students and our colleagues to be cautious about taking anything from Wikipedia as absolute fact, but we give the same advice for papers published in refereed journals and in books!

Our interest here, however, is not in the use of Wikipedia as a source (though we think it is perfectly acceptable for both student papers and dissertations), it is in the use of Wiki technology to support collaborative writing. There are a number of Wiki sites where you can either upload files your dissertation committee and research team can edit, or you can actually create those files using the writing tools on the website. If you would like to consider using a wiki with your dissertation team so that members can both edit and make comments on drafts of your chapters, there are several sites that offer free or very low cost wiki hosting. A few of them are:

http://www.wikidot.com/ Over 350,000 people use wikidot wikis and the website has a special service called Wikis for Education.

http://www.pbworks.com/ This services has free and fee based collaborative editing resources that offer more than the basic wiki resources. However it is still basically a wiki-style collaborative writing site. If the additional features suit your needs, Pbworks may be your preferred choice.

http://www.wikispaces.com/ This is one of the largest wiki hosting services with over a million wiki sites and over 2 million subscribers.

http://www.wetpaint.com/ This site is one of the easier to learn and use, and while free access involves advertising being presented to users, the advertising can be stopped by request if your wiki site is educational.

http://sites.google.com/ Google has its own wiki hosting service which is free to users.

Google has also created another online resources called Google Docs (http://docs.google.com) that is in some ways a competitor to the standard office tools like Microsoft Office's Word, PowerPoint, and Excel. Google Docs has similar programs that run online. Documents you create can be stored online or on your computer. While the Google Docs tools, such as the word processor, are not as powerful as Microsoft Word, they are sufficient to write a typical dissertation. The advantage of using Google Docs to write your dissertation is that the tools were designed for collaborative writing. Your dissertation chair and members of your committee, for example, can read your drafts online and edit as well as make comments on them. Also, if you know Microsoft Word already, Google Docs is compatible with the file formats for Word which means you and your dissertation team can write and edit using either Word or Google Docs. The choice between Google Docs and Microsoft Words' *Track Changes* tools for collaborative writing and editing will come down to personal preferences and needs. Dissertation chairs and committee members have traditionally done editing by marking printed drafts and adding notes and suggestions in the margins. If you and your chair decide to go to digital editing, Google Docs and the Track Changes options in Word are two alternatives you should consider. A third is Microsoft Office Live that includes many of the same features of Google Docs but, to us, does not feel as friendly or as usable, at least in its present form. You can sign up for Microsoft Live at http://www.officelive.com.

There are also hundreds of other collaborative writing tools—some that run on individual computers and others that are Internet based. The current crop includes Writeboard (http://writeboard.com/) and WriteWith (http://www.writewith.com/) as well as several programs that combine collaborative writing with project management tools that you may need if your dissertation is complex and requires coordinating the work of several groups (e.g., CentralDesktop at http://www.centraldesktop.com/, and Backpack (http://backpackit.com/). We will not attempt a review of these programs as they change quickly and new features are added to existing products on a regular basis. However, there are websites with information about such tools:

> http://www.kolabora.com/news/2007/03/01/
> collaborative_writing_tools_and_technology.htm
> http://www.kabissa.org/blog/collaborative-writing-tools-using-web-2-0
>
> http://crazeegeekchick.com/blog/27-free-must-have-online-
> collaboration-tools/ This site describes 27 "must have" collaboration
> tools that are free. They range from collaborative writing tools to
> brainstorming programs. Many of the 27 programs are very good for
> common dissertation project tasks.

Using Course Management Systems for Collaboration: Moodle and Blackboard

You are probably already familiar with programs that support online coursework. Two of the most popular today are Blackboard, which is a commercial product, and Moodle, which is an *open source* and therefore free program. Both Blackboard and Moodle were designed primarily to support instruction. They are both used to offer completely online courses, particularly at the college level, and also to support "mixed" courses that include some face-to-face classroom meetings as well as online components.

Blackboard (http://www.blackboard.com) and Moodle (http://www.moodle.com) are examples of a group of programs called course management systems or CMS. Most colleges and universities offer distance education programs today and the great majority use Blackboard, Moodle, or another CMS with similar features. If you have access to a CMS, it can also be used to support your dissertation project. Moodle, for example, has all sorts of tools such as forums, chat (you can "talk" to someone who is online at the same time by typing on your keyboard), file exchange, and collaborative editing through a wiki. Instead of creating a site on Blackboard or Moodle for a course, you set up a site for your dissertation and give it a name like "Jane Ochoa's Dissertation Site." Then you "enroll" each of your committee and research team members so they have access. Moodle even has options for organizing your team into groups that have different responsibilities and privileges. For example, one group might be able to edit drafts of chapters through the wiki tools while others would not.

The use of CMS for dissertation work is appealing because the current versions of course management systems have many features that support collaboration. You are not likely to need the tools for creating objective multiple choice tests, for example, but the tools for running discussion forums, for file exchange, and for collaborative editing will be useful, and having all the tools on one site is an advantage.

Chat Systems

Most communication services on the Internet are asynchronous which means that you and the person or group you want to communicate with do not have to be online at the same time. Chat is a different matter. You do need to be online simultaneously. Internet chats are like phone calls except that what is communicated is text instead of sound. Chats are infrequently used in scholarly work—it is hard enough to get people who work in the same building together for a face-to-face meeting. However, there are times when things can be accomplished by meeting electronically. One relatively easy way to do that is via chatting. Everyone gets on line and joins the chat. Then, as people type on their keyboards the other participants see their message on their screens.

IRC is short for Internet Relay Chat, and this system is one popular way of "chatting" online. Several companies have software that lets you join the hundreds of thousands of people who chat online every day. One of the most popular free systems is ICQ. You can learn about it at the company website: http://web.icq.com/. That same software can be used to support chats between two people and between small groups of collaborators who meet on line at a specific time.

Two other very popular chat programs are AIM's chat service (http://www.chat.aim.com) and Google's chat tools (http://www.google.com/talk). Any of these three chat services will meet your needs for online, text-based discussions with dissertation colleagues and partners. All of them support chats between more than two participants and they also allow you to "capture" the discussion so you can review it later or keep it for your records.

Brainstorming Programs: Another Way of Collaborating

Brainstorming programs are also called visual thinking software, mind mapping software, and graphic organizer software. Regardless of the name, the purpose of the software is to help you think by visually representing your current ideas. We discuss this type of software in another chapter but here we would like to mention one particular program, Webspiration. It is an offshoot of a brainstorming program that is very popular in schools named Inspiration. It is a powerful but easy to learn and use program for visually representing ideas, concepts, plans, and organizational structures. A version for children named Kidspiration is widely used in elementary schools. Webspiration is the company's effort to put the power of Inspiration online in a format that allows you to collaborate with others on the creation of anything from a conceptual map to a timeline for completing a project. You sign up for a Webspiration site on the home page (http://www.inspiration.com) and then invite your partners to join your Webspiration project. You can use the site to create anything from a timeline for the dissertation project to outlines for chapters to visual representations of the theoretical framework, the issue you are studying, or the solutions to the problem your action research group are considering. Currently Webspiration is in the beta stage of development and anyone can sign up to use it for free. Eventually, the company will probably move to fee-based access but there is no indication that will be soon.

SUMMARY

In this chapter we have discussed several issues related to the process of gathering and using both knowledge and perspectives about your research topic. We have suggested that you broaden your view of what you consider worthy sources and that you pay particular attention to professional as well as scholarly sources. Broadening the sources you consider worthwhile involves more work but, fortunately, there are a number of electronic and digital tools you can use to effectively and efficiently search for relevant sources. These include databases of abstracts, full-text databases of scholarly and professional literature, and many types of websites including gateway sites. To use these databases you will need to master the skills of doing online searches, which includes the use of Boolean algebra.

Strong search skills will, however, enhance your ability to use traditional abstract and full-text databases as well as search the Internet and use specialized databases such as Google Scholar and Google Books.

However, the search for content relevant to your dissertation is not limited to papers and books. People are also critically important resources and the final section of the chapter covered both simple (e.g., e-mail lists) and more complex (e.g., virtual reality) tools for interviewing, interacting with, and collaborating with others.

CHAPTER 6

SELECTING THE METHODS FOR YOUR DISSERTATION

The term "method" is defined in several ways. We are using it here to indicate two things:

- The general approach to your dissertation. An example of a general approach would be to "do" a case study dissertation, or a participatory action research dissertation, or a philosophical dissertation. Used in this way, the term "method" indicates a general approach to seeking knowledge. Sometimes the term "design" is used instead of "method" when talking about a general approach to doing research.

- The specific procedures for collecting and analyzing the data for your dissertation. This use of the term method is more specific. You might say, for example, that you are "doing participant observations" for your dissertation, or "open, semi-structured interviews," or 'doing a post-test only experimental study."

In this chapter we will explore methods at both levels, but the goal is not to teach you how to do research using all the methods discussed. That would require a book of encyclopedic length (and even then would not do the job very well). Instead, the purpose of this chapter is to make you aware of the major families of research methods that are useful in professional practice

Completing a Professional Practice Dissertation: A Guide for Doctoral Students and Faculty, pp. 177–195

dissertations. You will learn a little about how each method is used, and much more about the types of questions, problems, and contexts that are most appropriate, and inappropriate for a particular study. After reading this chapter you may want to explore several of the methods discussed before deciding which approach you want to use in your dissertation.

AN OVERVIEW OF METHODS OF RESEARCH AND SCHOLARSHIP

Because this book was written for professional practice doctoral students in many different disciplines, this chapter takes a very broad approach to research methodology. In a particular discipline, such as business, psychology, physical therapy, nursing, or education, even an overview research course will not likely cover all the methods presented in this chapter. One reason for the broad coverage here is to provide a multidisciplinary perspective. The other is that the barriers between different disciplines are becoming more porous to methods from other fields. The social sciences, for example, are now much more open to methods from the humanities and philosophy than they were even 20 years ago. You may, in fact, find a method developed in another discipline that appeals to you as a way of studying an issue or problem you are considering for your dissertation. If you do decide to explore a method that is innovative in your discipline or field, make sure you have the support of someone with experience using that method and be doubly sure that your dissertation committee accepts the method. And, because it is innovative, make sure the committee's support is not grudgingly given. You do not want the method to become an issue later in the dissertation process. Finally, we also suggest that if you use an innovative methodology that is unfamiliar to some of your committee members, include in your dissertation proposal more detail and more explanation of the method than is typical. Include several examples of how the method has been used in your field as well.

The breadth of methods covered in this chapter is illustrated in Figure 6.1. Seven different families of research methods are represented in the figure. There are two large families of research methods that are probably familiar to most professional practice doctoral students: quantitative and qualitative. Another family of quantitative methods, single-subject designs, were developed in a specialization of education and psychology called applied behavior analysis. They are less well known.

The other two methods families—philosophical inquiry and humanities research, are less familiar to doctoral students who are not in those fields. However, a number of methods from philosophy and the humanities are now gaining acceptance in the social sciences and professional fields.

A sixth family of research methods, clinical or applied research, is most closely associated with professional practice because these methods were developed specifically to improve practice. The seventh group of research methods is also very useful in professional practice research. That is reviews and syntheses of the literature. Many of the problems and critical decisions professional practitioners face call for an understanding of knowledge and procedures developed in several different disciplines. One way to contribute to our understanding of such problems and decisions is to review, organize, or synthesize the relevant literature, both scholarly and professional. This, unfortunately, is rare in the literature and even rarer as the sole focus of a dissertation. It is a valuable but underutilized approach to exploring important professional practice topics.

After this short overview, we will turn first to literature reviews as a research method for dissertations and then to quantitative research methods, which is one of the largest and currently the most "prestigious" frameworks for research in many disciplines. In the three chapters that follow, the five other families of research methods will be explored:

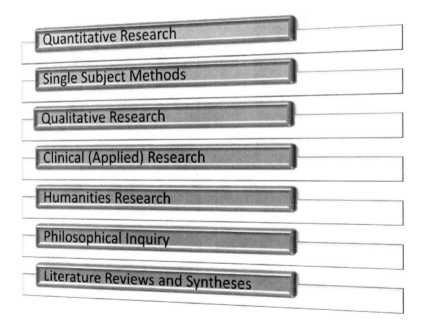

Figure 6.1.   The seven families of scholarship that are most relevant to professional practice research and scholarship.

Chapter 7. Qualitative Research Methods and Clinical (Applied) Research Methods

Chapter 8. Humanities Research Methods

Chapter 9. Philosophical Inquiry

LITERATURE REVIEWS AND SYNTHESES

Most of the research methods discussed in these chapters require you to narrow your focus to a specific issue, problem, or question. They help you concentrate on an issue like "Enhancing the participation of adolescent mothers in healthy child programs," "Evaluating a comprehensive program to support reluctant readers in the early elementary grades," or "Building a learning community climate in a state education agency." Doing a literature review takes you in the opposite direction. When you do a literature review for a professional practice dissertation, you identify a significant issue or problem that is complex enough to benefit from knowledge, procedures, and approaches drawn from a range of disciplines and professional fields. For example, if you focused on an issue like low attendance and high dropout rates in inner city schools the literature of several disciplines and professions would be relevant, including:

- Education
- Psychology
- School and Educational Psychology
- Sociology
- Social Work
- Anthropology
- Economics
- Urban Studies and Planning
- Poverty Studies
- Immigration Research

There are other relevant disciplines but even from this list you can see that practicing professionals who must make decisions about how to deal with low attendance rates, and/or high dropout rates, will have difficulty collecting and studying useful resources from so many different disciplines and professional fields. One way of enhancing access to those resources is to do a literature review that is organized around a problem or issue of professional practice.

In traditional five-chapter dissertations the second chapter is a review of the relevant literature, but "Chapter 2" reviews are typically not well suited to the purpose of informing professional practitioners. They are often little more than brief comments about one study after the other, with little effort to organize, synthesize, and analyze the available literature. Further, they typically focus on the research directly relevant to the dissertation study, and to the research methodology of the dissertation. Professional practice literature reviews should be broader, should keep the audience – professional practitioners and policy makers—in mind, and should draw from the research, the scholarly, and the professional practice literature. There is a need for such reviews in all fields of professional practice, and if your doctoral program encourages and supports this type of dissertation, we commend it to you for serious consideration.

If you would like more information on how to do literature reviews, there are many online resources as well as several books. Because a professional practice literature review is different from a traditional "research review" that is generally the focus of guides to doing reviews, there will be guidelines or directions in virtually all the available resources that we would disagree with. For example, some guides tell you to restrict your review to research studies that meet stringent criteria for quantitative research based on the scientific method. We disagree with that guideline because we consider many approaches to research and scholarship to be worthy of consideration. In a similar vein, quite a few guides either ignore or depreciate the value of the professional practice literature. Again, we find that literature worthy of attention and would expect it to be included in a professional practice literature review.

With that caveat, there are a number of publications on how to do literature reviews:

- Cooper, H. (1998). *Synthesizing research: A guide for literature reviews.* Thousand Oaks, CA: SAGE.
- Galvan, J. L. (1999). *Writing literature reviews.* Los Angeles: Pyrczak.
- Macauley, P. (2001). *The literature review.* Geelong, Victoria, Australia: Deakin University. Retrieved from http://www.deakin.edu.au/library/findout/research/litrev.php
- Language Center, Asian Institute of Technology. (n.d.). *Writing up research.* Retrieved from http://www.languages.ait.ac.th/EL21LIT.HTM
- Hart, C. (1998). *Doing a literature review: Releasing the social science research imagination.* Thousand Oaks, CA: SAGE.

- Pan, M. (2004). *Preparing literature reviews: Qualitative and quantitative approaches* (2nd ed.). Los Angeles: Pyrczak.
- Fink, A. G. (2004). *Conducting research literature reviews: From the Internet to paper* (2nd ed.). Thousand Oaks, CA: SAGE.
- Garrard, J. (2006). *Health sciences literature review made easy: The matrix method* (2nd ed.). Sudbury, MA: Jones & Bartlett.
- Galvan, J. (2006). *Writing literature reviews: A guide for students of the social and behavioral sciences.* Los Angeles: Pyrczak.
- Machi, L., & MvEvoy, B. (2009). *The literature review.* Thousand Oaks, CA: Corwin Press.

A good way of learning how to do good literature reviews is to read reviews. Below are a few that may be helpful but you will probably be able to find reviews in your field of practice:

- Cummins, J. (2003). Knowledge sharing: A review of the literature. Washington, DC: The World Bank Operations Department. Retrieved from http://lnweb90.worldbank.org/oed/oeddoclib.nsf/DocUNIDViewForJavaSearch/D9E389E7414BE9DE85256DC600572CA0/$file/knowledge_eval_literature_review.pdf
- John Jay College of Criminal Justice Research Team. (2002, June). *Child sexual abuse: A review of the literature.* Retrieved from http://www.usccb.org/nrb/johnjaystudy/litreview.pdf
- Atkins, S., & Murphy, K. (2008). Reflection: A review of the literature. *Journal of Advanced Nursing, 18*(8), 1188–1192.
- Lengnick-Hall, C. A., & Lengnick-Hall, M. L. (1988). Strategic human resources management: A review of the literature and a proposed typology. *Academy of Management Review, 13*(3), 454-470.
- Podsakoff, P. M., MacKenzie, S. B., Paine, J. B., & Bachrach, D. (2000). Organizational citizenship behaviors: A critical review of the theoretical and empirical literature and suggestions for future. *Research Journal of Management, 26*(3), 513-563.
- Finnema, E., Droes, R., Ribbe, M., & Tilburg, W. (2000). The effects of emotion-oriented approaches in the care for persons suffering from dementia: A review of the literature. *International Journal of Geriatric Psychiatry, 15*(2), 141-161.
- Savill-Smith, C. (2005). The use of palmtop computers for learning: A review of the literature. *British Journal of Educational Technology, 36*(3), 567-568.

- Thacker, S. B., Gilchrist, J., & Stroup, D. F. (2004). The impact of stretching on sports injury risk: A systematic review of the literature. *Medicine & Science in Sports & Exercise, 36*(3), 371-378.
- Mersch, P., Middlendorp, H., & Bouhuys, A. (1099). Seasonal affective disorders and latitude: A review of the literature. *Journal of Affective Disorders, 53*(1), 35-48.
- Krishnam, V., & Ulrich, K. (2001). Product development decisions: A review of the literature. *Management Science, 47*(1), 1-21.

Before moving on to quantitative research methods we want to make one more point about literature reviews. There is a statistically-based approach to doing research reviews that is called meta-analysis (Borenstein, Hedges, & Rothstein, (2009); Kulinskaya, Morgenthaler, & Staudte, (2008; Littell, Corcoran, & Pillai, 2008). While this approach is very useful for analyzing the empirical literature on a specific type of treatment, it is not appropriate for the type of professional practice literature review we have described here. Meta-analyses narrow your focus to the empirical research studies that meet all or most of the criteria for valid scientific studies and, if they are meaningful, the focus must be on one, or a narrow range of, treatment methods that have been promoted as effective for treating a particular problem or addressing a particular issue. Professional practice literature reviews broaden both the reviewer's and the reader's focus and are attempts to analyze and synthesize the current state of knowledge about a topic.

QUANTITATIVE RESEARCH METHODS

A simple way of explaining quantitative research is to say that it is research that uses numbers as data. However, as you will see, that is too simple an explanation because it ignores the fact that quantitative researchers tend to adopt foundational paradigms from a particular family, and tend to do research to answer a preferred set of questions.

Although there are hundreds of different methods for doing quantitative research, most fall into three broad categories: experimental studies, relationship research, and surveys. Of those three broad types, survey research is probably the most often used, although it is not always the most needed (see Figure 6.2).

Survey Research

Tens of thousands of studies are done each year using surveys. Surveys may be used to gather factual information such as the number of times a

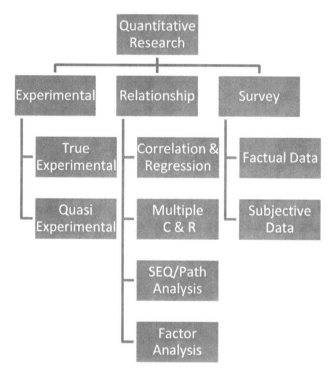

Figure 6.2.   The main methods of Quantitative Research.

teacher uses technology to support a lesson in a typical week as well as subjective data such as a teacher's opinion about Windows versus Macintosh operating systems. A relatively practical guide to doing survey research is Rea and Parker's (2005) book, *Designing and Conducting Survey Research: A Comprehensive Guide.* A shorter book on the same topic is Fowler's (2001) *Survey Research Methods.* A free, online guide to doing survey research was developed by the Center for Health Promotion at the University of Toronto. It is available at:

http://www.thcu.ca/infoandresources/publications
Surveys_Master_Wkbk_V2_Formating2008.09.03_Content2003.31.99.pdf

If you are like us and have trouble typing web addresses like the one above without making an error, you can simply do a Google search for the title, Conducting Survey Research, and include in the search the name of the organization—Center for Health Promotion. Another good online guide that is more of an introduction than a how-to manual is available at a Colorado State University website—http://writing.colostate.edu/guides/ research/survey/ .

If you are interested in learning about the opinions, knowledge, or circumstances of a particular group of people, surveys are one way of accomplishing that. Quantitative surveys are better for studies that begin with a prescribed set of survey items that will generate the responses you need to answer your dissertation questions. Surveys are not as good when the questions you need to ask participants are fuzzy, open, or require follow up questions based on a participant's answer to initial questions. In that case, open or semistructured interviews may be better.

One example of a dissertation that used survey data is Jesson McClinton's (2007) dissertation that was completed at Mississippi State University. Dr. McClinton wanted to know whether university faculty believed the features of a course management system contributed to better teaching and learning. To answer that question, he used an Internet survey to gather data from instructors at two universities about their experiences with, and opinions about, a popular course management system in use on their campuses.

Another survey dissertation was completed by Devrim Özdemi (2004) at Middle Eastern Technical University in Turkey. The focus was on how the adoption of a particular educational ideology influenced acceptance of technology in teaching and learning. One of the major sources of data was a survey completed by both teachers and graduate students. The survey is probably better described as a questionnaire because participants provided more than Yes/No or numeric responses. Several questions allowed them to provide much more detailed responses.

Relationship Research

A less common but still popular method is relationship research. Studies may look at correlations between variables like attitudes toward ecological issues and the likelihood of participating in recycling programs. Simple correlational research typically involves looking at the relationship between two or more variables. If the goal is to predict something like admission to a college, basic statistical procedures can be use to decide whether scores on certain tests (or other types of quantitative variables) predict things like maintaining a B average, or graduating within 5 years. This type of research is called regression analysis. More complicated relational research looks for relationships between, for example, multiple predictors and one or more factors the researcher wants to predict. For example, a study might take 15 different variables, each of which predicts college success, and calculate how well these variables, taken as a whole, predict success. Multiple regression and multiple correlation procedures are widely used in the health sciences.

Another type of relationship research is path analysis or structured equation modeling (SEQ). There are differences between these two procedures but they are essentially expansions of multiple regression and correlation techniques that give you much more sophisticated answers. For example, Kadijevich (2006) used path analysis to study whether different types of support for students preparing to be teachers had any influence on the students' interest in using technology. One finding of this study was that some factors being studied did not have a direct impact on the interests but they did have a positive impact indirectly. That is, they influenced other factors and those intermediate factors influenced the target attitudes. The last type of relationship research is factor analysis. One typical use of factor analysis is to organize a survey or test with many items into clusters of items that seem to assess a certain "factor." For example, Stuve and Cassady (2005) did a factor analysis on the NETS profiles of 956 teacher education students. NETS is the National Educational Technology Standards which is a set of skills, knowledge, and abilities the standards organization believes every teacher should possess. The standards are organized into six groups or factors. If the NETS standards are organized in a meaningful structure the authors reasoned that a factor analysis should empirically demonstrate that there are six factors and that the items in the NETS Profile that students complete should "load on", that is, be associated with, the factor they are a part of in the standards. The factor analysis did not confirm that. Instead, it found only two factors which the authors named Technology Self Concept and Policy and Professionalism.

Simple correlation and regression methods, multiple correlation and regression methods, path analysis, structured equation modeling, and factor analysis are all used regularly in dissertations from many disciplines. Advanced methods, from multiple correlation and regression to factor analysis, require considerable statistical expertise but the logic of these methods is not that difficult to learn. If you are interested in studying relationships between several different variables, simple or complex relational research methods may be appropriate. There are several excellent resources on both simple and complex relational methods. The second edition of Philip Bobko's (2001) *Correlation and Regression: Principles and Applications for Industrial/Organizational Psychology and Management*, covers basic and intermediate procedures with understandable explanations and good examples. Another useful book that covers a similar range of topics is Jeremy Miles and Mark Shelvin's (2000), *Applying Correlation and Regression: A Guide for Students and Researchers*. Books on advanced relational statistical procedures that are understandable without considerable background in the basic and intermediate procedures are hard to find. One book we recommend is the fourth edition of John Loehlin's (2003) *Latent Variable Models: An introduction to Factor, Path, and Structural Equation Analysis*. Loehlin's approach minimizes the use of complex equations to explain basic concepts and, instead, often uses graphical representations that are easier to grasp if you have an interest in these statistical procedures but a limited mathematical background. Another book, *A Beginner's Guide to Structural Equation Modeling* (Schumacker & Lomax, 2004) is also a good introduction to path analysis, structural equation modeling, and certain types of factor analysis, and it has the advantage of having a companion CD that includes the software for conducting many of the statistical procedures explained in the text.

If you would like to read a dissertation that used correlational statistics as a primary means of data analysis, Maretta Andreson's (2007) dissertation, completed at the University of Wollongong's School of Psychology, illustrates how correlational procedures can be used to test the meaningfulness of a theoretical framework. In this case, the framework evaluated was an explanation of how patients with schizophrenia progress through various stages of the illness and what factors influence recovery rather than continued decline. The model is based on positive psychology theory. If the model Dr. Andreson evaluated was supported by her research, it would provide a framework for structuring services to schizophrenic patients that support recovery that allows the patients to resume independent lives. The recovery theory she was studying involved both assertions about factors that support recovery and a sequence of stages a typical patient passes through on the way to recovery. She used correlational statistics to compare the progress of patients with the stages predicted by her theory, and she also correlated measures of the factors assumed by the theory to be important to recovery with actual recovery in a group of patients.

Another recent dissertation, completed at the University of Western Sydney in Australia, is an interesting example of how several advanced correlation/regression procedures were used to study the characteristics of bullying in school and factors that are associated with different roles such as bullying, being bullied, and being a bystander. Roberto Parada (2006) used factor analysis, structural equation modeling and several other statistical procedures to (1) develop a measure of bullying and related roles in schools, (2) look for factors that are associated with bullying and related roles, and (3) develop and evaluate the impact of a "whole school" intervention to reduce bullying in secondary schools. We recommend reading this dissertation because it is an example of the use of advanced correlation and regression procedures. However, had Dr. Parada been one of our students we might have suggested that any one of the three goals for this dissertation would have been a good dissertation. Students often propose doing much more in their dissertation than is needed for a worthy dissertation and there is nothing inherently wrong with that. However, we often suggest that students consider doing one component of their plan as a dissertation and consider the rest part of their research plans for the next few years.

Experimental Research

The last type of traditional quantitative research to be discussed is experimental. This approach, which is at the heart of the natural science model of research, involves dividing groups into one or more control groups and one or more experimental groups. After treatments are administered to the experimental groups a statistical analysis tells the researcher whether there are differences in the average scores of students in the experimental and control groups. Experimental studies must meet a host of requirements to be considered "true experimental" research. Most studies in professional practice dissertations do not meet all the requirements. In fact, most experimental studies in the social sciences do not meet all the criteria. The criterion most often not met is random assignment to groups. To be truly random, every person participating in the study must have the same chance of being assigned to any of the treatment or control groups. This is often impossible to do in studies conducted in the real world settings of professional practice and the result is frequently a "quasi-experimental" study that meets some, but not all, of the requirements for true experimental research. One of the authors of this book (Valenti, 1973) did a quasi-experimental dissertation. The purpose of the study was to compare the effectiveness of three instructional methods (the independent variable). Three different methods were compared—lecture, small group discussion, and independent study. The effectiveness of these three instructional methods were compared by collecting data from a student essay project. Several hundred students from a large metropolitan urban high school participated. The dependent variables, the ones the researcher wanted to change through better instructional methods, were (1) student knowledge of the content being taught, (2) student attitudes, and (3) actual performance on the essay. Because he wanted to generalize his findings to schools other than the school where the research was done, this was a quasi-experimental rather than a true experimental study. The students in the study were not randomly selected from the very large population of, say, students in American high schools today. Some of the data in this dissertation was quantitative and objective—such as a test over the content taught. Other day was more qualitative. For example, expert raters looked at the essays and graded them. One aspect of the study was, therefore, an analysis of whether different raters agreed on the quality of an essay (inter-rater reliability). The main data analysis procedure was an analysis of covariance (ANCOVA) which is a way of comparing two or more "treatment" conditions, in this case different teaching methods. ANCOVA is discussed in a bit more detail in Chapter 11. In Dr. Valenti's dissertation, by the way, there were no differences between lectures and small group discussions. However, students in the independent study group, who were given much more freedom to make decisions about their essays, did do better on some of the dependent measures. Specifically, they scored higher on measures of the ability to synthesize.

Few dissertations, and few research studies of any type in the human sciences, meet all the requirements for true experimental research. Most doctoral students doing experimental research are concerned that their dissertation research does not meet all the requirements for "true experimental" work, but keep in mind the fact that most of the experimental studies with sizable grant support also fail to meet some of the standards. It is much easier to meet the standards for experimental methods when the subjects are animals or steel beams or chemicals than when you are working with first graders, delinquent adolescents, or elderly heart patients.

However, when the purpose of your dissertation is to compare one way of dealing with an issue, problem, or goal with another way, experimental (usually quasi-experimental) methods must be considered as an option.

If you are interested in doing a quasi-experimental dissertation study, the book *Experimental and Quasi-Experimental Designs for Generalized Causal Inference* (Shadish, Cook, & Campbell, 2001) is highly recommended. However, the term "generalized causal inference" in the title means that the authors are focusing on research conducted to draw general conclusions that can be applied to other settings. This is a positivist reason for doing research. However, the methods and procedures described in this book are still applicable if you take an interpretive approach and look for local understanding rather than findings that are directly generalizable to other settings.

Many introductory research textbooks in the social sciences, including Punch (1998), also provide at least some coverage of quasi-experimental research methods. Also, Young Ju Lee's (2003) dissertation at the University of Tennessee is an example of a quasi-experimental dissertation study. In that research Dr. Young studied the impact of a program to enhance creative thinking in students. Her dissertation shows how quasi-experimental methodology can be used in a professional practice setting, in this case a s Korean school in Knoxville, Tennessee that served children of Korean, American and Japanese descent. It is also an example of a dissertation that is short and to the point. It is a total of 42 double-spaced pages, not counting appendices.

Another dissertation from the University of Tennessee that used a quasi-experimental design involved the evaluation of a degree-completion program for adults who were returning to college to finish a degree that was begun but not completed (Vos, 2003).

SINGLE SUBJECT RESEARCH

Another type of quantitative research that is separate from traditional quantitative methods but nevertheless solidly within the quantitative tradition, is single subject research. B. F. Skinner, a professor of psychology at Harvard University for much of his professional career, was the leading figure in one major effort to bring a radical form of positivism into psychology. He also introduced and championed the detailed study of the behavior of one living organism at a time. Skinner's favorite animal to study was the pigeon, in part because it was easy to set up a shiny aluminum disk the pigeon was supposed to peck an apparatus that automatically counted the number of pecks. Skinner is the founder of the experimental analysis of behavior movement and the *Journal for the Experimental Analysis of Behavior* is still in print today. Once the experimental analysis of behavior was established, many young psychologists and psychology graduate students were attracted to the field. Some of them decided to begin applying the theories and methods to the real world problems of humans. This led to the creation of the *Journal of Applied Behavior Analysis* that is also still in print. The Applied Behavior Analysts, or ABAs, developed and perfected several research designs for studying individuals or small groups. Tim Stocks (1999) at Michigan State University, has created a website that is a brief orientation to these research methods. He describes four commonly used designs (see http://www.msu.edu/user/sw/ssd/issd01.htm). The two most common are ABAB and multiple baseline.

ABA and ABAB Single Subject Designs

Figure 6.3 is an example of the typical type of data presentation for an ABA design. It was adapted from Tim Stocks' website. The first or A phase of an ABA design is Baseline. You observe an individual for several days and count a particular behavior. That behavior may be something like percentage of class time on task, the number of physical attacks on other

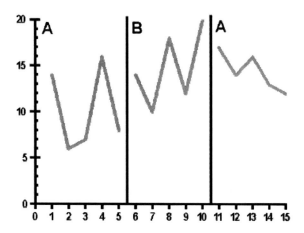

Source: Stocks (1999).

Figure 6.3.   Example of an ABA single subject design.

people in the room, the number of verbal outbursts or hallucinatory epi-
sodes, or any other behavior that can be counted. Once a baseline of the
behavior is established, the treatment phase begins (the B phase). In
applied behavior analysis research the treatment is often the systematic
delivery of some form of reward but other treatments are also studied. If
the behavior being measured seems to change then there is reason to
believe the treatment is effective. However, it is always possible that some
other factor was the real cause of the change in behavior. To test for that
possibility, a second A phase is established—sometimes called the
Reversal phase. The treatment is withdrawn while the behavior continues
to be counted. If it changes for the worse, that is strong evidence the treatment is a causal factor. The ABA method illustrated in Figure 6.3 could be
extended to another treatment condition so that the experiment ends
with a treatment phase instead of a reversal phase. That is called an ABAB
study.

Applied behavior analysis is not as popular today as it once was, but it
is still a major treatment method in special education and in the treatment of autism and some forms of mental illness. ABA and ABAB
research methods are worth considering when your dissertation research
is about the treatment of one, or a few, individual students, patients, or
clients. There is, however, a major limitation of these methods. If the
treatment you want to study is likely to result in a relatively permanent
change, then ABA or ABAB methods are not appropriate because the
design is based on the assumption that the impact of the treatment goes

away almost immediately after it has stopped. If your treatment method meets that criteria this type of single subject research may be an option to consider. For more information on this research design, Craig Kennedy's (2004) book, *Single Case Designs for Educational Research*, is a good resource. Toni Tripodi's (1994) book about using single case designs in clinical social work is another useful source of information as is Christopher Skinner's (2005) book for school psychologists. In addition to Tim Stock's website, there are hundreds of other websites on single subject designs as well as many published papers on the use of single subject designs in an unbelievable range of professional practice fields. For example, Janosky (2005) explained the use of single subject designs in medicine for practice-base primary care research.

Lizabeth Babson's (2007) dissertation at the Ohio State University is a good example of an ABAB study. The clients she studied were adults with chronic pain who were returning to work. She focused on the occurrence of "negative self statements" about pain that prior research suggested had an influence on a person's ability to deal with and overcome problems of chronic pain. Dr. Babson studied three clients who had complex chronic pain issues and had applied for worker's compensation because of the pain. After each client completed a baseline phase (A) she instituted a treatment to reduce the number of negative self statements (the first B phase). That reduced the number of negative self statements and she then instituted another baseline phase (A) in which treatment was withdrawn, followed by a second treatment phase (B). One of the interesting findings in this dissertation was that in the second baseline phase the number of negative self statements measured did not return to the level of the first baseline, which suggests that the treatment had an impact on that behavior even after it was withdrawn. This is probably the major weakness in ABAB designs—treatments that have a lasting impact may influence the target behavior during the reversal (the second A phase) phase and that complicates interpretation of the data.

Multiple Baseline Designs

The other popular design in this group is a multiple baseline. It is illustrated in Figure 6.4.

Each of the three graphs in Figure 6.4 represent the behavior of a separate individual or group. In essence these are three separate ABA studies. Note that each of the data points in Figure 6.4 is for 1 month, but multiple baseline studies more often measure and plot data on a daily basis or for a particular time during the day such as a class period, treatment session, or therapy period. The topmost graph has the shortest

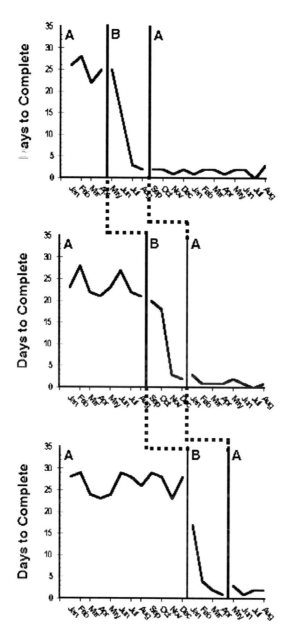

Source: Stocks (1999).

Figure 6.4.   Example of the results of a multiple baseline study.

baseline before treatment is instituted. However, when treatment is instituted for one individual or group, the other two individuals/groups are still in a no treatment or baseline condition. If the behavior improves in the top graph but not in the second and third, that is evidence the treatment has had an impact on the target behavior. Later, treatment will be started for the second individual or group, and even later for the third individual or group. Every time behavior changes for the better when treatment is introduced, that is evidence the treatment is effective. Figure 6-4 shows a second A condition (e.g., treatment was withdrawn) but many multiple baseline studies do not include this phase. Instead, they rely on the data from the staggered A and B phases to convince a reader that the treatment was effective. Note, by the way, that single-subject research methodology often relies on graphic representation of the data for analysis. No statistical tests are used in most of these studies.

An example of a dissertation that used a multiple baseline design was completed by Charles Heywood (2001) at the University of Auckland. He was interested in whether children with attention-deficit/hyperactivity disorder (ADHD) and Specific Learning Disorders (LD) or aggressive classroom behavior, would respond to a form of biofeedback. He studied seven boys, ages 7-12. A multiple baseline study was the core of his research but he also gathered several types of data and used other procedures as well.

SUMMARY

This chapter introduces five different families of methods for research and scholarship. The primary focus of the chapter is on quantitative methods, and that family has three members—experimental research, survey methods, and relationship studies. Today all three types of quantitative research are popular in virtually all areas of professional practice. They have a long history of both development and use, which means the procedures and processes involved in applying them to questions in applied research are relatively well established. Some of these methods are very complex and using any of them, even those that are relatively simple to implement, require thoughtful and careful decisions if you are to do research that meets the established standards for that method. However, because standards are so stringent, anyone who undertakes a quantitative professional practice dissertation will likely find it necessary to make difficult decisions that involve deciding which standards should receive priority in the design of the study and which can be violated without completely destroying the value of the research. Such decisions often do not involve obvious answers, and it will be important that you and your dissertation committee explore the options and reach a consensus before undertaking the research. Your oral defense is not the time to discover that several members of the committee do not agree with your decisions about how to conduct your dissertation research!

The fourth family of quantitative research methods discussed in this chapter, single subject designs, is less widely known and not often used in dissertation research. However, single subject designs have been around for decades and they are ideally suited to certain types of studies that focus on the impact of treatment on individuals or small groups. A critical issue, however, is whether the treatment effect will last after treatment ends. If it does, designs such as ABA or ABAB may be inappropriate. However, multiple baseline designs that involve only staggered baseline (A) and treatment (B) phases can be used to evaluate interventions that have an impact beyond the time when the treatment is in effect.

Finally, while a professional practice literature review is not often given serious consideration when students select a research method for their dissertation, there is much to commend this approach when the topic of the dissertation is a problem or issue of professional practice. Further, a growing number of professional practice doctoral programs are not only accepting, they are encouraging, dissertations that are literature reviews.

In the next two chapters, we will explore the large and diverse family of qualitative research methods. You will read about traditional qualitative methods, applied qualitative research methods, and some innovative methods such as emancipatory methods and design as research.

CHAPTER 7

TRADITIONAL QUALITATIVE RESEARCH METHODS

In the last 50 years there have been thousands of papers, hundreds of books, and innumerable conferences where the relative strengths and weaknesses of quantitative research methods have been compared to those of qualitative methods. Such discussions have not, however, generally focused on the worthiness of numeric data versus non-numeric data. There are issues about quantitative versus qualitative data, but much of the heat in what has come to be known as the "paradigm wars" is about the guiding frameworks, the theoretical foundations, and the purposes of research. Although they are important we will not explore the foundations of the paradigm wars here. There are a great many resources available, and all sides are well represented in the available literature (Willis, 2008, 2007). The purpose of this chapter is to introduce the major methods of qualitative research, identify the strengths and weaknesses of each, and the appropriate and inappropriate applications of those methods.

Figure 7.1 graphically represents the current families of qualitative research methods that are particularly applicable to professional practice dissertations. The traditional methods of qualitative research (observation, interviewing, historiography, and cast studies) have been developed in the social sciences and are all relatively mature. Applied qualitative methods, which are covered in Chapter 8, such as action research and design projects, are more recent developments. One expression of that

Completing a Professional Practice Dissertation: A Guide for Doctoral Students and Faculty, pp. 197–216

youth is the range of perspectives on how to do these methods well, and as debates about the appropriate reasons for doing particular types of applied research. The third category of qualitative methods, emancipatory methods, are even newer and less well developed. They represent what some call the "bleeding edge" of scholarship and there is considerable debate over the place of emancipatory research methods today. Participants in those debates take positions as extreme as *emancipatory methods are the only suitable methods for professional practice* to *emancipatory methods are not research methods at all, they are methods of political action and social revolution.* Emancipatory methods of qualitative research are also covered in Chapter 8.

We will begin in this chapter with an exploration of traditional qualitative methods, which are the least controversial, and end our coverage of qualitative methods in Chapter 8 with the most controversial—emancipatory methods.

As mentioned earlier, all the traditional qualitative methods developed in one of the social sciences. Figure 7.1 outlines the four groups of traditional methods. They involve observing in the field, asking questions or interviewing, doing historical research, and conducting case studies.

ETHNOGRAPHY (OBSERVATION IN THE REAL WORLD)

Ethnography (observation in the field) has been a major method of anthropology for over 100 years. Ethnographic methods have reached a very advanced level of sophistication and many different variants are now in use. The second edition of David Fetterman's (2007) book, *Ethnography:*

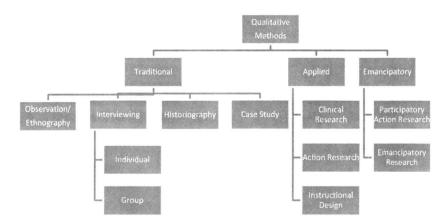

Figure 7.1.   The major families of qualitative research methods.

Step by Step, is one of many useful guides to doing this type of research. The book provides detailed examples and procedures for beginning ethnographers. In the first edition, Fetterman (1998) described ethnography this way:

> Ethnography is the art and science of describing a group or culture. The description may be of a small tribal group in an exotic land or a classroom in middle-class suburbia. The task is much like the one taken on by an investigative reporter, who interviews relevant people, reviews, records, weighs the credibility of one person's opinions against another's, looks for ties to special interests and organizations, and writes the story for a concerned public and for professional colleagues. A key difference between the investigative reporter and the ethnographer, however, is that whereas the journalist seeks out the unusual – the murder, the plane crash, or the bank robbery —the ethnographer writes about the routine, daily lives of people…. Ethnographers are noted for their ability to keep an open mind about the group or culture they are studying. This quality, however, does not imply any lack of rigor. The ethnographer enters the field with an open mind, not an empty head. (p. 1)

This form of research involves spending considerable time in the field—a school, a neighborhood, a clinic, a factory or business office—to name just a few settings where ethnographic research is practiced. The data gathered tends to be notes written by the observer as well as artifacts gathered from the field (e.g., minutes of meetings, examples of project plans, photographs, newspaper and television news reports). The purposes of such research is typically to develop an understanding of the setting where the research is being conducted. For example, Anna Pollard's (2008) dissertation at the Royal Melbourne Institute of Technology was an effort to better understand the types of professional development and training needs of literacy coordinators in Australian secondary schools. She based her research on constructivist and interpretive theoretical foundations and she used case study methodology, which is discussed later in this chapter, as a broad organizing framework for her dissertation. However, her major methods of collecting data were a combination of observation in high schools, including literacy programs, and interviews with literacy coordinators in those schools. Pollard summarized how she approached her research this way:

> In order to arrive at an understanding of what Literacy Coordinators in secondary schools in Victoria, need to know and be able to do when managing their programs, it is essential to capture the voice of the participants as they describe and explain both the knowledge and skills that they believe are essential to the role as well as the values and beliefs that inform their practice. Exploring and analysing the thinking of Literacy Coordinator participants

regarding what she/he needs to know and be able to do requires that the researcher collaborates with the participants in observing, documenting, reviewing and evaluating the Literacy Coordinators' practices and programs. Observation of the program in operation, analysis of documents and artefacts and the examination of the perspectives of other key stakeholders facilitates the triangulation of data and assists the researcher to tease out important themes that emerge from the study. (p. 82)

Specifically, Dr. Pollard collected data through several types of observations and interviews:

- In depth interviews with the Literacy Coordinator participants
- Key informant interviews/surveys
- Participant and nonparticipant observations
- Content analysis of school literacy policies and Charter/Strategic Plan, goals and priorities
- Analysis of artefacts. (p. 84)

Her methods chapter is well structured, informative, and provides a detailed description of her data collection methods as well as her theoretical foundations for the research and her practical approach to collecting and analyzing the data. Dr. Pollard's dissertation is one of many that is abstracted on the Networked Digital Library of Dissertations and Theses (http://www.ndltd.org/). The abstract on this site is linked to the full-text of the dissertation at http://adt.lib.rmit.edu.au/adt/public/adt-VIT20080514.122251/ .

This dissertation also illustrates the multilevel nature of many dissertations. The broad organizing framework was case study methodology. However, the case study involved the collection and analysis of several types of data including interviews (discussed in the next section), observations (some of which involved the observer participating in the activities being observed), and the analysis of a range of artifacts including some of the policy and strategic plan documents from the participating schools.

When Ethnographic Methods Are Appropriate, and Inappropriate

There are several traditions of ethnographic research and each has focused on different reasons for doing ethnographic studies. Critical ethnographers, for example, tend to use the method to identify and make public patterns of power and oppression in culture, society, group, or organization. For example, Janice Elliot (1998) did a nursing master's thesis at the University of Western Ontario titled, "A Critical Ethnography of the Experience of Menopause for Korean Women Living in Canada." Her study involved extended interviews with seven women and her focus was to understand how these women dealt with menopause in a setting where both Chinese and Western medical and cultural perspectives are influential and sometimes in conflict.

Interpretive ethnographers often do research to "tell the story" of a particular context. The result of interpretive ethnographic research is often a descriptive or narrative document that provides the reader with a better understanding of the focus of study. Beach (2005), for example, described the purpose of ethnographic research in education as a way of helping us know more "about how understandings are formed in instruction, how meanings are negotiated in classrooms, how roles and relationships are developed and maintained over time in schools and how education policy is formulated and implemented" (p. 1). These purposes are often accomplished through telling stories:

> Ethnographers produce storied versions of these things. These stories reveal, interpret and represent every day encounters, which ethnographers sometimes use in order to develop new education theory…. These stories are based on the minute-by-minute, day-to-day social life of individuals as they interact together and develop understandings and meanings by engaging in joint action and adapting to situations (p. 1)

Interpretive ethnographers may try to tell a story about what they study without adding much in terms of theoretical explanations. Some, however, do make generalizations from the data and try to offer conceptual and theoretical frameworks, based on their research, that both explain and give reasons for what has happened in a local context. These "local truths" are offered to readers of the research reports as sources of information that may, or may not be, useful when considering other contexts.

A third form, positivist ethnographic research, is more assertive. Positivist research typically uses the data collected to develop theoretical explanations of phenomena and patterns that were observed in one context. However, the purpose of the research is to develop explanations that apply broadly.

With three commonly used frameworks for doing ethnographic research, you are probably not surprised to learn that what are "appropriate" and "inappropriate" purposes for ethnography depend on the framework adopted. For example, interpretive researchers do not accept the positivist researcher's purpose of discovering broad, generalizable explanations because interpretivists believe context plays an influential role in human behavior. They believe there are few universal laws of human behavior to be discovered. On the other hand, critical theorists do not find a common interpretivist goal of developing an understanding of a local context very helpful. Critical theorists *know* there is oppression, inappropriate use of power to suppress groups and individuals, and conflicts in society that lead to social norms, rules, and even laws that privilege one group over others. A primary goal of critical ethnographic research is to show how that happens in a particular context and to promote change that leads to a more equitable and democratic society.

The end result is that whatever form of ethnographic research you undertake there will likely be scholars who consider your research inappropriate or irrelevant as well as scholars who think it is just the sort of work you should be doing.

Learning More About Ethnographic Methods

There are a number of websites with excellent resources on ethnographic methodology. These include QualPage (http://www.wualitativeresearch.uga.edu/QualPage/) which is a very large and useful site for information on virtually all forms of qualitative methodology. Click the *Ethnography* link on the left side of the home page to view many resources of the topic.

A short guide to ethnographic methods is available at http://www.sasu-penn.edu/anthro/CPIA/methods.html and Michael Genzuk has developed a very good overview of ethnographic methods that is available at http://www-ref.use.edu/~genzuk/Ethnographic_Research.html. There is also a complete anthropology course, *Seminar on Ethnography and Fieldwork*, that is available from the Massachusetts Institute of Technology, through its Opencourseware project. The web address is http://ocw.mit.edu/OcwWeb/Anthropology/21A-112Fall2003/Readingsindex.htm.

A more comprehensive introduction to ethnographic scholarship is the *Handbook of Ethnography* (Atkinson, Coffey, Delamont, Lofland, & Lofland, 2007). If you are interested in the use of ethnography within a critical theory perspective, Madison's (2005) *Critical Ethnography: Method, Ethics, and Performance* is available. Levinson, Foley, and Holland's (1996) book as well as Spindler and Hammond, (2007) present examples of ethnographic research in education. Finally, if you are interested in interpretive *ethnographic* methods, Norman Denzin's (1996) book, *Interpretive Ethnography: Ethnographic Practices for the 21st Century* is a good starting point.

INTERVIEWING

Few methods of research are conducted in so many ways, and for so many purposes, as interviewing. They range from the very structured questioning of a subject that yields little more than Yes and No answers to pre-structured questions to wide open interviews with very limited structure and few limitations on the content of questions or answers. The "structured interviewing" methods used in market research and political polling produce less useful data in professional practice research where open, less structured, approaches to interviews are typically more productive. Chapter 3, "Common Qualitative Methods" in the online textbook developed by the National Science Foundation (http://www.ehr.nsf.gov/EHR/REC/pubs/NSF97-153/CHAP_3.HTM) is a very good introduction to collecting data using open, flexible interviews (called "in depth interviews" in that text). The chapter also introduces ethnographic methods and the Focus Group method, which is a way of doing group interviewing.

Two useful books on interviewing are *Qualitative Interviewing: The Art of Hearing Data* (Rubin & Rubin, 2004) and *Interviewing as Qualitative Research: A Guide for Researchers in Education and the Social Sciences* (Seidman, 2006).

The data generated by interviews generally fall into two broad categories. Some researchers make notes during the interview and then write a summary after the end of the interview. The researcher's notes become the primary data for the research. The other approach is to record or videotape the interviews and then to analyze that raw data (plus researcher notes and comments). This second method is more time and labor intensive, often involving creating complete transcripts of each interview. This, however, may be worth the effort if you are looking for nuances in communication or complex patterns that may not become obvious to you until you do a detailed analysis of the transcripts. Fortunately, there are a number of computer programs to assist you in analyzing interview data and to look for patterns and relationships in your data.

Several of the dissertations discussed in the previous section on ethnographic methods used interview data as well. The use of observations in the real world as well as interviews of key participants is a popular approach. Akihiro Ogawa's (2004) dissertation at Cornell University illustrates this approach. He was interested in how a change in Japanese law and policy about nongovernmental organizations (NGOs) impacted their operation and their relationship to government policy and practices. Much of his data came from participation observations while he worked as a volunteer for an NGO in Japan but another critical source of data was "extensive interviews with NGO participants, Japanese NGO experts in academia, and government officials, attendance at workshops for NGO practitioners across the country, as well as discourse analysis of mass media coverage about NGOs."

Group Interviews: Focus Groups and the Delphi Technique

Interviewing individuals is common in professional practice research but some research calls for group interviewing methods. For example, if you would like to gather data that reflects the agreements and disagreements among a group, such as experts on a particular topic, the consumers of a particular service, or a particular level of staff in an organization (e.g., local staff, mid-management, upper level administration, policy makers) a focus group can be very useful. Focus groups generally consist of 5 to 10 people, led by a facilitator who is trained in focus group methods. The facilitator typically introduces questions to the group and guides the discussion. The end result is a report that summarizes the views, opinions, and disagreements expressed by members of the focus group. One relatively easy-to-read guide to focus group methods is Krueger and Casey's (2000) *Focus Groups: A Practical Guide for Applied Research*. Another is *Focus Group Research in Education and Psychology* (Vaughn, Schumm, & Sinagub, 2005). A useful reference about focus groups in medical research is Jenny Kitziner's paper from the *British Journal of Medicine* which is available online at http://www.bmj.com/cgi/content/full/311/7000/299 . There is also an online version of a book published by the International Nutritional Foundation for Developing Countries in cooperation with the World Health Organization and the World Bank. *A Manual for the Use of Focus Groups* is available online at http://www.unu.edu/Unupress/food2/UIN03E/uin03ee00/htm. This book emphasizes very structured focus groups (we prefer more flexible approaches), but it is a very good source of information on how to deal with the many details that need to be addressed to ensure a successful focus group study.

Finally, an online manual was developed at the University of Southern Maine with support from the Ford Foundation. Titled *The Focus Group Manual*, it is aimed at social services professionals who will be doing focus groups with low income families. The web address is http://muskie.usm.maine.edu/focusgroupmanual/ .

Another group interview method is the Delphi Technique, which is named after the home of the oracles in ancient Greece. The basic purpose of the Delphi Technique is to help a group to come to consensus on a set of questions. The participants may be experts on a particular topic, individuals who have had similar experiences or who have similar vested interests, or any group that can be a source of information about a topic that interests you. While Focus Group methods try to draw out individual opinions as well as disagreements, the purpose of the Delphi Technique is to get the group to come to consensus on a set of questions or issues. Skulmoski, Hartman, and Krahn (2007) described the Delphi Technique this way:

> The Delphi method is an interactive process to collect and distill the ... judgments of experts using a series of data collection and analysis techniques interspersed with feedback. The Delphi method is well suited as a research instrument where there is incomplete knowledge about a problem or phenomenon.... The Delphi method works especially well when the goal is to improve our understanding of problems, opportunities, solutions, or to develop forecasts.

Delphi studies are often conducted via e-mail today. The moderator creates a set of questions and sends them to the participants, usually experts or individuals who have experiences or other characteristics that qualify them for the study. The experts then respond to the questions and the moderator synthesizes the positions taken by the experts. In the first round of a Delphi study there are almost always points of agreement among the experts and points of disagreement. Because the goal is to reach a consensus the moderator creates additional questions that address the points on which there are important disagreements. Those questions, and a synopsis of what has been agreed upon, are then distributed to the participants. There may also be questions about points upon which it is unclear whether the group agrees or disagrees. The experts respond again and the moderator uses those responses to create another set of questions along with a new synopsis of agreements. This process continues until there is either substantial consensus or no further progress toward consensus seems possible.

The typical result of a Delphi study is a report that summarizes both the process and the results. In a very useful paper, Skulmoski, Hartman and Krahn (2007) discuss and offer advice on many of the decisions you must make to do a Delphi study. They cover issues such as how to select participants, how broad or narrow to make the questions, and when you have completed enough cycles. They also present an 11-step sequence that is helpful as you organize the process of conducting the research.

When The Delphi and Focus Group Techniques are Appropriate, and Inappropriate

If you are interested in doing your dissertation on a professional practice topic for which the knowledge base is not well codified, or has not been organized into a set of guidelines, statements, and rules, the Delphi

Technique is a very good way of tapping the expertise of practicing professionals who are excellent at dealing with the issue that interests you. Often professionals rely on their tacit knowledge and their experience but they may not have translated that tacit knowledge into formalized guidelines and rules for practice. In fact, some forms of professional practice may not even be amenable to such formalization. Delphi studies are a way of tapping such reservoirs of knowledge and expertise.

Perhaps the most often seen but inappropriate use of the Delphi method is to do your research with a group that does not have the expertise or experience to provide useful answers to the questions being asked. For example, suppose you study an organization that needs to make significant changes in the way it approaches clients—whether they be students, patients, community members, or other groups. If the members of the Delphi group do not have considerable experience in effective and successful ways of working with clients, and/or a knowledge of how other agencies have done this well, the results of the Delphi study are likely to be uninformed opinions rather than the consensus of knowledgeable participants. To be useful the participants should have expertise and relevant experience. Or, as an alternative you could do a Delphi study using participants who are clients. They could use their own experience with the organization to at least critique what has been done and perhaps make some suggestions about improvements. However, in this case, a focus group might be a better approach to tapping the experience of clients or customers. Use focus groups when you want to learn more about the views and opinions of a particular group but do not have a goal of reaching consensus based on the expertise of the participants.

If you would like to read a dissertation based on focus group methodology Jill Nolan's (1997) study at Ohio State University used focus groups to study the quality of life of older adults living in rural cooperative housing. If you are interested in the use of Delphi methods, an excellent beginning point is a paper by Skulmoski, Hartman, and Krahn (2007). It introduces the method and explains how it can be used in theses and dissertations. The paper also contains references to many dissertations based on Delphi methodology. It is available online at http://jite.org/documents/Vol6/JITEv6p001-021Skulmoski212.pdf .

HISTORIOGRAPHY

Historiography is the term for methods of historical research. Doing historical research, whether it be documenting local history or constructing a history with a broader perspective, is not common in dissertation work outside the field of history. Historical research is, however, a valued component of the scholarly and research literature in all professional fields. For example, an understanding of the historical relationship between public policy and professional practice is helpful in any field—particularly in times of transition or dissatisfaction. Two useful books on historiography are *From Reliable Sources: An Introduction to Historical Methods* (Howell & Prevenier, 2001) and the sixth edition of *Short Guide to Writing About History* (Marius & Page, 2009)

Appropriate and Inappropriate Uses of Historical Methods

Some time ago, one of the authors received a note from a graduate student at a university where he and his colleagues had created a doctoral program about 20 years ago. The student was doing a historical study of the development of that program and had many questions about the conditions and process involved in creating the new program. When the student finished his study the resulting paper made for interesting reading. This is an example of a "local" history. It documents what has happened in a particular situation. This paper linked local history to events occurring at the national level and also highlighted many relatively unique circumstances in the local context.

Such studies are helpful to three groups. Those who continue to work in the local context will find the information in a historical study helpful because it adds to our understanding of why things are as they are. Historical studies also help us understand the individuals, the groups, the issues, and the pressures that shaped and directed events. The other group that finds local history useful includes those interested in broader trends and issues. The study of a doctoral program's development at one institution is an example of how things happened during a particular time in the history of higher education in a state, region, or nation. When combined with other local histories, a "big picture" may emerge that helps us understand the way such developments are initiated and brought to fruition.

The third group that finds local history studies helpful is practitioners and policy makers in similar settings. While the knowledge generated by local histories does not automatically generalize to other settings, practitioners often find such studies useful because they add to the practitioners general knowledge of practice contexts. Understanding what happened in one context may help you understand your own context.

The second type of historical study that may be appropriate for professional practice dissertations is a historical analysis of trends, issues, contexts, or patterns related to professional practice in a particular field. Local practices are influenced by contemporary social, cultural, economic, and political policies and these all have a history. If we know that history we have a much better understanding of why things are the way they are, what options might improve professional practice, and how we might go about supporting and encouraging those options—from national and international policies to changes in day-to-day professional practice. While we were writing this chapter, for example, the new Obama administration was taking charge of the national government and more than one expert waxed eloquently on what we should know about the New Deal policies of the Roosevelt administration during the 1930s when the nation faced, not just a serious recession, but a depression. It is a cliché, but it is nevertheless true—those who do not understand the past are doomed to repeat it. Historical studies are thus worthy of consideration when you select a method for your professional practice dissertation.

A historical study is most appropriate when your topic is complex and has been influenced by significant historical movements and developments that are not well understood. Historical dissertations are not likely to provide "the answer" to contemporary issues of professional practice, but they do provide important knowledge and perspectives that contribute to the knowledge base that decision makers at all levels use when dealing with those issues. Thus, if you are seeking "answers" to contemporary practice questions historical studies may not fulfill your hopes. However, if the goal is to add to our understanding of the theoretical, practical, political, and cultural context in which contemporary decisions are made —either locally or nationally and internationally—historical research is one way to accomplish such a goal.

Sources of Additional Information About Historical Methods

The methods of historical research are relatively specialized but there are a number of useful guides. A short and informative introduction to the use of historical research methods is Elizabeth Dano's (2008) book, *Historical Research*. It is a good place to start. It is part of Oxford University Press' *Pocket Guides to Social Work Research Series*. Other recent books on historical research methods include Howell and Preveneir's (2001) book, *From Reliable Sources: An Introduction to Historical Research*, as well as George Igger's (2005) *Historiography in the Twentieth Century: From Scientific Objectivity to the Postmodern Challenge*. Two books from a publisher that specializes in history (Harlan Davidson) offer comprehensive overviews of historical research methods: Furay and Salevouris (2000) and Bundage (2002).

We particularly recommend the books by Elizabeth Dano (2008) and George Igger (2005) because they deal with the different theoretical and conceptual foundations for doing historical research. As a field, history has changed radically over the last 120 years, especially in terms of the foundational paradigms that guide historical research. It behoves anyone considering a historical dissertation to think carefully about the alternatives that emerged over the twentieth century. Both these books help you do just that.

If you would like to read some dissertations based on historiography the American Historical Association maintains a database of planned and completed dissertations at this address: http://www.historians.org/pubs/dissertations/index.cfm . Most of these dissertations were done by professional historians but there are examples in the database of dissertations about virtually every area of professional practice—including business, management, education, psychology, social work, and nursing.

CASE STUDY METHODS

Case studies are odd inventions because they aren't really a specific research method. Instead, they are really a conceptual *container* that is large enough for you to put in all sorts of methods. All the traditional qualitative methods mentioned thus far—observation, interviews, historical research—can be part of the data collection process for a case study, plus much more. As Stake (2005) put it, "Here and there, researchers will call anything they please a case study" (p. 445).

A case study is not about collecting a certain type of data; it is about why you are doing research. Again, quoting one of the authorities on case study method, Robert Stake (2005), "Case study is not a methodological choice but a choice of what is to be studied" (p. 435). Stake argues that it is "the case" that is studied rather than larger or smaller units. That means you look at a phenomenon holistically and in its natural context. It does not mean there is no analysis of the elements or components of a phenomenon but those aspects of a case study are there because they contribute to a better understanding of the phenomenon.

You probably noticed that we have used the term phenomenon, but we haven't really defined just what a *phenomenon* is. That is because it is difficult to provide a precise yet broad definition that gives you a good idea of all the sorts of things a case study can focus on. Perhaps the best way to do that is to provide some examples of phenomena that have been the focus of professional practice case studies:

- Eleanor Barnes' (1998) dissertation on an effort to coordinate and integrate the services of a large school district and those of supporting agencies in the community. It is available online at http://scholar.lib.vt.edu/theses/available/etd-23098-18255/unrestricted/front_section.pdf .

- Barbara Johnson's (2007) case study dissertation on the impact of leadership on literacy instruction in an elementary school. The full text of this dissertation, completed at Western Michigan University, http://www.wmich.edu/coe/elrt/proposals/index.htm. This site also has the dissertation proposal, the Institutional Review Board application for approval, and the PowerPoint presentation for the final defense. Several other dissertations, and related documents, are also available on this site including Ann Rae Kopy's (2006) case study of a school-university partnership.

- Melinda Lee Kreth's (1998) dissertation at Colorado State University looked at the experiences of women engineering students participating in co-op experiences. Her study included case studies of five women. Information on this dissertation, as well as many others from Colorado State, is available at http://wac.colostate.edu/theses/index.cfm?category=17 .

In spite of the fuzziness about just what a case study is, Robert Yin (2002) has written many good books on how to conduct case studies. He explains case study this way:

> The case study is but one of several ways of doing social science research. Other ways include experiments, surveys, histories, and the analysis of archival information. Each strategy has peculiar advantages and disadvantages, depending on three conditions: (a) the type of research question, (b) the control an investigator has over actual behavioral events, and (c) the focus on contemporary as opposed to historical phenomena.
>
> In general, case studies are the preferred strategy when "how" or "why" questions are being posed, when the investigator has little control over events, and when the focus is on a contemporary phenomenon within some real-life context. Such explanatory case studies also can be complimented by two other types—exploratory and descriptive case studies. (p. 1)

Many of the characteristics of case studies are appealing when you are doing professional practice research. The focus on studying a phenomenon *in context*, is very appropriate. The holistic approach is helpful because understanding professional practice calls for holistic understanding. The "how" and "why" questions noted by Yin are also very important questions though we would add additional questions that are appropriate for case study research such as "Did it happen?" "Was it successful?" and "Who supports what and why?" The wide range of questions that can be approached via a case study is one reason there are so many different reasons for using them in professional practice research. Yin (2002) talks about three types of case studies:

- **Explanatory**—Looks for reasons why a phenomenon happened the way it did. When the case study looks at a particularly unique or unusual situation it is sometimes called a critical instance case study. In such studies the researcher may not expect readers to generalize the findings broadly because the situation studied is valuable because the case being studied, though rare or relatively unique, is very important.

- **Exploratory**—An effort to develop more knowledge about a particular phenomenon with the expectation that the information gathered will be used to guide and shape additional research. Exploratory case studies are often abbreviated studies that are done to improve the focus and format of larger, more extended studies that may also be case studies or may use some other method. These are sometimes called pilot case studies.

- **Descriptive**—The purpose is to describe in some detail the setting and the phenomenon. Generalization and implications are typically left to the reader rather than undertaken by the researcher. A similar term is illustrative case study. For example, you might do a case study on one high school chemistry class that integrates many forms of educational technology to provide an example or illustration of how such a class works.

Various authors have described other types of case studies, some of which overlap with Yin's three types. This list was adapted from Willis (2008):

Program Evaluation—Case studies are often used as all or part of the process of understanding whether a particular project or program was "effective." When done from a positivist perspective the goal may be to determine whether "it worked" or not. Critical program evaluation tends to focus on whether "it worked" or not from the perspective of those in the program who are not in power. For example, a program to teach poor, inner city residents to qualify for jobs in a local factory might be considered a success in a positivist case study because many participants were hired by the factory. A critical case study of the same program might conclude it is a failure because it prepared participants for dead end and boring jobs where the workers are treated as cogs in the machine without power over their lives and without a voice in how the work situation is structured. An interpretive case study on the same project might present "multiple perspectives"—those of the factory managers, community leaders, the participants, local activists, and area politicians.

Program Implementation—Some case studies focus on the impact of a project or program. A related type of case study, program implementation, looks at the process of implementation rather than just the impact. Often done from an interpretive or critical perspective, program implementation case studies focus on how an innovation, reform, change, or even a reduction in services, occurs.

Positivist—In positivist case studies the goal is generally to use a single instance of a phenomenon (e.g., the progression of one teenage delinquent through the school, social service, and legal system of his or her community) to develop theories that can be generalized to other delinquents and other settings. Positivist case studies may also start with an existing theory and try to validate it by demonstrating that the case "fits" the theory.

Intrinsic—Intrinsic case studies are one of three types identified by Stake (2005). A case study is intrinsic

> if the study is undertaken because, first and last, one wants better understanding of this particular case. It is not undertaken primarily because the case represents other cases or because it illustrates a particular trait or problem, but instead because, in all its particularity and ordinariness, this case itself is of interest.... The purpose is not to come to understand some abstract construct or generic phenomenon, such as literacy or teenage drug use or what a school principal does. The purpose is not theory building—though at other times the researcher may do just that. Study is undertaken because of an intrinsic interest in, for example, this particular child, clinic, conference, or curriculum. (p. 445)

Instrumental—Calling a case study instrumental (which is Stake's second type) is appropriate

> if a particular case is examined mainly to provide insight into an issue or to redraw a generalization. The case is of secondary interest, it plays a supportive role, and it facilitates our understanding of something else. The case is still looked at in depth, its contexts scrutinized and its ordinary activities detailed, but all because this helps us pursue the external interest. (p. 446)

Cumulative—A cumulative case study involves the use of more than one case. For example, in a program evaluation case study, five or six participants might be studied and each of their case studies could illuminate the program. The result might be several themes that seem to cut across the cases, or the resulting study and report might illustrate how different the impact of the project is on different participants. Stake calls this a multiple case study or a collective case study.

The types of cases listed above do not exhaust the possible options; there are other lists in the literature with different types. Also, the types are not exclusive. A case study may well meet the criteria for several types. Perhaps the most important thought to take from reading the list is that one reason case studies are so popular in professional practice research is their versatility and flexibility. They can accommodate a wide variety of purposes and incorporate a wide range of data sources.

Doing Case Study Research

There are many formats for case study research and many of them are tied to the underlying paradigm that will guide the study. Critical theorists will do a case study differently than a positivist researcher, and an interpretivist will do one a bit differently than either critical theorists or positivists. One relatively general and flexible set of guidelines for doing a case study are described in Stake's (2005) chapter in the third edition of the *Handbook of Qualitative Research*.

When it comes to how you conduct a case study, Stake's (2005) advice is short and sweet, "Place your best intellect into the thick of what is going on" (p. 449). He provides more details, but this is not a bad summary because it emphasizes the fact that the researcher is the primary means of data analysis. The method of data analysis is reflection.

> In being ever-reflective, the researcher is committed to pondering the impressions, deliberating on reflections and records—but not necessarily following the conceptualizations of theorists, actors, or audience.... Local meanings are important, foreshadowed meanings are important and readers' consequential meanings are important. (pp. 449–450)

Often the data that is reflected upon is primarily observation, but it can include data from interviews, historical study, an analysis of artifacts, visual and structural information, and virtually any other form of data that seems relevant. Sometimes this data is coded in some way so that data relevant to particular issues or questions can be easily located. Or the researcher may take a more holistic approach to interpreting the data. In either case, the researcher will make multiple passes through the data, engage in reflection and re-reflection about the data, and keep in mind the need for validating the impressions and understandings that emerge from the case study. "Qualitative case study is characterized by researchers spending extended time on site, personally in contact with activities and operations of the case, reflecting, and revising descriptions and meanings of what is going on" (p. 450).

The Status of Case Study Research Today

For reasons mentioned earlier case studies are very popular in professional practice research. However, they are not always respected or accepted by traditional researchers who promote empirical and experimental methods as the gold standard for research in the social and human sciences. Doctoral students who do case study dissertations must sometimes deal with sharp questions about the value of case studies. It may be important to prepare yourself for such questions and also to include in your proposal and dissertation an extended discussion of your view of case study research, supported by references to relevant literature on this methodology. Resources such as Yin and Stake, which were discussed earlier, are helpful. We also recommend the work of a Belgian urban planner and theorist, Bent Flyvbjerg (2004). Flyvbjerg's (2001) book, *Making Social Science Matter: Why Social Inquiry Fails and How It Can Succeed Again,* is an extended statement of his view on why traditional social science research in the positivist tradition has not had a serious impact on society as well as his proposal about how to make social science research truly relevant and influential. This book, which has been widely debated, denounced, praised, and worshipped, is a very good source of information on the current debates about what social science research should, and should not, be. Another book, *Foundations of Qualitative Research* (Willis, 2007) may also be helpful in developing and supporting a perspective on why case study research is both worthwhile and valid as a method of professional practice scholarship. However, Flyvbjerg (2004) has written a paper that deals specifically with the status of case study research. He addresses the criticisms made by positivists and debunks a number of myths and "misunderstandings" about case study research. In his view, "conventional wisdom" about the case study method "if not directly wrong, is so oversimplified as to be grossly misleading" (p. 430). He wrote his paper to justify his heavy reliance on case studies and to refute the common, but inaccurate, criticisms of the method. He makes the point that case study methods are often criticized from a positivist perspective that assumes the only way to understand a particular instance or case is through the *theory-implications link*. That is, you must use a theoretical framework and the implications of that framework to analyze the specific case. If there is a match, the case supports the theory. Flyvbjerg rejected this line of argument and organized his discussion around five "misunderstandings." We recommend this paper if you need to justify the value of case study research.

Additional Resources on Case Study Research

In addition to the books and papers mentioned thus far there are many useful resources on case study methodology. The latest edition of Robert Yin's (2009) book, *Case Study Research: Design and Methods,* and Robert Stake's (1995) *The Art of Case Study Research,* are both good places to start your exploration. Another recent book, by Handcock and Algozzine (2006), was written specifically for novice researchers—*Doing Case Study Research: A Practical Guide for Beginning Researchers.* This book is both an introduction to case study research and a comprehensive guide to each step in a case study. For students doing dissertations, there is even a chapter on writing a proposal for a case study.

If you are considering a case study in education, Sharan Merriam's (1998) book deals specifically with case study methods in education. If a business related case study interests you, Hul and Hak's (2008) *Case Study Methodology in Business Research* is available. Although this book focuses primarily on using case studies to build and test theories, Chapters 10 and 11 are about using case studies in "practice-oriented research." Finally, Scholz and Tietje's (2002) book emphasizes the use of both quantitative and qualitative data in case studies and includes examples of case studies from several fields including neuropsychology, education, law, business, and environmental sciences.

Case study research is also the focus on several websites. One relatively comprehensive online guide to doing case studies is at Colorado State University. *Writing Guides: Case Studies* is at http://writing.colostate.edu/guides/research/casestudy/ com2b2.cfm. A briefer introduction to case study methods is a paper by Dan Bachor (2000) at http://www.aare.edu.au/00pap/bac00287.htm. In addition, a website at the University of British Columbia in Canada has a list of linked, online resources about different qualitative methods. There are many excellent ones on case study methods. The website is at http:// www.slais.ubc.ca/resources/research_methods/case.htm. Another site with links to papers on case study methods is at Southampton University in the United Kingdom (http://www.solent.ac.uk/library/subject/page210.stm). To get to the links for material on case study methods, click the *Electronic Resources for Information Research Methods* link and then click the drop down menu at the top of the page and select *2.3 Case Studies*. This site also has links for information on other qualitative methods.

SUMMARY

The traditional methods of qualitative research have been a mainstay of professional practice research for many years. In your professional field you will no doubt find examples of every type—ethnographic studies, interview research, studies incorporating historical methods, and case studies. Exploring how a particular method of qualitative research has been used in your own field should be one of your first steps in becoming familiar with any traditional qualitative method that interests you.

There are also a number of handbooks on qualitative methods that provide in-depth information on qualitative methods. The best known handbook, and one of the largest at 1,232 two-column pages of tiny type, is Denzin and Lincoln's (2005) *Handbook of Qualitative Research*, now in its third edition. This is not a book for the faint hearted. It is an intense and detailed exploration of many qualitative research methods as well as many different theoretical and conceptual frameworks for doing qualitative research. The book's 44 chapters were written by the world's leading experts on different qualitative methods. Those chapters cover everything from "Freeing Ourselves From Neocolonial Domination in Research: A Kaupapa Maori Approach to Creating Knowledge" to "Arts Based Inquiry: Performing Revolutionary Pedagogy." This is probably not the book to start your exploration of a qualitative method. However, once you have a good basic understanding of a qualitative method, chapters in the *Handbook* typically help you extend and deepen your understanding of that method.

CHAPTER 8

EMERGENT AND INNOVATIVE QUALITATIVE RESEARCH METHODS FOR PROFESSIONAL PRACTICE DISSERTATIONS

In the first two chapters on methods we followed the well-trodden pathways of traditional quantitative and qualitative research methods. In this third chapter on research methods for a professional practice dissertation we will turn off the main highways of methodology and introduce some of the emerging and innovative methods that are increasingly used by professional practice researchers. The chapter covers a number of qualitative approaches to research that are particularly suited to professional practice studies, including dissertation research. The following chapter, which is the last "methods" chapter, covers two additional families of research methods. One family which is covered in Chapter 9 is a group of methods that developed and were nurtured in the humanities but are now used in the social sciences, education, health care, and business to address problems and issues of practice. The other family is philosophical inquiry, a group of methods that is as old as recorded history, but ones that lend themselves to the study of certain types of contemporary professional practice problems.

Completing a Professional Practice Dissertation: A Guide for Doctoral Students and Faculty, pp. 217–237
Copyright © 2010 by Information Age Publishing

For some readers, part of the content of this chapter and the next will be very familiar because it has been incorporated into the core content of their discipline. However, exposure to this content is unpredictable. One doctoral program in educational leadership, for example, may emphasize research methods from the humanities, such as narrative inquiry, while students in another educational leadership doctoral program may complete the program without any familiarity with this method, or knowledge about how it can be used in applied educational leadership research. Similarly, one doctor of psychology, or doctor of nursing practice, program may cover a method like participatory action research in one or more courses (and require students to do projects using the method) while it is only mentioned in passing in another nearby program.

Lack of coverage of a particular method does not, however, mean that your doctoral faculty will not be open to working with you on a dissertation study that uses one of the research methods described in this chapter. Making choices about what content to cover in a doctoral program is always difficult because there is never enough time to include everything that should, or ought, to be covered. However, some faculty may have expertise in these methods already and others may be interested in collaborating with you on an exploration of both the topic you have selected for your dissertation and the research method.

All the methods introduced in this chapter have two features in common. First, they are all "emergent" rather than established methods. They thus have less of a history behind them, are less well defined and understood, and must often be justified carefully when submitting papers or reports to journals and agencies that do not have a history of considering studies based on these emergent methods. The second characteristic they have in common is that all of them are situated in the context of practice and all of them have as a primary goal the improvement of professional practice (though versions of some methods are also used in positivist ways to test theory and look for law-like generalizations).

Figure 8.1 is an overview of the five families and six specific methods that will be introduced in this chapter. The first and last family listed (professional practice knowledge and professional discourse) focus on the practitioner as a source of knowledge. The other three families include methods for identifying problems and developing solutions (action research), for studying potential improvements in practice (clinical research), and for designing resources that contribute to improved professional performance (design research).

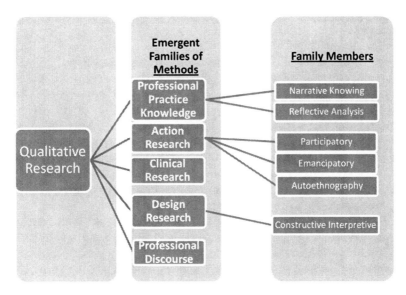

Figure 8.1. Emergent qualitative research methods of interest to professional practice dissertation students.

PROFESSIONAL PRACTICE KNOWLEDGE

In their book, *Practice Knowledge & Expertise in the Health Professions,* Joy Higgs and Angie Titchen (2001) lay out a framework for thinking about how to practice a profession that comes from *experience-in-practice.* Most of the health professions prepare students to enter the field through a combination of academic or classroom work and practical experience. In fact, most professions use one or more supervised practical experiences in their preservice preparation programs. Internships, practica, clerkships, residencies, studio experiences, student teaching, field experiences, and co-op experiences (aka cooperative education) are some of the names for this type of experience.

The type of knowledge developed through supervised practical experiences has been given many names. *Craft knowledge,* for example, is a popular term. Ruthven (2000) describes craft knowledge in the context of teaching as

> the professional knowledge which teachers bring to bear in their day-to-day classroom teaching. It is action-oriented knowledge, which is not generally made explicit by them; knowledge which they indeed find difficult to articulate, or which they may even be unaware of using. Through experimenting and problem solving in the course of teaching, and through re-presenting

their teaching and reflecting on it, teachers develop such craft knowledge. (para 4)

Higgs and Titchen (2001) use this term and suggest ways of enhancing craft knowledge in the health professions. *Reflection-on-practice, reflection-in-practice, reflective group supervision* of novice practitioners, and other forms of mentoring and collaborative exploration of practice are described and recommended. Reflective practice has also become a major model or metaphor for both teacher education and personal development in American education. The increasing emphasis on craft knowledge as opposed to scholarly knowledge in teacher education, and the use of reflection as a means of professional growth, is due in part to a shift in the ideas about what teaching and learning is.

Reflective approaches to professional practice are often contrasted with technical-rational approaches. The technical rational approach assumes that "good" professional practice involves following a set of rules derived from the available basic and applied research. Judging good practice is a matter of comparing what the rules derived from research say should be done with what the teacher actually does in the classroom (or a nurse does in the operating room, a physical therapist does in the clinic, and so on).

If you think of professional practice as a technical-rational process, there is little reason to seriously consider spending much time on research methods that try to capture the professional expertise of practitioners. That is because technical-rational views of professional practice assume good practice does not emerge directly from practice. Instead, it comes from the application of research findings to practice. On the other hand, if you consider professional practice to be a reflective process, there is every reason to capture and share the expertise of practitioners.

There are debates in the literature over whether or not craft knowledge can be distilled from conversations with practicing professionals and then distributed in some formal way to others. Kenneth Ruthven (2000) at Cambridge University in the United Kingdom thinks craft knowledge can be distilled. In fact, he proposes an approach to combining "scholarly" and "craft" knowledge that involves "eliciting and codifying craft knowledge [so] it can ... contribute to the development of scholarly knowledge" and "through the integration, tuning and restructuring of theoretical [e.g., scholarly] knowledge to the demands of practical situations and constraints" (p. 15).

Another term that is similar to the idea of craft knowledge is *tacit* knowledge. Imel (2003) defined tacit knowledge this way:

> In research studies from a variety of disciplines, tacit knowledge has been characterized as follows: personal, difficult to articulate fully, experience based, contextualized, job specific, held within, both known and unknown

to the holder, transferred through conversation and narrative, and capable of becoming explicit knowledge and vice versa…. It is an important component of the knowledge all workers have that allows them to perform their jobs.

Imel notes that there are also debates about whether tacit knowledge is just another form of knowledge that is yet to be extracted and distilled, or a distinct form that is likely to remain contextualized, difficult to articulate, and difficult to share. While it would be desirable to develop ways of making tacit and/or craft knowledge explicit and easily communicable, we think McInerney (2002) has a point when he asserts that it is more productive to put our energy into developing a "knowledge culture" where tacit knowledge is acquired informally and through dialog than to try and "extract" tacit knowledge and put it into artifacts such as reports or directives for distribution.

Creating and Disseminating Professional Practice Knowledge

If craft or tacit knowledge is important, and if it is difficult or impossible to codify or formalize, what is the best method of sharing it with other practitioners? In other words, what is the "method" for constructing and sharing professional practice knowledge. There are actually four common forms of professional practice knowledge in the literature today: (1) Guidelines and Standards Documents, (2) Narratives (narrative inquiry), (3) Reflective Analyses, and (4) Autoethnography.

Guideline and Standards Documents. Today there is an intensive push toward establishing "high standards" for everything from the knowledge gained in a high school American history course to the expertise of students graduating from doctor of nursing practice programs.

While standards and guidelines papers are popular in the literature, and many of them are helpful, we have not included them in Figure 8.1. We see them, not so much as emerging forms of qualitative professional practice knowledge, but as expressions of a more traditional approach in which authors offer readers "rules to follow." These rules may be based on the professional practice experience of one individual or small group, the collective wisdom of larger groups of both scholars and practitioners, or the implications of a particular theoretical position (e.g., distance education practiced from a constructivist perspective). Expressions of qualitative professional practice knowledge need to include enough context about where and how the knowledge developed to help readers make decisions about what they can take on board for their own situations. The general approach to communicating the knowledge also needs to be oriented less toward providing "the answers" and more toward contributing to the discussion of what seems important to consider when making professional decisions. The standards and guidelines approach does not do that very well. However, three other forms of qualitative inquiry seem particularly useful for expressing professional practice knowledge: narrative inquiry, reflective analysis, and autoethnography.

Narrative Inquiry. Narrative inquiry is storytelling. When used as a medium for communicating professional practice knowledge the storyteller embeds that knowledge in a rich description of the context in which the knowledge developed. In telling the story, the author may explicitly state the lessons learned or may leave at least some of the lessons implicit in the story but not extracted out. In either case, the way the story is told makes it clear that all the professional practice knowledge embedded in the story is subjective and contextual. We will explore narrative inquiry in more detail in the next chapter.

Reflective Analysis. Reflection as a means of personal and professional development has become very popular in education as well as many other professions. Much of the current popularity is due to the work of MIT professor Donald Schön who died in 1997. In the 1970s-1990s, he wrote many books on ways reflection can help us become better professionals, and his models and procedures are still some of the best understood and widely used. One of his early books was *Technology and Change: The New Heraclitus* (Schön, 1967). Heraclitus was the pre-Socratic philosopher from Ephesus who developed a systematic philosophy that proposed the essence of existence was not earth, wind, fire, or some other element. It was *change*. His most famous surviving quote is *"No man ever steps in the same river twice, for it is not the same river and he is not the same man."* In his book, Schön takes a similar position and proposes that we must accept and embrace change if we are to make progress. Many of Schön's later books (1995, 1990a, 1990b) deal with how reflection can revolutionize both professional practice and research to support and facilitate practice. Some groups have even developed technology-supported instructional resources to facilitate reflective practice. For example, a group at Harvard Medical School (McMahon, Monaghan, Falchuk, Gordon, & Alexander 2005) developed a set of simulators that present medical students with cases of ischemic heart failure and hypoxemic respiratory failure. Each of the three 90-minute cases were designed to encourage students to develop skills in comparative and reflective analysis. Another odd but interesting event related to the use of technology to support reflective practice was the granting of a U.S. patent in 2003 for a *Reflective Analysis System*, a computer program that supports the development of reflective practice skills on the part of practicing professionals (see http://www.patentstorm.us/patents/6626679.html for more information).

One element of the reflective model of practice proposed by Donald Schön is the use of reflections to communicate professional practice knowledge to others. For example, Wakkary (2005) conducted a reflective analysis of the how human-computer interface designers can deal with the complexities of the design process. Others have done reflective analyses of the way instructors at the Open University in the United Kingdom use distance education resources (Salmon, 2000) and of mathematics teacher education (Tzur, 2001). The journal *Reflective Practice*, which was established in 2000, is one of many sources of reflective practice articles on many aspects of education. There is also an online, open source journal that is freely available. The *Journal of Natural Inquiry and Reflective Practice* is available at http://www.und.nodak.edu/dept/ehd/journal/.

Papers about practice knowledge that use a reflective practice (also called "reflective inquiry") approach are accepted by professional practice journals in many fields and there are at least a hundred books and guides available on doing reflective inquiry in a wide range of professional disciplines. Many of the guides include suggestions about how to keep a written journal as part of reflective practice. These reflective journals are often used as the foundations for journal papers or dissertations based on a reflective analysis of practice. Reading some of the many examples of reflective analysis in the literature of your field is a good way to begin learning how to do this type of scholarship and to write a dissertation based on this approach.

If you do a dissertation based on reflective practice/reflective inquiry, there are three common approaches. One is to work with other professionals as they practice reflectively and write reflective journals. Your dissertation is then a distillation and analysis of the reflective work of the professionals you worked with. Clandinin and Connelly's (2000) book is both an excellent guide to how to do this work and a good example of the genre. The second approach to doing a reflective dissertation is to make yourself the reflective practitioner and to approach a problem or area of professional practice reflectively. In this approach your dissertation is an analysis and distillation of your own reflective journals. The Clandinin and Connelly book is also a very good resource for this approach but there are many others as well.

The third approach is probably the most common—to use reflective practice/reflective inquiry as one of the major sources of information in a dissertation organized around another method such as action research or narrative inquiry. These dissertations generally follow a format determined by the broader structure of a method such as participatory action research (PAR) and reflective journals become a source of data in the action research study. Rachel Eni Lawrenchuk's (2007) thesis is just such a study. She used PAR as the broad framework for her study of parental participation in a Head Start program for Cree and Ojibway children and she used reflection as a major component of the study.

Autoethnography. The third type of professional practice research method that lends itself to dissertation projects is autoethnography. It is similar to the second type of reflective inquiry research described above because the focus is on using ethnographic (observation) and reflective methods to analyze your own professional practice. Sarah Wall (2006), a doctoral student in sociology at the University of Alberta, described auto-ethnography as "an emerging qualitative research method that allows the author to write in a highly personalized style, drawing on his or her experience to extend understanding about a societal phenomenon" (Abstract section, para 1). We are considering autoethnography here in a more limited way—to explore issues of professional practice—but Wall's paper is a very good overview of the theoretical and conceptual foundations of auto-ethnogrpahy as well as a worthwhile introduction to how it is done.

If you would like to read a dissertation based on autoethnography, Laura Jewett's (2006) dissertation at Louisiana State University is a good example that is freely available. Dr. Jewett was a doctoral student in curriculum theory and she described the purpose of her dissertation this way:

> This dissertation, via autoethnography, couples experiences teaching multi-cultural education and learning to zydeco dance in order to explore semblances of intimacy across self and other; also, to consider the implications of such semblances in terms of thinking about curriculum and research. I use the term "semblance" to suggest that the intimacy at work in the embodied virtual worlds of zydeco, autoethnography, and curriculum can be a powerful as-ifness, or what Jerome Bruner ... might describe as a truth likeness. (p. vi)

That this is a dissertation outside the boundaries we have been accustomed to taking for granted is obvious even from the paragraph above. That it draws on the methods and ways of knowing that come from the humanities is obvious from the way Dr. Jewett wrote her dedication:

> His curriculum was sparse. Materials included a calculator, a tablet of typing paper, a blue mechanical pencil, a pack of Lucky Strikes, and one really rich problem. Growing up, I watched my mathematician father go about his business as a scholar. Now, as I trudge home from the university, weighted down like a pack mule with books and questions, I marvel at the curricular elegance of not even owning a brief case. My father was fond of telling people that the reason he became a mathematician was because one could do math anywhere: all you needed was dirt and a stick, and of course one really rich problem. My mother's curriculum is much rowdier and social. She is an

artist. In contemporary educational vernacular, her design is much more visibly hands on. When my mother wants to know, for example, how to anodize aluminum, re-stitch an oriental rug, or marry metals, she culls the registry of experts in her head, finds the person whose passion matches her interest, and puts herself in their way. Her ability to identify good teachers, place herself strategically inside their network of knowledge and live awhile is an organic lesson in ethnographic methods. I dedicate this dissertation to the memory of John W. Jewett, for all that he taught me, and to Conlee Jewett, for all that she continues to teach. (p. iii)

As Wall's (2006) paper indicates, doing autoethnographic research involves a critical rejection of theories of knowing that have dominated Western thinking for many centuries, and an acceptance of alternative theories that give more weight and more respect to the knowledge gained from thoughtful, reflective experience. Doing an autoethnographic dissertation calls for even more. It calls for a dissertation committee that is comfortable with, and supportive of, this emerging approach to scholarship. Fortunately, Dr. Jewett had two of the world's leading advocates of alternative ways of knowing, including autoethnography, and the theories that support it, on her dissertation committee—Dr. Bill Doll and Dr. William Pinar. If you decide to do an autoethnographic dissertation, make sure you have some strong and supportive committee members!

Two papers on autoethnography that are good introductions to the method and its use are Tracy Duckart's (2006) overview of this interesting form of scholarship and Roy Schwartzman's (2002) attack on the very narrow boundaries of accepted scholarship today He argues persuasively for using more methods from the humanities, including poetry. Autoethnographic work can be expressed in many forms, including poetry, short stories, and art. Other useful resources on autoethnography include Holman Jones' (2005) chapter in the *Handbook of Qualitative Research*. Another is the autoethnography entry in the online encyclopedia Wikkipedia (http://en.wikipedia.org/wiki/Autoethnography). Deborah Reed-Danahay's (1997) edited book, *Auto/ethnography: Rewriting the Self and the Social* is also very useful as is Swadener's (1999) paper on autoethnography in education.

PARTICIPATORY ACTION RESEARCH (PAR)

Some methods of working with and sharing professional practice knowledge tend to be focused inward—on the thoughts and cognitive processes of practitioners. That is true of narrative inquiry, reflective practice, and autoethnography. On the other hand, the focus of action research is more outward. *Action research* is a term that was coined in the late 1940s to describe systematic work in the field to solve a problem or answer an important question about professional practice. Kurt Lewin, the founder of social psychology, and one of the European Jewish intellectuals who came to America after the rise of Hitler in Germany, was concerned about authoritarianism and power relationships in a society. He developed the idea of action research as a way of improving professional practice that is more democratic than traditional research methods.

Lewin (1948) described his idea of action research this way:

> The research needed for social practice can best be characterized as research for social management or social engineering. It is a type of action-research, a comparative research on the conditions and effects of various forms of social action, and research leading to social action. Research that produces nothing but books will not suffice. (pp. 202-203)

Lewin wanted a research model that emphasized making an immediate difference in the real world. Action research would involve either selecting and implementing an action that would be studied to see if it made an important difference, or the study of a particular context or setting to develop knowledge that leads directly to action. Figure 8.2 summarizes the general model of action research proposed by Lewin.

Figure 8.2.   Kurt Lewin's plan for action research.

This is a recursive or iterative process in which a group (or an individual) goes through a process that begins with a general issue or problem. Then the group explores possible ways of addressing the problem or issue. This Reconnaissance phase may include many types of information gathering—from reviews of the relevant literature, to interviews, to brainstorming sessions, and much more. The third step, Planning, produces a plan for action that, hopefully, will address the problem or issue. That plan is implemented in the Action phase, and it is also evaluated. Usually, the action is not completely successful, and may even be a total failure. The next step is Revision of the Action Plan and then the cycle begins again. Action Research projects may go through many iterations of the basic cycle, but Figure 8.2 implies that the process within each cycle is linear. That is often not the case. Many of the activities in the action research cycle happen at the same time. You may, for example, be implementing and evaluating an action at the same time. Often, changes are made in the action while it is being implemented and evaluated. Thus, action research is more fluid and non-linear than Figure 8.2 implies. Figure 8.3 is an alternative representation of action research that emphasizes the iterative and nonlinear nature of the process.

Figure 8.3.   This representation emphasizes the nonlinear and recursive nature of action research.

Varieties of Action Research

Action research is an active and evolving approach to real world problems and there are many models to guide the action researcher. Many books and papers are available on this form of scholarship, but as you look at the literature on how to do action research it is important to know that different proponents begin with different theoretical foundations. The result is a set of models for action research that range from fairly authoritarian models where an expert basically tells practitioners what to do to solve a problem to collaborative models of action research that make practitioners full partners, and often the leaders, in the search for solutions to a problem of professional practice. We prefer open, collaborative models of action research and will therefore discuss in some detail one such model—participatory action research.

Participatory Action Research (PAR)

PAR involves the identification of a significant issue, the development of a collaborative group of stakeholders who are interested in exploring solutions or answers, and a period of careful study that often involves the development and implementation of potential solutions to a problem. PAR is typically a recursive process because a solution that is tried out often fails to achieve all that was hoped for it, and a new round of PAR begins with the development of a new solution (or the revision of an old one). Yoland Wadsworth (1998) has described how she sees PAR in relationship to traditional research.

> For me, participatory action research is not a different and separate matter from science at all, but constitutes a formulation of how I understand all science in the wake of the wave of thinking that is popularly being called the "new physics". This "new physics" or "new paradigm science" in the natural physical world seems to me to match a "new paradigm science" in the social world. I identify "participatory action research" not as an optional variant or specialist technique, but as one of the more inclusive descriptions of this new understanding of social science. (para 3)

While not everyone is as strong in their efforts to define all good research as participatory action research, Wadsworth's explanation of PAR is helpful:

> Essentially Participatory Action Research (PAR) is research which involves all relevant parties in actively examining together current action (which they experience as problematic) in order to change and improve it. They do this by critically reflecting on the historical, political, cultural, economic, geographic and other contexts which make sense of it.... Participatory action

research is not just research which is hoped will be followed by action. It is action which is researched, changed and re-researched, within the research process by participants. Nor is it simply an exotic variant of consultation. Instead, it aims to be active co-research, by and for those to be helped. Nor can it be used by one group of people to get another group of people to do what is thought best for them—whether that is to implement a central policy or an organisational or service change. Instead it tries to be a genuinely democratic or non-coercive process whereby those to be helped, determine the purposes and outcomes of their own inquiry. (What Participatory Action Research is—and is not! section, para 5)

Wadsorth's (1998) short paper is a good introduction to one method of PAR and it is available online at http://www.scu.edu.au/schools/gcm/ar/ari/p-ywadsworth98.html. While there are many versions of PAR, we think there are five relatively common characteristics:

- The focus is on improving a social situation.
- The general theme or focus is typically selected by the participating group as are solutions to implement, and conclusions about impact.
- Work occurs in the actual environment where the change is needed
- The process is participatory and involves the range of stakeholders who have an investment in a change for the better
- The process relies on reflection and is iterative.

For more information on PAR there are several books written to guide you through the process. Robin McTaggart (1997) is a PAR pioneer and his book, *Participatory Action Research: International Contexts and Consequences* is a good introduction. McTaggart wrote the first two chapters as introductions to PAR and the remaining chapters were written by practitioners in different countries around the world. An even more comprehensive introduction to action research, with an emphasis on PAR, is Peter Reason and Hilary Bradbury's (2001) *Handbook of Action Research.*

A number of other online and print resources on action research have already been mentioned. There are also several subscription journals on action research are also important sources of expertise and examples, including *Educational Action Research,* and *Action Research.* Online, open access journals include *Action Research International* (http://www.scu.edu.au/schools/gcm/ar/ari/arihome.html), *The Ontario Action Researcher* (http://www.nipissingu.ca/oar/), and *Action Research E-reports* (http://www2.fhs.usyd.edu.au/arow/arer/index.html).

We also recommend three very good online resources for action research. The Action Research site at Southern Cross University in Australia (http://www.scu.edu.au/schools/gcm/ar/) is a good place to start and a website at Goshen College has links to a large number of action research sites on the web (http://www.goshen.edu/soan/soan96p.html). Finally, a web resource at the University of Colorado Denver has many good links (http://carbon.cudenver.edu/Emryder/itc/act_res.html).

There are numerous examples of dissertations based on participatory action research. For example, Jane Henry's (2007) dissertation at the University of Tennessee—Knoxville used PAR to study women working in male-dominated professions. The dissertation

> tells the story of nine women who as media producer, engineer, scientist, minister, and/or college professor discovered a common journey and experience. It's not a story about "what should be" or "how it got that way," though some foundation is provided for these, but it is one of "what is" and "what we want to do about it now."
>
> PAR was an opportunity to reflect with other women about what it means to be a woman in each particular life and practice, from a position of gender complementarity/mutuality, reflecting together on how best to use relational skills toward effectiveness and an integration of public and private, thereby creating a Praxis of Womanhood. (Abstract section, para. 3

Other examples of dissertations based on PAR methodology have focused on parental involvement in literacy programs (Innes, 1999), and engaging marginalized students in their own education (Bland, 2006).

EMANCIPATORY RESEARCH

As noted earlier, methods that focus on professional practice knowledge tend to have an inward focus and action research tends to focus outward—on problems of professional practice. The third method we will discuss is emancipatory research and it has a different focus. Emancipatory approaches focus on social, economic, and historical relationships between groups and individuals. They are often based on critical or neo-Marxist theory and have the dual goals of (1) helping disenfranchised individuals and groups become *enlightened* about how the dominant groups control them and (2) helping disenfranchised and oppressed individuals and groups take more control of their own lives.

Emancipatory research (which is also called emancipatory action research (EAR) and even participatory action research) has additional broad goals, such as helping create a more democratic society that aims at social justice. Although EAR uses many of the same methods and approaches as other forms of action research, the foundational assumptions and framework is quite different. One of the best explanations of how critical theory can guide emancipatory research was written by Stephen Kemmis (2001) who is an Australian scholar and one of the founders of this form of research. He calls this approach "action research" but it is what we are calling emancipatory research. Kemmis considers what we call emancipatory research a form of action research, which is called *critical action research* or *emancipatory action research*.

> This form of action research aims not only at improving outcomes, and improving the self-understanding of practitioners, but also at assisting practitioners to arrive at a critique of their social or educational work and work settings. This kind of action research aims at intervening in the cultural, social and historical processes of everyday life to reconstruct not only the practice and the practitioner, but also the practice setting (or, one might say, the work, the worker, and the workplace). (p. 92)

Kemmis adds to traditional action research approaches the expectation that participants question the established goals and purposes of professional practice. Often this will lead to the conclusion that certain goals or purposes "may be limited or inappropriate given a wider view of the situation in which we live or work" (p. 92). This approach, which we are calling emancipatory research, is quite different in purpose and approach from two other forms of action research described by Kemmis, technical and practical (see Figure 8.4).

If you would like more information on the emancipatory paradigm and emancipatory action research one very helpful source is Kathryn Herr and Gary Anderson's (2005) book, *The Action Research Dissertation: A Guide for Students and Faculty.* This book covers all three approaches to action

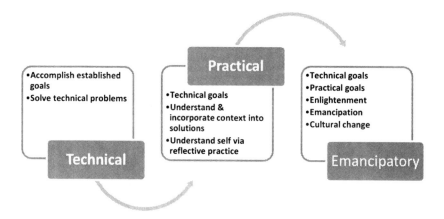

Figure 8.4.   The relationship between the three forms of action research. Bold text indicates the emphasis of each type of action research.

research (technical, practical, emancipatory) but it is particularly useful for graduate students interested in doing a dissertation based on either participatory action research or emancipatory research models. Another book that covers emancipatory as well as other forms of action research is *Action Research: Social Research for Social Change* (Greenwood & Levin, 2007). It combines an exploration of the foundational epistemologies of different forms of action research with detailed guidelines for how to do action research and how to write up action research reports.

CLINICAL RESEARCH

This form of scholarship is most often associated with medical research. It involves the study of real patients with real problems in the context of professional practice. Miller and Crabtree (2005) describe clinical research this way: "the clinical research space is created by focusing on the questions arising from the clinical experience and opens many possibilities for using the full range of qualitative data-gathering and analysis methods." The authors also suggest that clinical researchers have at least six different research styles available to them:

- experimental,
- survey,
- documentary-historical,
- qualitative field research,
- philosophical scholarship, and
- action/participatory research.

These methods should be used by clinical researchers to accomplish two major goals:

- "to deepen and contextualize the practical and ethical questions, concerns, and emerging understanding for healers and their patients and policymakers" and
- to "trouble the waters and seek change within the clinical research world itself" (p. 609).

As described by Miller and Crabtree (2005), clinical research has much in common with an approach called *design as research* (discussed in the next section) and with critical theory scholarship. However, clinical research has its own traditions, journals, and organizations. Miller and

Crabtree believe clinical research has unique demands that call for a diversity of methods.

> Research designs in clinical research inherently require multimethod thinking and critical multiplism, with the particular combinations of data-gathering and analysis/interpretation approaches being driven by the research question and the clinical context. There are infinite possibilities for integrating qualitative and quantitative methods, with the design being created for each study and the qualitative aspects often evolving as a study progresses in response to the emerging questions. Participatory research approaches, in particular, usually involve a more emergent design process. (p. 621)

The great majority of the methodology literature on clinical research assumes the work will be done in a health care setting. The comprehensive *Principles and Practice of Clinical Research* (Gallin & Obnibene, 2007) covers FDA rules about drugs and how to respond to media inquiries about a clinical trial. This book is also typical in that it emphasizes traditional quantitative, control-experimental group research methods. A welcome exception to this second characteristic is Crabtree and Miller's (1999) *Doing Qualitative Research*. Despite the nondescript and general title, the book covers many aspects of doing qualitative clinical research. Sections deal with topics such as data collection strategies, data interpretation strategies, and special methods for clinical research.

One of the best short introductions to qualitative clinical research is Miller and Crabtree's (2005) chapter in the *Handbook of Qualitative Research*. That chapter contrasts qualitative clinical research with traditional positivist models, and proposes a different model that emphasizes participatory inquiry (which leads to the "democratization of knowledge"), use of multimethods, crossdisciplinary collaboration, and "critical multiplism" which is a phrase that represents the broad skills of a generalist researcher. Those necessary skills include "negotiation, translation, theoretical pluralism, methodological pluralism, a community orientation, and comfort with and rootedness in clinical practices…. Critical multiplism assumes that multiple ways of knowing are necessary and that these options require critical thought and choice" (p. 619). A substantial part of the chapter is devoted to details of how to organize a qualitative or mixed clinical research study.

INSTRUCTIONAL DESIGN AS RESEARCH

Figure 8.1 at the beginning of the chapter includes instructional design (ID) as one of the emerging forms of qualitative research. And, like the other forms of research discussed in this section, ID has a unique focus. That focus is on the creation of learning or training materials. The list below is only a sampling of the types of materials that have been created using the instructional design process:

- A training program for officers of nuclear submarines on how to handle a crewmember experiencing a mental breakdown.
- A 2-day training program for emergency room staff on new methods of handling patients who have overdosed on legal and illegal drugs.
- A multimedia training package to teach adults to read.
- A digital video package to teach doctoral students to use qualitative research data collection strategies based on critical theory.
- Workshop materials, printed guides, and educational videos for nurses on proper care of different types of wounds.
- A corporate training package to prepare employees of a large retailer to use the new cash register software.
- An in-service-program for mental health professionals on short-term treatment of adolescents who are on the street.
- An educational program for young women on the dangers of cervical cancer and what they can do to reduce their risks.

These are only a few of the hundreds of thousands of resources that are created each year to support training and education efforts for students, the public, and professionals in many different fields. Instructional design is the process of creating such materials and ID is increasingly accepted as a suitable methodology for a dissertation. The result of an ID dissertation is not a new theory. Instead the result is new materials that can be used by trainers, teachers, staff developers, and groups responsible for professional development.

Thus far we have talked about ID as if it were one thing. There are actually several forms of ID, each based on a different theoretical framework and each proposing a somewhat different approach to the process of creating new educational resources. The three most common forms of ID are described below:

- **Traditional Instructional Design Models.** Several models of ID are all referred to as ADDIE models after the first letter of each of the five phases in the process (Analysis, Design, Development, Implementation, Evaluation). ID models in this group are also called instructional systems design (ISD) models because they are partially based on a version of systems theory. The most popular version of this type of ID model is the "Dick and Carey Model," which is named after the developers. The current edition of their book (Dick, Carey, & Carey, 2004) is an excellent guide to doing instructional design from this perspective. These models tend to be quite structured, to present design as a linear, step-by-step process, and to emphasize the importance of basing design decisions on the results of empirical research on how humans learn. These models also tend to be structured to produce traditional instructional materials.

- **The Design-Based Research (DBR) Models.** Traditional ID models such as Dick and Carey focus almost exclusively on the creation of useful instructional resources. DBR models, by way of contrast, try to do that too, and at the same time to advance both our basic or theoretical knowledge. The special issue of *Educational Researcher* (Vol. 32, No. 1, 2004) and the special issue of *Educational Technology* (Vol. 45, No. 1, 2005) contain articles that define what DBR is and what it attempts to do. The book edited by a group of scholars at the Universities of Twente and Utrecht in the Netherlands (Akker, Gravemeijer, McKenney, & Nieveen, (2006) is one of the first book-length treatments of DBR.

- **Constructivist-ID Models (C-ID).** ID models based on interpretive epistemologies and constructivist theories of teaching and learning have begun to appear in the last two decades (Cennamo, Abell, Chung, & Hugg, 1995; Cennamo, Abell, & Chung, 1996; Duffy & Cunningham, 1996; Lebow, 1993; Willis, 1995, 2000; Willis & Wright, 2000; Wilson, 1997). A book edited by one of the authors of this text (Willis, 2009) is a guide to doing constructivist ID research. It covers the foundational theories, describes a number of models for C-ID, and has four chapters of examples of how different groups have used C-ID models to create several forms of educational resources. C-ID models are more open, more flexible, and they tend to emphasize involvement of a range of participants and stakeholders in the ID process.

If creating a resource for your discipline or field would be an interesting dissertation topic for you, we recommend you explore some of the publications relevant to the type of ID model that appeals to you (traditional, DBR, or C-ID). Brandie Colon's dissertation at the University of Huston is one example of an ID dissertation. She used the R2D2 model of ID which is one of several C-ID models. An article based on the dissertation is available online (Colón, Taylor, & Willis, 2000).

PROFESSIONAL DISCOURSE

One of the often overlooked forms of scholarship and learning is the discussions professionals and scholars have in their day-to-day practice, at conferences and in workshops, through seminars, and in other settings where it is appropriate to "talk shop." While all of these are considered rather informal ways to disseminate ideas, they are, nevertheless, very important sources of understanding. It is important for every professional to join or develop one or more professional/scholarly communities that are a source of professional and scholarly knowledge and expertise. Often, practicing professionals become members of one or more local or regional groups as well as members of two or more national/international groups. Participation in communities where professional discourse is encouraged and expected is a critical component of professional growth as well as the beginning point for many innovations and changes in a field. At the end of her paper on changing how we think about teaching and learning, Jean McNiff (2002) commented that the changes she advocated in the relationship between scholarship and practice would be difficult to accomplish. To succeed:

> new discourses need to be established, and embedded within institutional and organizational life, discourses that celebrate the uncertainty of knowing and that award value to processes of personal and collective inquiry as practitioners engage, with their own inimitable originality of mind and creativity of spirit, in the creation of good lives in the interests of what Margalit (1996) calls "the decent society."
>
> And where do these new discourses begin? They begin as conversations among practitioners, among us, who have given thought to, and 'have a developed sense of what it is we are about. (Said, 2002, p. 364)

Can these forms of professional discourse become the focus of a dissertation? There are certainly a number of possibilities. Studies of the *process* of professional discourse use many different types of qualitative, and quantitative, research methods. There are also many studies that focus on how to improve professional discourse. These also use a variety of qualitative and quantitative research methods.

A third way of focusing on professional discourse is to document both the process and the outcome of professional discourse. When this is the focus, the methods discussed in the section on professional practice knowledge can be useful.

SUMMARY

This concludes our brief exploration of innovative qualitative research methods. Although these methods vary considerably in format, purpose, and means of implementation, all are well suited to addressing a range of questions related to professional practice. Selecting between them is a matter of matching the questions you want to ask with strong research methods for approaching those types of questions. This process is not a simple one, however, because advocates of different methods tend to see their preferred method as being appropriate for many types of questions, while proponents of other methods argue that their research methods are actually the best and alternatives have serious weaknesses. Rather than relying on what the experts say, we suggest you make yourself acquainted with potential research methods for your dissertation and carefully weigh the positives and negatives of each before making your decision. The choice involves issues at many levels, from theoretical and conceptual to professional and practical. For example, if the "best" method for your dissertation would involve a decade-long study, it may not be the "best" method from a practical standpoint. Similarly, using a method that would require you to spend several years being trained in that methodology is probably not a wise choice either. Finally, the decision about method should be one that is shared with your dissertation committee. The extreme of making your decision independently and insisting that the committee members go along with it even if they have grave doubts, is usually a mistake because you need the support and guidance of the committee to complete a strong dissertation. The other extreme, of simply adopting the method your chair or committee suggests, is also problematic because it does not provide you with the experience of carefully considering the options in a supportive environment where you can explore possibilities with the help of committee members. The choice of method should usually be one you and your chair/committee share and arrive at collaboratively.

CHAPTER 9

METHODS OF SCHOLARSHIP FROM THE HUMANITIES AND PHILOSOPHY

In this final chapter on potential research methods for a professional practice dissertation, we will explore two families of research methods that are not always covered in the research courses of professional practice doctoral programs. In fact, they are not always covered in the research Ph.D. programs of many fields outside the humanities and philosophy. In the Western intellectual tradition the Enlightenment was a watershed that put empiricism and the scientific method at the core of our search for new knowledge. And, during the eighteenth and nineteenth centuries, the status of the "scientific approach" was further enhanced by the astounding success of the natural sciences in making basic discoveries. The equally amazing success in converting those basic discoveries into technological advances that enhanced the capacity of humans to control their environment and produce goods and services that improved our living conditions, is yet another reason for the enduring appeal of the scientific method as *the* major source of new knowledge and understanding. When the social sciences such as sociology and psychology emerged in the nineteenth century there was considerable pressure to emulate the very successful natural sciences. Similarly, as professional practice fields like

Completing a Professional Practice Dissertation: A Guide for Doctoral Students and Faculty, pp. 239–260

social work and counseling psychology emerged in the nineteenth and twentieth centuries, it was natural for some to think of them as equivalent to technical fields like engineering but with a focus on humans instead of steam boilers or electrical systems. The term "social engineering" was even used to describe what these new professions, based on the "human sciences," did.

The result was a tendency for both the social sciences and the human services professions to form closer bonds with the natural sciences and applied fields like engineering than with the humanities and philosophy. For example, in the field of education, academic psychology was the major source of the theories, methods, and questions that guided much of twentieth century educational research. And for that same time period psychology itself was engaged in a deep and contentious debate about whether it was a "science" or not. American psychology generally took the position that psychology is a science in the same way that chemistry or physics is. Critics sometimes accuse American psychology of having a serious case of "physics envy" but the majority of American academic psychologists still believe that psychology is best considered a science with all the implications of that decision—including relying on research based on the scientific method that developed in the natural sciences.

The desire to be a science, and to be accepted by older and better established sciences, is one reason why psychology has been reluctant to embrace theories and methods from the humanities and philosophy. Many of the major historical figures of American psychology, for example, spent much of their professional lives trying to break the discipline away from philosophy. The first "psychological laboratory," for example, was created in a closet at Harvard University by William James who taught psychology in the philosophy department. James was one of the major theoretical figures in a uniquely American philosophy called pragmatism. Similarly, one of the founders of the progressive approach to educating children, and a contributor to the early psychology literature as well, was John Dewey, perhaps the most important American philosopher of the twentieth century. Many of the psychologists who came after James and Dewey were not as comfortable with close links to philosophy. That was particularly true of behaviorists.

When, beginning in the 1920s, the behaviorist movement in psychology successfully took over most of the major psychology departments in America, the discipline preferred and privileged the research theories and methods of the natural sciences over those of the humanities and philosophy. And, because many professional fields, including education and to a lesser extent social work and nursing, used psychology as a model for the types of research that were considered acceptable, as well as the proper questions to ask, the biases of American behavioral psychology tended to be transferred to research in education as well as other professional disciplines.

Throughout the twentieth century there were, of course, movements that attempted to link the social sciences and professional practice fields to both the humanities and philosophy, but they were generally limited to short bursts of popularity or to small specialty groups that were never able to shift the dominant trends in scholarship within the discipline or field of practice.

It was not until the last quarter of the twentieth century that the concepts and research methods of the humanities and philosophy began to have a major influence on professional fields like education, business, nursing, and others. Ironically, however, it was not because the traditional source of influence, American academic psychology, had changed. Dissatisfied with the traditional model of research that education had borrowed from psychology, more and more education researchers, both basic and applied, began to look for alternatives. The same was true in other professional fields such as nursing.

That search brought many to the humanities and philosophy. The result is a substantial increase in the use of research methods originally developed in the humanities and in philosophy. For example, nursing research has been a leader in the adoption of alternative research methods from the humanities.

With that introduction we will now turn to an examination of some of the more promising humanities research methods, followed by an exploration of methods developed in philosophy.

METHODS OF SCHOLARSHIP FROM THE HUMANITIES

Figure 9.1 presents the major forms of inquiry from the humanities that can be fruitfully applied in professional practice dissertations. All three families of humanities research methods—hermeneutic inquiry, narrative inquiry, and post-structuralist inquiry—are widely used in the social sciences today and are often adapted for use in studies that focus on professional practice. As you read this section you will note that, like the qualitative methods discussed in the previous chapter, each of the three families of humanities methods also tend to have a particular focus.

Hermeneutic Inquiry

Hermeneutic research involves a search for understanding, *verstehen* in German. For example, you might do a hermeneutic study of the patterns

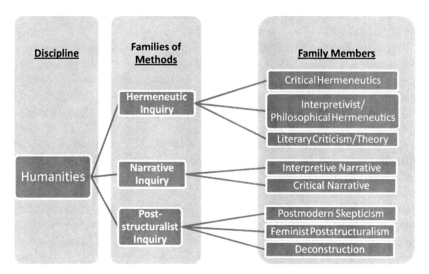

Figure 9.1.   Humanities methods of scholarship that may be useful in professional practice dissertation research.

of mental health services in the inner city of a large metropolitan area to develop an understanding of why the services are as they are. Contemporary hermeneutic methods developed from classical hermeneutics that were a way of studying sacred texts and the writings of the ancients. To understand an ancient text, it was not enough simply to translate the words of the text into a modern language. There were always questions about what the original author actually meant, and hermeneutics developed as a way of using context, historical knowledge, other writing from the era, contemporary commentaries and interpretations, and many other resources to develop a better understanding of a text. Today the term *text* means more than a document; it can mean a tradition, a set of policies or practices, or the social and cultural values of a particular group. Hermeneutic methods, for example, might be used to study a hospital manual for nurses that was used in 1849 in an effort to better understand the philosophy of treatment in 1849 and the roles of nurses within that framework.

Strands of Hermeneutic Research

There are three major strands of hermeneutic research methods that can be effectively used in professional practice research. The first is *critical hermeneutics* which is based on critical theory (also called neo-Marxist theory) but uses the methods of hermeneutics. Another is *philosophical hermeneutics* which is more compatible with interpretivist approaches that emphasize the subjective nature of knowing. The third approach, which is not always categorized as a hermeneutic method, is *literary criticism.*

Gadamer's (2004) *Truth and Method*, originally published in German in 1960, has become a classic statement of hermeneutic theory and practice:

> In the nineteenth century, the hermeneutics that was once merely ancillary to theology and philology was developed into a system and made the basis of all the human sciences. It wholly transcended its original pragmatic purpose of making it possible, or easier, to understand written texts. It is not only the written tradition that is estranged and in need of new and more vital assimilation; everything that is no longer immediately situated in a world—that is, all tradition, whether art or the other spiritual creations of the past: law, religion, philosophy, and so forth—is estranged from its original meaning and depends on the unlocking and mediating spirit that we, like the Greeks, name after Hermes: the messenger of the gods. It is to the rise of historical consciousness that hermeneutics owes its centrality within the human sciences. (p. 165)

Gadamer based his hermeneutics on the assertion that humans live in a world of sociocultural traditions that we have become alienated and estranged from and that hermeneutics helps us both understand ourselves and our traditions. In fact, we cannot understand ourselves without understanding our traditions and their history. Understanding is also mediated by language which means we must understand the critical roles of language in both constructing and carrying meaning. Gadamer emphasizes the importance of dialog and conversation in the search for understanding, and his discussions with students influenced his own writing. Gadamer often used art in his examples as he built a case for hermeneutics, and one of his major points was that *"all encounters with the language of art is an encounter with an unfinished event and is itself part of this event"* (p. 99). Gadamer used the German word, *dasein*, or "being in time" to emphasize that humans are understood within their place in the flow of history and experience.

Critical and Interpretive Hermeneutics

Two of the three forms of hermeneutics listed in Figure 9.1 refer to an underlying theory that guides the hermeneutic process—critical theory or interpretive theory. One way of thinking about the difference is Jürgen Habermas' (1971) division of human interests into three general categories. In his book *Erkenntnis und Interesse* (Knowledge and Human Interest) Habermas proposed that humans have technical interests, practical interests, and emancipatory interests (see Table 9.1)

**Table 9.1.   Habermas' Types of Human Interests and
the Associated Research Methods**

Human Interest	Research Method	Outcome
Technical	Empirical-Analytic (Positivist)	Instrumental Knowledge
Practical	Interpretive Hermeneutics	Practical Knowledge
Emancipatory	Critical Hermeneutics Emancipatory Research Methods	Emancipatory Knowledge and Procedures

Most of the content of Table 9.1 will be familiar to you from previous discussions. Habermas (1971), who helped build a critical social science, had two foundational commitments (McGee, 1998, p. 16):

> First, any acceptable social theory must contribute to the emancipation of both the thinker and humanity in general. The most prominent feature of society is its system of constraints, and the imperative duty of the social critic to minimize the effects of those constraints which cannot in reason be eliminated.... Second, any acceptable social theory must be amenable to bringing "empirical-analytical" thinking (social science) and "historic-hermeneutic" thinking (human science) "under one roof." This coexistence would not entail choosing causal analysis over interpretive understanding, or vice versa, "but of criticizing any pretension to universal and exclusive validity on the part of either, and of finding some sort of higher synthesis in which both have a place. (McCarthy, 1978, p. 140)

Habermas thus situates his perspective solidly within the paradigm of critical theory and interprets everything in ways that support his world-view. His hermeneutics is a *critical hermeneutics*. Gadamer (2004), on the other hand, has more faith in the possibility of understanding, including shared understanding between individuals and groups. That shared understanding can come from engaging in "conversations" or dialogs between people who begin the conversation with different views. Gadamer's approach is not dominated by the critical paradigm and it is not as skeptical as Habermas' view. Habermas, for example, believed that it was difficult, if not impossible, to engage in the types of dialog Gadamer advocated because the strongly held ideologies of the participants would cause them to artificially engage in dialog without actually buying into the purpose of free and open dialog. Thus, the possibility of such participants actually changing their beliefs was remote. Gadamer's approach is called *philosophical hermeneutics* but it could also be called *interpretive hermeneutics*.

If you are interested in doing a professional practice dissertation based on either interpretive or critical hermeneutics methods, two books that provide useful background information are Thomas Seebohm's (2004) *Hermeneutics: Method and Methodology,* and Yvonne Sherratt's (2005) *Continental Philosophy of Social Science.*

An example of an interpretive thesis in the area of city planning is Dianne Johnson's (2007) work at the University of Manitoba. Her focus was on how an urban renewal project in Winnipeg was implemented. Instead of doing a research study to discover The Truth about what happened when a plan to revitalize older neighborhoods was implemented, Dr. Johnson took an interpretive approach and gathered data on how members of different groups perceived the process of implementation. Her dissertation is a presentation of both the shared views of "what happened" as well as disparate views held by different groups. Judith Peters (2002) dissertation was also based on interpretivist theory. She studied the perceptions of participants in school-university partnerships about a support program designed to provide professional development opportunities for the region's teachers.

There are also a number of recent dissertations based on critical theory foundations. Some of these are traditional research studies that involve the collection and interpretation of data, but others are more conceptual and focus on philosophical and theoretical analysis. Robert Larson's (2009) dissertation in the area of educational leadership is an example of a dissertation that included both the collection and analysis of data (from an Internet survey) and philosophical/theoretical analysis. He looked at the question of equity in American education and used the theoretical and professional literature on leadership from a critical theory perspective to create a perspective on what it would mean to practice critical leadership and to support the values of equity and social justice. Larson then compared how practicing professionals in educational leadership view their own work with the critical leadership model he developed. He also used survey data gathered from participants in a statewide program to develop stronger education leaders as the background for developing what he described as a leadership for equity praxis model.

Literary Criticism and Literary Theory

Although not all literary criticism/theory is hermeneutic we have included it here because much of modern literary theory is a part of the hermeneutic tradition. Considering the origins of hermeneutics, it is, itself, a literary theory. Literary criticism, once primarily the domain of tweedy English professors and graduate students, has become a major force in the social sciences, and society in general. So much so, that Bressler (2007) began his book on literary criticism with this quote from Thomas McLaughlin:

Literary theory has permeated our thinking to the point that it has defined for our times how discourse about literature, as well as about culture in general, shall proceed. Literary theory has arrived, and no student of literature can afford not to come to terms with it. (p. 1)

Literary criticism, or literary theory, is not a single concept but a group of disparate approaches that try to tell us how to approach the interpretation and understanding of written, and spoken, communication. The target may be a speech, novel, short story, or an entire genre such as British Victorian novels. The target may also be the policy manuals of a corporation, the curriculum of a school district, the professional literature on a particular issue or topic, or the journal papers on an issue of practice such as ethics and the treatment of the poor. One of the most useful sources of introductory information on the various forms of literary criticism is Bressler's (2007) book. It provides a history of literary criticism but concentrates on the major threads of modern literary criticism in the West.

If you received a relatively traditional undergraduate education and completed a master's degree in a professional practice field, the jargon and concepts that populate the literary criticism literature may take some effort to master. Deconstruction, modernism, postmodernism, feminist theory, structuralism, poststructuralism, discourse analysis, and textual analysis are but a few of the terms that will need to be understood and put in context.

For much of the twentieth century the methods of literary criticism were used primarily in the humanities. However, as the social sciences began to question their foundations in the last half the twentieth century, social scientists began to look for ways of addressing questions such as the role of language in professional discourse, the subtle and not-so-subtle ways that biases and perspectives are communicated, and how language is used to empower some groups and oppress others. The rising doubt about certainties in the social sciences led to a new openness about research methods, such as literary criticism, that come from the humanities. As Ekegren (1999) put it:

In recent years, the problem of textuality and the importance of language has won recognition among certain social scientists. Textuality, then, pertaining to our possibility of gaining access to what is and what has been going on in the social realm....

With a few noteworthy exceptions, however, the situation in the social sciences is that the discussion on the relation between language, text, and the understanding of its texts is most conspicuous by its absence.

As to the understanding of the workings of language and text, there seems to be mainly two fields to turn to, literary theory and philosophy, and of course, the borderland where the two meet. (p. 2)

Ekegren's book is one place to start exploring the application of literary theory methods to questions that are important to social scientists and professional practitioners in the human services. Two books that focus specifically on research in the social sciences is Norm Faircloth's (2003) *Analysing Discourse: Textual Analysis for Social Research* and the edited book, *Discourse Analysis and Applications* (Bloom, Obler, De Santi, & Enrlich, 1994).

To read examples of this type of research in the social sciences see issues of three relatively new journals—*Discourse Process, Journal of Narrative and Life History,* and *Text.*

NARRATIVE INQUIRY

We discussed narrative inquiry in the previous chapter and will explore it in more detail here because it is one of the major methods from the humanities that is widely used today in the social sciences and in professional practice research.

Narrative inquiry is the second family of humanities scholarship. Narrative, or storytelling, is a form of expression in the humanities, with the short story and the novel being the most familiar forms of narrative. However, narrative is not simply a literary form:

We make narratives many times a day, every day of our lives. And we start doing it almost from the moment we begin putting words together. As soon as we follow a subject with a verb, there is a good chance we are engaged in narrative discourse. "I fell down," the child cries, and in the process tells her mother a little narrative, just as I have told in this still unfinished sentence a different, somewhat longer narrative that includes the action of the child's telling ("'I fell down,'" the child cries"). (Abbot, 2002, p. 1)

Many scholars believe narrative, telling stories, is the most fundamental way of communicating knowledge in human societies. That is illustrated in the ancient origins of the word. It is derived from the Sanskrit word *gna* that means *know* (p. 11). Narrative comes in many forms—from novels, anecdotes, and epics to films, plays, poems, and songs. Of course, not all poems or songs are narratives but many are. The country-western singer, Marty Robins, for example, was a master of narrative songs. His classic, *El Paso,* tells the story of a cowboy's love for Felina who dances in a cantina.

But narrative is not simply entertainment. In education, a novel written by Jean Jacques Rousseau in 1762, *Emile*, detailed how he would educate a child from infancy to adulthood. It is still in print and still read today because it expresses a theory of education that is advocated by some contemporary educational theorists. It begins with the sentence, "God makes all things good; man meddles with them and they become evil." The sentence sums up Rousseau's idea that eighteenth century European societies were corrupting the natural, inborn goodness of the citizenry, and the book lays out a plan for how to combat the undesirable effects of *civilization*. More recently the novel form has been used to communicate on socially relevant topics. Bebe Moore Campbell's (1995) novel, *Your Blues Ain't Like Mine*, is a good example. It is fiction based on the murder of Emmett Till, a young Black man from Chicago who was murdered in Mississippi while visiting his grandparents.

While the natural sciences (and the social sciences) have generally rejected the novel as a source of "knowledge" in the way an empirical study is a source of knowledge, several forms of postmodern thought have elevated narrative to a level equal to, or even superior to, other traditionally accepted forms of knowledge. Some theories of literature argue that narrative gives us a way of making sense of our lives that many other forms of knowledge do not. Because we are in the middle of living our lives, it is difficult for us to stand outside that life in order to understand it better. Stories are one way of "stepping outside" ourselves because we can identify with the characters and situations in the stories.

When we do that we begin to see ourselves through the narrative. Stories or narratives have been a way of communicating history and culture, and a way of understanding ourselves and the world we live in at least since Homer's *Odyssey* and the *Iliad*. However, the story fell on hard times when modernism severely restricted our "acceptable" sources of knowledge and understanding. Modernism privileged more objective, structured, and "scientific" sources of knowledge and it often relegated to the garbage bin of epistemology very personal and subjective sources of knowledge such as stories.

At the end of the twentieth century the social sciences and a number of professional fields became interested in the use of narrative as both a form of inquiry and a form of communicating the results of scholarly study to others. There is a growing literature of narrative scholarship that deals with a wide range of professional practice topics, and reading some of that literature is one of the best ways to learn to do narrative inquiry. That is because there is no hard and fast set of rules on how to do narrative inquiry. For every rule you could make, someone else could point to examples of very successful narrative studies that violate that particular rule. As Clandinin and Connelly (2000) put it in their book on narrative inquiry, "Our approach is not so much to tell you what narrative inquiry is by defining it but rather to show you what it is by creating a definition contextually by recounting what narrative inquirers do" (p. xiii).

While showing is better than telling when it comes to teaching about narrative inquiry, there are some important theoretical foundations. For example, Iran-Nejad, McKeachie, and Berliner (1990) describe two approaches to scholarship in education. One is *simplification by isolation*, which is a foundation of positivist research based on the scientific method. You keep everything constant except the one variable you want to study. Iran-Nejad, McKeachie, and Berliner argue that this has not worked. An alternative is scholarship based on *simplification by integration*. That is, instead of removing what we are interested in studying from the natural environment where it exists, we should acknowledge that removing it breaks the critical connections it has with other aspects of that context. Removing it changes its nature and destroys the possibility of knowing it in the rich and multifaceted way that will be most useful. Work in the natural environment allows us to maintain those connections and to understand them. Narrative inquiry is one of the major ways of doing the scholarship of *simplification by integration*.

Another foundation of narrative inquiry is the work of psychologist Donald Polkinghorne. In his book, *Narrative Knowing and the Human Sciences* (1988), Polkinghorne justifies narrative inquiry this way:

> Narrative is the fundamental scheme for linking individual human actions and events into interrelated aspects of an understandable composite. For example, the action of a narrative scheme joins the two separate events "the father died" and "the son cried" into a single episode, "the son cried when his father died." Seeing the events as connected increases our understanding of them both—the son cares for his father, and the father's death pains the son. Narrative displays the significance that events have for one another. (p. 13)

Narrative as Method

While we have used examples of narrative from literature, the fictional novel form is not often used in professional practice dissertation research. More often narrative scholarship is presented to readers in other forms— a case study, biography, autobiography, narrative ethnography based on observations in the field, or narrative papers based on the stories told by several informants. It is somewhat confusing to say that the result of narrative inquiry is narrative but it is nevertheless true. Narrative is both the name of a method of scholarship and the name of the resulting study. "Narrative inquiry entails a reconstruction of a person's experience in relation to others and to a social milieu" (Clandinin & Connelly, 2000, p. 39).

There are two very active communities of narrative research today. We will call them interpretive narrative inquiry (INI) and critical narrative inquiry (CNI) or counternarrative inquiry. Counternarrative is a term used to indicate people who write narratives are often trying to overcome and replace a more dominant narrative that defines them in ways they do not accept. These dominant narratives are sometimes called metanarratives because they exert control over members of a particular community of society. For example, in a culture with a strong metanarrative of male dominance and privilege, that metanarrative will influence not only the attitudes of men toward women but of women toward themselves and their relationships to men. A counternarrative would be a story told to overturn the metanarrative of male dominance.

There is no generally agreed upon term for these two families of narrative scholarship but we will use INI and CNI to distinguish them in this discussion. Interpretive narrative inquiry or INI is based on a foundation of interpretive theory that emphasizes the importance of the context and multiple perspectives in the search for meaning. Knowledge and knowing is local, relativistic, and social. One of the best introductions to this form of narrative scholarship is Clandenin and Connelly's (2000) book, *Narrative Inquiry: Experience and Story in Qualitative Research*.

CNI or counternarrative, is based on critical theory, especially standpoint theories in the critical tradition such as feminist inquiry. One of the best introductions to counternarrative in educational scholarship is Joy Ritchie and David Wilson's (2000) book, *Teacher Narrative as Critical Inquiry: Rewriting the Script*.

The two books both introduce narrative inquiry, both make heavy use of the work of the authors' students in colleges of education, and both believe narrative inquiry is a powerful way of both developing knowledge and of communicating it to others. There are, however, a great many differences in the suggestions and guidelines these two books offer because they are based on different theoretical foundations. If you would like to read dissertations that use narrative inquiry as a research method and/or as a way of communicating you findings, many new ones are published each year. An example is Anne Fry's (2002) dissertation titled, *Understanding Attempted Suicide in Young Women from Non-English Speaking Backgrounds: A Hermeneutic and Narrative Inquiry*. Dr. Fry interviewed women who had attempted suicide and used that data to develop a better understanding of their lives and their decisions. As she put it,

> Interpretation was predicated on the belief that life stories are statements about self-identity, and represent coming into being through the interaction

of coherence (the ability to establish connections between events, unifying themes, frames of reference and goal states), continuity (a longitudinal and sequential perspective on life) and connectedness (intrapersonal, interpersonal and transpersonal relationships). The paradox is that being unable to overcome the uncertainties of incoherence, discontinuity and problematic connectedness, participants were predisposed to act against self as a means of asserting agency. This understanding of attempted suicide represents a hermeneutic narrative reconceptualisation of the phenomenon, which places it outside discourses that sanction the language of psychopathology and provides a basis for developing alternative nursing theory and informing education and practice. (Description section, para 1)

Dr. Fry's work was based on the life stories or narratives of a group of women who made a decision to commit suicide. Dr. Fry stood "outside" that group and attempted to understand their experience. Another approach to hermeneutic and narrative research involves focusing on your own experiences and reflections in a particular situation. Margaret Duncan's (2000) dissertation is such a study. She used her own experiences and reflections about her work as an instructional designer involved in the creation of hypermedia multimedia materials. She used her experience as the foundation for proposing some guiding principles for the design of hypermedia/multimedia educational materials. An article based on her dissertation is available at http://www.ualberta.ca/~iiqm/backissues/3_4/html/duncan.html.

Poststructuralist Scholarship

To understand poststructuralism, the third form of scholarship borrowed from the humanities, you must first understand structuralism. Structuralism is one of the original frameworks for doing social science research when the different disciplines of social science were established in the nineteenth century. It is a search for the hidden but core structures of what you are studying. For example, the periodic table is the result of structuralist research in chemistry because that was an effort to define all the basic elements that make up the physical world and to show how they relate to each other in terms of several basic features such as atomic weight and density. When applied to humans or their behavior, the result of structuralist research is an attempt to define the "elements" of a phenomenon. For example, Freud was a structuralist when he divided the human mind into Id, Ego, and Superego. Piaget was a structuralist when he defined the cognitive stages through which children progress, and Skinner was a structuralist when he defined the two ways that humans learn—operant and classical.

Structuralists have focused on all sorts of human characteristics and the effort is always focused on finding universal knowledge about them. Piaget, for example, thought his cognitive stages were universal—all children go through them. Freud did not think the division of the mind into conscious and unconscious, or Id, Ego, and Superego, applied only to his patients in Vienna; they were universal categories. Similarly, some researchers looking for the "basic" or primary emotions from which all other emotions are constructed concluded there were four: fear, grief, love, and rage.

The number of the basic emotions illustrates a problem that eventually led many to abandon structuralism—the inability to reach a consensus on what is universal. While William James named four basic emotions—fear, grief, love, and rage—other scholars concluded there were fewer (pain and pleasure—Mowrer) or more (desire, happiness, interest, surprise, wonder, sorrow—Frijda). There is still no consensus on the question of how many basic or primary emotions there are.

In the humanities structuralists devoted themselves to discovering universals such as the ideal framework for a novel, the universal characteristics of poetry, and the 8 (or 10 or 5) story plots that are the foundation for all novels. Structuralism lost ground in the humanities because scholars began to doubt the universality of the conclusions pronounced by structuralists. The result was poststructuralism, which is still active today in both the humanities and the social sciences.

Poststructuralism is a rejection of the structuralist goal of finding universals—such as the number and names of the primary human emotions. Poststructuralists argue that the search for universals may be unworthy because experience and context may play an important role in things like the range of emotions a human may experience. There may be no universal set of "human primary emotions" for us to discover. Poststructuralists have not, however, given up the search for structure in human thinking, human behavior, social behavior, or cultural patterns. They continue to look for structures but they do not assume that the structures they find are universal. Poststructuralists present their findings as situated and contextual information. Another study, in a different context, might unearth a different structure.

Structuralists and poststructuralists both try to make public and visible a hidden structure. The difference is that structuralists look for universals while poststructuralists doubt there are universal structures. They look for "local" structures that are influenced by context, history, social norms, customs, and anything else.

In professional practice research poststructuralism often provides a framework for considering a question, but it does not necessarily provide a particular methodology. Elizabeth Henneman's (2008) paper titled

"Nurse-Physician Collaboration: A Poststructuralist View" is one good example of the use of poststructuralism as a guiding framework for professional practice scholarship. The relationship between nurses and physicians was traditionally defined as an unequal one in which the nurse is subservient to both the needs and the professional decisions of the physician. Henneman uses the poststructuralist theories of Michel Foucault to analyze traditional views of the nurse-physician relationship and to critique the limitations and restrictions those traditional views place on the way a nurse can participate professionally in health care. She uses poststructuralism to show that the traditional, physician-dominant roles are not universal and she proposes they are not conducive to quality health care.

Henneman's (2008) analysis is typically poststructuralist. She identifies a structure that is so deeply embedded in the culture of American health care that many take it as universal and correct. She attacks that structuralist perspective and proposes instead that the various forms of this traditional relationship are not universal but due to history, context, and power. In the last part of her paper she proposes an alternative structure for the nurse-physician relationship that is based on a collaborative model rather than a top-down, authoritarian model.

Poststructuralists often look for established cultural values, rules, and expectations that are treated as universals but are not. One of the most damaging such "universals in Western has to do with a woman's body image. In her book, *The Thin Woman*, Helen Masson (1998) used poststructuralist theory to analyze the cultural and social foundation for anorexia nervosa. Here is how Masson described her book:

> This book is about anorexia nervosa. It is about the distress that many girls and women in contemporary Western society experience around eating and not eating, around losing and gaining weight, being fat or thin, around being a woman. But this book is also about questioning the ways we currently understand these "anorexic" behaviours and experiences. It is about questioning the socially dominant 'mainstream' bodies of knowledge about 'anorexia' and about exploring new ways in which to theorize and research women's 'anorexic' practices and experiences. (p. 1)

Masson collected some data through a series of interviews with women who diagnosed themselves as having anorexia nervosa but her book is an example of how many different methods—from literary criticism to philosophical and theoretical inquiry—can be combined to address a topic. She first uncovers and makes public the unspoken but nevertheless powerful standards and expectations that are imposed on women in Western societies. She then proposes that illnesses like anorexia nervosa are not the result of psychologically weak or vulnerable women, but are instead the result of unreasonable and insidious cultural and social expectations. She uses several theories, including poststructuralism to accomplish this, and she finishes her work by developing a new theory to guide both professionals who work with women facing these problems and to push society toward a more enlightened approach. This too is guided by poststructuralist theory.

The scholarship of both Helen Masson and Elizabeth Henneman illustrate how poststructuralist theory can be used to guide professional practice research when the methodology used is drawn from a number of different fields. There is, however, one particular research methodology that is closely associated with poststructuralist theory. That is deconstruction. Deconstruction is a form of literary criticism that attempts to show that a text, broadly defined, contains within it not one clear message but many different messages, some of them contradictory to the main message the author may have intended. Deconstruction has the skeptical characteristic of postmodernism that raises doubt about the truth value of any type of proposed structure or pattern that purports to explain or define the basic nature of cultural or social life.

One example of the use of deconstruction in professional practice research is a study by Griffiths (2004) that was published in the *International Journal of Nursing Studies*. Griffiths used deconstruction to analyze two books, both of which were about "evidence-based practice," an approach to professional practice that is based on a technical-rational model of practice. It defines good practice as following the implications of empirical research. One text Griffiths deconstructed was itself a deconstruction of evidence-based practice while the other was a critique of the "relativistic" approaches to health care that poststructuralism and other postmodern theories represent. Griffiths' conclusions, based on a deconstruction of both texts, was not a total defense of either text. It was, instead, an effort to suggest ways of thinking about evidence-based practice in health care.

A third poststructuralist approach, poststructuralist feminist theory, involves applying the skeptical values of postmodernism and the rejection of universal frameworks of structuralism to issues specifically related to the lives of women. As McMahon put it:

> The post-structuralist feminist group denies any possibility of defining "woman" at all. Any attempt at definition (whether it comes from a misogynist male, a cultural feminist, or anyone really) is impossible without, according to post-structuralist thinking, reinvoking "mechanisms of oppressive power." For post-struturalist theorists, the idea of a subject being some basic anything is dependent on prevailing discourses that construct us creatures this way or that way, even to the point of constructing us in such a way as to have us believe we are in control—that (for many today "infamous") autono-

mous, coherent subject that is the product (construct) of humanist discourses. (para 1, item two)

Thus, when postmodern skepticism is applied to women's studies to combat efforts to define in any universal way what it is to be woman, that is feminist poststructuralism.

This concludes the section on research methods from the humanities. The final section of this chapter introduces methods suitable for professional practice dissertations that come from philosophy.

MODES OF PHILOSOPHICAL INQUIRY

Figure 9.2 illustrates the options when it comes to methods of dealing with philosophical topics, including those related to theory. Before looking at particular methods, however, it might, be appropriate at this point to discuss the differences between the questions that philosophical inquiry, theoretical scholarship, and rhetorical methods address. We suggest that philosophical inquiry addresses "foundational" questions. These are questions that must be answered, at least tentatively, before other questions can even be asked, much less answered.

For example, suppose you have decided that all this talk about hermeneutics, *verstehen*, and literary criticism is a crock. The Right answer to

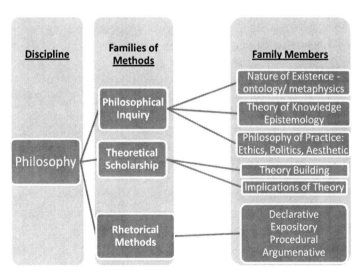

Figure 9.2.   Methods of philosophical inquiry that lend themselves to use in professional practice dissertations.

how you do good professional practice research is the scientific method. In stating that position about what good professional practice research is, you would be taking a positivist or postpositivist position on both what we *can* know (metaphysics) and *how* we can know it (epistemology). These questions and the answers you give are aspects of philosophy. If the adoption of the positivist scientific method is to make any sense whatever, it *must* be based on certain answers to questions that are at their core, philosophical. If the questions you want to address in your dissertation are philosophical, then philosophical inquiry may be an appropriate method for exploring them.

In contrast to philosophical inquiry that focuses on foundational or core questions, theoretical scholarship tends to focus on the intellectual space between philosophy and practice. For example, in psychology, a therapist's methods of doing counseling may be guided by the particular theoretical framework he or she has adopted. Many theories have been developed to guide the practice of psychotherapy and counseling: psychoanalytic, Adlerian, Jungian, client-centered, humanistic, existential, behavioral, cognitive, and many others. Two therapists who base their professional work on different theories may approach the same case quite differently. The same is true of virtually every professional practitioner—from actor, architect, and astrophysicist to teacher, theologian, and writer. There are many theories competing for the professional's allegiance and the way you practice your profession depends in part on the theory you adopt.

When theory is the focus of a dissertation the most common approach is to conduct an experiment or to use another form of traditional research to "test" whether the implications of the theory are supported when those implications are put into practice. The ways this is done were covered in Chapter 6. Here the emphasis is on the construction or reconstruction of theory and the marshalling of reasons why the theoretical perspective you propose is worthy of consideration.

In the social sciences, theoretical papers are more common than philosophical papers but the formats of philosophical and theoretical papers are often very similar. A philosophical/theoretical paper will generally:

- Focus on one major issue or a group of related issues.
- Lay out the position being proposed or defended and distinguish it from actual or possible alternatives.
- Marshall the evidence for the favored position. The "evidence" can take many forms—from other philosophical and/or theoretical papers/books, from an analysis of the logic behind the position, from an analysis of historical cases that seem to support the posi-

tion, from the opinions of people and organizations trusted by the readers, and so on.

- Address the existing and anticipated criticisms. Any important positions will be criticized and it is important to address as many of the major ones as possible so that readers, when faced with them, will already understand their meaning and how proponents of your position deal with them.

- Present any specious arguments in favor of your position and explain why they cannot be used to support the position, or actually detract from its appeal.

- Make sure readers understand the weaknesses of the alternative positions.

- Be sure to acknowledge weaknesses in the favored position as well and explain why readers should still favor it.

- Refine your favored position and distinguish it from similar but different positions if that is important. Point out why the position you propose is better than the close alternatives.

- Explain the implications of the position for the targeted readers. What difference will your favored position make in their professional lives if they accept your viewpoint? What will be the "costs" to them if they do?

The points above are relatively abstract but if you use them to analyze several papers from your field that deal with philosophical or theoretical questions, you can see how they are applied in practice. Theoretical papers may be quite broad, proposing or analyzing large "meta-theories" such as postmodernism or positivism. They may also focus on a mid-range theory with limited scope, such as the theories of psychotherapy and counseling mentioned earlier. The majority of theoretical papers are even more narrowly focused on mini-theories that seek to explain a particular phenomenon such as the achievement gap between majority and minority students or the relationship between crime rate and economic indicators. Regardless of the level of the theory you are dealing with, the elements of a philosophical/theoretical paper listed above will typically be required.

Although philosophical and theoretical dissertations are not common in professional practice doctoral programs, they do appeal to some students and some programs encourage them. An example is Matthew McDonald's (2005) dissertation on epiphanies—sudden and profound flashes of insight or understanding that can be life changing. Dr. McDonald used existential philosophy as a foundation for his dissertation and used the methods of philosophical inquiry and narrative inquiry to develop a better understanding of the epiphanies experienced by the participants he interviewed.

How Do We "Do" Philosophical Inquiry and Theoretical Scholarship?

Doing a philosophical or theoretical dissertation typically requires you to be familiar with three levels of knowledge: philosophical, theoretical, and professional. If you are writing a philosophical dissertation, it will be important to understand the implications of the philosophical position for theory and professional practice. And, if you are writing a theory dissertation on professional practice, the practices you will discuss will be based on supporting theories and the philosophical positions that are the foundation for those theories. You will find it difficult to write an influential dissertation without understanding the three levels (philosophical, theoretical and professional) and how they interact. Therefore, theory and philosophy call for considerable preparation before you start writing, and may call for much more library and online research before you are finished. In fact, as you track down important books and articles relevant to your topic, you are very likely to find that your focus is changing and that your viewpoint may also change. Writing a theoretical or philosophical dissertation is very much a learning process as well as a process of communicating. With that in mind, it is important to plan on doing several revisions of the dissertation and to be prepared to make drastic changes as you, and your thinking, progress. Another important aspect of writing this sort of dissertation is getting feedback from people who both support and disagree with your position. This can be very difficult to do – people with the necessary expertise are often busy and do not have free time. However, your dissertation committee has committed to do just that and the quality of your dissertation will very likely be increased significantly by careful and thoughtful critiques from both supporters and opponents. You will gain useful information from both.

A relatively straightforward philosophical dissertation on a problem of professional practice is the study by Julian Cross (2000) titled "*Return to Reality: A Causal Realist Approach to Re-construction in Science Teaching.*" In this dissertation Cross takes a stand that we should adopt the philosophical position of causal reality as a foundation for thinking about teaching science. Much of the dissertation involves an exploration of causal realism and its implications for science education.

Julian Cross' (2000) dissertation takes a broad perspective both in terms of the type of philosophy proposed and the focus—science education. In her thesis, Kyung Lee (1995) was more focused in terms of the theory being analyzed and the context in which it was applied. Dr. Lee's dissertation was an analysis of the ethical policy of "Do Not Resuscitate" as practiced by nurses and physicians on acute medical-surgical wards. Her dissertation is an exploration of the ethical dilemmas involved in implementing this policy as well as an examination of the philosophical underpinnings of one theory of human caring that is often used to support the policy.

WHAT ABOUT RHETORICAL INQUIRY?

Rhetorical inquiry is the third form of philosophical inquiry in Figure 9.2 at the beginning of this section. By the Middle Ages, rhetorical skills—the skills needed to persuade others—were the focus of a university education. The oral exam for the doctorate was not a setting where students presented new data and proposed new theories or treatment methods. Instead, they were public events where students could demonstrate their skills at debate and persuasive argument. In an era when books were very expensive, the emphasis was on speaking skills, but today the ability to convince others that your position on an issue is the correct one calls for both written and speaking skills. The literature of most fields of professional practice is filled with documents that are primarily rhetorical efforts to win you over to a particular position. And, people who both have something to say, and can say it well, are popular speakers at conferences, institutes, and workshops. However, while rhetorical skills are important in professional practice there are few dissertations based primarily on rhetoric. Dissertations should, of course, be well written, and your oral defense should be polished and convincing, but the skills of rhetoric should probably be considered supporting tools rather than the primary foci of a dissertation.

SUMMARY

This final chapter on potential research methods for a professional practice dissertation has taken you to the frontiers of methodology in most professional practice disciplines. Methods from the humanities such as literary criticism and deconstruction are not often taught in either research or professional practice doctoral programs. The same is true of methods of philosophical inquiry. The reason for that is not, however, a lack of relevance or usefulness. Methods from the humanities and philosophy lend themselves to some of the most important questions that face us as professional practitioners. The reason they have been so little used to date in applied and professional practice research is the barrier that was erected to wall off the social sciences (and the sciences) from, in the opinion of some, the undesirable and detrimental effects of the humanities and philosophy when the scientific method became the dominant, and in some disciplines the only suitable, way of searching for new knowledge. This metaphor of barriers reminds me (JW) of the Berlin Wall that was erected to separate two political and economic cultures, and it brings back memories of my trip to the Berlin Wall just as it was coming down. At Checkpoint Charlie I watched as young people on both sides took sledge hammers to the wall and knocked it down, piece by piece. I wanted to participate in that and, fortunately for me, the East German border guards had already learned the fundamentals of capitalism. For $5 they rented me a sledgehammer and showed me where to use it on a crack in the wall where big chunks could be easily knocked off. I still have those chunks, wrapped in a cloth and stored in a drawer, to remind me of the time when the wall came down.

The wall between the humanities/philosophy and professional practice scholarship is also coming down and the lowering of that barrier means you may have more choices for your dissertation, both in terms of the questions you ask and the methods you use to answer them.

CHAPTER 10

A PROCEDURAL GUIDE TO NAVIGATING THE DISSERTATION PROCESS

We have divided work on the dissertation into two broad categories. In this chapter we will discuss the *process* of doing a dissertation along with many of the decisions you must make about how that process will proceed from initial idea to a dissertation that has been successfully defended and submitted. In the following chapter we will focus on one of the core components of the dissertation—data collection and analysis.

EARLY DECISIONS

In Chapter 2 we discussed the different formats for a dissertation—from the traditional five-chapter model to the "three-article dissertation." The format for your dissertation is one of the foundational decisions that will influence other decisions you must make. For example, if you are doing a series of studies about a particular professional practice in your field, an "article" dissertation might be more appropriate if your work consists of several related but separate studies. On the other hand, if your dissertation is an evaluation of a particular project or program, then a five-chapter dissertation format might be more appropriate because the

Completing a Professional Practice Dissertation: A Guide for Doctoral Students and Faculty, pp. 261–300

dissertation "hangs together" as a single project. Thus, our advice is to begin thinking about how you will organize your dissertation work by tentatively selecting a format for your dissertation as well as a general topic and question.

Your Team and the Dissertation Proposal

Decisions about both the format of your dissertation and what your dissertation will be about should usually be made with your major advisor or dissertation chair. (See Chapter 4 for advice on selecting a chair as well as other members of the committee and Chapter 3 for suggestions on how to decide what your dissertation will be about.)

Let us assume that your major advisor does not have a planned program of well-funded research that you are expected to fit into. If your advisor did, your dissertation topic might be the next step in his or her program of research if your doctoral work is being funded by one of your professor's grants. That makes decisions simple and often helps ensure your major professor's continuing involvement and investment in the dissertation. However, it restricts your options and your choices. Assuming you not only have options and choices but are expected to bring some tentative ideas to your major professor for discussion, our advice is to identify two or three general topic areas and schedule a meeting. In that meeting between you and your major advisor (chair) you should outline the topics that interest you, explain why they interest you, and link them both to your major professor's interests and expertise as well as your career plans. Listen to what your chair has to say and take notes so that you can refresh your memory about major components of the discussion. If you and your chair select one of the several general topics as the "best" one to pursue, you can begin to explore what a dissertation on that topic might look like. A typical dissertation student may end up scheduling several meetings with his or her major professor before the skeleton of a dissertation proposal has been worked out. Again, keep notes and pay particular attention to any recommendations or questions your major professor seems to consider particularly important. One of the more irritating aspects of dissertation advising for faculty can be the necessity to ask a student over and over again to attend to an issue that must be addressed (at least in the opinion of the professor) before moving on to the next step.

These initial discussions will deal with four major areas—the topic of the dissertation, the purpose of the dissertation, the research methodology, and the roles of the dissertation committee as well as the larger "research team." As basic items like the topic, purpose, and research method become clearer, your chair may ask you to begin writing a proposal that will be presented to the dissertation committee. This can be part of the process of making decisions. Or, starting to write the proposal may come after you and your chair feel you have reached a tentative agreement on the essentials of your dissertation. In either case, writing the proposal will likely bring up questions that neither you nor your chair had considered, and additional meetings will be needed before the proposal is ready to be distributed before the proposal defense meeting.

When Do You Involve Your Dissertation Committee and Research Team?

Once you and your chair have narrowed down your options and selected a likely dissertation topic, purpose, and research method, there is a decision to be made. Do you meet with other members of your dissertation committee at this point, describe what you have in mind, and ask for their input? Or, do you write your proposal and then contact committee members for input? Or, do you write the proposal and schedule a defense of your proposal where you will, for the first time, receive feedback and critiques from committee members?

These three options are all common in professional practice doctoral programs. One may be the expected or required approach in your program. Each has its positive and negative points and the expectations of your program may be based on how those plusses and minuses play out in your particular program. For example, in a program where the faculty have outstanding expertise in different areas—topics, purposes, and research methods—it may make sense for you to work with your chair until the proposal defense. In another program, where the typical faculty member has expertise that cuts across particular research methods or topics, it may be better to get other committee members involved when you have a firm idea, or when you have a rough draft of the proposal.

Our advice is to consider carefully what is expected of you in the program, and when you have options about when to involve other members of the dissertation committee, consider whether they are more likely to make the best contributions by being involved early or later in the proposal process. Our bias is to get all the committee members involved early but to be sensitive to the level of involvement each individual committee member considers appropriate. Some dissertation members, for example, do not want to be involved until you and your chair have agreed that your proposal is "ready" for the other members to consider. Others want to be kept abreast of your general thinking and the basic direction you are taking. Still others want to be able to offer detailed advice throughout the decision making process. If you are not sure about how a particular member defines his or her role on the committee you can ask them directly, consult with your chair, or talk with other doctoral students who have worked with that faculty member on their dissertation. This last source of information is often the most accurate, but keep in mind that advisors may work differently with different doctoral students.

A related question is when you should involve people who are not members of your dissertation committee but who are critical to successful completion of your dissertation. Professional practice dissertations are often done in applied settings and that frequently requires the cooperation and support of several people—from the administrator responsible for the setting to other professionals who will be working with you on the dissertation. Our advice is to think very carefully about this broader "research team" and to involve them in the planning process as early as possible. Ideally, at least one person from the field will participate as a member on your professional practice dissertation committee.

However, some programs have rules that require all members of the committee to have doctorates, and that may mean you are not allowed to have the director of the clinic, or the principal of the school where you will do your research, serve as a member of your dissertation committee if they do not have a doctorate. In that case it will be very important for you to identify a "research team" that is larger than the dissertation committee and to decide how they will be involved in the planning and execution of your dissertation work. Many problems can be avoided this way. For example, if you are doing research in a school, the principal or collaborating teacher may note that you have scheduled a critical step in your research process in the middle of the annual high stakes testing period for the school—something you probably do not want to do. The input of professional practitioners is not, however, limited to technical issues such as schedules and timelines. Their experience and expertise is also a solid foundation for advising on every aspect of your dissertation—from topic to purpose to research methodology.

The expertise of professional practitioners has not always been welcome or encouraged in the university environment and if you are to make the best use of this source of guidance you may have to create supportive settings where that is encouraged. For example, holding "research team" meetings across the planning process at times that allow both committee members and the larger research team to attend can help build relationships between the university and field-based professionals. In addition, if your program allows members of your team to attend the proposal defense (and the dissertation defense), even if they do not have a doctorate and are not members of the dissertation committee, we suggest you invite and encourage them to attend. Some programs allow questions and comments from everyone who attends the proposal meeting, the only limit being that they cannot vote to approve or disapprove the proposal.

While we would prefer that professional practitioners with relevant expertise and experience be eligible for committee membership, the option of participating in the proposal defense, even without a vote, is better than not participating at all.

In any case, by the time you have written your proposal and are ready to schedule a meeting to defend it, you should have settled on two groups that will help you finish your dissertation—a dissertation committee that consists of a chair and one to three other members, depending on the rules of your program and institution, and a research team that includes the major players who are directly involved in both making your research possible and participating in it themselves. This latter group will likely be made up mostly of professional practitioners because most professional practice dissertations are done in the field.

Writing the Proposal

Two types of proposals are currently in widespread use in professional practice doctoral programs—the "full length," traditional proposal and the "short proposal." Figure 10.1 summarizes both types.

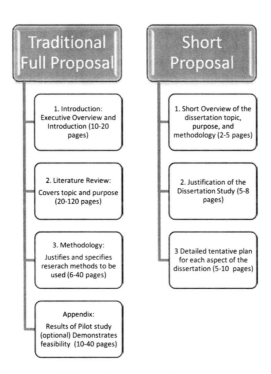

Figure 10.1.   Two types of dissertation proposals.

As you can see from Figure 10.1 the traditional full proposal is essentially the first three chapters of a traditional five-chapter dissertation. Once the proposal is approved, you collect your data, analyze it, and then write the fourth and fifth chapters—4. *Results* and 5. *Discussion*. In some cases one additional component will be added to a traditional proposal. That is a description of a pilot study using your research methods. Often, if there is some question about whether the research methods you plan to use will actually work and produce the type of data you are looking for, your chair may ask you to do an abbreviated "trial" run or pilot study to demonstrate that what you are proposing is workable. For example, if you are conducting phone interviews of a national sample of experts, you might conduct three or four interviews and in an appendix to your proposal show the type of data that was collected as well as how it can be analyzed to address the purpose of your dissertation. Often, when trial runs are done, you will make changes in your research methodology based on the trial. Incorporate those into the methodology chapter which is typically Chapter 3 but mention in the appendix what you originally planned to do and why you changed.

The traditional full proposal is still required today in a majority of research doctoral programs. One reason for justifying the creation of a document that can be over 200 pages long is that the dissertation committee must judge your ability to do everything—from mastering the relevant literature, to making sophisticated decisions about research methodology, to designing and implementing an appropriate data analysis and interpretation plan. The committee does that primarily by evaluating your dissertation proposal, and then your dissertation. As we have noted earlier, this type of dissertation proposal (and dissertation) often ends up being very long, and the skills needed to write it are not easily transferred to other forms of professional and scholarly writing. Even the step of converting a 250-page dissertation into two or three 25-page scholarly or professional papers for publication in journals can be difficult. Writing a paper often requires you to do the opposite of what you needed to do when writing the dissertation. For example, you might have to carefully select from (and reorganize) your 75-page dissertation literature review and produce a 3- or 4-page introduction to your study. Instead of demonstrating to your committee that you have located and reviewed virtually all the literature they consider important to your topic and purpose, you must show to the reviewers of your paper that you can select the most relevant prior literature, succinctly summarize the current state of affairs, and show why the research you have done is important and relevant enough to be published. These are two different types of writing for two different reasons.

Professional practice doctoral programs are increasingly allowing students to pursue other forms of both proposals and dissertations. We discussed the three article format in Chapter 3 and here we will introduce one type of short proposal format. The short format shown in Figure 10.1 is one of many you could use. If you follow the suggested page limits for a short proposal it would be between 12 and 23 pages (double-spaced). The proposal would begin with a short overview of what you want to do as your dissertation. This is followed by a justification of why this type of research is worth doing. The final section of the proposal is a tentative description of how the dissertation will be carried out. We say "tentative" because few applied dissertations, or applied research studies in general, are ever done exactly as planned. There should be some room for adaptation and adjustment based on what happens as you do your research.

The short proposal format in Figure 10.1 is, as noted earlier, one approach. There are many others and you will, of course, need to take into consideration the traditions and expectations of your program when creating the proposal. Another format that is very appealing is offered to Vanderbilt University doctoral students. This format is even more severe in terms of length than the one we suggest. It covers five major topics and is to be no more than ten pages long.

The two proposal outlines in Figure 10.1, and the Vanderbilt format summarized in Table 10.1, are three of many possible formats for dissertation proposals. You should, of course, pay particular attention to the expectations of your department and your committee, but the three described here illustrate the range of possibilities.

If you would like to read a number of dissertation proposals, most using qualitative methods from the social sciences, humanities, and philosophy, go to this University of Texas at Austin website: https://webspace.utexas.edu/cherwitz/www/ie/sample_diss.html. Another website of interest is at the Tepper School of Business at Carnegie Mellon University (http://www.tepper.cmu.edu/current-students/current-doctoral/dissertations/index.aspx). This site contains abstracts, proposals, and full-text copies of dissertations on many topics relevant to professional practice in business. For example, when we looked at this site in 2009, there were dissertations on the impact of sadness on the job, essays on information technology management, and studies of product design procedures. One appealing aspect of this site is that many of the dissertations are "article dissertations" and you can read both complete dissertations that use the article format as well as proposals to do this type of dissertation.

Table 9.1.   Vanderbilt Format

Title:

One Sentence Description

Abstract: from one paragraph to no more than 1 page

The Proposal (no more than 10 pages)

1. **"The problem, (hypo)thesis, and its significance** [emphasis added].... At the minimum the proposal should map out a coherent line of inquiry.... Show that the projected inquiry is restricted enough to be manageable and large enough to be significant. This section should answer the question: why is this a worthy project?"

2. **"Literature to which the project contributes.** Place the inquiry in the context of existing research on the subject or problem.... This section should answer the questions: who has worked on related questions, what insights have they gained, and how does this project contribute to those literatures?"

3. **"Resources.** Show that the resources necessary to carry out the project are available here at Vanderbilt or set out your plan for accessing those resources.... This section should answer the question: where are the materials I need to do this research?"

4. **"Method and procedure.** The student should indicate that the competencies necessary for carrying through the inquiry have been acquired and that the proposed method is adequate for the inquiry.... This section should answer the question: how will I do my research?"

5. **"Tentative chapter outline.** This section should answer the question: what are the parts of my project and in what order will I write them for my first draft?"

The Proposal Defense

A typical proposal defense begins with distributing the proposal to all committee members at least two weeks (longer is better) before the defense, making sure all committee members can attend, and announcing the defense through the procedures used by your program. Some universities have a website that shows the proposal and defense schedule for the next few weeks; other programs send out announcements via e-mail to all faculty and students, and still others put a printed announcement of each defense (often with an abstract) in the mail box of each faculty member and graduate student. If your program supports "open" defenses where everyone is invited to attend, you should already have attended the proposals of several other doctoral students and you should encourage doctoral student colleagues, as well as members of your research team, to attend your defense. Being the sole graduate student sitting on one side of a table facing three to five professors whose job it is to ask you difficult questions about your dissertation can be intimidating. One of the authors of this book remembers seeing an advanced doctoral student in my program at the University of Alabama getting ready to go in for his defense. He was someone all of us looked up to because he was a brilliant student with an outstanding career ahead of him. He was nervous, uncomfortable, and made several trips to the restroom because he was throwing up. He, of course, did very well in his defense. His major professor had approved his work and while the defense was not "easy," the outcome was never in doubt, except perhaps in the mind of this student. That this student could be so intimidated by the process simply indicates that it can be a stressful time for a student. It would be embarrassing at the least to "fail" a defense, and at worst it could mean the end of a student's pursuit of a doctorate. Thus, there is some stress involved in a defense despite the fact that it is very rare for a candidate to fail.

Having colleagues and friends in the room often makes you feel more comfortable and also contributes to a feeling that you have support in the room. And, if you have attended other proposal defenses you will also know that feeling stressed is typical.

Once the defense meeting begins, the chair typically makes a few comments and may even ask everyone, including you, to leave the room for a few minutes while the committee makes final decisions about how to proceed with the defense. Once everyone returns to the room, the chair generally asks you to make a short presentation of the proposal. We typically ask our doctoral students to do no more than a 10-minute presentation, but that guideline is almost never followed. If the presentation takes 15 minutes we are happy but when the half hour mark gets close we generally signal our students to wrap it up. If that doesn't work we will find some polite way to end the presentation and move on to the next segment of the defense.

That segment usually involves a round robin of questions from the committee members. If a student is nervous we will generally try to get a committee member who is likely to ask questions the student is comfortable with to begin the questioning. However, no matter who begins, all the members of the committee will have an opportunity to ask their questions. In a ritual that goes back to the Middle Ages, you will be expected to respond to all the questions asked of you. Your responses may involve providing additional evidence to support a position you have taken in the proposal, acknowledging that you think a question and the comments of a committee member raise issues that require a change in the proposal, disagreeing with the questioner's interpretation of what you have proposed, or defending a position that is in opposition to that taken by the questioner.

In most proposal defenses the great majority of questions are collegial and the dialog between you and the committee is reasonably friendly and supportive. In some proposal defenses, however, a committee member may take a very strong stance and insist that some aspect of your proposal — topic, purpose, methods—are unacceptable. When faced with strong opposition the first step is typically to make sure you understand the precise objection being made and why this committee member is making it. For example, suppose you have proposed a dissertation in which interviews with a group of professionals is a primary source of data and the committee member is saying that you must collect quantitative data and make it the primary focus of your dissertation. Ask yourself why this member has taken that position. If he or she is well known as a quantitative researcher and the objection is based on an assumption that quantitative data is always better than qualitative data, your response can acknowledge that there are different paradigms of research and that you have elected to work within a qualitative paradigm that values interview data because it is "rich and thick" as opposed to quantitative data. You may note that if you had adopted another paradigm you might well be advocating quantitative data. Then you might note that quite a few qualitative studies relevant to your topic are widely cited and respected in the literature. If, after extended discussion, it appears that there is one or more type of quantitative data that could be collected, a compromise may be to collect both types. Advocates of "mixed method" research often argue that collecting both types enhances the meaningfulness and quality of a study. On the other hand, if the committee member still pushes for a major change in the type of data collected your chair will probably intervene. He or she may defend your position, ask you questions that give you guidance about how to deal with the objection, or move the discussion to other issues. In any case, this is likely to be a point of discussion among the committee members later in the defense when they are voting to approve or disapprove the proposal.

Many doctoral students complete their defense without any strong objection that becomes an impasse. Avoiding such an impasse is one reason why we suggest you involve committee members in discussions of your dissertation ideas and the proposal before the proposal defense. Impasses happen most often when the committee members have not had a chance to talk with you about your dissertation before the defense meeting.

Another problem that happens occasionally is a debate that erupts between different committee members. Some doctoral students feel that as long as the professors are arguing amongst themselves rather than with them, that is fine. It means there is less time available to question the doctoral student and to raise other issues. Perhaps there is a bit of truth in this, but hard edged debates about whether your dissertation research is worthy or not, may lead to problems later on—either in the execution of your plan or at the final defense. It is better for you and your chair to know about strong objections and criticisms before the proposal defense meeting and to have worked them out. One way of working them out is to compromise and make changes in your research design, or focus, that satisfies the objections of a committee member. Another way is to remove the committee member and replace them with someone who shares your perspective and that of your chair. Of course, it is better to avoid having to do this by vetting potential committee members before they are appointed to the committee, but it is not always possible to anticipate every potential problem. A serious impasse, particularly where your chair and other committee members support your proposal, and one member does not, is often best handled by replacing the committee member. However, you cannot do that in the middle of a defense meeting; it should have been done before that. When you are in the defense the typical approach is to either make a compromise that allows the member to sign and approve the proposal, or to allow him or her to vote no. If a majority votes yes your proposal is approved in most programs (unanimity is rarely required) and you can begin your research. Then, after the defense meeting you replace the committee member, who will probably be happy with that solution.

In a proposal defense the question period can last from 45 minutes to hours, but eventually it will end and everyone except the dissertation committee will leave the room while the committee deliberates. This deliberation phase can last as little as a few minutes or as long as an hour. In the end, however, you and others will be invited back into the room and your chair will give you the result. That result will generally be one of three options:

1. *Fail* which means you will have to do the defense again. This is rare and in the several hundred proposal defenses we are familiar with at more than ten different institutions, we can only remember one that ended in a vote to fail the student.

2. *Pass with Revisions* means the committee has specified some changes that must be made to the plan of the dissertation but is approving your proposal. You can work on your dissertation but you must incorporate the changes recommended. This is the most common outcome of a proposal defense and it is the one you should expect. Make sure you and your chair clearly understand the changes expected by the committee and that you can explain at the final dissertation defense how those changes were incorporated into the dissertation.

3. *Pass* is not as common as Pass with Revisions. It indicates the committee is happy with the proposal as is.

Now that you have approval for your dissertation, you can begin work. Or, have you already begun?

When Do I "Start" The Dissertation Research?

We have presented the process of doing a dissertation as a linear process in which you prepare your proposal, defend it, and then start your dissertation research. That is how it works in some cases, but by the time many students defend their proposal they are already well into dissertation work. In an ideal world where everything happens when it is supposed to, you would start work on your dissertation *after* it has been approved by your committee at a formal proposal defense meeting. Once you have committee approval, you, in essence, have a contract with the committee, your program, and your institution that says if the dissertation work is carried out as described in the proposal, no one will change their minds later and decide that your dissertation plan wasn't good enough or appropriate. There is thus less chance that you will invest six months, or a year, in a dissertation project and then end up having to abandon it and start over. That is a very good reason to start your dissertation work after the proposal defense. Unfortunately, there are also lots of reasons to start before final approval of the proposal. One is that there is a great deal of preparatory work to be done before any collection of data. Professional practice dissertations often require collaboration, cooperation, and coordination among several agencies, organizations, and groups of professionals. Organizing that takes quite a bit of work and if you wait to do all that until after the proposal defense you may find that you cannot graduate in a reasonable amount of time. Waiting to make arrangements to do your dissertation until after the proposal defense also means you may run into unanticipated problems that require a major change in your research methodology, or even the purpose of your dissertation. It is better to have discovered as many of these problems as possible and to have dealt with them in the proposal – which means you need to do the prep work before the proposal defense.

There are also plenty of reasons to actually start collecting data before the proposal is approved. For example, if there are several types of data that must be collected before you can schedule a proposal defense, you have the choice of collecting the data when it is available or completely leaving it out of your dissertation. If the data is important, we advise you to collect it "early" even if changes in your dissertation that come from your committee may mean the data is not used or is not as important. (However, there is another aspect of preparing to do your research that *cannot* be omitted before collecting data. That is obtaining approval of your research plan by the institution's institutional review board or IRB. (that step will be discussed later in this chapter).

Some of our students have even started their dissertation research before final approval because the opportunity to study a particular issue of professional practice was time sensitive and could not be postponed until after the proposal defense. Suppose, for example, that the soonest you can schedule a proposal defense is in late October but the study you want to do requires that you begin a new program to work with students who are expelled from school for lack of anger control and violent outbursts. In order to use data from the previous school year you need to run the new program for the entire year. It must begin when school begins in late August or early September. In this example, delaying the research until the proposal defense would mean a one year delay—until the beginning of the next school year. Such delays are often not possible because of financial, economic, and job requirements that professional practice doctoral students face. The alternative is to talk with your chair and if he or she agrees, to let your dissertation committee, and your research team, know that you want to take advantage of the opportunity to do the research even though the committee has not fully approved the plan. You should make it clear that you understand this is a risk, that the committee may not approve the proposal, or may require changes that would mean the study you have already begun cannot be used as your dissertation. In most cases, advisors are likely to understand and be sympathetic about the dilemma you face. Many committee members will even work with you on identifying any issues that would be major problems for them and help you plan your research to address or deal with those issues.

If by chance one or more committee members strongly oppose "starting early" the decision is much more complicated. Our advice is to talk this over with your chair and seriously consider either delaying the start of your dissertation research or changing to another study that can be started after your proposal is approved. The ill-will generated by doing something that is strongly opposed by committee members can be difficult to overcome even if the research you do is worthwhile and successful.

WILL YOUR PROCESS BE LINEAR OR NONLINEAR?

Are you a linear thinker and actor? That is, do you tend to develop a plan that involves doing Step 1 first, then Step 2, followed by Step 3 and so on? Many people are and this approach is often recommended by authors of books about doing a dissertation and by dissertation advisors. A linear, sequential process helps you stay on track and to systematically complete all the work that needs to be done. Figure 10.2 illustrates a linear approach to doing your dissertation when you will be evaluating the impact of a particular treatment you want to study.

This linear model assumes that it is important to do earlier steps before starting later steps. For example, you complete your literature

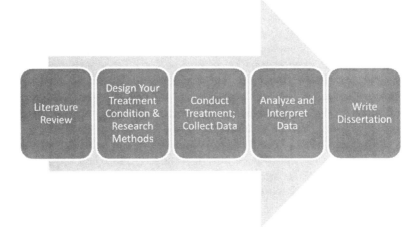

Figure 10.2.   A linear sequential, step-by-step plan for doing a dissertation.

review before designing the treatment condition and research methods. Similarly, you gather all your data before analyzing and interpreting it, just as you don't start writing your dissertation until you have analyzed/interpreted all the data. If this model makes sense to you; if it fits both your style of working and the type of research you will be doing, then by all means follow a linear plan.

On the other hand, if your approach to work, or the type of research you want to do, seems not to fit a traditional linear approach, consider alternatives. In their book on completing a qualitative dissertation, Bloomberg and Volpe (2008) describe the process in decidedly nonlinear terms. "In our experience, completing a dissertation is a rigorous and demanding process. It is iterative, unpredictable, and nonlinear" (p. xxii). They add that

> researchers never move in a linear fashion. Conducting research and writing a dissertation is not like strolling along a clearly marked path. Rather, it is a process that is iterative and recursive, looping back and forth, with many unanticipated events along the way. (p. xxii)

This applies even to your methodology chapter, which Bloomberg and Volpe designate as Chapter 3.

> Writing a dissertation is not a linear process. Rather, it is an iterative and recursive one that requires much back and forth, reminder notes to yourself, and memos to change, revise, and update what you have already written.

Chapter 3 is one of those chapters that must remain flexible and open to change right up to the very end. Frustration is inevitable, but don't despair! This is all part and parcel of managing and organizing the research and writing process. (p. 88)

While we agree with Bloomberg and Volpe (2008) that writing a dissertation is a nonlinear, iterative process, we also need to acknowledge that many advisors and many doctoral students disagree. They are much more comfortable working with a linear process that involves step-by-step completion of predetermined tasks. This view was expressed by Tara Kuther (n.d.) in her paper titled "Stop Procrastinating and Complete Your Dissertation!" She believes so many people do not complete their dissertation because they do not properly organize the process and manage their time wisely. She feels "the lack of structure is the difficult part of the dissertation because the student's role is to plan, carry out, and write up a research project (sometimes several). Structure must be applied in order to complete this task" (para 4). She proposes this solution:

> One way of providing structure is to view the dissertation as a series of steps, rather than as one mammoth task. Motivation may be maintained and even enhanced as each small step is completed. Organization provides a sense of control, holds procrastination at minimal levels, and is key to completing the dissertation. (para 5

However, even Dr. Kuther does not recommend starting at Step 1 and moving on to Steps 2 and 3 and so on. You can start with any of the steps. "Begin where you feel comfortable and fill in the gaps. You will find that you gain momentum with the completion of each small task. Feeling overwhelmed by any particular task is a sign that you have not broken it down into small enough pieces" (para 9).

Despite many guides that recommend a linear approach to your dissertation, in closing this section we will note that the authors of books on completing a dissertation in a wide range of fields are increasingly presenting students with non-linear, iterative models. In the field of business, for example, Reva Brown's (2006) book, *Doing Your Dissertation in Business and Management*, is based on a nonlinear model. As she put it,

> It is evident that the research process is more a matter of juggling balls in the air than following a logical route. A great deal of the time, you will be doing more than just one thing—you will be reading the literature while drafting your proposal, or learning how to run a computer analysis program while interviewing respondents. (p. 54)

Thus, we suggest you consider thinking of the dissertation process as nonlinear rather than linear. That means you might actually begin to analyze your data as soon as you have data to analyze. And, you might start writing your dissertation as soon as you have begun your study.

DOING THE RESEARCH: SOME PRACTICAL GUIDELINES

Doing research in applied settings like a business office, a hospital or clinic, a government agency, a school, or a college is a social and organizational process that requires you to consider many things that go beyond the basics of doing research. You must negotiate entry into the setting, for example. That is true even if you are doing your dissertation in the professional setting where you work. Doing your dissertation there will change your work pattern and also impact the work patterns and expectations of your supervisor and your colleagues. Building a collaborating community of supportive colleagues in the setting where you will do your dissertation is a critically important part of the research process, and it is not something that can be accomplished in a few hours. The way you gain entry into the research setting, build a supportive research team, and work with that team and other participants depends in part on the type of research you are conducting. However, no research method is exempt from the need to build working, collaborative partnerships with professionals and others in the research setting before undertaking your dissertation study. For guidance, we suggest you welcome mentoring from experienced researchers and look at the literature on how to conduct the type of research you are doing. For example, if you are doing action research, the literature contains information on several models of action research—from relatively authoritarian methods in which the researcher who comes in from the outside serves as an expert authority figure, to models of "participatory action research" and "emancipatory action research" that insist participants be equal partners with the researcher in all aspects of the research.

In the remainder of this section we will raise issues that are commonly encountered in professional practice dissertation projects.

Legal and Ethical Considerations

A consideration of legal and ethical issues is now an essential component on any plan to do a dissertation. That was not always the case and one reason why your chair and committee will probably insist that you pay particular attention to these issues is the number of times even experienced researchers have clearly violated the legal and ethical guidelines for doing research with humans. Virtually all the disciplines that prepare practitioners through professional practice doctoral programs have at least one set of ethical guidelines for research, professional practice, or both. A list of over fifty sets of ethical guidelines, from the American Academy of Clinical Neuropsychology to the World Medical Association, is available online at http://www.kspope.com/ethcodes/index.php. Most of the links in this list take you directly to the guidelines of a particular professional or scholarly organization. Below are links that will take you to the legal and ethical practice guidelines for a number of disciplines with professional practice doctorates:

- **Education:** American Educational Research Association. http://www.aera.net/aboutaera/?id=222 and http://www.aera.net/uploadedFiles/About_AERA/Ethical_Standards/EthicalStandards.pdf
- **Education:** Joint Committee on Testing Practices: http://www.apa.org/science/jctpweb.html
- **Nursing:** International Council of Nursing: http://www.icn.ch/icncode.pdf
- **Nursing:** American Nursing Association: http://www.nursingworld.org/MainMenuCategories/EthicsStandards/CodeofEthics/AboutTheCode.aspx
- **Marriage and Family Therapy:** American Association of Marriage and Family Therapy: http://www.aamft.org/resources/LRM_Plan/Ethics/ethicscode2001.asp
- **Psychology:** American Psychological Association: http://www.apa.org/ethics/homepage.html and http://www.apa.org/pi/multiculturalguidelines/homepage.html
- **Social Work:** National Association of Social Workers: http://www.socialworkers.org/pubs/code/default.asp
- **Sociology:** American Sociological Association: http://www.asanet.org/cs/root/leftnav/ethics/ethics

The links above are a good place to start learning about the legal and ethical guidelines for conducting research. There are also many papers and reports in the literature on specific aspects of legal and ethical practice. For example, the concept of informed consent has expanded and become more sophisticated over the past 30 years, and you should be aware of what the concept means today as well as how you should go about gaining informed consent from anyone who will be participating in your research. One good source of information about informed consent as well as samples of informed consent forms is a website maintained by Kenneth Pope at http://kspope.com/consent/index.php. Other issues for which there is considerable guidance in the literature include questions about the confidentiality of data from individual participants in research, multiple relationships that can lead to unethical conflicts (e.g., your dissertation involves collecting data on employees who work for you), and protecting the rights of vulnerable groups who participate in research such as prisoners, children, and the elderly. It is your responsibility to both familiarize yourself with the legal and ethical guidelines for conducting the type of research you are doing, and to discuss any issue you consider questionable with your advisor. In cases where the violation of guidelines is egregious and ignored by those responsible for ensuring that student research meets the appropriate guidelines, that may be a violation in itself and you may be responsible for reporting it.

Navigating the Institutional Review Board Process

Each institution that conducts research on human or animal subjects must also have a committee called an institutional review board, or IRB. The IRB is responsible for approving every research study that is conducted by faculty, scientists, and students at the institution. IRBs are relatively new in higher education. They have been operating for only a few decades and they are a response to the gradual realization that researchers and institutions need more guidance and structure when it comes to making decisions about what is ethical and legal with regard to research, and what is not.

Most colleges and universities have at least two IRB, one for animal research and one for human research. We will focus here on how human research is handled by an IRB. Figure 10.3 illustrates the general sequence of submission and approval.

Figure 10.3 is an abbreviated depiction of the process. For example, in educational research there is a category of research called "exempt" that involves the analysis of treatment methods that are commonly used in instruction and uses data that is commonly acquired as part of the normal process of teaching and learning. There are actually five types of research that are "exempt" from the IRB approval process:

1. Research conducted in a school or other educational setting that involves normal and well accepted educational practices. You may, for example, be studying the impact of common teaching and learning methods in either regular or special education classes. You could be evaluating accepted methods of classroom management, methods of teaching, or even different curricula.

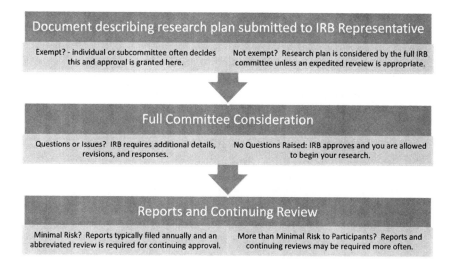

Figure 10.3.   A typical IRB approval and monitoring process for research.

2. Another exempt category is research that uses different types of standard educational tests as well as surveys, interviews, and observations. There are limits, however, on the exempt status of this category. You must complete the IRB process if your observations involve nonpublic behavior, if the data you collect and report can be connected to individuals, if the data you collect could subject participants to civil or criminal liability, or if disclosure of the data could damage the reputation, financial circumstances, or employability of a subject. On the positive side, this type of research is exempt if it involves the study of people who are elected or appointed officials, or people who are candidates for public office. And, finally, research of this type is exempt from the full IRB approval process if federal statute(s) require, with no exceptions, that all the data that could be used to identify specific individuals will be kept confidential before and after the research is completed.

3. A third type of study that is exempt is the collection or analysis of existing data such as documents, records, and pathological or diagnostic specimens. Again, however, there are restrictions on which studies are exempt. Such studies are exempt if the data being used is publicly available or if the information is collected and organized in a way that makes it impossible for individuals to be identified in any way.

4.   The fourth type of exempt study is one that involves research or demonstration projects that are either approved by or conducted by department or agency heads. To be exempt these studies must evaluate or study (1) public benefit or service programs, (2) procedures for obtaining the benefits or services of such programs, (3) potential changes to or alternatives to such programs or their procedures, or (4) potential changes in those benefits or services, or levels of payment for them.

5.   The last type of exempt research is taste and food quality studies that involve consuming food. The restrictions are that the food must be wholesome and does not contain any additives, or wholesome food that does not contain any additives or contamination in levels higher than is considered safe by the Food and Drug Administration, the Environmental Protection Agency, or the Food Safety and Inspection Service of the Department of Agriculture.

These five types of research studies that involve human subjects are "exempt" from a full IRB review because the federal guidelines consider them to involve "minimal risks" to participating human subjects. If you would like to read the federal guidelines that specify what types of studies are exempt, they are available online at http://www.hhs.gov/ohrp/humansubjects/guidance/45cfr46.htm#46.101. This isn't exciting reading unless you are a policy wonk or a very gung ho lawyer who is into writing such regulations.

There is one final set of limitations on whether a study can be exempted or not. If you plan to study individuals with limited capacity to provide informed consent, such as prisoners, children, or clients with limited cognitive capacity, you may be required to complete a full IRB approval process or to meet certain criteria. These criteria can include obtaining informed consent from the parents or legal guardians of children.

Please keep in mind that the decision about whether research is exempt or not cannot be made by the researcher or a research advisor. It is made by the IRB board – often by an individual or a subcommittee – and you must still submit a request to get your study exempted. That request usually involves a form that is shorter than the standard form, but it must still be submitted and approved by the IRB before you begin your research. If you would like to see forms used by different institutions to request an exemption, go to the following websites:

- http://www.irb.pitt.edu/Exempt/default.htm
- www.uhhospitals.org/Portals/6/docs/research/irb/forms/May_07/IRB_Policy_Exempt_Human_Research_5_2007.doc

- www.american.edu/sis/upload/exempt2008.pdf
- www.uab.edu/irb/forms/irb-exemption-review.doc

If your study does not qualify for exemption, there is another type of IRB review that many professional practice dissertation studies do qualify. That is an "expedited" review. An expedited review is shorter and less intensive than a full review. Expedited reviews were created for studies that present a minimal risk to humans participating in the study. Depending on the local rules and guidelines of your IRB, an expedited review may be handled by one member of the IRB or by a subcommittee. If you would like more information on what types of studies qualify for expedited IRB reviews, the following websites will be helpful:

- http://www.umbc.edu/research/HARPO/IRB/expeditedapplication.html
- http://www.rgs.uky.edu/ori/ORIForms/39-Issues_to_Address_When_Conducting_Expedited_Reviews.pdf
- http://researchintegrity.asu.edu/irb/apply/expedited.html
- http://www.hhs.gov/ohrp/humansubjects/guidance/expedited98.htm
- http://cflegacy.research.umn.edu/irb/applying/xrevcategories.cfm
- http://www.irb.cornell.edu/requirements/expedited.htm
- http://www.virginia.edu/vpr/irb/hsr/expedited_review.html

Starting the IRB Process

Many Institutional Review Boards require you to complete a training program before submitting a request to approve your research plan. Some institutions have their own face-to-face training sessions that are offered regularly throughout the year. Other institutions require you to complete the online training developed by the Department of Extramural Research at the National Institute of Health (NIH) titled *Protecting Human Research Participants*. A new version of this course was put online in 2008 and is required by many institutions and agencies before you can submit a research plan for IRB approval. You can sign up for this course at http://phrp.nihtraining.com/users/login.php. The course is divided into seven parts:

- Introduction
- History
- Codes and Regulations
- Respect for Persons

- Beneficence
- Justice
- Conclusion

The NIH course is an excellent way to become acquainted with the requirements and attitudes that are the foundations for legal and ethical research practice. We recommend you complete this online course even if you are not required to do so. The cases, examples, and discussions of common issues will sensitize you to problems that may come up as you make decisions about how to complete your research. The course is free and all that is required is to sign up on the website. The course includes tests that assess your mastery of the content and concepts presented in the course and are a very good way for you to test your own understanding. Your institution may require that you pass these tests, but should you fail one or more units, you can restudy the material and retake the test.

Still other institutions use other online training programs. For example, several hundred universities, colleges, and agencies (including units of the Department of Energy and the Department of Veterans Affairs) require all researchers to complete the training developed by the Collaborative Institutional Training Initiative (CITI). The web address of CITI is https://www.citiprogram.org and to use this site you must indicate you are affiliated with one of the participating organizations or institutions. These range from the Air Force Research Laboratory to Wright State University. CITI offers several levels of online instruction. There is one, for example, for members of an IRB. The course for researchers includes the following topics:

- Introduction
- History and Ethical Principles
- Defining Research With Human Subjects
- The Regulations and the Social and Behavioral Sciences
- Assessing Risk in Social and Behavioral Sciences
- Informed Consent
- Privacy and Confidentiality
- Records Based Research

At institutions that use the CITI training, you must complete the course and be tested over the content of the course before you can submit a research plan for approval.

Completing the required course on legal and ethical aspects of research is thus your beginning point. You *must* successfully complete the course and you *must* submit your research plan for approval.

A required reading in many of the courses on research ethics is the "Belmont Report" which is subtitled *Ethical Principles and Guidelines for the Protection of Human Subjects of Research*. It was published by The National Commission on the Protection of Human Subjects of Research in 1979. It is still relevant and important reading even if the training required by your IRB does not require it. It is available at http://www.hhs.gov/ohrp/humansubjects/guidance/belmont.htm. Much of what you will be required to do in order to protect your human subjects will be based on the requirements introduced in this document.

Completing the IRB Request Forms

Once you have completed the training required by your IRB, the next step is to work with your chair on completing an application for IRB approval of your dissertation. Many institutions require that you complete the form in collaboration with your advisor (we advise you do this even if it is not required) and some even require that the advisor be listed as the primary researcher rather than you. Be sure you understand both who is to submit the application and what must be included in the application. Start with the IRB website at your institution and download any instructions, examples, forms, and guides. Study them carefully and read examples of IRB applications made by others in your program that were successful. When you are ready to begin writing, work with your chair to create a draft. Make sure you understand all the rules and expectations of the IRB because a surprisingly high percentage of applications are returned because they do not contain everything the IRB needs, or the request is not in the format required by the IRB.

Another thing that often trips up doctoral students (and professors) is not knowing the schedule of the IRB. Don't submit your request for approval for a study that must start next week when the IRB will not be meeting for 4 weeks! Know the schedule of meetings and keep in mind that many research plans are not approved on the first cycle through the IRB. It make take two, even three cycles, before it is approved. That means you need to work backward from your start date and submit the approval request in time for it to be processed several times by the IRB. Not receiving approval on the first try can be frustrating, but it is better to anticipate it than to assume you have written the perfect request and that there will be no questions and no problems with approval.

Once your research plan is initially approved there will be reports to file and also continuing reviews, often on an annual basis if the study involves minimal risk to participants. If your study spans 2 years, that means you will need to submit reports and request at least one request for continuing approval. Don't forget to include the reports required by your IRB on your list of things that need to be done.

Problems With IRBs and Professional Practice Research

Despite the virtually universal agreement that IRBs are an essential component of the infrastructure that protects human subjects and helps ensure they are treated in a legal, ethical, and humane way by researchers, there are many papers and reports that express concern over the roles IRBs play in the research process. Most of the concern about IRBs comes from the social and behavioral sciences as well as applied fields like education and business. Many scholars see the core problem as the assumption made by many IRBs that the research they will approve is in the traditional experimental tradition where researchers "experiment" on subjects who do not participate in any of the decision-making procedures that led to the design of the experiment. When regulations and decisions are based on the assumption that this is the type of research that will be done, it can cause problems for researchers who use alternative methods. An example is the use of participatory action research (PAR) methods to conduct professional research in applied settings such as schools, agencies, and businesses. PAR and other methods such as cooperative inquiry are collaborative processes that mix the roles of "researcher" and "subject" in ways many IRB are unfamiliar with (and also uncomfortable with).

Other research methods used in the humanities and social sciences also run into trouble with IRBs because the methods are not part of the experiences of the members. Oral history, for example, involves doing detailed interviews with respondents and publishing the results. It is virtually impossible to maintain confidentiality because the rich and detailed information the participants provide will make it clear who the participant was even if real names are not used. If an IRB requires confidentiality, even when the participant knows that their oral history will be identified with them, many oral history studies cannot be done. Fortunately, in 2003 after input from American history associations, the federal government concluded that "oral history" was not actually research and therefore was not subject to IRB review. That decision is not always accepted by local IRBs and we feel it is better to accept that there are many forms of research, including oral history, and that IRBs must adapt their procedures to many forms of research rather than solving the problem by excluding important forms of research and scholarship from the process.

A related problem occurs when the researcher is a critical theorist who has a goal of exposing exploitation and the use of power to control groups without power. The Belmont report, mentioned earlier, has a "do no harm" requirement called "beneficence" that would make it difficult to do a study, for example, of the way Pacific Gas and Power systematically kept relevant information from the residents of a small California city and caused the deaths of many of them. This story was told in the movie, *Erin Brockovitch,* but when research studies that might uncover such behavior have been proposed, local IRBs have not always approved them. Recently, the guidelines for the IRB at the University of Missouri Kansas City were changed to make it clear that approval of such studies is acceptable:

> Akin to a journalist or lawyer, an historian is also responsible to a wider public to recover a shared past "as it really happened." In keeping with the public role of an historian in a democratic society, these responsibilities, especially when conducting narrative interviews, can necessitate a confrontational style of critical inquiry. So while historians do not set out to hurt their interviewees, oral historians are expected to ask tough questions in their interrogation of the past. (quoted from Social Sciences IRB and Oral History, University of Missouri Kansas City, http://www.umkc.edu/ors/irb/OralHistory.cfm)

You may want to read the UMKC document in full to get an idea of what the major issues are when it comes to doing applied research in the social sciences and humanities.

In fact, many scholars in the humanities and social sciences are concerned about the lack of representation from their fields on IRB and feel the result is regulations and requirements that are unsuited to the research they do. If you would like to read more about this issue, the *Institutional Review Blog,* which is subtitled "News and Commentary About Institutional Review Board oversight of the humanities and social sciences" is available at http://www.institutionalreviewblog.com/2007/01/why-not-make-irb-review-voluntary.html.

Another useful resource is a paper titled "The Qualitative Misfit: Evaluating the Interpretive Complexity of IRBs" (Corwin & Tierney, 2005). This paper is an analysis of the major issues involved in IRB supervision of innovative qualitative research. It is available at http://www.allacademic.com//meta/p_mla_apa_research_citation/0/2/0/1/0/pages20109/p20109-1.php. Corwin and Tierney address the problems that emerge from trying to apply regulations that were originally created to control biomedical research to the many forms of research and scholarship that are conducted in the humanities, the social sciences, and in professional practice. Corwin and Tierney cite many types of research but one they discuss is particularly relevant when it comes to professional practice dissertations. Case studies are popular as professional practice dissertations. Are case studies "research?" Here is what Corwin and Tierney say:

The position of case studies is less clear. Some scholars argue that case studies aim to contribute to generalizable knowledge, can cause risk to participants and thus are subject to IRB review; others argue that case studies do not rely on "systematic investigation" and generally invoke little risk and therefore should not be classified as research. Both sides concur that depending on how the IRB interprets research determines how case studies should be treated....

A practical result of this confusion is a logjam with regard to the approval process. The interpretation of IRB "rules" varies from campus to campus, and with different committees on the same campus. What was approved last year, or even last semester, may not gain approval this year. Graduate students, in particular, have faced delays in conducting research in large part because no one is certain how to proceed so that everything needs to be reviewed by a committee. Even if the process were optimal, the result is remarkably inefficient. (p. 10)

What To Do If Your Research Methods May be Unfamiliar to the IRB

Before offering advice on how to handle the types of problems discussed in the previous section we want to say that the vast majority of institutional IRBs are not difficult to work with and will go out of their way to help you make sure your dissertation research plan is the foundation for a meaningful and worthwhile research study that meets all the legal and ethical requirements. Regardless of the research methods you plan to use, it is likely that the IRB at your institution will be supportive and helpful.

There are, however, things you can do to help smooth the way through the IRB approval process. In our experience there are six things that can be very helpful:

- Work closely with your chair and others who have experience with the IRB process. In your program or department there will likely be professors as well as doctoral students who are very familiar with the IRB process. Those who have the time and are willing to help you create your own IRB proposal can be invaluable by offering suggestions, pointers, advice, and cautions.

- If it is appropriate at your institution, talk to the member of the IRB who represents your department, college, or area of research interest. For example, if you plan to do an ethnographic study and are in a college of education, the most likely IRB member to talk to will be the person who represents your department/college. However, suppose that person is a quantitative researcher who is most familiar with experimental research studies. In that case, you may also want to talk to the IRB member from an area like anthropology or sociology because those fields are where ethnographic methods developed, and that IRB member should be familiar with ethnographic methods and how to prepare an IRB proposal to do that type of research.

- Look at research plans that use similar methods and were approved by the IRB. Talk with the students or professors who submitted those plans about any issues that came up, how they were resolved, and whether the plan was handled through an exempt, expedited, or full IRB review. Use what you learn to guide you as you write your own plan.

- When you write your IRB proposal, if you are worried that members of the IRB may not be familiar with the research method you propose, help them become familiar, and comfortable, with it, by including more information about it than you might if you were proposing research methods that are routine and familiar to most IRB members. For example, describe in some detail the way the research method will be carried out in your study, and make sure you include information on other published research that used the same method. It may help if the research you cite was conducted by scholars at prestigious institutions the IRB members are familiar with. If there are journals devoted to publishing studies that use the type of research methods you will be using, mention them. For example, if you are doing a case study in an area like business and management, mention the *International Journal of Case Studies in Management*. If you are doing a case study in psychology, then *Clinical Case Studies* is an example of a journal that *only* publishes case studies. There are hundreds, if not thousands, of established journals that publish research based on a particular research method. They include *Action Research International, Applied Semiotics, Demographic Research, Discourse Analysis Online, Enculturation: A Journal of Rhetoric, Writing, and Culture; Ethnography, Folklore Studies, Forum: Sozialforschung / Forum: Qualitative Social Science Research, Grounded Theory Review, Journal of Contemporary Ethnography, Narrative Inquiry, Oral Tradition, Phenomenology and Practice, Philosophy of Mathematics Education Journal, Qualitative Report*, and the *Journal of Oral History Review*. There are also quite a few journals that focus on both a particular discipline or field of professional practice as well as families of research methods. They include *Educational Action Research, Education Policy Analysis Archives, Case Reports in Medicine, Complicity: An International Journal of Complexity and Education, Cultural Studies, CybrPsychology: Journal of Psychosocial Research on Cyberspace, Holistic Nursing Practice, International Journal of*

Collaborative Research on Internal Medicine & Public Health, International Journal of Qualitative Studies in Education, Journal of Applied Research in Higher Education, Journal of Case Research in Business and Management, Journal of Case Studies in Accreditation and Assessment, Journal of Critical Education Policy Studies, Journal of Humanistic Psychology, Journal of Phenomenological Psychology, Journal of Women's History, Pragmatic Case Studies in Psychotherapy, Qualitative Health Research, Qualitative Research in Psychology, Qualitative Social Work, Qualitative Sociology, Radical Pedagogy, and *Visual Anthropology Review.*

- If there are ethical guidelines for using the research method you have selected that the IRB may not be familiar with, mention them and indicate that your study meets those criteria.
- Finally, if there are articles or reports that address the issues likely to be raised by the IRB, ask your chair if copies of relevant papers should be attached to your proposal. In some cases, adding this material may be helpful, but in others the result may be more problems rather than less. Seek the advice of your chair on whether to do this or not.

In closing this discussion of the IRB approval process we want to emphasize again that while getting IRB approval often requires quite a bit of work, the idea of submitting your research plans to a group charged with making sure the studies conducted at your institution meet contemporary legal and ethical standards is sound and worthwhile. It is in the best interests of everyone involved, including you, to have your plans scrutinized by a knowledgeable group of experienced scholars and researchers.

DEALING WITH PROBLEMS

Few dissertations proceed so smoothly that there are no unexpected problems that must be addressed. Consider these two examples and think about how they might be handled.

Example 1: Informed Consent is Withdrawn

You are doing research in a sixth grade classroom where students are completing a social studies unit that involves problem-based learning in collaborative groups. Your procedures for obtaining consent from both the students and their parents or guardians were approved by the IRB and you have signed consent forms from all the parents/guardians of students in the class. However, 2 weeks into an 8 week study the parent of one of the children, who is not the custodial parent and who did not sign a consent form, comes to school and says they have learned their child is being videotaped in the classroom and that this is not acceptable. The parent, who speaks with the principal, insists that the videotaping be discontinued. Your research focuses on the type of interactions students engage in while working in their collaborative groups, so discontinuing the videotaping would probably mean you cannot continue your dissertation research. What do you do?

Example 2

Your dissertation involves studying the perceptions of active gang members in an inner city area. You want to understand how they justify their activities, how they perceive other gangs, the police, and the local schools. Your primary means of data collection is doing "street interviews" of gang members who are out in public in their neighborhoods. As you become more and more accepted by them, you realize that what they are telling you is becoming more "real"—that is, they seem to be telling you what they really think rather than what they believe you want to hear or what they say to justify their life style even if they don't really believe it themselves. This increased discomfort level leads to an unanticipated dilemma. Two of your informants are discussing how they justify attacks, such as drive by shootings of members of other gangs and people they perceive as threats to themselves or the gang. In that discussion you learn that a drive by shooting is planned for the following night. It will happen at an outdoor community basketball court where members of a rival gang will be playing a game. There are apartment buildings around the court, and young children as well as teens from the buildings are typically around the court watching the game. Your informants plan to drive by in a car and use two semi-automatic pistols to spray the court in an effort to kill or wound three members of the rival gang who are suspected of raping the sister of one of the gang members. What do you do?

The Best Approach: Anticipate and Avoid

We are not telling you anything new when we say that the best approach to dealing with unanticipated problems is to anticipate them and have a plan that either helps you avoid the issue or offers options for dealing with the problem. Of course, there is a contradiction in that since the term "unanticipated problems" means you could not anticipate them. Or does it? Actually, most of the unanticipated problems you will run across in your dissertation research probably could have been anticipated —or at least the possibility that they might occur can be anticipated. In the first example, we know that in this society the interaction between custodial and noncustodial parents can be a source of major conflict and frustration. Why should we expect that informed consent would be any different? There is always the possibility that a noncustodial parent may object to their child participating in a research study and the reasons are not always related solely to the nature of the study and the type of data being collected. On the other hand, obtaining consent before beginning the study from a noncustodial parent may initiate conflict rather than reduce it. What do you do?

One way to try and avoid this particular problem is to think of informed consent as a process rather than an effort simply to get a parent's signature on a piece of paper. The process includes sincere and extended efforts to inform parents about the study, the risks and benefits, and what will be done with the results. Studies that involve "minimal risk" to the student only require one custodial parent to sign the consent form. Studies that may involve more than a minimal risk, require both custodial parents/guardians to sign and that the process include obtaining informed consent from the child as well if they are eight years old or older. (If you would like to read instructions for obtaining parental and child informed consent as well as examples and sample documents please see the Tufts University resources at www.tuftsgloballeadership.org/files/resources/InformedConsentUnder18.doc). School districts also often have an approval process for doing research in a school and you may find the regulations and forms for the Clark County School District in Georgia helpful. They are at http://www.coe.uga.edu/adresearch/resources/human_subjects/Clarke_County_Guidelines.pdf.

The more collaborative, the more open, and the more supportive you are in helping parents and children understand what the research is all about and how they will participate, the less likely you are to end up with a problem like the one in the first example. Maintaining a close working relationship with school officials and your chair is also always important. When you become aware of a problem, notifying them and scheduling a meeting to discuss options should be one of the first things you do. However, suppose you have done everything "right" and you still have a noncustodial parent insisting that videotaping be stopped. There are several options but all involve talking with the principal and teacher at the school where you are working as well as with your chair. If the decision is to meet with the noncustodial parent, you may want to have several options in mind. For example, you could offer to mask the child's face, which is not difficult to do with digital video. Or, if that is not acceptable, you could offer not to videotape the small group that includes this child. Or, you could rely on audio tapes of that group. If you had five groups, video data would be available on only four of them. It is in the best interests of every-

one to settle an issue like videotaping a child in a way that satisfies everyone. That is in spite of federal regulations that do allow for one parent to
provide consent:

> Permission of one parent is sufficient if the other parent is deceased,
> unknown, incompetent, not reasonably available, or does not have legal
> responsibility for the care and custody of the minor child. (quoted from Johns
> Hopkins University Medicine website: http://irb.jhmi.edu/Guidelines/
> Federalobtainingparentpermission.html)

However, what one rule gives, another takes away. This quote is from also
from the Johns Hopkins website:

> What If Parents Disagree?

> If the investigator has succeeded in contacting the absent parent and that
> parent does not give his/her permission, or fails to sign and return the con-
> sent form, the child (or pregnant woman, fetus, or neonate, except in cases
> of rape or incest) may not be enrolled in the study, even if the parent who is
> present (or the pregnant woman, except in cases of rape or incest) has given
> permission.

In the case of a noncustodial parent who insists that he or she will not
consent, both federal and state regulations may be applicable and it may
be necessary to involve the institutional attorney in the discussions. The
details of the divorce agreement and how the legal custody of the child
has been worked out by the courts can be important in determining who
has the right to refuse consent and who does not.

However, when all is said and done, you may face the possibility of having to start the study over in another classroom. Keep in mind, also, that
the rules of informed consent are different from the rules of contract law.
For example, you cannot sign a contract to pay for a new car you have
purchased and then change your mind after you have driven the car for a
month. The rules of informed consent do, however, allow someone to
change their mind at any time, and you must, as part of the process of
obtaining informed consent, make participants and parents aware of that
right.

Now, what about the second unanticipated problem? How do you handle knowing that a crime will likely be committed? Here the issue is
broader than just the IRB rules and regulations. It involves two competing responsibilities—maintaining the confidentiality that is assured the
participant when he or she gives informed consent versus the protection
of society. State laws vary on the question of what you must do if you
become aware of an ongoing crime, a crime in the past, or a crime that

may happen in the future. What you are required to do by law may also depend on your profession. The "sanctity of the confessional" is a well established right of priests to keep what they are told in the confessional private under all circumstances. And, state laws may also extend such rights to other professionals such as therapists. There have, however, been challenges to the absolute right of confidentiality in the last 20 years for virtually all professionals, including the priesthood. For example, many states now *require* educators, physicians, and child welfare professionals to report to authorities even a suspicion of child abuse:

> Most therapists, whatever their discipline, agree that breaking confidentiality creates significant problems. It can destroy the therapeutic relationship and may risk a malpractice suit.... The ethical codes of the various helping professions (social work, psychology, religion, nursing, medicine, teaching, counseling, etc.) are intentionally vague, general, and elastic to cover all types of situations, but all take confidentiality very seriously (see, for example, the Code of Ethics of the National Association of Social Workers and the American Psychological Association's Ethical Principles of Psychologists). Confidentiality is so critical according to some theorists that psychotherapy may be worthless without it....
>
> However, all states now have reporting laws which require therapists to break confidentiality and report any child abuse suspicions to law enforcement or child protection agencies. All state laws therefore require putting the "child's best interest" above the therapeutic relationship. Maine and Maryland are the only states that allow therapist discretion in deciding whether to report. In the others, the therapist is mandated to report based upon "suspicion." There is no leeway permitted for discretionary judgment. (Schultz, 1990, paras. 1, 2)

Over the past 30 years the rules and regulations concerning when you must notify authorities, even when there is an assurance of confidentiality, have shifted toward allowing, and in some cases, requiring, notification when protecting the public from violence, death, or even severe financial or economic loss. In the situation we are discussing here the researcher has learned that a crime, that may involve murder or serious physical injury, is planned. If the participants have been informed that everything they say will be held in the strictest confidence, then reporting to the authorities will be breaking that promise. In her book on counseling criminal justice offenders Masters (2003) suggests the following approach to such situations:

> Counselors should inform offenders what procedures, if any, are in place to ensure confidentiality. It is also wise to discuss with offenders the way in which the agency requires the criminal justice counselor to deal with the treatment

notes and records. The counselor should not make unrealistic promises of unqualified confidentiality to establish a climate for good offender relationships. Such practices will destroy relationships when the counselor has to break confidentiality because of the law or agency policy. (p. 20)

In research the concept of informed consent means that participants are aware of the limits of confidentiality, such as legal requirements that certain types of information must be communicated to authorities. Without that knowledge, they cannot give informed consent. Although the laws vary from state to state, four common exceptions to confidentiality are:

- You learn about criminal behavior that has happened or may happen, including economic crimes such as fraud.
- There is an imminent danger that a participant will harm him or herself or someone else.
- Child abuse or neglect has happened or is happening.
- You receive a court order to reveal what you know.

Again, the laws vary from state to state and while these four exceptions to confidentiality may seem simple, they are not so simple when it comes to applying them to a particular situation. In addition, different professions have developed various approaches to dealing with them. Psychiatrists, for example, have created a procedure for handling threats made by patients. If a patient says he or she is going to kill or physically harm someone after release from a short term therapy program, the psychiatrist is, in most states, legally obligated to notify the person who has been threatened. As a first step, the psychiatrist will try to get the patient to make the contact and tell the person about the threat. Then the psychiatrist may also talk with the person being threatened. However, if the patient refuses to cooperate, the psychiatrist is still obligated, both ethically and legally, to make the target of a credible threat aware of that threat.

Up to this point, the issue of confidentiality versus the protection of the public seems complex. However, it also seems relatively clear. If you have credible knowledge of a threat to the public most states require you to report it either to the person being threatened or to the authorities, or both. Similarly, many states have laws that require most people to report prior crimes or crimes likely to be committed in the future. Before moving on to another topic, however, consider what Robert Weiss (1995) has to say about "confidentiality issues" in his book, *Learning from Strangers: The Art and Methods of Qualitative Interview Studies:*

We guarantee respondents confidentiality. Indeed, we put the guarantee into our consent forms. Furthermore, one element of the implicit research partnership we establish with a respondent is a commitment that the respondent will not be damaged because of his or her participation in the interview. Are there any circumstances in which an interviewer would nevertheless be justified in passing on interview information to whoever might be the appropriate authorities—the police, the respondent's psychiatrist, a state agency for the protection of children? Suppose a respondent confesses behavior that is criminal? Should the respondent be reported to the police? What if the respondent is homicidal? Or suicidal? What if the respondent is harming others? What if the respondent is harming children?

I have never interviewed anyone who gave me reason to believe he or she planned a homicide or suicide or was involved in child abuse. If I had, I believe I would have made an effort to contact appropriate authorities. I have interviewed people engaged in criminal behavior, including several who were engaged in illegal drug use, a few who were involved in occasional theft from retail stores, and one man who a year before our interview had committed armed robberies. (The man was a drug user who had been desperate for money.) I did not report any of these respondents to the police and would have resisted efforts to make their interview reports available as evidence against them. I hope I am not vulnerable to charges as an accessory after the fact, but I think in those cases I could responsibly honor my pledge of confidentiality.

More difficult was the problem posed by a woman respondent who was HIV positive. She said that all her life, from the time she was a child, she had been treated brutally by men. Contracting HIV from a boyfriend was only the most recent instance. Now she wanted to get even with the whole male sex. She visited barrooms every evening to pick up men with whom she could have intercourse, in the hope that she would infect them. The woman's sister had already reported her to a public health agency, mostly because she wanted the woman stopped before she was hurt by some man she had tried to infect. The public health agency did nothing.

In our final interview, I learned the woman was no longer seeking revenge through sex. She had met a man who had become her steady boyfriend and who remained with her even after he was told – by that same sister – that she was HIV positive.... If in our final interview the woman had reported continuing her campaign to spread HIV among men, I would have told her to stop. I can't believe that would have done much good, but I would have told her anyway. I also would have discussed her report with the head of the clinic where she was being treated, with the thought of devising some way to interrupt her behavior.

Until the woman herself resolved the issues, the problem of what to do with information that a respondent was trying to spread HIV infection to others was the most difficult dilemma I have faced in a lifetime of interviewing. (pp. 131-132)

Weiss (1995) also discusses one of the most common solutions to limitless assurances of confidentiality—that of specifying the limits when obtaining informed consent:

> It might seem that dilemmas associated with confidentiality could be avoided by noting in the consent form the conditions under which confidentiality will be breached. A statement might be made ... that a serious threat to adult life or to the well-being of children would justify suspension of the investigator's commitment to confidentiality. In fact, some research review boards require such statements.

> Noting in the consent form that confidentiality may not be absolute can help, but it will not fully resolve the problem. If an interview produces evidence of a threat to the well-being of the respondent or others, the investigator would still be required to assess the threat's credibility. If the investigator believes the threat to be genuine and yet unlikely to be implemented, should action to forestall it nevertheless be taken, to be on the safe side? Issues of judgment remain, no matter what's in the consent form: Just how credible is the threat? Is useful action to forestall it possible? What would be the cost to the respondent and to the study of any action undertaken? What are the possible costs of inaction? (p. 133)

Weiss' comments highlight the complex and difficult nature of making decisions about unexpected problems that can arise in the course of any research study. Note, however, that there is quite a bit of published literature as well as directions in the guidelines and laws about research that are directly relevant to both the examples we have used here As a student completing a dissertation, you have both extra resources and extra responsibilities when facing such decisions. You have the additional resources of experienced researchers on your dissertation committee, including your chair, who have committed their time and expertise to helping you complete a dissertation ethically and legally. When dilemmas and problems arise, and they likely will, be sure to make use of your committee as well as other resources available to you locally and in the literature. Also, because you are likely a novice researcher it is one of your responsibilities to seek guidance more quickly and perhaps more often than an experienced researcher might. This can make the difference between a dissertation remembered for its problems and one that "went smoothly."

DO YOU NEED A HARD OR SOFT RESEARCH PLAN?

We have already discussed this issue but it bears repeating that just as there are two extreme ways of interpreting the U.S. constitution (strict constructionism versus loose constructionism) there are also two ways of treating a research plan. The strict constructionism approach is typically advocated by positivists who privilege the scientific method as the best source of new knowledge. Positivist and postpositivist theory has within it some assumptions about what determines the believability of a research study's results that make it critically important that no substantial changes be made once a research plan has been agreed upon and the study begun. If changes are made, they, according to positivist theory, call into question the believability (validity and reliability) of the study's results.

On the opposite end of this continuum there are the loose constructionists, mostly interpretivists and critical theorists, who argue just the opposite. They propose that as we do a research study we learn more and more about both our research methods and our topic. And, if we are most ignorant about both method and topic when we begin, they argue that it makes little sense to set in stone the research plan made at a time when we are most ignorant. This group advocates remaining open and flexible in terms of the topic, purpose, methods, and procedures of the research so that you can take advantage of your increasing knowledge to develop the best study possible.

You can probably see the problems either of these positions presents to a student trying to get a research plan approved by a dissertation committee. Strict constructionists on the committee may be appalled by the idea that what is in your research plan is little more than "what I might or might not do depending on how I feel when doing the dissertation," while loose constructionists on the committee may wax eloquently on the topic of why "it is crazy to force the student to stick with a plan even after he/she has realized the result would be an inferior, even useless, research study that becomes simply a hoop to jump through rather than real research." Of course, these are expressions of extreme views but they do illustrate the importance of the underlying beliefs held by opposing sides. Fortunately, in our experience most dissertation committees are made up of people who are all closer to one end of the continuum than the other, or when the committee does have representatives along the whole continuum they have been able to work together to reach satisfactory compromises. However, whether the dissertation proposal you present is "set in stone" or a "reasonable beginning" should be a topic of discussion with your chair and probably with your committee.

Our advice is to try and negotiate a plan that is flexible, one that allows you to make major changes even after the study has begun. However, because this is a dissertation, major changes should be done with the participation and support of your research team, including your chair and probably other members of the dissertation committee. If you are interested in an example of a dissertation that did change drastically while the doctoral student was working in the field, we recommend the movie *Never Cry Wolf,* which starred Charles Martin Smith as a young doctoral student researcher sent into the wilds of the Arctic to prove what his dissertation chair and many others already knew—that the decline of the caribou population was due to the wolves who were killing too many of them on the caribou's annual migration. The movie is essentially the story of how Smith's character begins collecting data that will prove the hypothesis in his proposal only to realize that not only is the hypothesis wrong, the data he is collecting is not what he should be collecting. He designs a new study—by himself because he is living in the wilds thousands of miles from his university and without any means of communication or transportation until the float plane comes for him in the brief summer when the lakes unfreeze and the plane can land to pick him up.

HOW WILL YOUR PLAN BE EXPRESSED?

The question that is the heading for this section may seem odd because we have been talking about creating a written proposal. Isn't that how you will "express" your research plan? Yes, the written proposal is usually the official and authorized version of your plan, but there are other ways of depicting a research plan. These other methods are generally used because they help you keep a complex project well organized and on schedule, and they provide some backup to your memory so that you don't forget to do something essential. The three additional ways of presenting and following your research plan all involve using computer software. Three types of software will be discussed here: flow charting programs, brainstorming software, and project management software.

FlowCharting Software

Flowcharting has been used for decades to do things like design a piece of software "on paper" and graphically represent it. Flowcharting has also been used to create graphical representations of a project or a system. There are many flowcharting programs and they cost anywhere from hundreds of dollars to nothing. The 2007 and later versions of Microsoft Word, for example, have built-in flowcharting software that is part of the SmartArt options under the Insert menu at the top of the screen. A list of 23 other stand-alone flowcharting programs, most of them commercial programs, is available at http://www.qualitydigest.com/march97/html/f3.htm. SmartDraw is one of the better ones and the publisher offers a free 30-day trial (http://www.smartdraw.com). Another is Microsoft's Visio (http://www.visio.com) which has a 60-day free trail (http:// office.microsoft.com/en-us/visio/ \)

There are also quite a few free flowcharting programs available. They include StarUML (http://staruml.sourceforge.net/en/), Dia (http:// live.gnome.org/Dia), and Graphviz (http://www.graphviz.org/).

Brainstorming Software

Some people lump flowcharting programs and brainstorming software together in one large group because both types let you create visual representations of your ideas. We think the difference is worth keeping. Flowcharting programs are more structured and require you to work within tighter limitations. Thus, if you like structure, and the structure of the program you are using fits the work you are doing— such as creating a timeline for completing all the components of your dissertation—then you may prefer to use a flowcharting program. On the other hand, if you want a more open and flexible program, one that expects you to make many of the decisions about how tasks and steps in a research plan will be graphically represented, then brain storming programs may be your cup of tea. Brainstorming programs are also called concept map programs, idea mappers, and mind mapping programs. Popular commercial brainstorming programs include MindJet (http://www.mindjet.com), Inspiration which is a commercial product and NetSpiration which is currently free to use (http:// www.inspiration.com), and mindapp6 which currently costs less than $30 (http://www.mindapp.com). Free programs that may help you create a graphic representation of your research plan include Freemind (http:// www.freemind), Spinscape (http://www.spinscape.com), and VYM or View Your Mind (http://www.insilmaril.de/vym/). Some people find the ability to graphically represent their research plan very beneficial. Others find it more trouble than it is worth. We suggest you look at a few of the flowcharting and brainstorming programs and decide for yourself whether either type of program will be useful as you do your dissertation research.

Project Management Software

We have presented the three types of software in order, from simple to complex. This final category is the most complex. Project management programs were created to help manage complex projects of all types—from building a 100 story skyscraper to negotiating an international treaty. Proj-ect management programs are widely used in business, and they are often used to manage large, complex research projects as well—especially those with multiple sites that take several years to complete. Whether this type of software will help you manage your dissertation research depends on both your work habits and the complexity of your dissertation. Dissertations based on a relatively simple research plan probably don't need the support of project management software. However, some moderately complex and very complex research projects are easier to complete successfully when you use project management software.

If you are interested in exploring this type of software, one useful resource is a website called "Top Ten Reviews" (http://project-management-software-review.toptenreviews.com/) where the 10 most popular project management programs are compared. Programs reviewed include Microsoft Project, MindView, Project Kickstart, Rational Plan, Milestones, Fusion Desk, and VIP Team To Do List. Prices range from $50 to just over $500. Although the review ranks the most expensive program, Microsoft Project, the best, that overall assessment may not fit your needs. Reading the reviews and thinking through how you would use project management software to manage your dissertation work could point you to a less expensive product that meets your needs. One site with information and links on hundreds of different project management programs is part of the CNET website—http://download.cnet.com/windows/project-management-software/. When we checked this site there were 176 free programs as well as an even larger number of commercial project management programs discussed.

As noted, there are also free, and almost free, project management programs that may meet your needs at little or no cost. For example, Mingle: Agile Project Management and Collaboration, is free if you will have no more than five users (http://studios.thoughtworks.com/). That could include you and your dissertation committee. OpenProj (http://openproj.org/) is free for any number of users, as is TaskJuggler (http://www.taskjuggler.org/), and OpenWorkbench (http://www.openworkbench.org/). Information on several other free project management programs is available at http://en.wikipedia.org/wiki/List_of_project_management_software. This site lists commercial as well as free (open source) programs and provides links to their websites. It also includes information on programs that support collaboration, resource management, and document management. Depending on the type of dissertation you are doing, these other types of software may also be helpful.

SUMMARY

The procedures involved in completing a professional practice dissertation are complex and multifaceted. There are decisions that must be made early, such as what format your dissertation will use and how your dissertation committee and research team will participate in the process. There are also questions of timing, and major tasks to complete such as writing and defending your proposal, and obtaining approval from your local IRB.

You will also need to negotiate with your committee the meaning of your research plan. Is it set in stone, or is it flexible and open—or something in between these two extremes? And, even when you have done everything "right", there may be unanticipated problems that crop up that must be handled. These problems may not have obvious, cut-and-dried solutions to them. However, the stronger your working and collegial relationships are with your committee and your research team, the more likely you are to have the resources and support needed to handle those unanticipated problems.

Finally, if your research is complex you may want to consider using a computer program to help you manage the research process. Flowcharting, brainstorming, and project management programs are all potentially useful for managing your dissertation research.

CHAPTER 11

THE DATA COLLECTION AND ANALYSIS PROCESS

We should begin this chapter with a statement of what it is not about. It is not a detailed guide about how to analyze every possible type of data you might collect for your dissertation research. That would be impossible and, even if possible, it would be a poor substitute for the many outstanding books, papers, training experiences, internships, research team projects, advisors, and mentors who are much better sources of such guidance.

The chapter is also not even a definitive guide to how you should collect your data, regardless of type. Again, it would be impossible to provide all the details you need about collecting the many different types of data that may become part of a particular dissertation. What we will do instead is focus on some of the issues of data collection and analysis that, in our own experience as dissertation chairs and advisors, have been problematic for too many students. The chapter is organized around some of those issues along with our advice about how to handle each one.

Researchers collect hundreds of different types of data—test scores, recordings of interviews, field notes of observations, and videos of work and learning settings. All types of data have one thing in common. They need to be gathered and organized in a way that reduces the likelihood of errors, mistakes, and loss. The data you collect for your study should be organized into a "data set." Organizing the data is the first step in the

Completing a Professional Practice Dissertation: A Guide for Doctoral Students and Faculty, pp. 301–323
Copyright © 2010 by Information Age Publishing
All rights of reproduction in any form reserved.

analysis phase of a study. Data sets can contain anything from thousands of test scores to the transcript of an interview with a single individual. Regardless of the type of data you collect, it is imperative that you develop a sensible, and understandable, way of organizing the data. A large shoebox full of scribbled notes on pages torn from a yellow pad does not usually qualify as a "sensible and understandable" way of organizing your data. More is required if you are to avoid losing some of the meaning in the data you are collecting.

ANTICIPATING DATA NEEDS

Organizing and safeguarding your data means you have data to organize. However, in our experience, dissertation students often make two mistakes when thinking about the data they need for their dissertation. One mistake is to think about what data is needed after it is too late to gather several important types of data. If you do not anticipate data needs until you are in the middle of doing the data analysis, it will be too late for many types of data. Think about data needs early. Before you collect any data, tell yourself the imaginary story of how you completed the entire dissertation process. Make it detailed enough for you to include both the types of data you collect and how you analyzed, interpreted, and wrote up your work. As you tell yourself that story, write down all the types of information and data that will be helpful.

The second common mistake is to narrowly focus on a few types of data that will be formally analyzed and interpreted. For example, you may plan to videotape the interactions of a professional group deliberating a practical decision, or a group of clients discussing their response to new services offered by an agency. There are sophisticated ways of analyzing such data, but there may also be other information associated with the data that is also very valuable. For example, if each member of the professional group writes a reflective analysis of the meeting, that can often clarify viewpoints and sensitize you to issues that are not apparent from the video. Or, notes from a discussion with the social worker who organized the client group may elicit information that puts the results of that group meeting in context (such as noting that the person who led the group has a very good rapport with the clients and that some of the things they said in the meeting may have been in support of his or her work rather than their assessment of the services being delivered by the agency).

So, the advice we offer here is to "think early about data needs and think broadly about the types of data you need to collect." In the remainder of this section we will discuss some of the types of data that you may want to collect. These sources are often neglected by dissertation students, especially when the data is only available in the early stages of the dissertation.

Early Data

Data available only at the initiation of a study is often lost because the researcher does not think about collecting it until the data is no longer available. This is particularly true of research conducted in applied, professional settings. For example, interviews of clients or service providers about what they expect or anticipate when a new program, structure, or approach is instituted cannot be done after the fact. They must be done before the change is made. There are many other types of "early data" that, if gathered, will turn out to be very useful. Consider what might be helpful and include it in your plan for data collection.

Researcher Notebook

Another important data source that is too often left out of the plan is a researcher notebook. Such notebooks are often kept by both basic and applied researchers in fields like engineering because they become part of the patent application process. And, in cases where there is a disagreement about who actually invented or discovered something, the notebooks of the respective claimants often become one of the most valuable sources of data. In the field of semiconductors, for example, debates about who invented the integrated circuit (Jack Kilby at Texas Instruments or Robert Noyce at Fairchild Semiconductor) dragged on through the courts for years. Similarly, the university where the first electronic computer was invented is still the subject of considerable debate (University of Pennsylvania versus Iowa State University).

The importance of researcher notebooks when it comes to inventions is illustrated by this quote:

> Kilby began to write down and sketch out his ideas in July of 1958. By September, he was ready to demonstrate a working integrated circuit built on a piece of semiconductor material.
>
> Meanwhile up in northern California, a recently formed company Fairchild Semiconductor under the leardership of Robert Noyce began making silicon transistors, which at the time had to be wired together by hand after they were produced. It was a cumbersome, laborious process, and it soon

became clear to Fairchild's founders that the commercial success of their venture rested on the development of a better production method.

Noyce, in his capacity as director of research and development, joined Fairchild co-founder Gordon Moore in investigating methods of connecting transistors that would eliminate after-production wiring. After a time, they developed a theory that seemed plausible, based on the idea of combining transistors in a solid block of silicon. Noyce began making notes in his lab notebook, unaware that a similar theory had already been arrived at the summer before in the laboratories of Texas Instruments, where a young scientist named Jack Kilby had spent months wrestling with the same problem. (Idea Finder, 2007, paras. 1-3)

Even if the researcher notebook you keep for your dissertation does not play an important role in court cases or the history of an emerging technical field like integrated circuits, it can be a very important source of data for you when you begin to analyze data and write up your results. A researcher notebook should be a bit like a diary that tells the who, what, when, and why of what has happened that day or week on your dissertation project. Provide enough information in each entry so that you can understand and interpret what you have said at a later date when thousands of other events related to your dissertation have clouded your memory of specific days and weeks. Some of the more important things to put in your researcher notebook is information on any changes made in what you are studying, changes in the data collected, and changes in the data analysis procedures. These may change drastically in the course of a dissertation study and it is important that you have documentation of when these changes occurred, what changes were made, and why they were made. Be sure, also, to include information on who you talked to about the changes and whether they were in agreement or not. Often, you will make changes upon the recommendation of a committee member, especially your chair. Make sure that information is in your researcher notebook!

Contemporary Researcher Reflections

We see the researcher notebook as containing the details of your dissertation journey: what happened, when it happened, and why. Some advisors also expect you to include in that notebook your reflections about the research. These reflections may include tentative explanations, ideas about what should be studied or explored in more detail, and questions that come to mind. We prefer such reflections to be in a separate document but they can also be conveniently incorporated into the researcher notebook. In either case, the goal is to get your thoughts down while things are fresh. These reflections should be done in a contemporary time frame, not a few weeks later when you get around to it. Think of these reflections as something you need to do each day during particularly active periods of work. You might actually add reflections to this file several times a day when you, for example, collect data in the morning, meet with your chair in the early afternoon, and then spend part of the evening organizing and looking at data. Researcher reflections often guide the "next steps" in the research process but they can also be a source of data when you are explaining the emergence of your understanding and explanations of the data you have gathered.

Contemporary Researcher Observations and Comments

When doing a study in an applied professional setting such as an office, school, or institution you may be there on an almost daily basis for weeks or months. Another type of data you should collect is contemporary observations and comments. If you meet with the chair of a department, with clients receiving the new services that were implemented for the dissertation study, or virtually any other type of contact in the setting that causes you to think about what is happening, write about it in your Observations and Comments file. This can, of course, be combined with your reflections, but we have separated it here to make the point that this is a different type of data. What you observe, and your interpretations of those observations, are important and will likely be very useful in the analysis and write up phase of your dissertation. However, under the stress of getting everything done, many dissertation students put off doing observations and comments—usually by telling themselves they will get that done "this weekend" or "early next week." Soon a month has passed and the observations and comments are no longer contemporary. As they say, "Just do it!"

Contemporary Participant Reflections, Observations, and Comments

Another type of data that is often overlooked comes from participants. If you are doing a study of using new methods in a classroom, for example, what do the students and the teacher think about them when they are implemented, when they are "up and running" and when they have become a standard part of the classroom routine? Asking students and teachers to write reflectively at several points during the implementation process often yields very valuable data. Comments you hear while observing in the classroom are also valuable (if you write them down and remember them) as are the observations of students and teachers who talk with you about the innovation you are studying or your research project in general. Again, these need to be contemporary rather than retrospective because human memory is fallible and fleeting. What you "remember" about a comment made a month ago may not be what you "remember" if you write a note in one of your notebooks twenty minutes after meeting with a teacher or group of students.

Artifacts

Finally, there are many different types of artifacts—from meeting minutes to student projects to business plans to newspaper articles, to photographs and video, to virtually any other type of text or visual or audio data that is relevant to your dissertation research. For example, suppose you are studying a new method for teaching nurses on a unit to administer a particular type of treatment to patients with a specific disease. Your focus is the teaching method, not the treatment. A video clip of the nurses being taught the method would be valuable, particularly if it captures all the innovative steps and procedures involved in the new teaching method. You may be thinking at this point, "I can't put that in a dissertation so why do I need to go to the trouble of collecting that type of data?" There are two reasons. One is that having the video will help you write up the teaching method in a way that communicates how it is different from "traditional" methods. Second, you are likely to make a number of presentations of your dissertation research. Having a video about the teaching method you studied will communicate what you are talking about much better than virtually anything else—including a verbal description of the method. Further, more and more online journals are accepting video data, which means you would be able to include the video in a paper based on your dissertation should you publish in an online journal (and if you obtained the correct permissions from all the participants in the video).

Artifacts relevant to your dissertation study are most difficult to collect at the end of your research when you are beginning to do your final data analysis. They are easiest to do as soon as the artifacts become available. While we have not always followed our own advice to collect artifacts when they become available or when it is possible to create them, we advise you to follow our advice because we have lived to regret our own failures!

With that last piece of advice about collecting data we will turn to another important, if somewhat boring, topic – how to safely store your data.

DATA STORAGE GUIDELINES

As you collect data, it *should be* stored in a safe location and on a stable medium. A cardboard box of data files on DVD discs in the trunk of your Ford Expedition parked in the lot of a Miami school in August does not qualify. In fact, one doctoral student we know left the Mercedes her father gave her parked on a side street near the university and lost a very nice leather briefcase laying on the back seat. That was bad enough but inside it was the sole copy of some critical data. With that in mind, we will expand our advice. As you collect your dissertation data, store it in a safe location, on a stable medium, and keep more than one copy of your data in more than one location.

Handling data today usually means storing it in some sort of computer file. Virtually all forms of data—from numbers to video clips—are either in electronic form from the beginning or can be converted to electronic form. Even when the data is something like handwritten notes, you can use a scanner to convert them to computer files.

When it comes to safeguarding their data, many dissertation students don't go much further than storing their original data on their computer's hard drive and making another copy on a thumb drive, a disc such as a DVD or Blu-ray, or an external hard drive. We think this is not enough. Often the backup files are on a DVD or external hard drive that is close to your computer. Lose the computer through theft, a fire, or an accident, and you may lose the backup data as well.

We suggest you add two levels to your efforts to safeguard your data. First, where possible don't get rid of any of your original data. If clients fill out forms that provide demographic data, don't throw those forms away after you transfer them to computer files. If you administer tests, gather survey data, or conduct interviews that are video or audio taped, keep the original data in a secure and safe place like a safe deposit box. Such boxes are not that expensive and they provide an additional level of protection should something happen to your computerized data files.

The second level of protection involves backing up your data files more than once and making sure that a complete backup is kept "off site." There are many forms of off site data storage these days, but there are a growing number of services that were created specifically to store your computer files. Services designed for large organizations are expensive but there are many data storage services for individuals. Microsoft's Live service (http://www.officelive.com) is one service that provides file backup as well as several other options. You can, for example, use Microsoft Live to share the latest version of your dissertation with your advisor or committee. A similar service is Mozy (www.mozy.com). It also gives you a number of features beyond data storage that will be of interest to doctoral students and if you do not need more than 2 gigabytes of storage, it is free. More than that costs about $5 a month. The website "TopTen Reviews" has an evaluation of the 10 most popular data storage services on the web at http://online-storage-service-review.toptenreviews.com/. If you want to use an online service we suggest reading the reviews there before making a choice. As you make your decision consider more than the cost of the service. Look at the interface. How easy is it to select which files and folders on your computer you want to upload to the file storage service? Does the system work easily enough so that you won't forget or put it off? Automated backup is probably the best option, but you also need to be able to make an unscheduled backup of important files when they are created or changed.

There are simpler ways to store data on the web, such as attaching files to an e-mail message and sending them to yourself. Although we have used this method ourselves, it is not as safe as using an online data storage service. Also, don't forget that if you download your e-mail messages and attachments to a mail management system such as Microsoft Outlook, those files are stored on your computer's hard drive, not on the Internet. If your hard drive crashes you may lose all the files stored there.

WHAT TOOLS WILL YOU USE TO ORGANIZE YOUR DATA?

Before you take precautions to protect your data, you have to create it. In a typical professional practice dissertation, five types of software can be used to create and organize your data files: word processing programs, statistical packages, qualitative data analysis packages, database programs, and electronic spreadsheets. Each type of software is suited to a particular type of data. For example, word processing programs such as Microsoft Word, Corel WordPerfect, and OpenOffice are good for creating text files. Data such as field notes, interview summaries, commentaries, and annotations of papers you have read are all appropriate targets for word processing. A program like Microsoft Word has enough features to be used for some simple forms of qualitative data analysis if the data is primarily text.

On the other hand, if you will be collecting quite a bit of quantitative data, you will need something other than a word processor to organize and analyze that data. There are many general purpose statistical analysis programs such as SPSS that will both create data files and conduct a bewildering array of analyses on those files. If your quantitative data analysis needs are minimal, you may even be able to use a spreadsheet program like Excel to create the files and do the analysis.

There are also hundreds, if not thousands, of specialized data analysis programs designed to support a particular form of data analysis. Content analysis, for example, is a way of analyzing text data such as interview transcripts or historical data, and there are many programs for that purpose. See the website—http://courses.washington.edu/socw580/contentsoftware.shtml—at Washington University for a list of some of the content analysis programs. Harald Klein's website, *Text Analysis Resources* (http://www.intext.de/TEXTANAE.HTM) also has links to programs designed specifically for content or text analysis.

There are also programs to support many other data analysis methods, both qualitative and quantitative. The best way to find appropriate programs is generally to ask an experienced researcher or do a search on the Internet. The Washington University website mentioned above, in fact, lists many different types of software for analyzing qualitative data.

Before considering general purpose programs for qualitative data analysis we want to mention one more specialized type of software. Surveys are so popular in business, advertising, and social science research that many different software packages have been created to analyze survey data. Some are very, very expensive and designed for organizations that do surveys for hundreds of clients. There are, however, a number of less expensive programs that help you organize your survey data and analyze it. A website at Harvard University medical school (http://www.hcp.med.harvard.edu/statistics/survey-soft/) is a good place to start a search for survey analysis software. Also, it is becoming more and more popular to do surveys online. One free and relatively powerful online survey system is BIRAT—the Balch Internet Research and Analysis Toolkit (www.birat.net). BIRAT manages the entire process of doing surveys—from creating a survey to collecting and analyzing the data. It was the result of a professional practice dissertation done by one of our students at Louisiana State University, Charles Balch. Another popular online survey tool is SurveyMonkey (www.surveymonkey.com) that also helps you create, use, collect and analyze data from surveys administered online.

In addition to specialized data analysis programs for qualitative data such as text, there are also a few general purpose programs for qualitative data analysis. The four most popular are Atlas.ti (www.atlati.com), Ethnograph (http://www.qualisresearch.com/), and two programs named NUDIST and NVivo (http://www.qsrinternational.com//default.aspx). These are the "big four" of general purpose qualitative data analysis at the moment but they are each quite different in how they work as well as the purposes and types of analysis they do best.

A final type of software that may be useful to you is a database. Databases were one of the first types of computer software developed for business use and they are still powerful ways of organizing sets of data that include both quantitative and qualitative data. Data from questionnaires, very structured interviews, public records, and historical records are often best analyzed and explored using a database like Microsoft's *Access* or competitors like dBase or Paradox.

As you can see there are quite a few options when it comes to analyzing dissertation data and good choices will save you time as well as provide a higher quality of data. Your advisor and committee will likely be an important source of guidance in making decisions about what type of software to use for organizing and analyzing your data. However, unless your dissertation is relatively straightforward, you are likely to end up using several programs because you will collect several different types of data.

ENSURING THAT YOUR DATA IS ACCURATE

There is an old saying in computer science (at least old in terms of how long computer science has existed). "Garbage in, Garbage out!" It means that if you enter meaningless data or instructions into the computer, the best you can hope for as output from the computer is garbage. This also applies to dissertation data. If in the process of collecting, organizing, and analyzing your data, there is a problem that turns it into garbage, the best you can hope for from your data analysis is garbage. There are many examples of how mistakes in data handling led to very serious mistakes. One that has been deadly in the recent past is a problem with a drug often administered to premature infants. It is also administered to adults as well but in much larger doses. Because the bag of medicine for adults and infants is the same color (until recently) there have been errors that resulted in an infant receiving an adult dose because the dosage is one range for infants (e.g., .1 to .5 milliliters) and in a larger range (e.g., 1 to 5ml) for adults. Using the adult range for infants has resulted in a number of deaths. Another recent mistake that resulted in the lost of a $125 million Mars Lander involved a computer program that was created by two teams, one that used metric measurements and another that used English measures. The result was instructions to the Mars Lander that made no sense and the mission was a failure.

We have all probably watched enough Law and Order television programs to know that there is a "chain of evidence" protocol that police use to protect the integrity of the evidence they gather. Most of the time in television shows, the chain of evidence issue is used by defense attorneys to get evidence suppressed that would otherwise convict their client. However, the O. J. Simpson case, that the whole world seems to have watched, is a real world example of how critical it is that the keepers of data maintain its integrity so that it is both accurate, and believable. We generally do not have such dramatic issues when it comes to the data you collect for your dissertation, but there are important steps you should take when collecting and organizing your data. We have already discussed the need to backup data files and store them "off site." Here are some additional steps that will help assure that you have accurate, and properly organized data to analyze.

CREATE A CODEBOOK FOR YOUR RESEARCH

A codebook, is basically a guide to all your data. It tells you what data is stored where, the organizational structure of the data, when it was collected, and the nature of each piece of data. For example, if you collect demographic data on participants and organize that data into a spreadsheet file, your codebook might include information on the name of the file with demographic data, the location of the original file and the backups, and details of how it is organized. For example, if you forget whether the Gender data in column 3 of the spreadsheet uses "1" for Female or Male, you should be able to look in your codebook and discover that column three is not about gender at all. It is about whether the participants are patients or health care workers. Gender data is in column 13 and F means female, M means male. Codebooks save time and they save you from silly data analysis mistakes that can be both embarrassing and lead to serious errors in analysis and interpretation.

Regardless of the type of data you collect, each source of information should have its own unique code. If all your sources are individuals, you can simply assign a participant number to each individual. If some sources are groups—such as participants in a group interview, you should also have a unique number (or set of letters) for each interview. For example, if you did a focus group interview with six people, your number for that might be DELPHI06 and you would add that information to the codebook so that you could quickly see that DELPHI06 was a group interview held on January 18, 2011. The codebook would include details such as who participated (perhaps only their participant ID numbers if information about them is already in the codebook), the time and place of the meeting, who facilitated the focus group, and so on. When you enter this information in your codebook, it may seem to be a waste of time because everything is so fresh in your memory. However, 6 months later when you are trying to remember details that are no longer fresh, the value of the codebook will be much more apparent.

It is easy to see how demographic data and quantitative data like test scores can be handled in a codebook. If test scores are part of an SPSS file you need only indicate in the codebook that the entering ACT score of a student is in the ninth column of the SPSS data file named "Admissions-ACTDATA" and that the score range is from 13 to 31. Providing a score range helps you check your data for inaccuracies. If a test score range, for example, is 56 to 136 and a score is entered as 242, you know that score is incorrect and you can guess that whoever entered the data probably hit the number keys at the top of the keyboard just to the right of 131 (entering 242 means tapping the keys just to the right of 1, 3, and 1.

When you use non-numeric data, such as transcripts of interviews, observation notes, artifacts such as committee meeting minutes, and video, audio or image data, the way information about it is entered in the codebook is a bit messier but nonetheless important. This data may be stored in anything from a U-Haul moving box to a digital videotape or a computer file. Regardless of the location, it should be documented in your codebook along with enough information to help you remember just what this data is and how it was collected.

Finally, as with other files, it is a good idea to backup you codebook and store it "off site."

Create Participant Data Files

At the same time you are creating a codebook (which will probably change as you rethink how to organize your data and what data needs to be collected), you will need to create participant data files. Those files contain raw data from each source. If most of your data is quantitative, a spreadsheet may be the best way to organize and store your data. However, many professional practice dissertations involve the collection of several types of data. In that case a spreadsheet may not be suitable or it may be one of several ways of storing and organizing your data.

In some studies the data will all be from individuals and if there are many pieces of quantitative data you may store the data from all your participants in one spreadsheet file or a file created in a statistical analysis program like SPSS or SAS. In other cases, you may have huge amounts of qualitative data from a few individuals. In that case you may create files for each individual participant. Those files for individual participants may contain everything from transcripts of interviews to notes of observations of the participant, reflective pieces written by the participant, and data such as the results of examinations and tests. Regardless of how you organize you data files, your codebook should provide all the information needed to find each piece of a particular participant's data set.

Decisions about how to organize and store your data will also depend on the type of software you use to create participant data files. For example, qualitative data analysis programs such as Atlas ti, NUD*IST, and NVivo all have flexible data file systems that can handle many different types of qualitative (and quantitative) data. Some, such as Atlas ti and NVivo, can accommodate both the storage and analysis of video and image data as well as text.

Another convenient way of organizing and managing multiple files of data is to use a "relational" database program. Database programs come in two general formats—flat file and relational. Flat file databases work, essentially, on one file of data. Everything you do in that database will be about the data stored in that one file. Relational databases are different. They let you store data in many different files. For example, one of your relational database files could be "CityCommissionVideo" and it could contain the video of all the meetings of the city commission that you obtained from the local government open access channel. Another database file, such as your participant data file, might contain links to those videos. For example, if one of your individual participants is a member of the city commission, there would be links in his or her data file to the relevant city commission video files. If you have many sources of data that are interrelated in ways that may become confusing, consider using a relational database to organize and keep track of it. The disadvantage of using a regular relational database program to store qualitative data is that databases do not have built-in features for analyzing the data using standard qualitative research methods. Depending on how you approach your data analysis (which is discussed later in this chapter) that may not be a problem. However, in comparing a relational database to a qualitative data analysis program like NVivo, the qualitative analysis program may have many advantages, depending on how you do your analysis. The down side to programs like NVivo and Atlas ti is that they are generally more complex and difficult to learn than relational databases (though these are not easy to learn either).

Ensure Data Integrity: Catch and Correct Errors

When you are dealing with quantitative data there are a thousand ways for errors to creep in. These range from simple data entry errors to mistakes that allocate whole sets of data to the wrong subject or participant. Once, while in intensive care for a heart problem, I (J. Willis) was woken up by a nurse in the middle of the night to take several pills. I managed to get my eyes open wide enough to see that the colors displayed in this set of pills were not familiar to me and I made that point. After checking further the nurse giggled and said they were for the patient in the next room and she would bring mine in a minute. Had I been a little sleepier when I was handed the cup of pills and a glass of water, there is no telling what the result might have been. I doubt this mistake, which should have been written up in the log of that hospital wing, was ever officially recorded. However, errors such as the one I experienced are not uncommon in health care:

> An average of 195,000 people in the USA died due to potentially preventable, in-hospital medical errors in each of the years 2000, 2001 and 2002, according to a new study of 37 million patient records that was released today by HealthGrades. (Loughran, 2004, para. 1)

If there are so many deadly mistakes in a field like health care, where professionals go to great lengths to keep them to a minimum, there is certainly the possibility of significant mistakes in the data collected for a dissertation. One of your jobs as a dissertation student is to take precautions that will reduce the possibility and likelihood of data errors. Some ways of reducing errors, such as creating a codebook, have already been discussed. There are also others that are simple but important. For example, if you are entering data in a spreadsheet and you want to erase data in a cell, *and leave it blank,* click on the cell to make it active and then press the Backspace key. Then press Enter and any data in the cell will be deleted. There are other ways to try and erase data in a spreadsheet cell but they do not always leave the cell blank.

There are many other ways to spot and correct inaccurate data in a spreadsheet file or a data file in programs like SPSS. You should use these because manually entering data in a spreadsheet, or any other computer form, is notoriously error prone. Most people will make at least a few mistakes, and some will make many mistakes. The final step in entering quantitative data is to check it for accuracy. There are several ways to do that:

Use Fresh Eyes for Error Detection. Correcting errors in a set of data often comes at the end of a long and boring session of data entry. You are tired, you are more willing to take shortcuts, and you are more willing to skip or minimize the effort you put into finding and correcting errors. Our advice is to make error checking the first thing you do in a new session, after you have had some rest, instead of the last thing you do at the end of a data entry session. You will be more careful, more serious, and less likely to let a mistake or two slip by.

Look for Outliers. If you scan the data in a column that should only contain numbers from 3 to 6, anything else is an outlier—a number that should not be there. If you find a 2 or a 9 in that column, there is a data entry error. Each column of numeric data can be scanned for outliers that fall outside the range of acceptable numbers for that variable.

Get Someone Else to Check For Errors. Some errors are systematic and you will make them again when you check for errors in data you entered yourself. However, someone else may not make that systematic error and will spot it when they check data you have entered. Where this type of error is possible, get someone else, who takes the task seriously, to check your data for errors.

Consider Double Entry Data Checks. A particularly rigorous way of checking for errors in quantitative data is to enter the data twice in two different files and the run a check to see that the files are exactly the same. Some statistical analysis programs, such as SAS, have a command for doing this. There are also stand-alone programs for doing double entry checks. EasyEntry is one example. The website for this program is http://wwweasyentry.com.

Double entry can also be used to check for errors in text data such as the transcripts of interviews. For example, interview data could be transcribed into two Microsoft Word files and differences checked with the *Compare Documents* command under *Track Changes*. Text data is rarely checked this way because of the cost of transcribing interviews twice and because small errors like typos and incorrect punctuation are not as significant in qualitative data analysis as errors in quantitative data.

However, we should also note that Microsoft Word can be used to check quantitative data as well. When you have a small amount of quantitative data to process, one way to enter it into a spreadsheet or statistical analysis program is to create a "comma separated data file." That will be a set of numbers, with each number separated from the next by a comma. Each group of numbers (e.g., the data for one subject) will end with a carriage return code (pressing the Enter or Return key generates this code). All spreadsheet programs and most statistical analysis programs accept comma separated files. Before transferring the file to another program, you can use the *Track Changes, Compare Documents* command of Word to compare the two data files to see if they are exact duplicates. Word can show you where the files are not alike and thus pinpoint errors. It is often a good idea to have two different people enter the data to avoid idiosyncratic but consistent mistakes (e.g., reading a 7 in the data as a 2).

Oral-Visual Checks, and Better. Finally, there is the tried and true method of having someone call out the data while a second person visually checks the data to verify that it is accurate. There is a scene in the original movie (Woolf & Zinneman, 1973) version of the Frederick Forsythe novel, *Day of the Jackal,* when the French intelligence service agents are trying to figure out what one of the OAS agents said while being interviewed. Unfortunately, the conditions of the interview were so severe the agent died before he could be convinced to explain what he had said. The original transcript of the interview now seems incorrect on a critical point and, because the OAS (Organization of American State) agent is now dead, the French intelligence service agents are left to try and figure out what was actually said by listening again and again to the recording of the interview. This scene points out how easy it is to mishear or misinterpret what someone has said in an interview. One common way of checking your interpretations of an interview is to do a "member check." That is you ask the person you interviewed to look at your interpretations and comment on them. Some researchers also ask those they interview to look at the transcript and make any additions or corrections or comments they like. The focus here is not so much to make sure every word is transcribed as said; it is, rather, to make sure you understand what the person being interviewed intended. It is a higher, but also more important, purpose.

Another way of addressing the potential for misunderstanding text and other forms of data is to ask someone who works from a different theoretical perspective to read both the data and your interpretation. The comments from this person may alert you to ways some of your theoretical or ideological stance has influenced you that you were not aware of. However, that does not mean you must take on the theory/ideology of your colleague—who is also working from his or her own vantage point. It simply means you need to acknowledge that how you interpreted the data is influenced by your foundational beliefs and assumptions.

INTERPRETATION AND ANALYSIS OF YOUR DATA

In discussing things like having someone who works from a different theoretical perspective look at your data and your analysis, we have already begun to explore the process of data analysis and interpretation. As with other sections in this chapter, we will not attempt to provide a thorough guide to analyzing all the possible types of data that might be used in a professional practice dissertation. Instead, we will emphasize some of the larger issues that strongly influence many specific decisions and practices.

Decisions About Data Analysis Procedures

The process of deciding how to analyze quantitative data is quite different from how you think about qualitative data analysis and we will deal with them separately in this section.

Quantitative Data Analysis

Quantitative data analysis procedures have been established and regularized over the past 100 years, and even newly developed methods tend to fit into the established patterns, assumptions, and existing theoretical frameworks of quantitative methods. There are, to be sure, plenty of debates and disagreements over how a certain type of quantitative data should be analyzed and interpreted. However, even where there are disagreements, the logical and argumentative paths to each opinion are well travelled and familiar to those who specialize in that type of analysis. For example, the field of parametric statistical analysis has many rules about when a procedure like a standard analysis of variance (ANOVA) is appropriate, when alternatives such as analysis of covariance (ANCOVA) are better, and when the structure of the data is not suited to any type of parametric analysis. Some scholars focus on "nonparametric" statistical procedures because they do not require the data to meet so many criteria before it can be analyzed and the results considered valid. However, the literature is filled with guidance about how to deal with a Tukey test that is significant and thus that indicates the distribution pattern of parts of your data diverge too far from the "normal distribution" (or from other parts of your data set). Some experts advise that violations of the assumptions of parametric statistical procedures should not to be taken very seriously because they usually do not seriously distort the results. Such experts thus urge you to do your ANOVA or *t*-test anyway. Other experts will tell you the nonparametric alternatives to the parametric statistics are too weak and that while using parametric statistics when some of the assumptions are violated does present a problem, it is probably better in most cases to go ahead with parametric statistical analyses. And, still other experts will tell you that violations must be considered serious and that the nature of applied quantitative research often requires you to use nonparametric procedures that are based on very few foundational assumptions about the pattern and distribution of the data to be analyzed.

The question of whether your quantitative data is suitable for parametric statistical analysis versus nonparametric procedures is only one of many decisions that can come up as you propose and then defend your dissertation. Our advice on how to handle this is more pragmatic than theoretical or ideological. First, get input and advice from your chair. If he or she advocates strict adherence to the rules about using parametric procedures—whether they involve comparing groups (e.g., *t*-tests, ANOVA, ANCOVA) or involve calculations of correlations and regression statistics (e.g., Pearson correlation coefficients)—follow your advisor's lead. For example, the nonparametric equivalent of an ANCOVA is usually the Kruskall-Wallis H Test and the equivalent of a Pearson correlation is the Spearman Rank Correlation Coefficient Analysis. On the other hand, if your chair is comfortable with a liberal interpretation of the foundational assumptions, then go ahead and use parametric statistics. However, make sure you include in your proposal and your dissertation a justification of the decisions you made as well as some quotes from the literature that justify your decision. Of course, as noted earlier, you can find quotes and logical justifications in the literature for any of the three general decisions you will make (ignore violations, justify a "the better of two evils" decision, or take violations seriously and use nonparametric statistics). What is important is not that you find the Right solution in any broad and universal sense. Your job is to first satisfy your chair and then to satisfy your committee. Keep that in mind, and once you have made your decision in collaboration with your chair, include information about, and justification of, that decision in your proposal and your dissertation. Give the committee a chance to wrestle with the issue and to raise any differences of opinion well before you defend your finished dissertation. In our own experience we have seen committees come to a different conclusion in the proposal defense about how a student should analyze dissertation data than was proposed by the student. This is not generally a major problem, but the proposal defense is the latest point in your dissertation project that such discussions should be initiated. After that, there should be general agreement between you and your committee concerning the data analysis procedures.

Qualitative Data Analysis: The Atomistic—Holistic Continuum

If your primary data is qualitative—such as interviews, observations, field notes, and artifacts—the choices of how to analyze them can be overwhelming. Qualitative data analysis in the social sciences has been around for a long time but in the last 30 years these methods have emerged from enclaves such as social anthropology, urban sociology, and the humanities to become mainstream methods used by thousands of researchers in applied fields such as business, education, nursing, engineering, and applied psychology. If you were to spend a year carefully reading every chapter (all 1,136 double column pages in very small print) in the third edition of the *SAGE Handbook of Qualitative Research* (Denzin & Lincoln, 2005) you could probably identify several hundred distinct methods of analyzing qualitative data. They range from highly structured approaches such as content analysis to very open and holistic approaches that are similar to reviewing a play or musical composition.

We recommend the latest edition of the *Handbook* to you as a definitive source of information about all the major and most of the minor qualitative data analysis procedures that can potentially be used to analyze your qualitative dissertation data. However, when making a choice about the particular methods you will use, we also recommend you consider these three factors carefully:

- **Suitability to your purpose.** Different methods provide different types of information and thus are not interchangeable. Think about why you are collecting your data first, what you want to understand when you have analyzed it, and then ask yourself what sorts of data analysis procedures will be the most helpful in developing that type of understanding.

- **Acceptability to Your Committee.** A second very important factor is how your dissertation committee, especially your chair, views the methods you are considering. Ideally, you should select your data analysis methods in collaboration with your chair. After that, the methods should be shared with and explained to your committee, either before or during the proposal defense. Differences of opinion, suggestions about variations in how a method or procedure is applied, and alternatives or additions to the main data analysis procedures proposed, should all be addressed either before or during the proposal process. At least by the end of the proposal meeting your committee should be agreed on how you will analyze your qualitative data.

- **Knowledgeable and Experienced Support.** Even better than just committee approval, however, would be approval from a committee that includes members with extensive experience using the methods you have selected. That applies especially to your chair but many dissertation committees have a chair and a "methods expert" who has agreed to share his or her expertise with you as you use a procedure or method that member knows well. If no one on your committee has experience with the methods you will be using, our advice is to add someone with that expertise or get someone who is not a member to mentor you. It is much better, but not always possible, to have your methods expert actually serve as a dissertation committee member. When they are, they can sometimes help when slippery questions arise related to data analysis, and when they are not, you must defend by yourself the decisions you made based on the advice of an expert who has no vote on your dissertation.

The Atomistic—Holistic Continuum

There are hundreds of different ways to analyze qualitative data but they all tend to fall along a wide continuum that is anchored on one end by what we are calling an atomistic approach (Willis, 2007) and by a holistic approach on the other. The atomistic approach tends to be based on a "code and retrieve" method of data analysis. For example, you might use a qualitative data analysis program like NVivo to "code" your interviews. When a person says "The police officer just assumed because I was a young Hispanic out after midnight in a residential neighborhood that I was guilty of something," such a statement might be coded as "prejudice" or "profiling" or some other code you have created to derive meaning from you interview data. When you have coded all your data, programs like NVivo have sophisticated retrieval methods that allow you to search for all the statements in your interviews (or selected types of interviews) that were coded as examples of Prejudice or Profiling or whatever code that interests you. Qualitative data analysis programs also let you cross check codes. For example, you would be able to look up all instances of the Profiling code based on whether the police officer was white or minority. Some programs like Atlas ti even let you develop a theoretical explanation of your data and then test it against the patterns (e.g., relationships between codes) in your data.

These methods, which all fall under the broad "code and retrieve" approach to qualitative data analysis, have been around for a long time. However, until computer software for analyzing qualitative data became widely available about twenty years ago the process was often a time-consuming manual process that involved writing each sentence from an interview on an index card, putting the codes that applied to that sentence at the top of that card, and then trying to find patterns by looking at all those cards one after the other while you created stacks of coded cards that seemed to be showing a particular pattern in the data. Software like Atlas ti and NVivo have revolutionized this type of qualitative data analysis.

In fact, it is not a stretch to say that virtually all the programs for qualitative data analysis support the code and retrieve approach. That, however, is not the only approach to qualitative data analysis. On the other end of the continuum is what we are calling holistic data analysis. Critics of qualitative data analysis software often focus on what the software was designed to do—support a code and retrieve method of data analysis. They oppose this method and thus oppose software that supports it. Many of these critics believe that extracting snippets of the data, such as sentences from an interview, do serious damage to that data because the meaning of any particular sentence is must be derived from the meaning of that sentence *in context*. If you take the sentence out of its context, you lose some of its potential meaning. Scholars who take this view advocate holistic data analysis. For example, you might carefully read the interview transcripts and make notations about ideas and possible explanations as you read. Then you read again, and again, and so on while you write and revise your emerging understanding of what the interviews are telling you. The results of this type of holistic analysis is often a reflective explanation of what you feel you have learned from a careful study of the interviews, supported by material drawn from them to illustrate the points you are trying to make. You could say that while code and retrieve methods put the locus of data analysis in a procedure, the holistic approach puts that locus in the mind of the researcher. One of the foremost advocates of holistic methods in education is Elliot Eisner (1997) at Stanford University. His most recent book, *The Enlightened Eye: Qualitative Inquiry and the Enhancement of Educational Practice*, is both a justification of holistic analysis and an explanation of how it is done using Eisner's Connoisseurship model.

An example of code and retrieve methods of data analysis is the use of a method called grounded theory or the constant comparative method. A current guide to this method is Cathy Charmaz's (2006) book, *Constructing Grounded Theory: A Practical Guide Through Qualitative Analysis*. Charmaz explains grounded theory methods this way:

> Grounded theory methods consist of systematic, yet flexible guidelines for collecting and analyzing qualitative data to construct theories 'grounded' in the data themselves. The guidelines offer a set of general principles and heuristic devices rather than formulaic rules ... thus, data form the foundation of our theory and our analysis of these data generates the concepts we construct. Grounded theorists collect data to develop theoretical analyses from the beginning of a project. We try to learn what occurs in the research setting we join and what our research participants' lives are like. We study how they explain their statements and actions, and ask what analytic sense we can make of them.
>
> Grounded theorists start with data. We construct these data through our observations, interactions, and materials that we gather about the topic or setting. We study empirical events and experiences and pursue our hunches and potential analytic ideas about them. Most qualitative methods allow researchers to follow up on interesting data in whatever way they devise. Grounded theory methods have the additional advantage of containing explicit guidelines that show us how to proceed. (pp. 2-3)

The "how to proceed" of grounded theory data analysis usually begins with a process of developing a set of codes (or using an existing set) and coding the available data. While you are coding you develop explanations, hypotheses, ideas, and questions. These become your first, tentative explanation of what the data is telling you. This is your first theory. In some grounded theory studies you reach your first theory by analyzing a part of your data—say 5 of 20 interviews. Then you use your tentative theory as a guide to analyzing another 5 or so interviews. Did the analysis of the code patterns and text of the interviews completely confirm your first theory? Probably not. You will probably need to revise or reformulate aspects of your first theory—or even throw it out completely and develop another one that is congruent with the data from both your first and second sets of interviews. Then you analyze another set of interviews that have not yet been analyzed—using your second theory as a framework. Does the analysis of these interviews support your second theory? Probably not, so you revise your theory and analyze more data.

Another way grounded theory may be done is to analyze all the data, develop your theory, then analyze the all the data again using your revised theory. In either case, you can see how grounded theory provides the researcher with a somewhat structured and organized way of approaching the analysis of qualitative data. Charmaz's (2006) book is one of many that will guide you through the process of doing a grounded theory data analysis. Many scholars, including doctoral students beginning their first major research project, find the structure and guidelines of grounded theory comforting and supportive. Dissertation students often feel uncomfortable with the looser and more open model of holistic data analysis because so much of what you do to analyze the data happens inside the head of the researcher. That is, of course, in keeping with Eisner's idea of the researcher as a *connoisseur*. Eisner compares the researcher as connoisseur to the role of a wine expert who reviews a new vintage or to a critic who reviews a new play or movie or musical composition. However, many doctoral students are not yet ready to take on such a role. Also, there are diverse opinions about the value of atomistic and holistic ways of analyzing qualitative data. Some are strong advocates of atomistic methods while others prefer holistic approaches. The three authors of this book fall all along the continuum. One prefers methods like grounded theory that come from the atomistic end of the continuum, one falls somewhere in the middle and is relatively eclectic, and the other is a shameless promoter of holistic data analysis methods.

SUMMARY

In this chapter we have discussed some of the important issues that must be addressed when collecting and analyzing your dissertation data. There are, for example, important sources of data that are often overlooked or ignored—especially if it is only available early in the dissertation process.

There are also data sources such as researcher notebooks as well as researcher and participant reflections and observations that provide very useful data, especially if they are contemporaneous. However, with the pressure of getting everything done to complete a dissertation many of these sources get a lower priority and sometimes are not tapped. We urge you to keep them in your plan and to make sure they are collected.

Regardless of the quality and amount of data collected, it is only useful if it is well organized and safely stored. Procedures like creating a codebook for your data contribute to good organization, and steps like backing up all data and keeping at least one copy "off site" reduce the likelihood of data loss.

Good organization of data also means selecting the right tool for the type of data you are collecting. Word processing programs, statistical analysis programs, qualitative data analysis programs, spreadsheets, and databases are all potential tools for data storage and organization. However, these programs are best for different types of data and different purposes. You will want to consider your choices of tools carefully when it comes to organizing, storing, and analyzing your data. And, of course, you should incorporate a range of error detection and correction procedures into the process of collecting and organizing your data.

Finally, there are decisions about the type of data analysis procedures you use that do not have agreed upon and universal answers. Different groups of scholars will have different opinions. The most important group of scholars for you is your dissertation committee. The data analysis procedures you decide to use should emerge from discussions with your chair and should be agreed to by your committee. Even better than agreement on your data analysis methods is the presence of expertise on your committee. Ideally, several of your committee members will be experienced users of the methods you have selected.

CHAPTER 12

THE DISSERTATION WRITING PROCESS

HOW DO YOU "WRITE" A DISSERTATION? KEEP YOUR FOCUS!

All of us have had the experience of starting out to do a particular task and, hours later, realized that we have been sidetracked and are no longer focusing on that task. Something else has attracted our attention and, sometimes without even realizing it, we have shifted our focus. This happens often when it comes to dissertation work. One of the peculiar characteristics of the dissertation process is how compelling some things become that were frequently ignored before the dissertation became so important. Housework, such as cleaning the bathroom, arranging the bookshelves, or putting up curtains that have been in the closet for more than a year, can become so critical that the task commands a doctoral student's attention when plans called for hours of work on some aspect of the dissertation. If you find yourself concerned about the waxy buildup on your kitchen floor, or the disorganization apparent in the way you have run cables from your computer to you peripherals, this may be a sign of *dissertatus avoidus*—a psychosocial malady that is surprisingly prevalent among dissertation students, even those who proclaim loudly and often that their dissertation has their highest priority. There are lots of reasons for this problem and they vary from student to student. Doing a disserta-

Completing a Professional Practice Dissertation: A Guide for Doctoral Students and Faculty, pp. 325–346

tion calls for a significant shift in working patterns, especially if you have just spent 2 years taking courses with other students and having the schedule of the classes, the tasks to be completed, and the timeline for completion, set by someone else. Now, along comes the dissertation and it can be a solitary activity that also requires you to make, on your own, many decisions about time allocation, what to work on now, and when to contact your advisor or committee. Other possible causes of *dissertatus avoidus* include worries about the ability to complete the dissertation successfully, the huge amount of work that has to be done to finish, and competing demands for available time. Sometimes doing something like cleaning the apartment, which has never been a priority, is a way of avoiding harder choices such as spending the weekend on a family outing versus sending the family on a picnic while you stay at home or go to the library and work on your dissertation.

And, just as there are multiple causes for *dissertatus avoidus*, there are also multiple ways of getting over it. You may already know what works for you, but there are also some "treatments" that seem to work well for quite a few dissertation students. One is to try and avoid making your dissertation a solitary action. Join or form a dissertation work group that meets regularly and offers both psychological support and professional help. Such groups are based on the idea of writing groups to support novelists or academics writing scholarly papers. Other approaches include attending conferences where there will be sessions on doing your dissertation, or attending workshops at your institution on how to do a dissertation. Sometimes setting subgoals such as finishing a draft of your methods chapter, or getting all the consent forms done and filed, will help you make progress. Each subgoal accomplished is both fulfilling and psychologically uplifting. Keeping in contact with your chair is also helpful, especially if he or she provides encouragement and helps you see the work as doable.

Beware of Simple and Simplistic Advice

We have offered our share of simple and simplistic advice in this book but we nevertheless want to warn you that such advice is as often wrong for you as it is right—perhaps more often wrong! There are three types of advice we find particularly problematic.

Any "One-Size-Fits-All" Advice is Probably Wrong

If you are given what amounts to a recipe for doing your dissertation and told that if you follow this recipe you will undoubtedly be successful, be particularly cautions about adopting such a plan. Doing a dissertation is at the same time an intensely personal and social process. You are at the center of that process but you will be engaged with a number of groups—your chair and committee, your professors, your colleagues in the field, and participants in your dissertation project. You are a unique individual and the groups you interact with as you plan and complete your dissertation are also unique. That must be taken into consideration when creating and implementing a plan to finish your dissertation. A student working on a dissertation is more like an artist creating an original painting than someone who has purchased a "paint by number" kit and is dutifully daubing the specified color in each of the numbered spaces on the canvas that came with the kit.

Writing Your Dissertation in 3 Weeks (or 3-Minutes a Day)

Some sources of advice focus on setting up a particular timeframe and schedule for writing your dissertation. Perhaps it involves working an hour a day, or three hours a day, but you are told that following a particular regimen will assure success. That may be true if the author of the advice were writing your dissertation but it may not be true for you. As you think through how you will approach writing your dissertation give serious thought to your work habits and patterns. If they have been successful in the past, they may also work for writing your dissertation. If you recognize weaknesses or problems in your work habits that will need to be overcome to complete your dissertation in a reasonable timeframe, think through how to address them. Talk with friends, colleagues, partners, and your dissertation chair. Then, as you write, monitor yourself and identify any problems that come up. Think about how to deal with the problem(s) and try out one or more solutions. Keep working both on completing the different dissertation tasks and on handling any problems you see. If you look back on a month and see that you have made very little, if any, progress, talk with others. Listen to people who know you well and look for insights they may have that will help you get beyond a barrier or problem and start productive work again on your dissertation. What you don't want to do is adopt a plan prescribed for everyone without thinking carefully about how it fits you.

Linear Plans Are Essential, Not!

We have discussed linear versus nonlinear plans for doing a dissertation in a previous chapter but it bears repeating here that some people work better when there is a linear plan and some do not. Again, we would emphasize that the decision about whether you follow a linear plan or a nonlinear one depends on many factors including your own personality and work habits, the nature of your dissertation, and the nature of the context in which you will do the dissertation. It is not a simple decision but it is a personal rather than a universal one.

SOME USEFUL GUIDELINES

Now, having warned you against simple and simplistic advice, we will proceed to offer you just that. We offer seven simplistic suggestions in this section for your consideration, knowing that some or all of it may not apply to you, to your type of dissertation, or to your particular context.

Keep the Audience in Mind

English professors are fond of telling students that one of the most important factors in good writing is the ability to keep the audience in mind. If you are writing a paper on a new treatment for ear infections in children, the paper you write will be quite different if the audience is parents rather than pediatricians. The advice about keeping your audience in mind also applies to your dissertation, but the question that many students do not answer correctly is "Who is my audience?" We think the answer to that question should be clear and simple. Your primary, most important, most powerful, and most influential audience is the dissertation committee. If your parents, the president of your university, and the bulk of the Republican (or Democratic) Party all think your dissertation is terrible, it will still be accepted and your will still receive your doctorate if your dissertation committee likes and approves it. That is a reality that should never be far from your thoughts. Thus, write your dissertation for your committee. The members are your audience.

Select an Appropriate Style

Different committees may have different preferences for the style you use when writing a dissertation. Below are a few styles that are in widespread use today:

Sterile Academic Style

Far too many dissertations are still written in stilted, difficult-to-follow academic style that distances the dissertation from the reader in ways that only an academic who is steeped in this style could appreciate. Sometimes, students adopt this style because they think it is what is expected of them. Sometimes that is true! But more often, the dissertation committee will accept such a style but, in reality, would prefer another.

Comfortable Academic Style

Another style that is becoming much more popular is still academic. It takes the topic seriously, relates the dissertation study to the existing literature, and thoughtfully lays out sophisticated ideas that may be difficult for lay readers to understand but are both interesting and understandable to academics who know the topic of the dissertation. For many dissertations, especially theoretical and empirical dissertations, this is probably the style most committees would prefer.

Journalistic Style

"Journalistic" dissertations are written in a format that is easy to read. This applies to readers who are insiders such as academics who specialize in the topic, and readers who are not specialists but who have an interest, and some background. Complex ideas and concepts are explained in commonly used language rather than academic language, and less demands relative to general and specific knowledge about the topic are put on the reader. More is explained, introduced, and linked to the dissertation research. Such a dissertation could be read, for example, by an undergraduate student who is interested in the topic and has completed no more than one college course on a related topic. Theoretical and empirical dissertations in the positivist tradition rarely use this style. Many committee members may consider it less scholarly than a dissertation should be. It is occasionally used in writing dissertations about professional practices, especially if is likely to be read by practitioners with relevant experience but limited exposure to the theoretical and conceptual aspects of the topic. If you are thinking about using a journalistic style for your dissertation, make sure it is acceptable to your dissertation committee.

Narrative Inquiry and Storytelling

Until about 25 years ago, most of the American social sciences and professional fields like education focused on a certain type of knowledge—it was abstract, universal, and disconnected from the context in which the knowledge developed. Things have changed in the last 25 years, however, and there is an increasing respect for narrative inquiry, which was discussed in previous chapters, and for the type of knowledge that develops through narrative inquiry. Dissertations based on this approach will generally "tell a story" which means the knowledge and understanding is communicated through the story that is told. Because narrative inquiry and storytelling involves a commitment to paradigms and ideologies that are not yet mainstream in many doctoral programs, you will want to work closely with your dissertation committee on the plan for a dissertation that is based on narrative inquiry and storytelling. Fortunately, professional practice doctoral programs are often much more comfortable with this approach than traditional research doctorates.

Persuasive Style

Occasionally a student will want to write a dissertation that is primarily an effort to persuade the reader that an approach, idea, or model is clearly the best option given particular professional situations or decision points. The entire dissertation, which many include a case study or some other form of research, is aimed at persuading the reader to join with the author in advocating a particular change or idea. That is, in fact, often the purpose of a dissertation but dissertations are not often written in ways that make this purpose blatantly obvious. At one extreme, a committee may insist that you maintain a stance of strict objectivity. You do not use "I" or "We" in the dissertation and when you state a particular position you also offer alternative positions and arguments. A middle ground is to emphasize one position but to acknowledge that there are alternatives, even if they are not explored in detail. Dissertations based on rhetorical efforts to persuade do exist but they are not very common. Most committees will want you to take at least a "middle ground" approach if not an "objective" approach. The acceptance of a persuasive style of dissertation also depends on the field of study as well as the inclinations and comfort zones of the committee members.

Philosophical Inquiry

Related to but different from the persuasive style is philosophical inquiry. Such a dissertation involves presenting alternatives and explaining the foundations of these alternatives. And, either concurrently or sequentially, you select or develop an alternative that you prefer, marshal your evidence for it and deal with all the likely objections to it from opposing philosophical and theoretical perspectives. The "alternative" you are discussing may be a professional practice, a theoretical approach to professional practice, or a philosophical foundation for practice. What characterizes philosophical inquiry is not so much the topic but the way you approach the topic. Instead of doing quantitative, empirical research, or a narrative inquiry, you "think" about the topic and build a case for your viewpoint by analyzing other people's viewpoints and describing why yours is better. Philosophical inquires are not very common in professional practice dissertations but our impression is that the reason is more often that students are uncomfortable doing them than because the dissertation committee would not allow this style and form of dissertation.

To summarize, there are quite a few styles for writing a dissertation and the one you select should fit you, your topic, and be acceptable to your dissertation committee.

Develop Your Own Writing Style

We have emphasized the need to consider your dissertation committee's preferences and comfort zone when selecting a dissertation style, but there is a dark side to that as well. The authors of this book were all pushed into writing dissertations in styles that were close to the "sterile academic" style described above. None of us became a basic researcher in a field where that style was then necessary to be published. Ron became a principal and then a superintendent of schools. Jerry became a college professor with an emphasis on applied rather than basic research. Deborah became a college professor, education specialist in the federal government, and international change agent. All our career choices call for a much more informal and comfortable style of writing than "sterile academic" and the dissertation experience actually distracted us from the goal of developing a written communication style that fit our career goals and needs. In some cases it took four or five years after our doctorates to rid ourselves of the bad habits learned while completing a dissertation in a format that was expected by the committee. Fortunately, our experiences were several decades ago and as dissertation advisors ourselves we are much more flexible when it comes to style. Our advice is to consider the wants and preferences of your dissertation committee but if you think it is possible to convince them that other styles than the one(s) they prefer are worth considering, try to use the dissertation experience to help develop your own style and make it better.

Write, Get Feedback, Write, Get Feedback

Reading advice on how to write can be useful, but writing and responding to feedback is an even better approach. Writing is generally a major requirement of doctoral programs and every paper your write, individually or collaboratively, is an opportunity to get feedback and advice. When you submit a paper, ask your professor to offer suggestions on how the paper could be improved.

Professors are not the only sources of feedback, however. Form a writing group and get your fellow students involved in critiquing and offering suggestions about papers. Reading someone else's work and offering suggestions helps you think about writing, and the critiques of your papers will help you identify common problems that many people see when they read your work. If there are optional courses on writing that are part of your doctoral program, take them. If they are required, great—make the best use of them. If they don't exist, inquire about whether the faculty is interested in offering them before you graduate. Writing is one of the critical skills of professional practice and quite a few doctoral students (and professors!) can benefit from a concerted effort to improve their writing skills.

Know When To Stop

There is a story about Whistler, the painter, that even after he sold a painting and it was proudly hung on the walls of the owner's home, Whistler would sometimes visit and while there make additional changes to the painting. Whistler found it difficult to let go and consider the painting finished. Some dissertation students have the same problem and it happens at two points. One is during intermediate stages of writing when there is a rough draft of a chapter or two that should be passed on to the chair for review. Some students are reluctant to do that. They keep "polishing" and tweaking the drafts, sometimes for months. Professors have different levels of tolerance concerning how rough a draft they will work on, but their lack of tolerance is rarely the reason why students delay submitting a draft. There are many reasons for holding back a draft but all of them hold up progress on the dissertation. You need feedback from your chair in order to make the next revision and the sooner you get that feedback the better. If you are having difficulties submitting a draft to your chair, ask a trusted colleague or a professional editor to read it first and offer suggestions. Make the changes that seem important and then submit the draft chapters to your chair. Submitting drafts can become a bottleneck in the writing process so it is important that you get beyond any reluctance you have to submit a draft once you have written it and then revised it one or two times.

The other phase when this problem arises is when it is time to turn in a draft of the entire document. The same problems and issues can arise here, but because you are dealing with the entire dissertation, the time delay can be greater because you are working on a longer document. Again, the issue needs to be dealt with quickly so that you do not lose a great deal of time. One solution to this issue is to hire an editor.

Get a Real Editor! Pay for Quality!

Dissertation students, especially in professional practice doctoral programs, are typically older and with family as well as work responsibilities. Completing a doctorate involves sacrifice on the part of the student and his or her family. One aspect of the sacrifice is the financial burden placed on the family. Even if the student can continue to work full time, the tuition and other expenses of a doctoral program are significant. That is one reason why students often resist the suggestion to pay for the professional services of an editor who knows about editing dissertations. Yet, we will argue that if you are having trouble writing your dissertation you may actually save money in the long run by hiring a qualified editor. Working with a writing group or getting a friend or spouse to read and edit your work may help, but paying for the services of a top notch editor can save you both time and money in the long run.

Our only advice about hiring an editor is that you do not simply turn over your draft to an editor and then pick it up after it has been polished and "fixed." Instead, work with the editor and use the experience to learn how to write better. Don't simply accept any change the editor makes. Instead, ask them to explain their recommendations and tell you why the way you wrote a sentence, paragraph, or chapter was problematic. A good editor, who is also a good writing tutor, can help you develop communication skills that you will use for decades after completing your doctorate.

To select an editor we advise that you interview several and to learn enough about their approach to be confident you can work with them as well as learn from them. Keep in mind also that making price the primary deciding factor may eliminate from consideration some outstanding editors who know what they are worth and are comfortable setting their prices at a premium level. The highest priced editor is not necessarily the best editor for you, but the lowest priced editor is not necessarily the "best buy" either.

Remember, Finishing is the Immediate Goal!

When one of the authors of this book did his dissertation a distinguished professor on his committee disagreed strongly on how some achievement tests should be administered to the emotionally disturbed children he was studying. In essence, the argument was over whether to follow the directions for administering that achievement test precisely or to modify the directions to take into consideration the common characteristics of emotionally disturbed children. The distinguished professor insisted that the directions be followed precisely. In contrast, Jerry argued that we would get better data about these students' achievement levels if we modified the testing conditions. The committee reached an impasse. However, Jerry's primary goal, and it should be your goal as well, was to finish the dissertation. Jerry did the testing as the distinguished professor insisted way and completed the dissertation. (However, Jerry also did another study that is still cited in the literature that showed the alternative approach approach was more informative and accurate when evaluating emotionally disturbed children.)

The dissertation is one step in a doctoral program, which is one step in a career. When you are in a doctoral program, and working on your dissertation, it is easy to lose sight of the fact that your dissertation is not what you will be doing for the rest of your life. It occupies your time and your mind in a unique and comprehensive way, but it does that for a year or so. After that you begin a new phase of your career and the dissertation's importance fades as other opportunities and challenges replace it. Finishing your dissertation is thus an important but relatively short term goal. Remember, the goal is finishing, not "winning" or "conquering" or anything else—it is finishing. And, considering the tens of thousands of ABDs in the world, finishing is a difficult and honorable goal.

THE DEFENSE: PREPARATION AND PARTICPATION

You have scheduled your defense for three weeks from this Thursday; you have completed your "final" draft before the defense, made copies and distributed them to each of the committee members, and now you are thinking about how to get ready for the defense. We think this may be a time when you can relax a bit and unwind. Talk to your chair about questions he or she expects to come up in the defense. Prepare for them carefully and try and anticipate some questions yourself that you will be ready to answer. If traditions of your program allow it, talk to each person on your committee after they have read your dissertation and make notes about things you need to bone up on before the defense. Keep in mind, however, that in a typical dissertation defense, the student is the most knowledgeable person in the room when it comes to the topic of the defense. You began preparing for the defense when you started reading papers and talking to professors and practitioners about your dissertation topic. What you have done up to this point is much more important than what you will do between now and three weeks from now when you defend your dissertation at a public meeting.

A traditional defense involves you making a 10 to 30 minute presentation (traditions vary from program to program) on your dissertation study. In most instances, all the members of your committee will have read the dissertation and made some notes about the questions they want to ask. Occasionally, however, there will be one member who, for one reason or another, has not read the dissertation. He or she is present and wants to participate in the questioning in ways that do not embarrass anyone, but that professor will be depending on your presentation to provide enough orientation and information to conjure up a few meaningful questions to ask you. Make sure you help a committee member in such a situation by making an informative presentation that presents both some of the scope and the details of the dissertation.

Once the presentation is over, the round of questions begins. The process is similar to the proposal defense so will not be repeated here. Our advice about how to handle difficult questions or issues is also the same as it was for proposal defenses.

When the questions are finished and the committee has voted behind closed doors to approve or disapprove your dissertation, you and any guests are invited back into the room and it is traditional for the chair to be the first person to greet you as "Dr. ____." Other members will join in with congratulations and then the committee will settle back into routine and explain their vote. Usually the vote is to accept the dissertation with some revisions that will be supervised by either the chair or the entire committee. It is best if your chair has that responsibility, but if the committee will also be involved you will need to make sure you get the revisions to everyone and that they all approve. More often, all the members sign your dissertation approval form at the end of the meeting and they leave it to the dissertation chair to see to it that you make the required revisions satisfactorily. Sometimes the chair does not sign the approval form until the revisions are satisfactorily made.

Once revisions are made, you must submit a properly formatted dissertation to the appropriate campus office. Some offices still require paper copies but more and more require electronic copies in a standard format such as Microsoft Word, RTF, or PDF. Adobe's PDF is currently the most popular electronic format but you must follow the directions and requirements of your institution. Usually, there will be someone who approves the format of your dissertation and accepts your submission. There will be fees to pay, an abstract that will be submitted to a dissertation archive service such as ProQuest, and assorted forms to fill out. Then, you are finished! Congratulations!

One common contribution some faculty make to a final defense is a heavily edited copy of your dissertation with grammar, spelling, and punctuation corrections. There may even be a professor who has identified all your sins against the APA guidelines for citations and references. Thank them for their help, take their copies so you can find all the corrections that need to be made, and promise that you will return a clean and corrected copy of your dissertation to them. Traditionally, your chair receives a bound copy of your dissertation while committee members receive an unbound copy. Our advice is to give all members of your committee a bound copy. It is small recompense for the effort they have invested in your dissertation, and it is an indication that you appreciate their efforts. If your institution requires the submission of electronic dissertation copies only, we suggest you consider having bound copies of your dissertation done by one of the "print on demand" services such as LuLu. LuLu can produce softbound or hardbound copies of your dissertation a very low cost to you (see www.lulu.com for more information on how to submit a PDF version of your dissertation to LuLu for printing).

AD—AFTER THE DISSERTATION

Finishing a dissertation is such a momentous occasion, one that calls for much celebration and joy, that after finishing it can be difficult to start up long postponed aspects of life and begin "living normally" again, whatever that means. In this section we will discuss some aspects of living normally after a dissertation.

Therapy, Recovery, and Freudian Repression of the Memory

We wrote this section only half in jest. The dissertation process can be stressful and the opportunity to talk with someone about the process, to work out your feelings and understanding of what happened, and to begin to think seriously about the future, is often a needed step in the AD or After Dissertation phase of your life and career. This may be done with your partner or lover, with one or more sympathetic colleagues, and with a trusted mentor or advisor. It can also be done with a counselor who does this type of work professionally. It is probably not so important who you talk to as it is that the experience is helpful to you. Many people want to handle difficulties, stresses, and traumas by themselves because they fear others will consider them weak or unstable if they know you are going to counseling. There is also a streak of pioneer individualism and independence in the American psyche that does not always serve us well. If you think it will be helpful, talk to someone, or talk to several people, including a professional counselor. Often the process of talking about things helps you finalize your understanding, your reality, of the dissertation process. That then becomes a foundation for thinking about your future. However, this is an individual decision. If your dissertation experience was minimally stressful, if you are usually successful working out issues on your own and that is the approach you prefer, talking to others, including a counselor, may not be needed.

For many people there is also an aspect of forgetting. If the joys and pleasures of doing your dissertation gradually sharpen as time passes, while the stresses and problems fade and become less sharp, that is not necessarily a bad thing. Moving your dissertation out of the center of your life makes more room for other aspects—your relationships and family, your career and professional goals, your interests and pleasures.

Follow-Up Work

Before you leave your dissertation behind completely, think about any follow up work that needs to be done. Did the study open up new opportunities, new possibilities, in your work? At your company, organization, or institution? Is there a "next step," or several next steps, that should be done if you want to build on your dissertation and accomplish something larger than the dissertation study itself? Some people do a dissertation and make it the launching point for the next decade or more of their professional life. For others the dissertation tells them something else—that there are other avenues, other frontiers in their career, they want to pursue. If possibilities do emerge from your dissertation, now is the time to think about how to turn the possibilities into plans and actions. In the next section we will address one common "follow up" to your dissertation —how to disseminate your findings to others.

DISSEMINATING YOUR RESEARCH

A typical response to finishing a dissertation is to stare at the finished copy for a few days and then put it on a shelf for a year or two. Those years can stretch into decades for many dissertations. However, if you can overcome the reluctance to do any more on your dissertation after it has been approved and submitted, we have some suggestions about how to get the word out about your research.

The Dissertation

Naturally, the dissertation itself is the most comprehensive and detailed presentation of your research. If someone is interested in your topic, they may want to read the entire dissertation and the best way to enable them is to make it available online for downloading. Services like ProQuest provide this service for a fee readers must pay, but you are also free to make your dissertation available through services that are free to anyone who wants to read your dissertation. Many colleges and universities, for example, have an online library of dissertations completed at their institutions. Here are, for example, the web addresses of online dissertation repositories at several universities:

http://www.uflib.ufl.edu/etd.html University of Florida

http://www.pitt.edu/~graduate/etd/ University of Pittsburgh

http://www.lib.virginia.edu/etd/ University of Virginia

http://www.wvu.edu/~thesis/ West Virginia University

There are also a number of online depositories that carry dissertations from many different institutions. One is the *Networked Digital Library of Theses and Dissertations* (NDLTD) (http://www.ndltd.org/ndltd/find). This is a large project, which originated at Virginia Tech University, that encourages and supports the creation of electronic theses and dissertations, and the dissemination of those documents via the Internet. Most of the files are in the Adobe Portable Document Format (PDF). Many, but not all, of the dissertations in this archive are available without charge. If you would like to explore NDLTD's *Electronic Thesis and Dissertation* archive the home page address is http://scholar.lib.vt.edu/theses/. If you decide to submit your dissertation to one additional archive beyond any required by your institution we recommend this one.

The *Theses Canada Portal* (http://www.collectionscanada.gc.ca/thesescanada/s4-230-e.html) has information on over 300,000 theses and dissertations from Canadian institutions. Over 50,000 are available electronically. Not to be outdone, the U.K.'s *Index to Theses* (http://www.theses.com/) has information on over half a million theses and dissertations that go back as far as 1716. Some of these are accessible online in full text either for free or for a fee.

Another useful site if you are looking for dissertation repositories is the Registry of Open Access Repositories (ROAR) at http://roar.eprints.org/. This is a list of links to repositories for preprints (rough drafts of papers before they are accepted by a journal) and dissertations/theses. The first link on the list is *Addis Ababa University Electronic Theses and Dissertations*, which has over 1,500 entries and the last is the *Universidad de Boros—Repositorio Instructional—Tesis Doctoral*.

If you would like to make your dissertation widely available to anyone interested in reading it, there are several approaches. First, make sure you use your institution's online repository if there is one. Then, put a PDF version of your dissertation on your website, along with a list of descriptor terms that search engines can use to find it. After that do an online search using phrases like "search engine placement," "website submission service," or "search engine optimization" to find articles that tell you how to make sure the major search engines have indexed your site so that your dissertation will be found when someone searches for information on relevant terms.

A third way to increase the exposure of your dissertation is to use one of the services that make it available in either print or electronic form. Dissertation.Com is one such service. This service takes your PDF dissertation file and distributes it to interested readers as if it were a book. It sells print and electronic copies and gives you 20-40% of the sales price. The advantage of Dissertation.Com is that your dissertation has an ISBN number which is how bookstores identify a particular book. While this may generate some sales of your dissertation, more people will probably find it through the ProQuest online system that many universities use to distribute dissertations (http://www.proquest.com then click on the "UMI Dissertations Publishing" link at the bottom of the page). This service has been around for decades and it has been a traditional way of distributing printed copies of dissertations. If you read the abstract of a dissertation in reference publications like *Dissertation Abstracts International*, you could jot down the number of a dissertation and order it from UMI for $25 to $65. It arrived in a week or so. Almost all the dissertations produced at American universities were available through UMI because students were required to submit a copy to UMI for archiving. Today, this service has been updated to allow online access, and most universities still use this method as a way to make dissertations available to a wider audience. When you finish your dissertation you will probably need to complete a set of forms giving your institution permission to submit your dissertation to the ProQuest/UMI system. If the forms give you the option of making your dissertation freely available (as opposed to restricting the full text to a certain group such as faculty and students at your university) we suggest you make it freely available. If you goal is to share what you have learned in your dissertation research, it is generally desirable that there be no restrictions on who can read it.

If your university does not participate in the ProQuest/UMI service you can still submit your dissertation as an individual. Just follow the directions on the website. There are two major advantages and one significant disadvantage to the ProQuest/UMI system. The first advantage is that the system now accepts both document files and multimedia files. If your dissertation is a 125 page dissertation and two hours of video stored in digital files, both the dissertation and the video files will be available to readers. This is a relatively new feature of this service, but it is one that will become standard in the near future as we expand our ideas of what a dissertation can contain beyond black ink on white paper.

The second advantage is that it has a very good search system that potential readers can use to find your dissertation. The disadvantage is that once found, searchers will have to pay a fee to read the dissertation. They may even have to pay a fee to do the search. The *ProQuest Dissertations and Theses* database is probably available online through your university library portal, but if not, even searching will require you to subscribe to the service. And, if you want to read more than the abstract of a particular dissertation, you may have to pay for that too unless your institution has a license that provides free access to the full text of the dissertation.

Finally, we will repeat the advice we gave earlier in this section. If you submit your dissertation to just one additional archive, we recommend Virginia Tech's Electronic Thesis and Dissertation service which is at http://scholar.lib.vt.edu/theses/. This service seems to be a well established, stable, and long term resource for free access to dissertations.

Traditional Presentations

The second most common way of presenting the results of a dissertation is at a conference, and the most common support for a presentation is a Microsoft PowerPoint file. There are many guides in the literature about how to create a strong PowerPoint presentations but the average quality of presentations at scholarly and professional conferences suggests they are more often written than read. A well organized, lively, and interesting PowerPoint presentation adds visual interest and appeal to a presentation, but if it is poorly organized, hard or impossible to read or see details, and distracting because of either too little or too much information, the result is frustrating. Many veteran conference attendees consider it a good day if of six presentations they attend, one is "pretty good" and another is "great." Of course, a traditional PowerPoint presentation, even if good, will not overcome other problems or difficulties in the presentation, but they can be one important element of a strong presentation. We suggest you read some of the guides for creating good presentations, and don't let your conference presentation be the first time you have made a PowerPoint presentation. Practice in your classes, in your dissertation proposal and defense, and become comfortable with both the technology and how you will control the flow of the presentation.

Finally, keep in mind that while 99.99% of PowerPoint presentations are linear—they start with slide 1 and proceed sequentially to the last slide, PowerPoint does not require linearity. You could, for example, start a presentation with a brief overview of your research project and then move to a slide where five or six links will take you to different topics about your work. You can ask the audience what they would like to hear about first and then move to that section. This provides for some audience involvement in the decision about what to present. After you finish with that section, you can return to the screen with links and ask what the audience wants to explore next.

New Media Presentations

A new media presentation is simply a presentation that involves more than text and simple graphics. PowerPoint, for example, has multimedia features that are rarely used. You can add audio, video, and links to Internet sites, to a PowerPoint presentation. This is not often done in conference presentations but it should be. A 30-second video clip of an aspect of your dissertation work may be much more informative than a 5-minute verbal description, for example. Presentations that effectively use several types of media are more appealing, and often more informative, than a straight lecture supported by a linear PowerPoint presentation.

If you outgrow the feature set of PowerPoint and want to do even more sophisticated new media presentations there are advanced programs like Dreamweaver and Director that are used by professionals to produce sophisticated presentations, online video shows, and television commercials. These programs are generally difficult to learn and should probably be used only after simpler programs like PowerPoint cannot keep up with your ideas for innovative presentations.

Publishing Papers From Your Dissertation

If you wrote an "article" dissertation, the papers that constituted the bulk of your dissertation document may already be in print. The articles in many such dissertations are often submitted for publication before the dissertation defense and, despite the notoriously long period between submission and publication that many journals suffer from, your papers may actually be in print before your defense (which means you will need to obtain permission from the journal to reprint the article(s) in your dissertation).

On the other hand, if you did an article dissertation and have not yet submitted the papers to a journal for publication, we advise you do so quickly. Once you have received the final pieces of advice about editing your dissertation, make those changes, submit the dissertation to your institution, and then take a week or two to decompress. After that, pull out each of the papers in your dissertation, make one more stab at revising them, format them in the style required by the journals you have selected, and then ask your dissertation chair to read and critique them "one more time." If your chair has been heavily involved in the dissertation work, consider whether he or she should be listed as a second author. There may even be other members of your dissertation committee, or a professional practitioner who worked with you in the setting where you did your research, who also deserve coauthorship. If you are unsure about whether coauthorship is deserved or not, we advise erring on the side of generosity. Make the offer to your chair, or anyone else who was heavily involved in the dissertation as a contributor to the intellectual process or the data collection and analysis process. Once co-authorship questions are resolved, submit your papers to journals you and your chair believe are appropriate.

If you did a traditional 5-chapter dissertation, the process of converting the 200 or so page document into one or more journal articles will be more arduous and frustrating. The first step is generally to decide how the dissertation should be split up. Is there just one article in it? If so your task is to convert 200 pages into a single 15 to 30 page paper. The result is often a paper that painfully shows its origins as a dissertation because the paper is arrived at simply by chopping off huge chunks of the dissertation until only 25 or so pages are left. Elements of the dissertation, such as formal statements of hypotheses remain, and most of the text is taken directly from the dissertation. That is often a mistake because the writing style of a dissertation is different, and the purpose of a dissertation is different—a point that was made in an earlier chapter.

We advise another approach to converting a dissertation to a single paper. Find a paper you consider very good that is about a topic similar to your dissertation topic—such as the evaluation of a program, a study of the social interactions in a classroom or office, or interviews with youth offenders. Use that paper as a model and write your paper based on the model but using your information, data, and conclusions. This forces you to think like the writer of an article instead of the author of a dissertation. When you finish the first draft, put away the model; then read your draft paper carefully and make revisions. Once that second draft is finished, ask someone else to read it—such as your dissertation chair. Consider any advice offered and make the changes that seem sensible and reasonable to you. After a second round of revising and getting feedback from others, finish the paper and submit it to a journal. The most likely response from the journal is either a polite rejection or a recommendation to revise the paper and resubmit. In either case, read and think through the recommendations and comments of the reviewers. Some may seem silly or out of place, some may be obviously based on a misunderstanding or misinterpretation of what you have said in the paper, and some may be very valuable and on the mark. Don't ignore everything but the "on the mark" comments. All the comments, wrong, misguided, or accurate, should be considered. If you don't revise the paper to help readers avoid misguided conclusions, for example, the next set of reviewers may make the same mistakes. It is your job to make sure the paper effectively communicates what you intend.

If you find yourself upset at remarks the reviewers have made, especially if you have a hard time finding *anything* that seems sensible to you, this may be a sign of being too sensitive to criticism. Get someone else who isn't your mother or devoted partner to read both the paper and reviews. This should be someone you trust, who is sensitive to your feelings, but who will help you find useful guidance in the reviews for revising your paper. Then, revise your paper, get two or three people to read both your revision and the reviewer recommendations. Use their feedback to make a final revision and submit the paper again. If the journal that reviewed your paper asked you to resubmit, do that. Remember, however, that some journals send the revised paper out to a new set of reviewers. It is not unusual for a revised paper to be reviewed quite differently—you may even find that the new reviewers are critical of some of the revisions the first set insisted you make! Reviewing papers for journals is much more of an art than a science, and some people swear it is an occult art.

If your revision is not accepted, use the additional feedback to go through another cycle of revision, and submit the paper to another journal. Finding a home for a paper is a complex process that involves many things beyond the quality of your work. There must be a match between the purpose of the journal and the topic of your paper, between the style and tone of the paper and the journal's preferences, between the audience of the journal and the audience you wrote the paper for, and so on. The reason many papers based on dissertations go unpublished is not because the papers are "bad" but because the authors gave up before finding that elusive match between the paper and journal. And, of course, finding the match also means responding to the suggestions for revision made by reviewers.

Now what about the situation where the dissertation seems to contain more than one paper? How do you decide what papers are hiding out in the pages of your dissertation? There are several approaches to this question. The simplest is probably to break out papers based on the chapters of the dissertation. For example, three papers that might emerge from a dissertation that involved the evaluation of a new treatment or teaching method might be:

1. A review of the literature on the topic that is written for a particular audience such as researchers studying the new method or treatment or practitioners trying to make decisions in professional practice.

2. A detailed description of the treatment or method with information on how it can be implemented, problems and issues that will probably need to be addressed, and the types of support and training needed to support a successful implementation. Such a paper would probably be published in a practitioner journal rather than a "research" journal.

3. A paper on the evaluation of the treatment or method. In such a paper the focus is on the details of the research method, the data analysis, and the interpretation of the results as well as a discussion of the implications of the study. Such a paper might be published in either "applied research" or practitioner journals.

There are, of course, other ways of dividing up a dissertation into articles. The nature and structure of your particular dissertation will determine what is possible and feasible. There are also a number of papers in the literature on how to convert a dissertation to one or more journal articles (or a book). Here are a few we recommend:

http://www.apa.org/monitor/dec99/ed1.html "Unpublished? Try Your Dissertation." Advice about psychology dissertations.

www.apa.org/journals/authors/guide.html *This guide, from the American Psychological Association, is an excellent overview of the process of preparing articles for submission to journals. Of particular interest is a section on Converting the Dissertation into a Journal Article. Read it carefully!*

http://ezinearticles.com/?Turn-Your-Dissertation-Into-A-Book-Manuscript-By-Creating-Engaging-Chapters&id=446348 Converting your dissertation to a book is often more difficult than you might think but worth considering. If you would like a somewhat cynical view of the dissertation to book process written by an editor at a university press, see Alex Holzman's paper at http://aaupblog.aaupnet.org/?p=16. He also reviews two books on how to convert your dissertation to a book and finds both useful.

http://www.colorado.edu/geography/foote/geog5161/notes/AA-Chapter-13-Activities.doc. *A series of short papers that deal with many of the intricate aspects of converting a dissertation to articles.*

Social Networks and Professional Communities

Because the dissertation is a document, we tend to focus on documents as the logical extensions that emerge from a year or two of dissertation work. It is true that articles, conference presentations and papers, and even a book, can emerge from a dissertation chrysalis. However, the work you have done on your professional practice dissertation is also part of your preparation to join, or rejoin, the professional practice communities that exist online, locally, regionally, and nationally. In each field of professional practice there are online professional groups—who sponsor websites, online communities, wikis, blogs, social network sites, and virtual communities. There are so many such groups that making a good choice about which two or three to join becomes very important. Sometimes a bit of shopping is called for. You may join several online groups and then discover that just one or two fit your interests. However, once you have found your niche, these groups are an important aspect of your professional development—both as a contributor to the work of the group and as someone who benefits from the work of others.

In a similar vein, there are local, regional, national, and international organizations in every professional field, and the choice of which ones to join is just as difficult as the selecting online groups. Professions, however, are dynamic and changing entities. Participating in organizations that are part of that dynamic is a component of ongoing professional development. Why not make completing your dissertation a transition point in your career where you stop and consider which groups to join and become active in?

SUMMARY

Writing a dissertation requires that you focus on the work required over an extended period of time. Distractions that seem so appealing that they drag you away from the dissertation can become a problem—even if they never were before—and it can feel like there are almost as many books and papers on writing a dissertation as there are dissertation students. Many of these guides prescribe surefire ways to overcome writer's block, reduce dissertation stress, and make the dissertation process painless, easy, and even fun. Beware of simple and simplistic advice, including ours! Both you and the dissertation process are complex, not easily understood, and exist in a particular context that has its own history and traditions. It is highly unlikely that any universal piece of advice or any standard recipe for doing your dissertation, will apply to everyone and every situation. Consider the advice offered, but consider too your strengths and weaknesses, and the context in which you are completing your dissertation.

Major decisions about the process, such as whether to follow a linear or nonlinear model, will need to be made individualistically, not adopted

346 J. WILLIS, D. INMAN, and R. VALENTI

because this or that guide says linear, or nonlinear is always the right way to do it. Even issues like what style of writing you adopt should be considered in light of the traditions and expectations of your program as well as your own style and the types of writing you will do after graduation.

We offer one last common but simplistic piece of advice to you that is just as subject to our warnings as any other. That is to write a lot before beginning your dissertation and to get as much feedback and advice as possible. Use the feedback to improve your writing and continue that process as you write your dissertation. Participating in dissertation writing groups, hiring a good editor who teaches you as well as helps you edit your dissertation, attending conference sessions on dissertation writing, and participating in campus workshops about completing your dissertation are all potentially effective ways to enhance the quality of your dissertation.

Once your final predefense draft is completed and the time of your dissertation defense set, we advise you to slow down and rest a bit. Yes, prepare for the defense but take some time off as well. Come to the defense rested, and ready.

Once you are "Dr. ___" there may be additional things to do such as submit your dissertation to one or more archives where people can find it, prepare and make presentations about your research at conferences, prepare and submit journal articles based on your dissertation, and take time to think about follow up work based on your dissertation.

CHAPTER 13

THE TECHNICAL ASPECTS OF YOUR WRITTEN DISSERTATION

Completing a dissertation calls for an extensive combination of intellectual and social skills plus some critical personality attributes that include the ability to maintain sustained levels of focused, intensive work over long periods. You do all this in a culture that makes you the person primarily responsible for setting your timetable, deciding what needs to be done next, and who you need to talk to or meet with. You may be completing your dissertation in a program that has many forms of support and encouragement—a major advisor who is invested in your success, an ongoing group of dissertation students who meet regularly, seminars where students present their ideas for discussion, and so on. Or, you may be in a program where your are expected to do much of your dissertation work "on your own" without much support, encouragement, or guidance. Unfortunately, the research on doctoral student's perceptions of their programs suggests that programs are, on average, closer to the "on your own" extreme than the "richly supportive" alternative.

As a doctoral student you are, however, entitled to a certain level of support, and one of the tricks of the trade is to figure out how to get that support in programs where it does not happen automatically. Unfortunately, we know more about inappropriate and unsuccessful ways of getting that support than we do appropriate ways. Aggressively

Completing a Professional Practice Dissertation: A Guide for Doctoral Students and Faculty, pp. 347–375

demanding support, or publicly criticizing faculty members or the program, are more likely to reduce support rather than improve it. However, waiting for your major advisor or chair to contact you and offer help is also a common, but unsuccessful, approach to getting support. We suggest that you maintain regular contact with your chair. "Regular contact" may mean once a month at some points in the dissertation process and weekly face-to-face meetings at other, busy, times. Set up these meetings at least a month in advance and then, a day or two before the meeting, send your chair an e-mail message saying that you will see him or her, giving the day, time and place. Make sure there is actually something to discuss at the meeting and come in with at least an informal agenda that lists the major questions, decisions, or issues you need to discuss. In the meeting, listen to what your chair tells you, take notes so that you don't forget something important, and make sure you let your chair know what you have done relative to the action items discussed in your previous meetings. For example, if you were supposed to check out Chapter 3 in a book your chair recommended, let him or her know the book is not in the library but you have submitted an interlibrary loan request and should have it in a few days.

Most of the advice, support, and mentoring you will receive while completing your dissertation relates to the intellectual, scholarly, and professional aspects of your work. There is another aspect of the dissertation process, however, that most of us hate to deal with but which is, nevertheless, a necessary evil that must be mastered and addressed if you are to finally, and proudly, place a copy of your dissertation on the desk of someone who calmly signs a form that says you are finished! That person does not judge the academic or professional quality of your dissertation. He or she decides whether you have followed all the technical requirements your institution has for completed dissertations. As you near the end of the process it may seem that meeting the technical requirements for formatting and structuring your dissertation will take more time and effort that actually doing the dissertation research. This chapter will help you reduce the burden of meeting those technical requirements and we will begin with a discussion of what software you will use to write your dissertation.

SELECTING A WRITING PLATFORM: MICROSOFT WORD AND ITS ALTERNATIVES

So many students write their dissertation using a version of Microsoft Word that it is not an exaggeration to say that "almost all" dissertations in the United States are written in Word. There are many reasons for that. Word has been the dominant word processing program for over a decade and during that time it has further distanced itself from competitors like WordPerfect, which is now distributed by the Canadian company, Corel. Each new version of Word has additional features, additional power, and, unfortunately, additional "bugs" and annoyances that plague the user. Word is also part of the most popular "office" suite of programs. Microsoft Office, depending on what version you have, includes spreadsheet (Excel), database (Outlook), mail management (Outlook), presentation (PowerPoint, and desktop publishing software (FrontPage).

Because of the dominance of Microsoft Office and Microsoft Word, most doctoral students begin work on their dissertation already knowing Word at least at an intermediate level. And, despite Word's little quirks and its predilection to crash at inopportune moments, most of us are comfortable trusting it with our most important writing—in part because it has a number of features to protect us from disasters. Those features include automatic backup and recovery procedures you can use to salvage a copy of your file should the current copy be damaged beyond repair, or lost because of a computer crash.

Word also has several features that make writing your dissertation easier and less time consuming. We will discuss both why you need those features and how they work in Word. They include:

Templates. You can create or install a template that defines how each element of your dissertation should be formatted. That is, you can tell Word how each paragraph you call a "main heading" or a "reference" should look. Once you have a template, you can format virtually every part of your dissertation automatically rather than by hand. Many institutions have created Microsoft Word dissertation templates you can download and use to format your dissertation according to the rules of your program and institution. For example, if your institution specifies that main headings (often called H1 headings) should be centered in first letter capitals (e.g., Heading rather than HEADING or heading), 14 point bold, and in the Times New Roman font, you need do little more than put your cursor somewhere in a line of text that is a main heading and click the H1 style in a list of "tags" on the screen. All the required formatting for a main heading will be applied to that line of text.

Over the years Word has added little extra features that go beyond the basic concept of a document template. For example, since most main headings are followed by regular text (called Normal or BodyText), Word lets you specify what style should follow a main heading, or any other style. In the case of a main heading when you start to write the next paragraph after a main heading (H1) it will be formatted in the Normal or BodyText style—which is almost always the correct format.

If your program or institution has a dissertation template for Word, use it. It will save you time and make it much easier to ensure that your dissertation is consistently formatted. If you format every instance of a main heading, for example, by hand, there is a good chance some of the main headings will be different from others and you will have to go through the entire document to find the nonconformists. On the other hand, if you decide the style for a main head should be changed from 14 point bold type to 12 point bold type, you can modify the template and Word will automatically find and update every instance of a main heading to match your new specifications. There is no need to search through the entire document and manually change every main heading individually. Make sure, however, that any changes you make to the template are within the format requirements at your institution.

Front matter Support. Every dissertation has a set of "front matter" which is material that comes before the body of the dissertation. A typical dissertation contains the following front matter:

Title Page
    Signature Page (if it is not included on the title page)
        Abstract
            Dedication Page
                Table of Contents (TOC)
                    List of Figures
                        List of Illustrations
                            List of Tables

The exact content of the front matter for a dissertation will vary from institution to institution, but these five elements are usually included in one form or another. A template will usually include a sample title page and signature page that shows you exactly how they should look. All you have to do is enter the correct text for your dissertation (e.g., dissertation title, names of committee members, and so on). There may also be a sample dedication page where you can substitute the placeholder text with your own. Our advice, by the way, is to include a dedication page that thanks those who have contributed to your efforts on the dissertation and your doctoral program. Be generous. And thank family and supportive friends as well as colleagues and the members of your dissertation committee, your research team, and anyone else who played a significant role.

The help a template provides for the title page, signature page, and dedication page is useful, but Word's built-in support for the contents, figures, and illustrations lists is where it can save you hours of work. The Table of Contents (TOC) command in Word lets you identify the paragraph styles you want included in your table of contents. That command also lets you specify the way your TOC will look. For example, suppose your institution requires a TOC to include the title of each chapter and the main headings within each chapter. Word's TOC command lets you specify that any paragraph formatted with the "ChapterTitle" style (or whatever name you use) and any paragraph formatted as "H1" or "Main-Head," depending on your template, will be included in the TOC. Once you have made all your decisions, Word will automatically build a TOC for you. And, if revisions cause the TOC to be out of date, you can automatically update it. You do the same thing with the lists of figures, tables, and illustrations. If each caption for a figure is formatted with a "Figure-Caption" tag you can use Word's TOC commands to build a List of Figures that include the captions and page numbers for all the figures in your dissertation. You do the same thing to create your List of Illustrations. (However, Word also has an "insert caption" command under the References tab that lets you add a caption and then create a table of figures or illustrations that includes all the captions.)

The TOC command is one of several "advanced" Word commands that takes a little effort to learn, but the time it saves is substantial. Further, using it reduces the number of errors that always sneak in to a document when you do this type of work manually. Let the software do this work!

Document and Page Layout Commands. Most people are familiar with standard layout options such as margins. A typical dissertation is formatted with either 1" or 1.5" margins on all four sides. One common exception is that the left margin has an extra half inch margin. That is because most dissertations are printed on one side of the page and then bound on the left. The extra half inch keeps the left side of the text from being hidden by the binding. That extra space on the left margin to accommodate binding is called the "gutter."

Margin settings are part of the Page Layout commands in Word and there are several other important page layout options as well as commands under other tabs at the top of the Word window that you may need to use when formatting your dissertation.

Sections. A typical dissertation generally has three main sections:
Front Matter (discussed above)
Main Body (all the chapters)
Back Matter (appendices, supplementary documents, "about the author")

When it comes to formatting your dissertation this tripartite division of the dissertation would be unimportant except for one thing—there are differences in the way the three sections are formatted. For example, some dissertation guides require that all the front matter material have page numbers in Roman numerals (e.g., XIV or xiv) while the main body of the dissertation, and the back matter, have page numbers that are Arabic (e.g., 14). The problem with this is that some word processing programs do not allow you to format some pages with Roman numeral page numbers and some with Arabic. There are work-arounds, such as writing and printing each component of the dissertation as a separate document and then assembling the final printed copy manually. That complicates things, however, if you must submit an electronic copy of your dissertation.

Word solves this problem with the Section command. If you click the Page Layout tab at the top of the window and then click Breaks, you will see options for both Page and Section breaks. Page breaks are handy for ending a chapter and making sure the next chapter begins on a new page. A Section break is a bit more complicated. For example, suppose you have a draft of your dissertation that includes the Front Matter as well as all the chapters in the main body of the dissertation. You now need to format the Front Matter and Main Body, and the guidelines call for a different format for these two sections (e.g., Roman versus Arabic page numbers in the Footer). That is easy to do. At the end of the last page of Front Matter, insert a Next Page Section Break. This will designate the Front Matter of your dissertation as Section 1 and the Main Body as Section 2. Now you can format these two sections separately. You can, for example, specify Roman page numbers in the footer for Section 1 (Front Matter) and Arabic page numbers in Section 2 (Main Body). We will not try to provide a complete tutorial about how to do this here—there are already many good guides both online and in print for all the advanced features of Word. What is important is that you know this feature is available and that it can save you time as well as reduce the frustration that often comes with trying to format your dissertation so that it follows all the detailed criteria for appearance and form.

Another use of the Section command is to make space for large tables that do not fit on a standard 8.5 by 11 page in the "portrait" mode. Portrait mode is when the lines of text are across the 8.5" width of the page. With one and a half inch left and one inch right margins each text line is about 6 inches. In "landscape" mode the text lines flow across the 11" width of the page, which means with 1.5" left and 1" right margins, the width of each line is 8.5 inches instead of 6. This extra 2.5 inches can sometimes make the difference between a table that doesn't fit well and one that is easily read and understood. To orient a table so that it is displayed and printed in landscape mode, first create a new section (on a new page) and use the Page Layout/Orientation command to format the new section as Landscape rather than Portrait. Don't change any other settings. Then create your table on that page. Finally, use the Section command again to start a new page and return to the Portrait mode. Your oversize table (or illustration, chart, graph, or whatever) will print in landscape mode but the text on the pages before and after will be in portrait mode.

Headers and Footers. Another feature of Word, and most modern word processing programs, is the automatic control of headers and footers. The header and footer commands in Word are under the Insert command. If your doctoral program supplies a template for formatting your dissertation, the specifications for headers and/or footers will probably be built into that template. If not, you will want to follow the directions in your institution's dissertation formatting guide and create the correct format in the template you design. Word has several standard formats for headers and footers you can select from, but it also allows you to create a unique format from scratch. Most dissertation templates will require you to format aspects of the header or footer manually. For example, your formatting requirements may specify that the first page of each chapter should not have a footer or header. Or the footer/header for the odd and even pages may need to be different. There are options in Word that let you specify headers and/or footers for first pages in a section, odd numbered pages, and even numbered pages. Also, when you are formatting footers and headers, there are options for whether they apply only to a specific section or to the entire document. However, once all that is done, Word will automatically format your headers and/or footers correctly.

Formatting Citations and References. In most fields of professional practice, citations and references are the source of more errors and variations in both dissertations and journal articles than any other element of the document. A *citation* is what you put in the text of your document to indicate the source you are using or quoting. A *reference* is what you put at the end of your dissertation or chapter that provides all the necessary publication details about each work you have cited. From this relatively simple task, a whole industry of training manuals, guides, computer programs, and workshops have emerged to help you correctly cite and reference the sources you use in your dissertation. The task is not simple because there are hundreds of different types of sources and the way each one is cited or referenced can be different. Most of us learn how to cite and reference a book with one or two authors and scholarly articles with a few authors. Even these seemingly simple sources, however, may have variations, such as a book that is edited or a journal article that is available online rather than in printed form. With those variations come detailed rules about how the source should be cited and referenced.

There are, in fact, several sets of rules that specify how a citation and reference should be made. In different fields the specifications of the Modern Language Association (MLA), the Chicago manual of style, or the guidelines in one of Kate Turabian's books on writing term papers, theses, and dissertations are considered the "standard" by which citations and references are evaluated for correctness. However, the most common set of rules in the social sciences and education as well as many other areas of professional practice is the American Psychological Associations guidelines. The most recent edition of the *Publication Manual of the American Psychological Association* was published in 2009. According to the rules in that manual, it would be cited (American Psychological Association, 2009) as shown in the parenthesis because the author is the organization rather than an individual. The correct reference for this book is:

American Psychological Association. (2009). *Publication manual of the American Psychological Association* (6th ed.). Washington, DC: Author.

Students completing their dissertation generally take one of two approaches to getting the citations and references "right." One way is to buy and study one or more guides such as the current edition of the APA manual (or any of the other good guides available online or in print). Few, if any, writers actually learn and remember all the rules for citing all the different types of sources, however. There are too many details. Studying your guides carefully before writing does familiarize you with the guides though, and that makes it easier to find the rules and examples when you're unsure about how to cite or reference a source (which will likely be very often if you're like the rest of us).

The other approach to getting citations and references correct is to hire someone who is an expert to check and correct them. While it is a good learning experience to do it yourself, the completion of a dissertation is not exactly a walk in the park and getting someone else to check your citations and references relieves you of one major source of irritation and hassle. Our advice, however, is to ask your consultant to make handwritten corrections you then enter into your dissertation file. That way, you learn from your mistakes rather than simply having them fixed by your expert.

To help you manage citations and references, Microsoft Word has a set of commands under the References tab at the top of the window. The "Citations and Bibliography" commands let you enter information on a source and, with Word's help, correctly cite and reference that source. Word lets you select any of ten different guidelines—from MLA to APA— and it automates the process of creating a list of references that are, hopefully, formatted correctly. We do not use Word's features for managing citations and references, perhaps because we began writing in a period when all that was done manually. We still do it manually but you may find Microsoft's options increase you accuracy and save you time. Try them and make your own judgment.

There are also many other computer programs that help you correctly format citations and references including CiteWrite, EndNotes, Inflight Referencer, Owl Citation Software, Perrla, Reference Point Software templates, ScholarWord, Style Ease, and TopStyle Pro. Many of these programs work inside Word by adding commands to the program, but there are more and more programs available that go beyond helping you create correctly formatted citations and references. These programs let you build and manage a database of resources relevant to your research. They are variations on a group of programs generically called "content management systems" and you enter information into a database. However, once the database is organized and set up, you can search it electronically for information. The weak link in these programs is that your ability to search the database depends on how well you organized the database in the first place. Many people find the effort required to build the database is not worth the effort. An option we occasionally use is brainstorming software such as MindMap, IdeaFisher, MindJet, Inspiration, Freemind, and SmartDraw. These programs let you organize your information in a flexible way—for example, you might have a node in your "map" of information for "theories" and another for "program models." The advantage of brainstorming programs is that you can change the structure of the map you are creating as you become more familiar with the structure of the knowledge you are studying. You might, for example, find that "theories" is too broad and that you need to create two different nodes—"grand theories" and "theories of professional practice" with grand theories under a category called "Foundations" and the other under a category called "Professional Practice." This is not difficult to do with brainstorming programs.

Before moving on to another topic, we want to recommend that you purchase the latest version of the APA publication manual if you will be formatting your dissertation in APA style. Although the sixth edition is better organized and easier to use than the fifth edition, it is still a substantial book that will require some searching to find the specific information you are looking for. However, the manual contains information on all aspects of formatting, not just citations and references. It has become "the" style manual for dissertations in many fields and if your program requires that dissertations follow APA guidelines, you should own a copy this manual even if you use another, more user friendly manual, as your primary resource for citations and references.

Formatting Footnotes/Endnotes. Most professional practice dissertations do not use footnotes, which are much more popular in the humanities and in fields like philosophy. There are, however, occasions when a footnote is the best way to provide certain types of information. For example, some readers may need additional information but including it in the text will be distracting to most readers. Putting the information in a footnote is less disruptive but readers who need the information can go to the end of the chapter and read the footnote.

Microsoft Word supports both "footnotes" and "endnotes" and the difference is where the note appears in a document. Footnotes are at the bottom of the page and endnotes appear at the end of the document or at the end of a section. Footnotes in dissertations typically appear at the end of a chapter which means they are "endnotes" in Microsoft Word jargon. Therefore, if you format each chapter as a section, any footnotes (endnotes) in that chapter will be printed at the end of the chapter if you tell Word that is where you want them to appear. Within the text of the chapter a superscripted number will alert the reader to the availability of each endnote/footnote.

Collaborative Editing: Word's Track Changes Command

There are many ways to work with someone who is editing your dissertation. The traditional standard is for your chair and other editors to read your drafts and make comments in the margins as well as corrections in the text. You then meet with your editor who discusses the recommended changes with you. Then you use the edited chapters to make revisions to your original file. (And, of course, when you finish editing a file you immediately make backups!)

Another way to work with your editor is to use the Track Changes command in Microsoft Word. That command is under the Review tab at the top of the Word window. When Tracked Changes is switched on, one or more editors can make any changes they wish as well as add notes, comments, and messages. When the revised file comes back to you, it will show every change made by the editors and you can decide whether to accept the edit or not. Some people love the way Track Changes works while others hate it. We suggest you check it out for yourself and if you and the people who are editing your chapters are comfortable with it, consider using it as a part of your writing and revision process. The question of how you work with editors was also covered in Chapter 12 where several other options, including Google Docs and Office Live were discussed.

Alternatives to Word

Almost all dissertations are composed in one or another version of Word but there are alternatives. WordPerfect was once a worthy competitor to Microsoft Word and the two programs split the word processing software market without either totally dominating the field. WordPerfect, however, fell behind Word about a decade ago and while it remains a very powerful program it is no longer a serious competitor to Microsoft Word.

Most people who use the current version of WordPerfect do so because they used earlier versions and are comfortable with the program. Word-Perfect has all the high level features needed to write and edit a typical dissertation.

Another option that once competed with Word is also distributed by Microsoft. Microsoft Works is a cheaper, less powerful, suite of programs that covers much of the same ground as Microsoft Office, which includes Word. Works is less well known and less powerful than Word and if the choice is between these two programs, we recommend Word.

A more difficult choice when selecting a program for writing your dissertation is between Word or WordPerfect and more advanced programs that are more, rather than less, powerful when it comes to formatting documents. These programs were once called "desktop publishing" programs and were used to create everything from advertisements and posters to magazines, journals and books. Programs like InDesign and QuarkXpress are most useful when you are creating something like a magazine where each page is a combination of complex graphics, text, and illustrations that must be integrated into a pleasing whole. Both have many commands for doing just that, but dissertations that look like an issue of *Vanity Fair* or *GQ* magazine are not well accepted. We expect dissertations to be formatted simply. Boring may not be an overstatement of the formatting expectations. Thus, unless your doctoral program, and institution, is on the avant garde of dissertation formatting, the considerable time it takes to learn programs like InDesign or QuarkXpress may well be wasted on your dissertation.

THE STRUCTURE OF THE DISSERTATION

We have discussed the typical format of a dissertation in previous chapters but two options are worth visiting again here. They are the five-chapter model and the "article dissertation."

Traditional and Professional Practice Five-Chapter Models

A traditional research dissertation has five chapters—Introduction, Literature Review, Methodology, Results, and Discussion. This particular set of chapters is best suited to traditional research studies rather than professional practice dissertations. An option for a professional practice dissertation that used action research methods to develop a solution to a problem of professional practice could include these chapters:

1. **The Problem of XXX.** Provides an overview of the professional practice problem (represented by "XXX") being addressed, and summarizes your dissertation work including the results. This chapter is like an executive summary.

2. **The Context of Research and Practice.** Introduces readers to the context where you did your dissertation. Provides enough detail for readers to understand the setting, its history, the groups and individuals who were most important to the study, and the relationships as well as interactions among the various groups.

3. **The Action Research Process.** Introduces and justifies the particular method of action research you used in your dissertation.

4. **The Search for Possible Solutions to XXX.** In this chapter you describe what happened in the cycles of action research, including the results as judged by the participants. This chapter is often written as a narrative—a story told about each phase of action research. Often this chapter integrates the story of the action research project with discussions of how the team was influenced by the relevant literature and other sources of professional and scholarly knowledge. Thus, instead of a separate "review of the literature" chapter the sources become part of the story of how the team made decisions about practice.

5. **A Reflective Analysis of the Project.** In this chapter you reflect on what you learned about the problem and the process. Did the action research project succeed? How? Why? Did different stakeholder groups view the process, and the outcomes, differently? Why? Overall, did the action research methodology help the group address the professional practice problem? How does what your action research project came up with compare to approaches to the problem that are proposed in the literature? How do you understand what happened in the action research project? Does your understanding reflect the application of an existing theory? Or a new one? Explain. Would your understanding be helpful to practitioners in other settings? How? What needs to be considered when thinking about how what you learned might be used in another context?

This is one example of a format for a five chapter professional practice dissertation, but it is not a universal model. Different purposes, different research methods, and different audiences (e.g., policy makers, practitioners, professional development trainers) may call for different dissertation formats. We suggest, therefore, that when you are considering the format for your dissertation, make your decisions about purpose, method and audience first. Then ask yourself what dissertation structure and format fits those decisions. The result may be a dissertation with relatively unique chapter structures and content. That is fine if there is a good fit with the purpose, process, and audience for your dissertation!

TAD—The Three Article Format Dissertation

An alternative to all the five-chapter formats that is a good fit for many professional practice dissertations is the TAD or "three article" dissertation. We discussed this format in earlier chapters and we recommend it here because (1) the format allows you to write parts of your dissertation as articles that can be submitted directly to journals for publication, (2) it encourages you to complete papers while you are doing your coursework and field experiences, and those papers can become part of your dissertation, and (3) the type of writing you do for a TAD dissertation may be closer to the type of writing you will do as a practicing professional after completing your doctorate.

In an editorial published in the journal, *Qualitative Health Research*, Morse (2005) noted both the trend toward article dissertations and their advantages:

> Increasingly, the dissertation requirement for a doctoral degree is changing from a monograph-style research report to a set of interrelated publications. University regulations for this requirement differ. Some require three, and others four or even five articles. Some insist that these articles be accepted for publication as a requirement for graduation; others that they be presented in publication format, ready to be submitted after the student's defense. This requirement has been led by the hard sciences, in which the reporting of several experiments as short articles is logical and efficient. But how does this requirement change the qualitative dissertation?

> First, for students, this option has considerable advantages. Pragmatically, students skip the painful process of synthesizing, condensing, and segmenting a 200-plus-page [dissertation] document into 15-page articles. They graduate with a vita boasting publications or articles in press rather than scrambling to get articles "out" during their first year as faculty members. Therefore, in their new appointments, they can focus on getting a research proposal funded, teaching, and becoming a faculty member.

Professor Morse was thinking of the article dissertation from the point of view of students who will become professors and researchers, and she has some concerns about TADs. While she points out some of the advantages of article dissertations in the quote, her ultimate conclusion is that article dissertations are a bad idea for people planning careers as academics. She prefers the traditional "monograph" model of a five-chapter dissertation.

What about doctoral students planning careers as professional practitioners? Despite Morse's (2005) view, we think the advantages are substantial for them. In addition to the three advantages we mentioned earlier, most publications about professional practice are journal articles rather than monographs or books. Thus, it makes sense to do a dissertation that consists primarily of articles that can be submitted to journals without having to go through the difficult and time consuming rewrite that converts a 200+ page dissertation into two or three articles.

A typical format for a TAD has five parts:

1.   **Introduction:** About five pages that introduce the three articles and explain how they relate to each other.
2.   **Article 1.**
3.   **Article 2.**
4.   **Article 3.**
5.   **Conclusion**: Five to 10 pages that tie the articles together, discuss the implications of the research presented in the articles, and suggest a line of exploration and study the dissertation author might pursue after graduation that is related to the work presented in the three articles. Five to 10 pages should usually be sufficient.

Remember the fictional action research dissertation used earlier as an example of how the chapters in a five chapter professional practice dissertation might be organized and structured? Suppose that dissertation was a TAD instead. Here is one way it could be a Three Article Dissertation:

1.   **Introduction:** Describes the professional practice problem and provides an overview/introduction to each article in the dissertation. This can be done in about five pages.
2.   **Article 1. *XXX: Linking A Persistent Problem to Potential Solutions.*** This paper could be an analysis of the professional practice problem selected by the doctoral student for in depth study. The paper could be written originally for a doctoral course. The paper might provide readers with an overview of the problem, lay out the common approaches to dealing with the problem, and link solutions as well as explanations to their theoretical foundations. The end of the paper might offer some practical guidance to practitioners based on the available research and professional practice literature.

3. **Article 2:** *An Action Research Study of XXX in a Mental Health Center.* The second paper could be an article that describes the action research project that focused on developing and trying out solutions to the professional practice problem in a particular professional practice context such as a mental health center.

4. **Article 3: A Manual of Practice: Addressing the Problem of XXX.** Suppose the third paper is a manual for practitioners that was created during the action research project to help practitioners implement a potential solution to XXX. If that solution seemed to work well, the manual might become the third "article" in the dissertation. It could also be published on one of the sites that distribute practitioner oriented resources on the web. Other options for the third paper include one on the policy implications of the solution developed through the action research project, or an analysis of the action research process itself and how it might be improved to address the problems of professional practice.

5. **Conclusion:** In this final section of the dissertation the three papers would be discussed in terms of their contribution to the literature on the XXX professional practice problem as well as how to approach problems of professional practice using one of the action research methods. In this section the doctoral student might, for example, discuss the particular strengths of the action research model used in the dissertation and suggest strengths as well as weaknesses in the approach plus the types of professional practice problems that seem best suited to action research.

Formatting the Article Dissertation

The first and last sections of an article dissertation are generally formatted according to the same rules as a five-chapter dissertation. Some institutions also require each article to be treated as a dissertation chapter and formatted accordingly. Others allow you to format your three articles according to the requirements of the journals they have been, or will be, submitted to. Louisiana State University takes an intermediate position and allows you to use a different format for the articles, but you must select one of the journals you will submit an article to and use those formatting requirements for all three articles even if one or two of them will go to different journals.

Ideally, you should be able to format the articles one time and use the resulting document in both your dissertation and for submission to journals. That is not always possible, however, and you must check local requirements to determine how to format your TAD.

FORMATTING DETAILS

Most institutions have two levels of formatting details. One is at the institutional level. There will be a manual or guide that has all sorts of arcane and specific rules you must follow. And, because these vary from one institution to another there is no way around learning these rules yourself or hiring someone with intimate knowledge of them to edit your dissertation.

Institutions do not, however, typically provide all the rules in a local document. There are too many details that must be specified and the document would be too long. Instead, the institution will say something like, "dissertations should be formatted according to the rules of the latest edition of the *Publication Manual of the American Psychological Association.*" This is both good and bad. It is bad because there is another huge set of formatting criteria to learn and use consistently. It is good because the APA guidelines, or any other widely used guides, are national/international standards and there are many sources of information and support you can tap to figure out some of the details that are confusing.

We will not attempt to cover even the most general aspects of APA format requirements here. As noted earlier there are many good resources available online for free and in many different books on the subject. What we will do is cover a few important areas that seem particularly prone to problems or misunderstanding.

Margins and Gutters

Margins are the white space around the four sides of a page where no text appears. Many dissertations have 1" margins on all four sides. Quite a few have 1" margins on all sides except the left, which has a 1.5" margin to give some extra room for the binding. You will occasionally see directions for a one inch margin on all four sides and a half inch "gutter" on the left. The gutter is simply the extra margin added to the side of the paper that will be bound. When a dissertation is printed on one side of the paper, a 1.5" left margin is the same as a 1" left margin plus a .5" gutter on the left. However, if your dissertation will be printed on both sides of the paper, as a book is, things are more complicated. When printed only on one side, all the pages will be bound on the left side. However, if your dissertation is printed on both sides of the paper, the odd numbered pages will be bound on the left side and the even numbered pages bound on their right side. In this case you should set your margins and the gutter separately. For example, if you set margins to 1" all around and then set the gutter margin to .5" the odd pages will have half an inch of extra space on the left and the even pages will have an extra half inch on the right.

Typography: Fonts, Points, and Leading

Typography is something you can get a PhD in, but for most of us there are just three terms that should be understood: font, points, and leading. A font is a set of characters that share a set of characteristics. The two most common families of fonts are Serif and Sans-serif. A Serif font has curves and artistic elements that appeal to many readers. Here is an example of Serif font—the very popular Times New Roman:

Times New Roman font. The size is 16 points.

Notice the flourishes on the ends of the T and the R. These are serifs. Now look at the Sans-serif font below—Arial.

Arial Font. The size is 16 points

Note that the Arial font has no serifs. Note too that these two fonts differ in more than just the presence or absence of serifs. There are tens of thousands of fonts in use today but many dissertation guides specify either one required/preferred font (e.g., Times New Roman) or a limited range of fonts. Times New Roman, which is a serif type, and Arial, which is a sans serif type, are two of the most commonly used fonts in dissertations. Often the guidelines specify Times New Roman for body text and Arial or Helvetica for headings.

Fonts are created using many different formats and that can cause problems when you must create and submit your dissertation in an electronic format such as Adobe's PDF. Some font formats are easier to convert to pdf than others. If you have several versions of the font you will use on your computer, select the one that is in the TrueType (TT) format to avoid problems later. If you do not have a TrueType version of the font, Type 1 versions should also work. Using common, widely available fonts like Times New Roman, Helvetica, and Arial also reduces the likelihood of problems.

The second term you should know is points. The vertical size of text is measured in points. The two examples above are both 16 point type. There are approximately 72 points in an inch and most dissertations use 10, 11, or 12 point type for the main text. If your institution gives you a choice, we recommend that dissertations of 75 pages or less be printed in

12 point type while longer documents use 10 point type. However, if your dissertation will be viewed primarily as an online document 10 point type may be preferred even for short documents.

The third term you should know is leading. Leading is also measured in points and it is a measure of line spacing. Word processing programs like Microsoft Word let you set line spacing crudely with options like single space, double space, and so on. Most also allow you to set spacing in points, which is much more precise. If someone says they printed a document "10 on 12" that means the font size is 10 points and each line is 12 points (roughly 10 point type and 2 points of spacing between the lines of type). Dissertations have traditionally been printed double spaced and the great majority of doctoral programs still insist on double spaced text (except perhaps for quotations that are single spaced). Double spacing is helpful when someone is editing your dissertation because there is room to make notes and corrections between each line. Double spacing the final version is less helpful. A dissertation is more readable when the text is single spaced which means the leading is 2 points more than the font size, and the dissertation is also shorter. If your institution allows you to use a line spacing other than double spacing, we recommend that you do. The University of St. Gallen in the United Kingdom, for example, specifies ten point type if you use the sans serif Helvetica font with line spacing that is 1.2. This is another way of saying "10 point type on a 12 point line." If you use a variation of the Times Roman font, St. Gallen specifies 10 point type on a 1.3 line which means the type will be 10 points and the line spacing or leading will be 13 points.

The University of Tennessee, Knoxville allows dissertations that are single, one and a half, or double spaced and recommends 10 or 12 point type. Where these are the options we recommend using "single spacing" which is close to 10 point type on 12 point leading, or 12 point type on 14 point leading. Many books are printed in 10 point type with leading of 12 or 13 points and printing your dissertation "10 on 12" or "10 on 13" should produce a readable document. If you use a larger size, such as 12 rather than 10 point type, your leading should be a least 2 points larger but no more than 4 points larger. You can try out several options to see how a page looks before making your final choice. However, remember that most local dissertation guides put limits on your options and you are most likely to end up using 10 or 12 point type and double spacing because that is what most institutions currently require.

Paragraph Formatting

In Microsoft Word a template includes specifications for general requirements such as margins but the focus is on detailed specifications for different types of paragraphs. Keep in mind that a paragraph can be anything from a single letter on a line to pages of text. A paragraph is nothing more than at least one character followed by a carriage return (the code generated when you press the Enter or Return key). Paragraph styles or "tags" let you apply several formatting specifications (e.g., font and size, bold, italics, justification, indenting, spacing before and after the paragraph, tab settings) in one step. For a dissertation, the template should contain specification at least for the following paragraph styles (though the names of the styles may vary):

BodyText: This style defines how the primary text paragraphs should be formatted. Dissertations generally indent the first line of each new paragraph but do not add any extra space between paragraphs. This style is often the same as the "Normal" style in a template and some people tend to use them interchangeably. Our advice is to pick one, BodyText or Normal and then use that one style for all the ordinary text paragraphs. Using one or the other means if you decide to change the formatting of ordinary text paragraphs you only have to change one style and the change will apply to all those paragraphs. (Note: Sometimes, the "Normal" style is used in disesertation templates instead of a BodyText style.)

BodyTextNoIndent: There will be times when you need a new paragraph that is formatted just like BodyText but without the first line indented. For example, you may put a figure or table in the middle of a paragraph which means the text after the table or figure should not be indented because it is a continuation of the paragraph that began before the table or figure.

H1 or Main Heading: Often centered, 14 or 16 point type, and printed in bold. Some guides specify that body text use a serif font such as Times New Roman while headings are in a sans serif font like Helvetica or Arial. Main headings generally have extra space above the heading to separate it from preceding text and some extra spacing after the heading to signify that this is a major shift from one topic to another.

H2 or SubHeading: Subheads may also be centered and printed in bold but use a smaller type than main headings. They also have less extra space above and below the heading.

H3 or SubSubHeading: This is a minor heading and is usually printed flush left in 12 or 14 point type. It may be bolded and there will be some extra space above the heading but not necessarily below.

H4: Many guides do not allow four levels of heading but if it is permitted it is a good idea to set one up in your template. An alternative is to use a "run-in" heading like the ones used here to identify the paragraph styles. **H4:** is an example of this type of heading. Typically the end punctuation for a run-in heading is a colon or a period.

DissertationTitle: This style will only be used once or twice in a dissertation but there is still an advantage to having all the rules for how a title should be formatted set up in a tag so that you do not have to remember those details. Apply the style to your title and it is automatically formatted.

Dissertation Subtitle: This tag is optional unless you will be using a subtitle as well as a title and your institution has different criteria for the subtitle.

Chapter Title: All chapter titles should be formatted the same way and this tag will do that for you. It is also important that you apply this style to every chapter title because Word will use the tag to locate every chapter title when you create your table of contents.

Chapter Subtitle: Another optional tag, but it may be needed if your institution requires chapter subtitles to be formatted differently from the chapter title.

Reference: This tag does not format your references according to MLA or APA guidelines. Instead, it is a general style you apply to references after the APA or MLA rules have been applied. For example, your institution may require references to be in 10-point Times New Roman with all except the first line indented (called a hanging indent) .4 inches. The Reference style can do all that for you.

Author: An optional tag, but some templates include this because there are specific rules for how the author's name should appear on the title page.

Quote: Institutional dissertation guides treat long quotes in different ways. Some, for example, require that quotes be printed in smaller type, be indented on the right and left, and be single spaced. Others only require that long quotes be indented. This style should apply all the rules at your institution to a long quote.

IllustrationCaption, TableCaption, FigureCaption: These three styles are used to format the captions of common elements in a dissertation such as tables and figures. The formatting requirements may be exactly the same for all the captions in your dissertation but you should use the correct style for each type of caption. Don't, for example, apply a TableCaption style to a figure caption. That is because Word uses these captions to create the List of Figures, List of Tables, and List of Illustrations in your front matter. If you tag a figure with a TableCaption style that figure will end up in the list of tables rather than figures.

FIGURES AND ILLUSTRATIONS

We are becoming a society that increasingly expects information to be provided by, or at least supported by, visual as well as text and numeric data. In the scholarly and professional literature charts, figures, and illustrations have long been used to present information. Before personal computers and programs that create sophisticated graphics, the process involved creating charts and figures by hand—something a commercial artist did—or using rub-on letters and lines made by companies like Letraset to produce charts and graphs.

Fortunately, there are many different ways to produce graphics for your dissertation today. One of the simplest ways, if you are using the latest version of Microsoft Word is the Illustration commands under the Insert tab. For example, the SmartArt command simplifies the process of creating hundreds of different types of graphs and illustrations, and the Chart command does the same for everything from a simple pie chart to a complex radar chart. All of the illustrations in this book were created with the SmartArt command in Microsoft Word 2007. For your dissertation, you may not need anything else to create useful and informative graphics that look very professional.

Statistical analysis programs such as SPSS also have graphics packages associated with them and many dissertation students take advantage of those features if they use a program like SPSS to analyze their data. There are also specialized programs for creating graphics. Some are general purpose programs that are appealing because of their flexibility and power. Popular programs in this group include Photoshop, Paint Shop Pro, and Corel Draw. There is also another group of programs that are also powerful but they are easier to learn and use because they are more structured and tend to give you choices and options rather than a blank screen where you are free to create anything you want. The problem with the freedom is that you have to learn a lot about the program before you can translate your idea for a chart or graph into the real thing.

There are hundreds, no thousands, of programs that automate the process of creating professional-looking charts. Many programs even focus on one type of chart—such as Gnatt charts, organization charts, or flow charts. If the graphics options of Microsoft Word and programs like SPSS are not sufficient, one or more of the specialized programs, some free and some commercial, may fit your needs. Your chair or a colleague may be able to recommend a program or you can do a search on the Internet for programs that create the type of illustrations you need. Keep in mind, however, that some programs, such as 3-D, CAD-CAM, and virtual reality software can be both expensive and very difficult to learn.

A final type of software for creating illustrations that you may want to consider is brainstorming or concept mapping programs. There are many of these programs but their purpose is to represent ideas and concepts visually. These programs are a unique combination of structure and flexibility. They are structured because they help you create only a limited range of visual representations such as concept maps. They do that well but are useless if you want something else, such as a pie chart. On the other hand, they are very flexible because as your concepts and ideas change it is easy in most brainstorming/concept mapping programs to change your visual to represent your current thinking.

What About Video and Animation?

Today dissertations at most institutions are restricted to what can be represented in ink on paper or, at best, represented in files and formats such as Adobe's PDF standard that was created primarily to make text materials readable on almost any computer. PDF files now have the capability to support color graphics, audio, and video, but the origins of the PDF standard's as support for text-based documents is still very apparent. Over the next decade or two dissertations are likely to enter a new phase in which they become disconnected from their origins as printed text documents. As that occurs the importance of word processing programs for writing dissertations will decrease and programs for creating multimedia documents will replace the venerable word processor as the tool of choice. Today, that market is dominated by programs like Adobe Director but as we noted earlier, the power and flexibility of such programs is wasted on the traditional dissertation. However, when a dissertation is more like a documentary film, a music video, a video game, a fashion magazine, or a French movie that appeals primarily to intellectuals, then Adobe Director and similar multimedia development environments will be much more relevant to a student completing a professional practice dissertation. In the meantime, if your institution requires dissertations to be submitted electronically, there may also be room for video and other forms of content that do not fit within the traditional "ink on paper" requirements that have been in place for almost two hundred years.

ASSEMBLING THE DISSERTATION: MANUAL OR AUTOMATIC?

As you write your dissertation, do you create one large file that contains every chapter? Or do you create separate word processing files for each chapter and for the front and back matter? There are advantages to both approaches, but we recommend you create separate word processing files for each chapter. There are two reasons for that. The first is that as word processing files become larger the word processing software tends to become less stable and to crash more often. This seems particularly true of Microsoft Word running on computers with average or less than average amounts of memory. The second reason is that saving chapters in separate files offers some protection from both user errors (you make a mistake) and computer crashes (lightning strikes, catastrophic failure of a hard drive or motherboard). However, regardless of the approach you take—one file or chapter files—you should make multiple backup copies of your files with at least one stored on your computer and one stored on an external device such as a USB thumb drive that will not be stored in the same building as your computer. We also recommend that you save current versions of each file to an online location. You can do that by sending an e-mail to yourself with the file as an attachment or by using one of the free data storage sites on the Internet. All this may seem like silly overkill that takes caution to the extreme. That attitude disappears the first time you lose all your work on a chapter and have to begin from scratch because something happened to your original file that was not backed up.

If you follow our suggestions and create files for each chapter, you will eventually want to "assemble" all the chapters into a single document. There are several ways to do that. The simplest, which we do not recommend, is to cut and paste each file into a document that will be the entire dissertation. This is tedious and prone to mistakes. Another way to do it is detailed online at the My Digital Life website. Go to:

> http://www.mydigitallife.info/2007/12/05/combine-and-merge-multiple-documents-in-microsoft-office-word-2007/

and follow the directions in the article titled "Combine and Merge Multiple Documents in Microsoft Word 2007." This approach involves using the Object command under the Insert Tab. Other online guides for combining files are at:

> http://helpdeskgeek.com/office-tips/merge-combine-multiple-word-documents/

> http://www.gaebler.com/How-to-Combine-Multiple-Word-Documents-into-One-Document.htm

There is also a file named Boiler that works with many versions of Word. It lets you create a new document by combining several Word files, such as the files that contain your chapter documents. You can download this file from http://www.gmayor.com/downloads.htm. The name of the file is Boiler.zip and you will have to "unzip" this file before you can use it.

FORMATTING THE THREE MAJOR
SECTIONS OF YOUR DISSERTATION

There are five different groups of formatting and style rules for a dissertation. Some are general and apply to the entire document. For example, the rules for page size, margins, and gutter size typically apply to all parts of your dissertation. Other rules are specific to the front matter, the body of the dissertation, the back matter, or specific components such as tables or figures. In this section we will discuss a few issues relevant to the three major components of a dissertation—front matter, body, and back matter.

Front Matter: Title Page, Second Title Page, TOC, Table List, Figure List, Preface, Dedication

One example of how detailed the guidelines for front matter can be is the specificity of the University of Michigan directions for a dissertation title page (see http://www.rackham.umich.edu/downloads/oard/ Dissertation_Format_Guidelines.pdf). Between the title of the dissertation (ALL CAPS or First Letter Caps, centered, 10 or 12 point type, Courier, Ariel, or Times New Roman) and your name (First, Middle Initial only, and Last name) the word "by" in all lower case must be centered. By or BY are incorrect. The University of Michigan rules also require different margins for the title page (2.5" top, 1.5" left, and 1" right and bottom) than for the body of the dissertation (1.5" left, all others 1" except for a 2" top margin on the first page of each chapter). The University of Michigan even specifies where the line breaks should be in the statement:

> A dissertation submitted in partial fulfillment
> of the requirements of the degree of
> Doctor of Philosophy (English Language and Literature)
> in The University of Michigan
> 2009

Note that the institution is The, not the, University of Michigan. Details, details! And many of the details are local, not universal. You must learn what goes in the front matter of your dissertation and how it should be formatted at your institution.

Main Body

Within the main body of the dissertation areas pay attention to the rules about how the first page of chapters are formatted. Some guidelines for chapter first pages require a different top margin, omit page numbers, or forbid headers or footers.

Rules also vary about how many levels of headings are allowed—usually from three to five. Some institutions enforce the rules strictly ("No more than three levels, no exceptions!") while others look the other way if additional levels make sense even if the rules specify fewer levels than you used. Check informally with your major advisor and other students who have already successfully submitted their dissertations before you decide to use five levels of headings even though the rules say four are the maximum allowed.

Finally, one of the trickiest formatting tasks in the body of your dissertation will be tables. The APA guidelines for tables are long and detailed, and most institutions will expect tables to be formatted according to the APA rules. However, there may be exceptions to those rules and there may be options.

If you are using Microsoft Word to write your dissertation, the table commands built into Word can save you time and stress. Unfortunately, creating tables using Word's table commands does not automatically format the tables according to APA rules. Fortunately, there are several online guides to using Word's table commands to create "APA tables:"

http://www.runet.edu/~jaspelme/443/spring-2007/
How_to_Make_an_APA_format_Table_in_Word.pdf

http://academics.hamilton.edu/psychology/home/SPSSInstructions/
CreatingTablesinMSWord.doc

http://core.ecu.edu/psyc/wuenschk/Help/ThesisDiss/th-word.doc

Perhaps the most important thing about formatting the body of your dissertation is to learn the rules of formatting provided by your institution and automate the process of following those rules whenever possible. Using a template is one very important way of doing that. It allows you to tell the program which text is a "level 3 heading," for example, and then let the word processor apply all the formatting rules to that text.

Back Matter: Author Bio, Index, Appendices

Many dissertations include substantial back matter organized into appendices. Typically, each appendix will begin with a cover page that includes the letter or number of appendix and the title:

Appendix C

Patient Directions for Supplemental Treatment

The content of the appendix begins on the next page. Most institutions permit some variation in the appendices because you are often reproducing original materials that should appear as they did when they were used in the research. However, margin requirements are usually enforced to prevent parts of the appendices being too close to the bound edge to be readable.

Another back matter component that is read more often than you might think is a short author biography. If an author bio is permitted at your institution we suggest you provide one that gives enough detail about your background, experience, and professional interests to make you a "real" person to someone reading your dissertation. This is one area where you can add a personal touch.

BINDING, COPYRIGHT, AND
SUBMISSION TO PROQUEST AND OTHER WEBSITES

The final steps in the dissertation process are mostly bureaucratic in nature but nevertheless necessary. If your institution requires submitting several printed copies of the dissertation to a campus office, there will be a set of directions for doing that. You may, for example, be told that your dissertation must be bound at a particular bindery that has the correct covers and materials. If not, companies like

PHD Bookbinding (www.phdbookbinding.com),

Thesis on Demand (www.thesisondemand.com) and

C & H Bookbinding (www.chbook.com)

are three of the many companies that do dissertation binding for many colleges and universities.

If your institution requires an electronic copy of your dissertation, the most commonly required file format is Adobe's Portable Document Format (PDF). Anyone who downloads and installs Adobe's free Reader software can read a PDF document, including your dissertation if it is available to them as a PDF file. If your dissertation was created in Word, WordPerfect, or some other word processing program there are several ways to create a PDF file. Some word processing programs, like

OpenOffice and WordPerfect, can "export" your dissertation to a PDF file. There is also an "add on" available from Microsoft that converts your Word file to a PDF file (go to the Microsoft website—www.microsoft.com— and search for "Microsoft Save as PDF or XPS"). The option of working within your word processor to create a PDF file works well in some cases and poorly in others. Word's PDF conversion has the worst reputation for bugs and problems while OpenOffice and WordPerfect seem to do a much better job. However, your institution may require that a particular program be used to convert your dissertation to PDF. The most common requirement is the current version of Adobe's Acrobat software, which is not free. However, most institutions that require dissertations be submitted in a PDF file have Acrobat software available for that purpose.

Another step in submitting your dissertation is to establish copyright. Actually, by writing the dissertation you have established copyright under current law. There is no longer a requirement that you pay a fee or submit a copy to the U.S. Copyright Office to formally copyright your dissertation.

The directions from your institution for creating front matter often tell you where a copyright notice should be placed (e.g., "Copyright 2020, Joan Garfield"). While omitting even this notification does not mean you lose copyright, it is still a good idea to include this notice somewhere in the front matter. The typical location is just after the title page but there are variations from institution to institution.

Ironically, one of the first things you will do after submitting your dissertation is to give permission to companies like ProQuest to make and distribute copies of your dissertation to others. Because you own the copyright, you will need to give permission to your institution, ProQuest, and perhaps others, to legally reproduce your dissertation. You own the copyright which means you can permit others to use some of your rights—such as the ability to distribute the dissertation to others.

Dissemination: Free Access or Restricted?

The last topic we will discuss in this book is the question of access to your dissertation. As discussed in previous chapters there are many ways to make your dissertation available to others. Some options provide free and open access to anyone while others are restricted in one way or another. For example, the ProQuest online access system for dissertations charges a fee to access and download the full text of your dissertation. Other sites let you restrict access to people with IDs from your doctoral institution. For example, Rensselaer Polytechnic Institute gives doctoral students two access options:

If you select the 'Standard" agreement, the electronic copy of your thesis or dissertation will be available only to current Rensselaer faculty, staff and students; and Rensselaer will only allow the abstract of your work to be viewed by people outside of Rensselaer. You might want to choose this option if you plan to try to find a commercial publisher for your thesis or dissertation. (quoted from http://library.rpi.edu/update.do?artcenterkey=1389)

The standard agreement, as you can see, restricts access. Another option does not:

If you select the Creative Commons agreement, you authorize Rensselaer to permit the electronic copy of your thesis or dissertation to be viewable and available for download to anyone in accordance with the terms identified in a Creative Commons License 3.0. The license specifies that anyone who views and subsequently uses a copy your thesis or dissertation must attribute the work to you, cannot use the work for any commercial purpose, and cannot modify your work in any way without obtaining your explicit permission.

You might want to choose the Creative Commons option because it potentially provides you with faster professional recognition than is gained by using traditional distribution channels. This can be useful for individuals seeking to establish their artistic credentials. However, it is important to note that a Creative Commons License 3.0 is not "revocable," i.e. you cannot change this decision later. Your thesis or dissertation may also be considered as "published" by some entities because you made it available to the general public. Finding a publisher may be harder; and in some European jurisdictions, other intellectual property rights, such as your filing for patent protection, will be affected. (quoted from http://library.rpi.edu/update.do?artcenterkey=1389)

Our advice is to select the least restrictive option for disseminating your dissertation unless there are very important reasons for not doing so (e.g., the results of your dissertation research involves an invention or concept that may be patented). We also advise you to take advantage of several sites where dissertations can be submitted and made available to others. Submit your dissertation to these sites, particularly ProQuest, because they help potential readers find your dissertation. ProQuest is probably the most commonly used site by anyone looking for dissertations on a particular topic, and that popularity plus the ability to do sophisticated searches on the ProQuest site makes it a must-use site for disseminating your dissertation. Your institution may include all the steps for submitting your dissertation to ProQuest in the institutional process of acceptance. If not, you can go to http://www.proquest.com/en-US/products/dissertations/submitted_authors.shtml and follow the directions there.

However, restricted sites should not be the only way to access your dissertation. Internet search engines can index the full text of your dissertation when it is stored on your own website and dissertation archive sites in your doctoral department and institution. These are thus excellent places to store electronic copies of your dissertation so that others will find and use it. A dissertation is an effort to contribute to our understanding of the world we live in and sharing that understanding with others is the final step in a process that began when you decided that studying for a doctorate might be a good idea.

REFERENCES

Abbott, H. P. (2002). *The Cambridge introduction to narrative.* Cambridge, England: Cambridge University Press.

Akker, J., Gravemeijer, K., McKenny, S., & Nieveen, N. (2006). *Educational design research.* London: Routledge.

American Association of Colleges of Nursing. (2004). *Position statement on the practice doctorate in nursing.* Retrieved from www.aacn.nche.edu/DNP/pdf/DNP.pdf

American Association of Colleges of Nursing. (2005). Frequently *asked questions concerning the AACN position statement on the practice doctorate in nursing.* Retrieved from www.aacn.nche.edu/DNP/AboutDNP.htm

American Association of Colleges of Nursing. (2006). *The essentials of doctoral education for advanced nursing practice* (Draft V). Retrieved from www.aacn.nche.edu/DNP/pdf/Essentials5-06.pdf

American Psychological Association. (2009). *Publication manual of the American Psychological Association* (6th ed.). Washington, DC: Author.

Andresen, M. (2007). *The experience of recovery from schizophrenia: Development of a definition, model and measure of recovery.* Unpublished PhD dissertation, School of Psychology, University of Woologong. Retrieved from http://www.library.uow.edu.au/adt-NWU/public/adt-NWU20080703.161126/

Aspland, T. (2002). Framing graduate supervision and examination in the professional doctorate at QUT. In A. Goody, J. Herrington, & M. Northcote (Eds), *Proceedings of the 2002 Annual International Conference of the Higher Education Research and Development Society of Australasia.* Perth: Higher Education Research and Development Society of Australia.

Atkinson, P., Coffey, A., Delamont, S., Coffey, A. Lofland, J., & Lofland, L. (2007). *Handbook of ethnography.* Thousand Oaks, CA: SAGE.

Averett, P. (2004). *Parental communications and young women's struggle for sexual agency. Dissertation submitted to the Faculty of Virginia Polytechnic Institute and State University in partial fulfillment of the requirements for the degree of Doctor of Philoso-*

phy in Human Development. Retrieved from http://scholar.lib.vt.edu/theses/available/etd-12142004-161236/unrestricted/AverettDissertation.pdf

Ayers, M. (1918). Disputations. In *The Encyclopedia Americana*. New York: The Encyclopedia Americana Corporation.

Babcock, J., Green, C., & Robie, C. (2002, January). Does batterers' treatment work? A meta-analytic review of domestic violence treatment. *Clinical Psychology Review, 23*(8), 1023-1053.

Babson, L. (2007). *Effects of self-monitoring of negative self statements with chronic pain patients*. Unpublished PhD dissertation, Ohio State University. Retrieved from http://www.ohiolink.edu/etd/view.cgi?acc_num=osu1195144188

Bachor, D. (2000). *Reformatting reporting methods for case studies*. Retrieved from http://www.aare.edu.au/00pap/bac00287.htm

Barnes, E. (1998). *Linking integrated services with schools: A case study*. Doctoral dissertation, Virginia Polytechnic Institute and State University. Retrieved from http://scholar.lib.vt.edu/theses/available/etd-23098-18255/unrestricted/front_section.pdf

Beach, D. (2005). *From field work to theory and representation in ethnography*. In G. Troman, B. Jeffrey, & G. Walford (Eds.), *Methodological issues and practices in ethnography* (pp. 1-18). San Diego, CA: Elsevier.

Blake, R., & Mouton, J. (1964). *The managerial grid: The key to leadership excellence*. Houston: Gulf Publishing.

Bland, D. (2007). *Researching educational disadvantage: Using participatory research to engage marginalized students with education*. Unpublished PhD dissertation, Queensland University of Technology. Retrieved from www.eprints.qut.edu.au/16434

Bland, D. (2007). *Researching educational disadvantage: Using participatory research to engage marginalized students with education*. Unpublished PhD dissertation, Queensland University of Technology. Retrieved from www.eprints.qut.edu.au/16434

Bloom, R., Obler, L., De Santi, S., & Ehrlich, J. (1994). *Discourse analysis and applications*. Mahwah, NJ: Erlbaum.

Bloomberg, L., & Volpe, M. (2008). *Completing your qualitative dissertation*. Thousand Oaks, CA: SAGE.

Bobko, P. (2001). *Correlation and regression: Principles and applications for industrial/organizational psychology and management* (2nd ed.). Thousand Oaks, CA: SAGE.

Borenstein, M., Hedges, L., & Rothstein, H. (2009). *Introduction to meta-analysis*. Hoboken, NJ: Wiley.

Bowen, W. G., & Rudenstein, N. L. (1992). *In pursuit of the PhD*. Princeton, NJ: Princeton University Press.

Brannen, S. J. (1996, October). Comparing the effectiveness of gender-specific and couples groups in a court-mandated spouse abuse treatment program. *Research on Social Work Practice, 6*(4), 405-424.

Bransford, J., Brown, A., & Cocking, R. (Eds.). (2002). *How people learn: Brain, mind, experience, and school*. Washington, DC: Commission on Behavioral and Social Sciences and Education of the National Research Council, National Academy Press.

Bressler, C. (2007). *Literary criticism: An introduction to theory and practice* (4th ed.). Upper Saddle River, NJ: Pearson Prentice Hall.

Britt, E. (2008). *Enhancing diabetes self-management: Motivational enhancement therapy.* Unpublished doctoral dissertation, University of Canterbury. Retrieved from http://library.canterburh.ac.nz/etd/adt-NZCU20080314.124830

Brodie, L. (2001). *The Hermeneutic approach to museum education program development.* Unpublished dissertation, Department of Curriculum Studies, University of Saskatchewan. Retrieved from http://library2.usask.ca/theses/available/etd-10212004-002539/

Brown, R. (2006). *Doing your dissertation in business and management.* Thousand Oaks, CA: SAGE.

Brown, G., & Atkins, M. (1988). *Effective teaching in higher education.* London: Methuen.

Brundage, A. (2002). *Going to the sources: A guide to historical research and writing.* Wheeling, IL: Harlan Davidson.

Campbell, B. (1995). *Your blues ain't like mine.* New York: One World/Ballantine.

Cennamo, K. S., Abell, Chung, M. & Hugg, W. (1995). A "Layers of Negotiation" model for designing constructivist learning materials. *Proceedings of the Annual National Convention of the Association for Educational Communications and Technology (AECT), Anaheim, CA, 95,* 32-42.

Cennamo, K. S., Abell, S. K., & Chung, M. L. (1996, July-August). A "Layers of Negotiation" model for designing constructivist learning materials. *Educational Technology,* 39-48.

Chapman (2002). Comment. Quoted in S. Taylor & N. Beasley (Ed.), *A handbook for doctoral supervisors* (p. 64). New York: RoutledgeFalmer.

Charmaz, C. (2006) *Constructing grounded theory: A practical guide through qualitative analysis.* Thousand Oaks, CA: SAGE.

Clandinin, D. J., & Connelly, F. M. (2000). *Narrative inquiry: Experience and story in qualitative research.* San Francisco: Jossey-Bass.

Colón, B., Taylor, K., & Willis, J. (May, 2000). Constructivist instructional design: Creating a multimedia package for teaching critical qualitative research. *The Qualitative Report, 5*(1/2). Retrieved from http://www.nova.edu/ssss/QR/QR5-1/colon.html

Corwin, Z., & Tierney, W. (2005). *The qualitative misfit: Evaluating the interpretive complexity of IRBs.* Retrieved from http://www.allacademic.com//meta/p_mla_apa_research_citation/0/2/0/1/0/pages20109/p20109-1.php

Crabtree B., & Miller, W. (1999). *Doing qualitative research.* Thousand Oaks, CA: SAGE.

Crosby, D., Stills, S., & Nash, G. (1970). Love the one you're with. *On Crosby, Stills, & Nash, G.* [box set] [CD]. New York: Atlantic Records. (1991)

Cross, J. (2000). *Return to reality: A causal realist approach to re-construction in science teaching.* Unpublished doctoral dissertation, University of Melbourne. Retrieved from http://eprints.infodiv.unimelb.edu.au/00002048/01/Cross.pdf

Damrosch, D. (2006). Vectors of change. In C. Golde & G. Walker (Eds.), *Envisioning the future of doctoral education* (pp. 34-45). San Francisco: Jossey-Bass/Carnegie Foundation for the Advancement of Teaching.

Dano, E. (2008). *Historical research.* New York: Oxford University Press.

Denzin, N. (1996). *Interpretive ethnography: Ethnographic practices of the 21st century.* Berkeley: University of California Press.

Denzin, N., & Lincoln, Y. (Eds.). (2005). *SAGE Handbook of Qualitative Research* (3rd ed.). Thousand Oaks, CA: SAGE.

Dick, B. (1996). *Scientist practitioner* (Paper 14). Retrieved from http://uqconnect.net/~zzbdick/dlitt/DLitt_P14scip.pdf

Dick, W., Carey, L., & Carey, J. (2004). *The systematic design of instruction* (6th ed.). Boston: Allyn & Bacon.

Duckhart, T. (2006). *Authethnography.* Retrieved June 4, 2007, from http://www.humboldt.edu/~tdd2/Autoethnography.htm

Duffy, T., & Cunningham, D. (1996). Constructivism: Implications for the design and delivery of instruction. In D. H. Jonassen (Ed.), *Handbook of research for educational communications technology* (pp. 170-198). New York: Simon & Schuster.

Duke, N., & Beck, S. (1999). Education should consider alternative formats for the dissertation. *Educational Researcher, 28*(3), 31-36.

Duncan, M. (2000). *Principles of multimedia design: An authethnographic study of one designer's experience.* Unpublished PhD dissertation, Queensland University of Technology, Brisbane, Australia.

Eisner, E. (1997). *The enlightened eye: Qualitative inquiry and the enhancement of educational practice* (2nd ed.) Englewood Cliffs, NJ: Prentice Hall.

Ekegren, P. (1999). *Reading of theoretical texts.* New York: Routledge.

Elkana, Y. (2006). Unmasking uncertainties and embracing contradictions: Graduate education in the sciences. In C. Golde & G. Walker, (Eds), *Envisioning the future of doctoral education* (pp. 65-96). San Francisco: Jossey-Bass/Carnegie Foundation for the Advancement of Teaching.

Elliot, J. (1998). *A critical ethnography of the experience of menopause for Korean women living in Canada.* Master's thesis in nursing, University of Western Ontario. Retrieved from htp://www.collectionscanada.gc.ca/obj/s4/f2/dsk2/tape17/PQDD_0007/MQ30722.pdf

Faircloth, N. (2003). *Analysing discourse: Textual analysis for social research.* New York: Routledge.

Feder, L., Wilson, D., & Austin, S. (2008). *Court-mandated interventions for individuals convicted of domestic violence. Volume 12 of the Campbell Systematic Reviews, 12.* Oslo, Norway: The Campbell Collaboration. Retrieved from http://db.c2admin.org/doc-pdf/Feder_DomesticViolence_review.pdf

Fetterman, D. (1998). *Ethnography step by step.* Thousand Oaks, CA: SAGE.

Fetterman, D. (2007). *Ethnography step by step* (2nd ed) Thousand Oaks, CA: SAGE.

Flyvbjerg, B. (2001). *Making social science matter: Why social inquiry fails and how it can succeed again.* Cambridge, England: Cambridge University Press.

Flyvbjerg, B. (2004). Five misunderstandings about case-study research. In C. Seale, G. Gobo, J. Gubrium, & D. Silverman, (Eds.). *Qualitative Research Practice* (pp. 420-434). Thousand Oaks, CA: SAGE.

Fowler, F. (2001). *Survey research methods.* Thousand Oaks, CA: SAGE

Fry, A. (2002). *Understanding attempted suicide in young women from non-English speaking backgrounds: A hermeneutic and narrative inquiry.* Unpublished PhD Dissertation, University of Western Sydney. Retrieved from http://handle.uws.edu.au:8081/1959.7/643

Furay, C., & Salevouris, M. (2000). *The methods and skills of history: A practical guide* (2nd ed.). Wheeling, IL: Harlan Davidson.

Gadamer, H. G. (2004). *Truth and method* (2nd revised ed.). New York: Continuum.

Gall, M., Gall, J., & Borg, W. (2006). *Educational research: An introduction* (8th ed.). Boston: Allyn & Bacon.

Gallin, J., & Obnibene, F. (2007). *Principles and practice of clinical research* (2nd ed.). Burlington, MA: Academic Press.

Gatfield, T., & Alpert, F. (2002, July) The supervisory management styles model. *Quality Conversations, Proceedings of the 25th HERDSA Annual Conference, Perth, Western Australia, 7-10*, 263.

Gelso, C. (2006). On the making of a scientist–practitioner: A theory of research training in professional psychology. *Training and Education in Professional Psychology, 5*(1), 3-16.

Gerber, B. (2000). Consideration of an alternative dissertation format. Educational Perspectives. In P. A. Rubba, J. A. Rye, P. F. Keig, & W. J. DiBiase (Eds.). *Proceedings of the annual meeting of the Association for the Education of Teachers in Science* (Akron). Retrieved from http://www.ed.psu.edu/CI/Journals/2000/AETS/26Gerber.rtf

Glenn, D. (2008, December 5). Psychology departments are changing. *Chronicle of Higher Education, LV*(13), A1, A10-A11.

Golde, C., & Walker, G. (Eds.). (2006). *Envisioning the future of doctoral education: Preparing stewards of the discipline.* San Francisco: Jossey-Bass/Carnegie Foundation for the Advancement of Teaching.

Green, H., & Powell, S. (2005). *Doctoral study in contemporary higher education.* Maidenhead, England: The Society for Research into Higher Education/Open University Press/McGraw-Hill Education.

Greenwood, D., & Levin, M. (2007). *Action research: Social research for social change.* Thousand Oaks: CA: SAGE.

Griffiths, P. (2004). Evidence-based practice: A deconstruction and postmodern critique. *International Journal of Nursing Studies, 42*(3), 355-361.

Grigoratos, A. (2006). *A narrative exploration into the world of ill fathers who have lost a limb due to diabetes.* A mini dissertation submitted in partial fulfillment of the requirements for the degree, Magister Artium Counseling Psychology in the Faculty of Humanities, Department of Psychology, University of Pretoria. Retrieved from http://upetd.up.ac.za/thesis/available/etd-11052007-104428/unrestricted/dissertation.pdf

Habermas, J. (1971). *Knowledge and human interest.* Boston: Beacon Press.

Handcock, D., & Algozzine, R. (2006). *Doing case study research: A practical guide for beginning researchers.* New York: Teachers College Press.

Hastings, B. (1999). Cognitive, contextual, and personality factors in wife abuse. Doctoral Dissertation in Psychology, Kansas State University. Retrieved from www.dissertation.com/library/1120664a.htm

Henneman, E. (2008). Nurse-physician collaboration: A poststructuralist view. *Journal of Advanced Nursing, 22*(2), 359-363.

Henry, J. (2007). *Scenes from the margins: A participatory action research study about the praxis of womanhood as a different way of working in male-dominated professions.* Unpublished Ph.D. dissertation, University of Tennessee—Knoxville. Retrieved from http://etd.utk.edu/2006/HenryJane.pdf

Hernandez, L. (1996). In search of a dissertation committee: Using a qualitative research approach to study a lived experience. *The Qualitative Report, 2*(4). Retrieved from http://www.nova.edu/ssss/QR/QR2-4/hernandez.html

Heron, J. (1996). *Co-operative inquiry: Research into the human condition.* Thousand Oaks, CA: SAGE.

Herr, K., & Anderson, G. (2005). *The action research dissertation: A guide for students and faculty.* Thousand Oaks, CA: SAGE.

Hersey, P., & Blanchard, K. (1988). *Management of organizational behavior: Utilizing human resources.* Englewood Cliffs, NJ: Prentice-Hall.

Heywood, C. (2001). *An assessment of EEG biofeedback for the remediation of attention-deficit hyperactivity disorder.* Unpublished PhD dissertation, University of Aukland. Retrieved from the University of Aukland library website at http://researchspace.auckland.ac.nz/docs/uoa-docs/rights.htm

Higgs, J., & Titchen, A. (2001). *Practice knowledge & expertise in the health professions.* Burlington, MA: Butterworth-Heineman.

Hill, H. (2002). Comment. Quoted in S. Taylor and N Beasley (Ed.), *A Handbook for Doctoral Supervisors* (p. 64). New York: Routledge.

Holman Jones, S. (2005). Autoethnography: Making the personal political. In N. Denzin & Y. Lincoln (Eds.), *Handbook of Qualitative Research* (pp. 763-791). Thousand Oak, CA: SAGE.

Howell, M., & Prevenier, W. (2001). *From reliable sources: An introduction to historical research.* Cornell, NY: Cornell University Press.

Hul, J., & Hak, T. (2008). *Case study methodology in business research.* Oxford, England: Butterworth-Heinemann.

Idea Finder. (2007, April 17). Integrated circuit. Retrieved from http://www.ideafinder.com/history/inventions/integratedcircuit.htm

Iggers, G. (2005). *Historiography in the twentieth Century: From scientific objectivity to the postmodern challenge.* Middleton, CT: Wesleyan University Press.

Imel. S. (2002). *Tacit knowledge. Trends and Issues Alert No. 46.* ERIC Clearinghouse on Adult, Career, and Vocational Education. Retrieved June 3, 2007, from http://www.eric.ed.gov/ERICDocs/data/ericdocs2sql/content_storage_01/0000019b/80/1b/41/cc.pdfhttp://www.cete.org/acve/

Innes, S. (1999). *A family literacy initiative using participatory action research in Manilla, Phillipines.* Unpublished PhD dissertation, University of Calgary. Retrieved from http://www.collectionscanada.gc.ca/obj/s4/f2/dsk1/tape7/PQDD_0019/MQ47949.pdf

Iran-Nejad, A., McKeachie, W., & Berliner, D. (1990, Winter). The multisource nature of learning: An introduction. *Review of Educational Research, 60*(4), 509-515.

Janosky, J. (2005, September). Use of single subject design for practice based primary care research. *Postgraduate Medical Journal, 81*(959), 549-551.

Jewett, L. (2006, May). *A delicate dance: Authethnography, curriculum, and the semblance of intimacy.* PhD dissertation, Department of Curriculum and Instruction,

College of Education, Louisiana State University, Baton Rouge, LA. Retrieved March 29, 2009 http://etd.lsu.edu/docs/available/etd-03082006-153046/unrestricted/Jewett_dis.pdf

Johns, C. (2004). *Becoming a reflective practitioner: A reflective and holistic approach to clinical nursing, practice development, and clinical supervision.* Oxford, England: Blackwell.

Johns, C. (2007). *Engaging reflection in practice: A narrative approach.* Oxford, England: Blackwell.

Johnson, B. (2007). *Leadership-influenced practices that impact classroom instruction related to writing: A case study of a successful elementary school.* Doctoral dissertation, Western Michigan University. Retrieved from http://www.wmich.edu/coe/elrt/proposals/index.htm

Johnson, D. (2007). *An analysis of the Manitoba/Winnipeg Community Revitalization Program implementation process.* Master of City Planning Thesis, University of Manitoba. Retrieved from http://mspace.lib.umanitoba.ca/dspace/handle/1993/1243

Kadijevich, D. (2006) Achieving educational technology standards: The relationship between student teacher's interest and institutional support offered. *Journal of Computer Assisted Learning 22*(6), 437-443.

Kemmis, S. (2000). *Educational research and communicative space.* The 2000 Radford lecture. Presented at the annual conference of the Australian Association for Research in Education, Sydney, University of Sydney.

Kennedy, C. (2004). *Single case designs for educational research.* Boston: Allyn & Bacon.

Kopy, A. (2006). A case study of the efficacy of a University Cohort Group in a small urban school district. Doctoral dissertation, Western Michigan University. Retrieved from http://www.wmich.edu/coe/elrt/proposals/index.htm

Kreth, M. (1999). *Talking to text and sketches: the function of written and graphic mediation in mechanical engineering design.* Doctoral dissertation, Colorado State University. Retrieved from http://wac.colostate.edu/theses/index.cfm?category=17

Kulinskaya, E., Morgenthaler, S., & Staudte, R. (2008). *Meta-analysis: A guide to calibrating and combining statistical evidence.* West Sussex, England: Wiley.

Kuther, T. (n.d.). Stop procrastinating and complete your dissertation! *About.Com: Graduate School* (online publication). Retrieved from http://gradschool.about.com/cs/thesiswriting/a/diss.htm

Krathwohl, D. (1994). A slice of advice. *Educational Researcher, 23,* 29-32.

Krueger, R. & Casey, M. (2000) *Focus groups: A practical guide for applied research* (3rd ed.). Thousand Oaks, CA: SAGE.

La Belle, T. (2004, April). *Credential inflation and the professional doctorate in California higher education.* Berkeley, CA: Center for Studies in Higher Education, University of California Berkeley. Retrieved from http://cshe.berkeley.edu/publications/publications.php?id=75

Larson, R. (2009, January 1). Educational leadership development for equity: Enhancing a critical theory of action. *Dissertation abstracts international. A. The Humanities and Social Sciences, 69*(7), 2547.

Lawrenchuk, R. (2007). *Parental participation in a Cree and Ojibway Head Start program: Development of a conceptual framework.* Unpublished MSc thesis, University of Manitoba. Retrieved from http://mspace.lib.umanitoba.ca/dspace/handle/1993/1205

Lebow, D. (1993). Constructivist values for instructional systems design: Five principles toward a new mindset. *Educational Technology Research and Development, 41*(3), 4-16.

Lee, K. (1995). *Do not resuscitate: Bioethical and nursing perspectives.* Unpublished master's thesis, University of Western Sydney. Retrieved from http://handle.uws.edu.au:8081/1959.7/7672

Levine, A. (2005). *Educating school leaders. The Education Schools Project.* Retrieved from http://www.edschools.org/pdf/Final313.pdf

Levinson, B., Foley, D., & Holland D. (Eds) (1996). *The cultural production of the educated person: Critical ethnographies of schooling and local practice.* Albany, NY: SUNY Press.

Littell, J., Corcoran, J., & Pillai, V. (2008). *Systematic reviews and meta-analysis.* New York: Oxford University Press.

Loehlin, J. (2003). *Latent Variable models: An introduction to factor, path, and structural equation analysis* (4th ed.). Mahway, NJ: Erlbaum.

Loughran, S. (2004, August 9). In hospital deaths from medical errors at 195,000 per year USA. *Medical News Today.* Retrieved from http://www.medicalnewstoday.com/articles/11856.php

Lovitts, B. (2006). Making the implicit explicit: Faculty's performance expectations for the dissertation. In P. Maki & N. Borkowski (Eds.), *The assessment of doctoral education: Emerging criteria and new models for improving outcomes* (pp.163-187). Sterling, VA: Stylus.

Lewin, K. (1948). *Resolving social conflicts: selected papers on group dynamics* (Gertrude Lewin, Ed.). New York: Harper & Row.

Masson, H. (1998). *The thin woman: Feminism, poststructuralism and the social psychology of anorexia nervosa.* New York: Routledge.

Madison, D. (2005). *Critical ethnography: Method, ethics, and performance.* Thousand Oaks, CA: SAGE.

Margalit, A. (1996). *The decent society.* Cambridge, MA: Cambridge University Press.

Marius, R., & Page, M. (2009). *Short guide to writing about history* (7th ed.). New York: Longman.

Masters, R. (2003). *Counseling criminal justice offenders* (2nd ed.). Thousand Oaks, CA: SAGE.

McCarthy, T. (1978). *The critical theory of Jurgen Habermas.* Cambridge, MA: The MIT Press.

McDonald, M. (2005). *Epiphanies: An existential and psychological inquiry.* Unpublished doctoral dissertation, University of Technology, Sydney, Australia. Retrieved from http://epress.lib.uts.edu.au/dspace/handle/2100/264

McIntyre, A. (2008). *Participatory action research.* Thousand Oaks, CA: SAGE.

McGee, M. (1998). Phronesis in the Gadamer versus Habermas debates. In J. Sloop & J. McDaniel (Eds.), *Judgement calls: Rhetoric, politics and indeterminancy* (pp. 13-41). Boulder, CO: Westview Press.

McInerney, C. (2002). Knowledge management and the dynamic nature of knowledge. *Journal of the American Society for Information Science and Technology 53*(12), 1009-1018.

McLinton, J. (2007).*The perceived impact of WebCT technology as an instructional delivery system among college instructors.* Unpublished PhD dissertation, Mississippi State University. Retrieved from http://sun.library.msstate.edu/ETD-db/theses/available/etd-03122007-232436

McMahon, M. (2003). *Cultural and post-structuralist feminism.* Retrieved June 28, 2007, from http://webpages.ull.es/users/mmcmahon/textos/feminisms.htm

McMahon, G. T., Monaghan, C., Falchuk, K., Gordon, J., & Alexander. E. (2005, January). A simulator-based curriculum to promote comparative and reflective analysis in an internal medicine clerk clerkship. *Academic Medicine, 80*(1), 84-89.

McNiff, J. (2002, October). *Realising a knowledge base for new forms of educational theory in Irish universities.* Paper presented at the All Ireland Society for Higher Education, Dublin Institute of Technology. Retrieved June 3, 2007, from http://www.jeanmcniff.com/aishe.html

McTaggert, R. (1997). *Participatory action research: International contexts and consequences.* Albany, NY: SUNY Press.

Merriam, S. (1998). *Qualitative research and case study applications in education.* San Francisco: Jossey Bass.

Miles, J., & Shelvin, M. (2000). *Applying correlation and regression: A guide for students and researchers.* Thousand Oaks, CA: SAGE.

Miller, W., & Crabtree, B. (2005). Clinical research. In N. Denzin & Y. Lincoln (Eds.), *Handbook of Qualitative Research* (3rd ed., pp. 605-639). Thousand Oaks, CA: SAGE.

Morgan, K., & Libner, K. (2004, June). Ph.Digital? Lessons from the history of the doctorate and the dissertation. In *Proceedings of the Seventh International Symposium on Electronic Theses and Dissertations, Lexington, KY.* Retrieved from http://uky.edu/EDT2004/abstracts5.html and full paper available at /www.uky.edu/ETD/ETD2004/libner/Libner-Morgan-ETD2004.pdf

Morse, J. (2005). Feigning independence: The article dissertation. *Qualitative Health Research, 15,* 1147.

Moses, I. (1992). *Expectations and standards in postgraduate supervision* [Video Tape]. Brisbane, Australia: The University of Queensland.

National Science Foundation. (1997). *User-Friendly Handbook for Mixed Method Evaluation.* Washington, DC: Directorate of Education and Human Resources; Division of Research, Evaluation and Communication; National Science Foundation. Retrieved from http://www.nsf.gov/pubs/1997/nsf97153/start.htm

Nguyn, T. (2005). *Development of new cooling methods for grinding.* Unpublished doctoral dissertation, University of Sydney. Retrieved from http://hdl.handle.net/2123/1689

Nolan, J. (1997). *Examination of the quality of life of older adults living in rural cooperative housing.* Unpublished PhD dissertation, Ohio State University. Retrieved from http://www.seniorcoops.org/intro.html

Norcross, J., & Castle, P. (2002). Appreciating the PsyD: The Facts. *Eye on Psi Chi, 7*(1), 22-26. Retrieved from http://www.psichi.org/pubs/articles/article_171.asp

Ogawa, A. (2004). *The failure of civil society? An ethnography of NPOS and the state in contemporary Japan.* Unpublished PhD dissertation, Cornell University, Ithaca, NY. Retrieved from http://ecommons.cornell.edu/handle/1813/134

Özdemi, D. (2004). *The effects of educational ideology upon technology acceptance.* Unpublished PhD dissertation, Middle Eastern Technical University, Ankara, Turkey. Retrieved from http://etd.lib.metu.edu.tr/upload/2/12604992/index.pdf

Papert, S. (1994). *The children's machine: Rethinking school in the age of the computer.* New York: Basic Books.

Parada, R. (2006). *School bullying: Psychosocial determinants and effective intervention.* Unpublished PhD dissertation, School of Education, University of Western Sydney. Retrieved from http://handle.uws.edu.au:8081/1959.7/17413

Pearson, M., & Brew, A. (2002). Research training and supervision development. *Studies in Higher Education, 27*(2), 135-150.

Peters, J. (2002). *Complexity of school university partnerships participants' perceptions of the Innovative Links projects in South Australia.* Unpublished PhD dissertation, University of South Australia. Retrieved from http://arrow.unisa.edu.au:8081/1959.8/25030

Pironet, F. (2001). The relations between insolubles and obligations in medieval disputations. In M. Yrjönsuuri (Ed.), *Medieval formal logic: Obligations, insolubles and consequences* (The New Syntheses Historical Library, Vol. 49, pp. 95-114). New York: Springer/Kluwer Academic.

Polkinghorne, D. (1988). *Narrative knowing and human sciences.* Albany, NY: SUNY Press.

Pollard, A. (2008). *The professional development and training needs of literacy coordinators in secondary schools in Victoria, Australia.* Unpublished PhD dissertation in the College of Education, Royal Melbourne Institute of Technology. Retrieved from http://adt.lib.rmit.edu.au/adt/public/adt-VIT20080514.122251/

Prewitt, K. (2006). Who should do what? Implications for institutional and national leaders. In C. Golde & G. Walker (Eds.), *Envisioning the future of doctoral education* (pp. 23-33). San Francisco: Jossey Bass/The Carnegie Foundation for the Advancement of Teaching.

Punch, K. (1998). *Introduction to social research: Quantitative and qualitative approaches.* Thousand Oaks, CA: SAGE.

Rea, L. & Parker, R. (2005). *Designing and conducting survey research: A comprehensive guide.* San Francisco: Jossey-Bass.

Reason, P., & Bradbury, H. (Eds) (2001). *Handbook of action research.* Thousand Oaks, CA: SAGE.

Reed-Danahay, D. (Ed.). (1997). *Auto/ethnography: Rewriting the self and the social.* Oxford, England: Berg.

Ritchie, J., & Wilson, D. (2000). *Teacher narrative as critical inquiry: Rewriting the Script.* New York: Teachers College Press.

Robbins, M. (n.d.). *El Paso* (music video). Retrieved from ttp://www.last.fm/music/Marty+Robbins/_/El+Paso

Rubin, H., & Rubin, I. (2004). *Qualitative interviewing: The art of hearing* (2nd ed.). Thousand Oaks, CA: SAGE.

Ruthven, K. (2000). Towards synergy of scholarly and craft knowledge. In *Proceedings of the annual meeting of the Annual Conference on Didactics of Mathematics*, Potsdam, 2000. Retrieved June 3, 2007, from http://webdoc.gwdg.de/ebook/e/gdm/2000/ruthven_2000.pdf

Said. E. (2002). *Power, politics, and culture: Interviews with Edward Said*. New York: Vintage Books.

Salmon, G. (2000). Computer mediated conferencing for management learning at the Open University. *Management Learning, 31*(4), 491-502.

Shadish, W., Cook, T., & Campbell, D. (2002). *Experimental and quasi-experimental designs*. Boston: Houghton Mifflin.

Schön, D. (1967). *Technology and change: The New Heraclitus*. New York: Delacourt.

Schön, D. (1995). *The reflective practitioner: How professionals think in action*. New York: Basic Books.

Schön, D. (1990a). *Educating the reflective practitioner: Toward a new design for teaching and learning in the professions*. San Francisco: Jossey-Bass.

Schön, D. (1990b). *The reflective turn: Case studies in and on educational practice*. New York: Teachers College Press.

Scholz, R., & Tietje, O. (2002). *Embedded case study methods: Integrating quantitative and qualitative knowledge*. Thousand Oaks, CA: SAGE.

Schumacker, R., & Lomax, R. (2004). *A beginner's guide to structural equation modeling* (2nd ed.). Mahway, NJ: Erlbaum.

Schultz, L. (1990). Confidentiality, priviledge, and child abuse reporting. *IPT Journal, 2*. Retrieved from http://www.ipt-forensics.com/journal/volume2/j2_4_5.htm

Schwartzman, R. (2002, Fall). Poeticizing scholarship. *American Communications Journal, 6*(1). Retrieved June 4, 2007, from http://www.acjournal.org/holdings/vol6/iss1/special/schwartzman.htm

Seebohm, T. (2004). *Hermeneutics: Method and methodology*. Norwell, MA: Kluwer.

Seidman, I. (2006). *Interviewing as qualitative research: A guide for researchers in education and the social sciences*. New York: Teachers College Press.

Senge, P. (2006). *The fifth discipline: The art and practice of the learning organization* (2nd ed.). New York: Doubleday.

Scott, D., Brown, A., Lunt, I., & Thorne, L. (2004). *Professional doctorates: Integrating professional and academic Knowledge*. Maidenhead, England: Open University Press/McGraw Hill Education.

Sherratt, Y. (2005). *Continental philosophy of social science*. Cambridge, England: Cambridge University Press.

Shulman, L., Golde, C., Bueschel, A., & Garabedian, K. (2006). Reclaiming education's doctorates: A critique and a proposal, *Educational Researcher, 35*(3), 25-32.

Skinner, C. (Ed.). (2005). *Single subject designs for school psychologists*. New York: Routledge.

Skulmoski, G., Hartman, F., & Kran, J. (2007). The Delphi method for graduate research. *Journal of Information Technology Research, 6*, 1-21. Retrieved from http://jite.org/documents/Vol6/JITEv6p001-021Skulmoski212.pdf

Slattery, P. (1997, September). *Postmodern curriculum research and alternative forms of data presentation*. Public seminar/occasional paper presented to The Curricu-

lum and Pedagogy Institute of the University of Alberta. Retrieved from http:/
/www.quasar.ualberta.ca/cpin/cpinfolder/papers/slattery.htm

Smith, A. (2001, January 1), A program assessment in domestic violence. Dissertation Collection for Tennessee State University. Paper AAI30224633.
Retrieved from http://e-research.tnstate.edu/dissertations/AAI3024633/

Sorkin, D. (1983, January-March). Wilhelm von Humboldt: The theory and practice of self-formulation (Bildung, 1971-1810). *Journal of the History of Ideas,*
44(1), 55-73.

Spiro, R. J., Coulson, R. L., Feltovich, P. J., & Anderson, D. K. (1988). Cognitive
flexibility theory: Advanced knowledge acquisition in ill-structured domains.
In *The tenth annual conference of the cognitive science society.* Hillsdale, NJ: Erlbaum.

Spindler, G., & Hammond, L. (2007). *Innovations in educational ethnography.* Mahwah, NJ: Erlbaum.

Spiro, R. J., Feltovich, P. J., Jacobson, M. J., & Coulson, R. L. (1995). Cognitive
flexibility, constructivism, and hypertext: Random access instruction for
advanced knowledge acquisition in ill-structured domains. In J. Gale & L.
Steffe (Eds.), *Constructivism in Education* (pp. 85-108), Hillsdale, NJ: Erlbaum.

Stake, R. (1995). *The art of case study research.* Thousand Oaks, CA: SAGE.

Stake, R. (2005). *Multiple case study analysis.* New York: Guilford.

Stern, D. (1996). *Wittgensetin on mind and language.* Oxford, England: Oxford University Press.

Stocks, T. (1999). *Introduction to Single Subject Designs.* Retrieved from http://
www.msu.edu/user/sw/ssd/issd01.htm

Stuve, M., & Cassady, J. (2005). A factor analysis of the NETS performance profiles: Searching for constructs of self-concept and technology professionalism.
Journal of Technology and Teacher Education. 13(2), 303-324.

Stringer, E. (2007). *Action research* (3rd ed.). Thousand Oaks, CA: SAGE.

Svedberg, G. (2002). *Nursing traditions in Swedish psychiatric care during the first half*
of the 20th century. Doctoral dissertation, Karolinska Institutet, Sweden.

Swadener, B. (1999). Critical personal narrative and autoethnography in education: Reflections on a genre. *Educational Researcher, 28*(6), 21-26.

Taylor, S., & Beasley, N. (2005). *A handbook for doctoral supervisors.* New York: RoutledgeFalmer.

Tollefson, D. R., & Gross, E. (2006). Predicting recidivism following participation
in a batterer treatment program. *Journal of Social Service Research, 32*(4), 39-
62.

Tripodi, T. (1994). *A primer on single-subject design for clinical social workers.* Washington, DC: National Association of Social Workers Press.

Tzur, R. (2001, December). Becoming a mathematics teacher-educator: Concep-
tualizing the terrain through self-reflective analysis. *Journal of Mathematics*
Teacher Education, 4(4), 259-283.

Valenti, R. (1973). *A comparision of three levels of teacher-student interaction in secondary*
education programs for tenth grade students. Unpublished PhD doctoral dissertation, New York University.

Vaughn, S., Schumm, J., & Sinagub, J. (2005). *Focus group interviews in education*
and psychology. Thousand Oaks, CA: SAGE.

Voida, A. (2008). *Exploring a technological Hermeneutic: Understanding the interpretation of computer-mediated message systems.* Unpublished doctoral dissertation, School of Interactive Computing, College of Computing, Georgia Tech University. Retrieved from http://smartech.gatech.edu/handle/1853/24744

Voss, M. (2003). *Bridging thought communities: Implications of membership in degree-completion groups for the self-concepts of adult students.* Unpublished PhD dissertation, College of Education, University of Tennessee, Knoxville. Retrieved from http://etd.utk.edu/2003/VosMatthew.pdf

W. K. Kellogg Foundation. (1998). *W. K. Kellog Foundation Evaluation Handbook.* Battle Creek, MI: Author.

Wallston, K. A., Wallston, B. S., & Devellis, R. (1978). Development of multidimensional health locus of control (MHLC) Scales. *Health Education Monographs, 6*(2), 160-170.

Wadsworth, Y. (1998). *What is Participatory Action Research?* Paper #2. *Action Research International.* Retrieved June 6, 2007, from http://www.scu.edu.au/schools/gcm/ar/ari/p-ywadsworth98.html

Wakkary, R. (2005). Framing complexity, design and experience: A reflective analysis. *Digital Creativity, 16*(2), 65-78.

Wall, S. (2006). An autoethnography on learning about autoethnography. *International Journal of Qualitative Methods, 5*(2), Article 9. Retrieved [DATE] from http://www.ualberta.ca/~iiqm/backissues/5_2/html/wall.htm

Weiss, R. (1995). *Learning from strangers: The art and method of qualitative interview studies.* New York: Free Press.

Wenger, E. (1998). *Communities of practice: Learning, meaning, and identity.* Cambridge, MA: Cambridge University Press.

Whitehead, A. F. (1929). *The aims of education and other essays.* New York: The Free Press.

Willis, J. (1995). A recursive, reflective instructional design model based on constructivist-interpretivist theory. *Educational Technology, 35*(6), 5-23.

Willis, J. (2000). The maturing of constructivist instructional design: Some basic principles that can guide practice. *Educational Technology, 40*(1), 5-16.

Willis, J. (2007). *Foundations of qualitative research.* Thousand Oaks, CA: SAGE.

Willis, J. (2008). *Qualitative research methods in education and educational psychology.* Charlotte, NC: Information Age.

Willis, J. (2009). *Constructivst instructional design (C-ID): Foundations, models, and examples.* Charlotte, NC: Information Age.

Willis, J., & Wright, K. (2000, March/April). A general set of procedures for constructivist instructional design: The New R2D2. *Educational Technology, 40*(2), 5-20.

Wilson, B. (1997). Reflections on constructivism and instructional design. In C. R. Dills & A. A. Romiszowski (Eds.), *Instructional development paradigms* (pp. 63-80). EnglewoodCliffs, NJ: Educational Technology.

Woolf, J. [Producer] & Zinneman, F. (Director). (1973). *Day of the jackal* [Motion picture]. United States: Universal Studios.

Yin, R. (2002). *Case study research: Designs and methods* (3rd ed.). Thousand Oaks, CA: SAGE.

Yin, R. (2009). *Case study research: Design and methods.* Thousand Oaks, CA: SAGE.

Young, J. (2003). *Effects of divergent thinking training/instructions on Torrance Tests of Creative Thinking and creative performance.* Unpublished PhD dissertation, College of Education, University of Tennessee, Knoxville. Retrieved from http://etd.utk.edu/2004/LeeYoungJu.pdf

Yrjönsuuri, M. (Ed.). (2001). *Medieval formal logic: Obligations, insolubles, and consequences.* New York: Springer/Kluwer Academic.

ABOUT THE AUTHORS

Dr. Jerry Willis is professor and associate dean of education in the School of Social and Behavioral Sciences at Marist College in New York. He received his PhD in child clinical psychology from the University of Alabama and completed his internship at the University of Kansas Medical Center. Over the past 3 decades he has developed new doctoral programs at a number of institutions and participated in major revisions of doctoral programs at several others. He has also published scholarly papers on graduate programs to prepare professional practitioners, as well as on the dissertation process. He has directed dissertations at a number of institutions including Texas Tech University, the University of Houston, Iowa State University, the University of British Columbia, and Louisiana State University.

Dr. Deborah Inman is associate professor of educational leadership at Manhattanville College and one of the founding faculty members for the college's doctoral program in leadership. Her EdD is from Teachers College, Columbia University, and she has extensive experience as a supervisor of applied doctoral dissertations. She has taught, or held leadership positions, at a number of institutions including New York University, Teachers College, and the University of North Florida. She also served as codirector of the Oxford International Round Table on Educational Policy. She also served as director of the Institute on Educational Governance, Finance, Policymaking and Management in the Office of Education Research and Improvement (OERI) of the U.S. Department of Education.

Dr. Ron Valenti is an associate professor at the College of New Rochelle in New York and the director of the St. John Fisher College executive leadership doctoral program on that campus. He received his PhD from New York University and served as a teacher, principal, and superintendent in several districts. He has been an active participant in a number of professional organizations related to leadership, and he has taught in graduate programs at several institutions for the last 20 years. As a practicing professional he has worked on a number of applied research projects and served on the committees of doctoral students completing professional practice dissertations. Currently he teaches doctoral research courses in the program he directs, and supervises a number of professional practice dissertations.

INDEX

Breinigsville, PA USA
24 July 2010
242378BV00003B/3/P